D0453904

HANDBOOK OF

UNITED STATES COINS

R.S. YEOMAN

EDITOR
KENNETH BRESSETT

74th Edition
2017

An Illustrated Catalog of Prices Generally Paid
by Dealers for All American Coins—1616 to Date

Containing Mint records and wholesale prices for U.S. coins from 1616 to the
present time, including colonials, regular issues, commemoratives, territorials,
gold, bullion coins, Proof sets, and Mint sets. Information on collecting coins—
how coins are produced—mints and mintmarks—grading of coins—location of
mintmarks—preserving coins—starting a collection—history of mints—and interesting descriptions of all U.S. copper, nickel, silver, and gold coins. Illustrated.

Handbook of United States Coins™
THE OFFICIAL BLUE BOOK OF UNITED STATES COINS™

THE OFFICIAL BLUE BOOK and OFFICIAL BLUE BOOK OF UNITED STATES COINS are trademarks of Whitman Publishing, LLC.

WCG™ • OCG™

Printed in the United States of America.

© 2016 Whitman Publishing, LLC
3101 Clairmont Road • Suite G • Atlanta GA 30329

OCG™ Collecting Guide   Whitman®

Scan the QR code at left or visit us at www.whitman.com for a complete listing of numismatic reference books, supplies, and storage products.

CONTENTS

INTRODUCTION

3

CONTRIBUTORS TO THIS EDITION

Editor: Kenneth Bressett. Special Consultant: Philip Bressett.

Whitman Publishing extends its thanks to these members of the coin-buying community who have contributed pricing for this year's *Handbook of United States Coins.* Their data were compiled and then reviewed by editor Kenneth Bressett, consultant Phil Bressett, and Jeff Garrett. This process ensures input from a broad range of dealers and auctioneers from across the country—experts who buy, sell, and trade coins every day and know the market inside and out.

Gary Adkins
Mark Albarian
Dominic Albert
Buddy Alleva
Richard S. Appel
Mitchell A. Battino
Richard M. August
Lee J. Bellisario
Mark Borckardt
Larry Briggs
Bill Bugert
H. Robert Campbell
Elizabeth Coggan
Alan Cohen
Gary Cohen
James H. Cohen
Stephen M. Cohen
Steve Contursi
Adam Crum
Raymond Czahor
John Dannreuther

Sheridan Downey
Steve Ellsworth
Gerry Fortin
John Frost
Mike Fuljenz
John Gervasoni
Dennis M. Gillio
Ronald J. Gillio
Rusty Goe
Ira M. Goldberg
Lawrence Goldberg
Kenneth M. Goldman
J.R. Grellman
Tom Hallenbeck
Ash Harrison
Brian Hendelson
Brian Hodge
Jesse Iskowitz
Steve Ivy
Amandeep Jassal
Joseph Jones

Donald H. Kagin
Bradley S. Karoleff
Jim Koenings
Richard A. Lecce
Julian M. Leidman
Stuart Levine
Kevin Lipton
Denis W. Loring
Dwight N. Manley
David McCarthy
Robert T. McIntire
Harry Miller
Lee S. Minshull
Scott P. Mitchell
Michael C. Moline
Charles Morgan
Casey Noxon
Paul Nugget
Mike Orlando
John M. Pack
Joseph Parrella

Robert M. Paul
Joel Rettew Jr.
Joel Rettew Sr.
Greg Rohan
Maurice Rosen
Mark Salzberg
Gerald R. Scherer Jr.
Roger Siboni
James Simek
Rick Snow
Scott Sparks
David M. Sundman
Anthony Terranova
Troy Thoreson
Rich Uhrich
Frank Van Valen
Fred Weinberg
David Wnuck
Mark S. Yaffe

Special credit is due to the following for service in past editions of the *Handbook*:

David Akers
John Albanese
Michael Aron
Richard A. Bagg
Mitchell A. Battino
Jack Beymer
Q. David Bowers
J.H. Cline
Tom DeLorey
Silvano DiGenova

Kenneth Duncan
John Feigenbaum
Ron Guth
John Hamrick
Gene L. Henry
Karl D. Hirtzinger
James J. Jelinski
A.M. Kagin
Mike Kliman
Robert Lecce

David Leventhal
Andy Lustig
Robert Mish
Charles Moore
Richard Nachbar
Chris Napolitano
John M. Pack
William S. Panitch
William P. Paul
Tom Rinaldo

Leonard R. Saunders
Mary Sauvain
Richard Schwary
Craig Smith
William J. Spencer
Lawrence R. Stack
Steve Tanenbaum
Jerry Treglia
Douglas Winter

Special photo credits are due to the following:

Douglas F. Bird, Steve Contursi, Bill Fivaz, Heritage Auctions, Ira & Larry Goldberg Coins & Collectibles, Tom Mulvaney, the Museum of the American Numismatic Association, Numismatic Guaranty Corporation of America (NGC), Brent Pogue, Sarasota Rare Coin Gallery, the Smithsonian Institution, Rick Snow, Spectrum, Stack's Bowers Galleries, Superior Galleries, Anthony Swiatek, and the United States Mint.

Since 1942, annually revised editions of the *Official Blue Book of United States Coins™* have aided thousands of people who have coins to sell or are actively engaged in collecting United States coins. The popular coin-folder method of collecting by date has created ever-changing premium values, based on the supply and demand of each date and mint. Through its panel of contributors, the Blue Book has, over the years, reported these changing values. It also serves as a source of general numismatic information to all levels of interest in the hobby.

The values shown are representative prices paid by dealers for various United States coins. These are averages of prices assembled from many widely separated sources. On some issues slight differences in price among dealers may result from proximity to the various mints or heavily populated centers. Other factors, such as local supply and demand or dealers' stock conditions, may also cause deviations from the prices listed. While many coins bring no premium in circulated grades, they usually bring premium prices in Mint State and Proof. Extremely rare and valuable coins are usually sold at public auction, and prices vary according to current demand.

THIS BOOK LISTS PRICES MANY COIN DEALERS WILL PAY.

Premium prices are the average amount dealers will pay for coins (according to condition) if required for their stock. This book is not a retail price list.

IF YOU HAVE COINS TO SELL

Whitman Publishing, LLC, is not in the rare-coin business; however, chances are that the dealer from whom you purchased this book is engaged in the buying and selling of rare coins—contact them first. In the event that you purchased this book from a source other than a numismatic establishment, consult your local telephone directory for the names of coin dealers (they will be found sometimes under the heading of "Stamp and Coin Dealers"). If you live in a city or town that does not have any coin dealers, obtain a copy of one of the trade publications (such as *Coin World* [www.coinworld.com] or *Numismatic News* [www.numismaticnews.net]) or check the Internet in order to obtain the names and addresses of many of the country's leading dealers. Coin dealers who belong to the congressionally chartered American Numismatic Association (and who must abide by its code of ethics) are listed at www.money.org.

You will find current average *retail* valuations of American coins (the prices you can expect to pay a professional coin dealer) in the latest edition of *A Guide Book of United States Coins™* by R.S. Yeoman, edited by Kenneth Bressett. Coin collectors popularly call this the "Red Book." Pricing in even greater detail is included in *A Guide Book of United States Coins, Deluxe Edition.*

HOW TO READ THE CHARTS

A dash in a price column indicates that coins in that grade exist even though there are no current sales or auction records for them. (The dash does *not* necessarily mean that such coins are exceedingly rare.) Italicized prices indicate unsettled or speculative values. A number of listings of rare coins do not have prices or dashes in certain grades. This indicates that they are not available or not believed to exist in those grades.

Mintages of Proof coins are listed in parentheses.

Italicized mintages are estimates.

COLLECTING COINS

Numismatics or coin collecting is one of the world's oldest hobbies, dating back several centuries. Coin collecting in America did not develop to any extent until about 1840, as our pioneer forefathers were too busy carving a country out of wilderness to afford the luxury of a hobby. The discontinuance of the large-sized cent in 1857 encouraged many people to attempt to accumulate a complete set of the pieces while they were still in circulation. One of the first groups of collectors to band together for the study of numismatics was the American Numismatic Society, founded in 1858 and still a dynamic part of the hobby (www.numismatics.org). Lack of an economical method to house a collection held the number of devotees of coin collecting to a few thousand until Whitman Publishing and other manufacturers placed low-priced coin boards and folders on the market in the 1930s. Since that time, the number of Americans collecting coins has increased many-fold.

THE PRODUCTION OF COINS

To collect coins intelligently it is necessary to have some knowledge of the manner in which they are produced. Coins are made in factories called "mints." The Mint of the United States was established at Philadelphia by a resolution of Congress dated April 2, 1792. The act also provided for the coinage of gold eagles ($10), half eagles, and quarter eagles; silver dollars, half dollars, quarter dollars, dimes (originally spelled "disme"), and half dismes or half dimes; and copper cents and half cents. The first coins struck were one-cent and half-cent pieces, in March of 1793 on a hand-operated press. Most numismatic authorities consider the half disme of 1792 the first United States coinage, quoting the words of George Washington as their authority. Washington, in his annual address, November 6, 1792, said, "There has been a small beginning in the coining of the half dimes, the want of small coins in circulation calling the first attention to them." Though the half disme is considered America's first coinage, it was not the first coinage produced by the Mint; these coins were produced off premises in July of 1792 before the mint was completed. In the new Philadelphia Mint are a number of implements from the original mint, and some coins discovered when the old building was wrecked. These coins included half dismes, and the placard identifying them states that Washington furnished the silver and gave some of the pieces to his friends as souvenirs.

Prior to the adoption of the Constitution, the Continental Congress arranged for the issuance of copper coins under private contract. These are known as the 1787 *Fugio coppers* from their design, which shows a sundial and the Latin word "fugio"—"I Fly" or, in connection with the sundial, "Time Flies." The ever-appropriate motto "Mind Your Business" is also on the coin.

In the manufacture of a coin, the first step is die preparation. Dies for early federal coinage were prepared by hand; generally, letters and numbers were added with punches, while portraits and other designs were engraved into the die. Eventually, eagles, Liberty heads, and the like were also added with hubs and punches. After about 1836, many dies were made from masters, which contained all elements except the date and, if applicable, the mintmark. The addition of an element to a master die ensured its consistent placement throughout the life of the die. Today, many design tasks are performed with three-dimensional computer graphics. Mint artists are known as sculptor-engravers, and their work takes place mainly at the Philadelphia Mint. The dies are made of soft steel, which is hardened after the impression is received. The die is then dressed or finished to remove imperfections and make it suitable for coining. A typical die for production coinage can be used to strike hundreds of thousands of pieces. Dies for special issues such as Proofs are replaced more often.

The hand method of cutting dies accounts for the many die varieties of early United States coins. Where the amount of coinage of a given year was large enough to wear out many dies, each new die placed in the coining press created another die variety of that year. The dies being cut by hand, no two were exactly alike in every detail, even though some of the major elements such as the head or wreath, were sunk into the die by individual master punches. Of the cents dated 1794, more than sixty different die varieties have been discovered.

Thousands of dies are now used by the mints of the United States each year, but they are all made from one master die, which is produced in the following manner:

After the design is settled upon, the plaster of paris or wax model is prepared several times the actual size of the coin. When this model is finished an electrotype (an exact duplicate in metal) is made and prepared for the reducing lathe. The reducing lathe is a machine that works on the principle of the pantograph, only in this case the one point traces or follows the form of the model while another much smaller point in the form of a drill cuts away the steel and produces a reduced-size die of the model. The die is finished and details are sharpened or worked over by an engraver with chisel and graver. The master die is used to make duplicates in soft steel which are then hardened and ready for the coining press. To harden dies, they are placed in cast-iron boxes packed with carbon to exclude the air, and when heated to a bright red are cooled suddenly with water.

In the coinage operations the first step is to prepare the metal. Among the alloys that have been used are the following: silver coins, 90% silver and 10% copper; five-cent pieces, 75% copper and 25% nickel; one-cent pieces, 95% copper and 5% zinc. (The 1943 cent consists of steel coated with zinc; and the five-cent piece of 1942–1945 contains 35% silver, 56% copper, and 9% manganese.) Under the Coinage Act of 1965, the composition of dimes, quarters, and half dollars was changed to eliminate or reduce the silver content of these coins. The copper-nickel "clad" dimes, quarters, half dollars, and dollars are composed of an outer layer of copper-nickel (75% copper and 25% nickel) bonded to an inner core of pure copper. The silver clad half dollar and dollar have an outer layer of 80% silver bonded to an inner core of 21% silver, with a total content of 40% silver. Current cents are made from a core of 99.2% zinc, 0.8% copper, with a plating of pure copper. Dollars are composed of a pure copper core with outer layers of manganese-brass.

Alloys are melted in crucibles and poured into molds to form ingots. The ingots are in the form of thin bars and vary in size according to the denomination of the coin. The width is sufficient to allow three or more coins to be cut from the strips.

The ingots are next put through rolling mills to reduce the thickness to required limits. The strips are then fed into cutting presses which cut circular blanks of the approximate size of the finished coin. The blanks are run through annealing furnaces to soften them; next they move through tumbling barrels, rotating cylinders containing cleaning solutions which clean and burnish the metal; and finally into centrifugal drying machines.

The blanks are next fed into a milling machine which produces the raised or upset rim. The blank, now called a *planchet,* is now ready for the coining press.

The planchet is held firmly by a collar, as it is struck under heavy pressure varying from 40 tons for the one-cent pieces and dimes to 170 tons for silver dollars. Upper and lower dies impress the design on both sides of the coin. The pressure is sufficient to produce a raised surface level with that of the milled rim. The collar holding the blank for silver or clad coins is grooved. The pressure forces the metal into the grooves of the collar, producing the "reeding" on the edge of the finished coin.

HOW A PROOF COIN IS MADE

Selected dies are inspected for perfection and are highly polished and cleaned. They are again wiped clean or polished after every 15 to 25 impressions and are replaced frequently to avoid imperfections from wear. Coinage blanks are polished and cleaned to assure high quality in striking. They are then hand fed into the coinage press one at a time, each blank receiving two blows from the dies to bring up sharp, high-relief details. The coinage operation is done at slow speed. Finished Proofs are individually inspected and are handled by gloves or tongs. They also receive a final inspection by packers before being sonically sealed in special plastic cases.

Certain coins, including Lincoln cents, Buffalo nickels, quarter eagles, half eagles, eagles, and double eagles, between the years 1908 and 1916, were made with Matte Proof (nickel and silver) and Sand Blast and Satin Proof (gold) finishes. These later Proofs have a dull frosted surface which was either applied to the dies, or produced by special treatment after striking.

MINTS AND MINTMARKS

In addition to the Philadelphia Mint, the U.S. government has from time to time established branch mints in various parts of the country. At present, branch mints operate in Denver, West Point, and San Francisco. Starting in 1968, Proof sets as well as some of the regular coins were produced at the San Francisco Mint and Assay Office. The Denver Mint has operated since 1906. A mint was operated at New Orleans from 1838 to 1861 and again from 1879 to 1909. Mints were also in service at Carson City, Nevada, from 1870 to 1893; at Charlotte, North Carolina, from 1838 to 1861; at Dahlonega, Georgia, from 1838 to 1861; and at San Francisco since 1854. The U.S. government also supplied a mint in the Philippines (M mintmark) in the early 1900s.

Coins struck at Philadelphia before 1979 (except 1942 to 1945 five-cent pieces) do not bear a mintmark. Historically the mintmark was used only for branch mints. Modern exceptions include the Lincoln cent and the Kennedy half dollar, which both use the P for Philadelphia. All coins struck after 1967 have the mintmark on the obverse. The letters signifying the various mints are as follows:

C—Charlotte, North Carolina (gold coins only; 1838–1861)
CC—Carson City, Nevada (1870–1893)
D—Dahlonega, Georgia (gold coins only; 1838–1861)
D—Denver, Colorado (1906 to date)
O—New Orleans, Louisiana (1838–1861; 1879–1909)
P—Philadelphia, Pennsylvania (1793 to date; P not used in early years)
S—San Francisco, California (1854 to date)
W—West Point, New York (1984 to date)

The mintmark is of utmost importance to collectors because, historically, coinage of the branch mints has often been much smaller than quantities struck at Philadelphia. Many early coins of the branch mints are very scarce.

SLABBED VERSUS UNSLABBED COINS

In this handbook, values from under $1 up to several hundred dollars are for "raw" coins—that is, coins that have not been graded and encapsulated by a professional third-party grading service. Coins valued near or above $500 are assumed to be third-party graded. A high-value coin that has not been professionally certified as authentic, graded, and encapsulated by an independent firm is apt to be valued lower than the prices indicated.

The general effect of third-party grading and authentication has been to increase buyers' and sellers' comfort levels with the perceived quality of rare coins in the marketplace.

Coins in high grades that have been certified (professionally graded and guaranteed authentic) and encapsulated ("slabbed") may be valued significantly higher than similar coins that have not been so treated. In today's marketplace, "raw" or non-certified coins, are usually valued at less, except for modern U.S. Mint and bullion products.

DISTINGUISHING MARKS

The illustrations and explanations in this section will help the collector identify certain well-known varieties.

Half Cents of 1795–1796 Showing Location of Pole to Cap

The end of the pole lies parallel with the lines of the bust, which is pointed. On some coins, the pole is missing due either to engraver error (while cutting the die) or to an error in "relapping" (when the die is ground to remove wear, clash marks, etc.).

Pole to Cap   **No Pole to Cap**

Stemless Wreath Variety of Half Cents and Large Cents

For this variety, the difference is on the reverse side. Illustrations show both Stemless and Stems to Wreath types for comparison—stemless wreath found on the 1804, 1805, and 1806 half cents; and on the 1797, 1802, and 1803 large cents.

Stemless Wreath   **Stems to Wreath**

1864 Bronze Indian Head Cent With "L" on Ribbon

A small "L," the initial of the designer James B. Longacre, was added to the Indian Head design late in 1864 and was continued through 1909. For coins in less than Fine condition, this small letter will often be worn away. The point of the bust is rounded on the 1864 variety without "L"; the bust is pointed on the

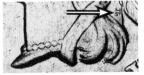

variety with "L." The initial must be visible, however, for the 1864 variety to bring the higher premium. If the coin is turned slightly so that the portrait faces the observer, the highlighted details will usually appear to better advantage.

Designer Initials, Overstrikes, Die-Doublings, and Date Varieties

During 1909, initials appeared on the reverse of the Lincoln cent.
Starting in 1918, they appear below the shoulder.

Prior to 1990, mintmarks for all mints were usually applied directly to working dies at Philadelphia in a hand-punching operation. Occasionally, a die was accidentally marked with one letter on top of another.

Dies are produced by impressing the raised coin design of a hub into the end of a cylinder of steel. In early years the Mint made use of old dies by repunching the dates on their dies with new numbers. That practice was stopped prior to 1909. Since that time, all overdated coins have been the result of errors that occur when two different-dated hubs have been used in die preparation, and one is impressed over the other by accident.

1938-D, D Over S,
Buffalo Nickel

1918-S, 8 Over 7,
Standing Liberty Quarter
A variety of this kind is rarely found in coinage of the 20th century.

1942, 2 Over 1,
Mercury Dime

1955, Doubled-Die Obverse
Lincoln Cent

Large Date Cent
(1960)

Small Date Cent
(1960)

Large Date Cent
(1982)

Small Date Cent
(1982)

COUNTERFEIT COINS

Recognizing a spurious coin can be made easier through the use of common sense and an elementary knowledge of the techniques used by counterfeiters. It is well to keep in mind that the more popular a coin is among collectors and the public, the more likely it is that counterfeits and replicas will abound. Until recently, collector coins valued at under $100 were rarely replicated because of the high cost of making such items. The same was true of counterfeits made to deceive the public. Few counterfeit coins were made because it was more profitable for the fakers to print paper money. Today, however, counterfeiters in Asia and elsewhere create fakes of a surprising variety of coins, most notably silver dollar types, but also smaller denominations.

Coin dealers will rarely buy coins of exceptional rarity or value without being 100% certain of authenticity. Professional authentication of rare coins for a fee is offered by commercial grading services, and by some dealers.

Replicas

Reproductions of famous and historical coins have been distributed for decades by marketing firms and souvenir vendors. Most replicas are poorly made by the casting method, and are virtually worthless. They can sometimes be identified by a seam that runs around the edge of the piece where the two halves of the casting mold were joined together.

Counterfeits

For many centuries, counterfeiters have produced base-metal forgeries of gold and silver coins to deceive the public in the normal course of trade. These pieces are usually crudely made and easily detected on close examination. Crudely cast counterfeit copies of older coins are the most prevalent. These can usually be detected by the casting bubbles or pimples that can be seen with low-power magnification. Pieces struck from handmade dies are more deceptive, but the engravings do not match those of genuine Mint products.

Die-struck gold coin counterfeits have been mass produced overseas since 1950. Forgeries exist of most U.S. gold coins dated between 1870 and 1933, as well as all issues of the gold dollar and three-dollar gold piece. Most of these are very well made, as they were intended to pass the close scrutiny of collectors. Many gold coins of earlier dates have been counterfeited, and all coins dated before 1930 should be carefully examined.

Silver dollars dated 1804, Lafayette dollars, several of the low-mintage commemorative half dollars, and the 1795 half dimes have been forged in quantity. Minor-coin forgeries made in recent years are the 1909-S V.D.B.; 1914-D and 1955 doubled-die Lincoln cents; 1877 Indian Head cents; 1856 Flying Eagle cents; and, on a much smaller scale, a variety of dates of half cents and large cents. Nineteenth-century copies of colonial coins are also sometimes encountered.

Alterations

Coins are occasionally altered by the addition, removal, or change of a design feature (such as a mintmark or date digit) or by the polishing, sandblasting, acid etching, toning, or plating of the surface of a genuine piece. Among U.S. gold coins, only the 1927-D double eagle is commonly found with a spuriously added mintmark. On $2.50 and $5 gold coins, 1839 through 1856, New Orleans O mintmarks have been deceptively altered to C (for Charlotte, North Carolina) in a few instances.

Over a century ago, five-dollar gold pieces were imitated by gold plating 1883 Liberty Head five-cent coins without the word CENTS on the reverse. Other coins commonly created fraudulently through alteration include the 1799 large cent and the 1909-S; 1909-S V.D.B.; 1914-D; 1922, No D; and 1943, Copper, cents. The 1913 Liberty Head nickel has been extensively replicated by alteration of 1903 and 1912 nickels. Scarce, high-grade Denver and San Francisco Buffalo nickels of the 1920s; 1916-D and 1942, 42 Over 41, dimes; 1918-S, 8 Over 7, quarters; 1932-D and -S quarters; and 1804 silver dollars have all been made by the alteration of genuine coins of other dates or mints.

Detection

The best way to detect counterfeit coins is to compare suspected pieces with others of the same issue. Look at the photographs in this book for comparisons. Carefully check size, color, luster, weight, edge devices, and design details. Replicas generally have less detail than their genuine counterparts when studied under magnification. Modern struck counterfeits made to deceive collectors are an exception to this rule. Any questionable gold coin should be referred to an expert for verification.

Cast forgeries are usually poorly made and of incorrect weight. Base metal is often used in place of gold or silver, and the coins are lightweight and often incorrect in color and luster. Deceptive cast pieces have been made using real metal content and modern dental techniques, but these too usually vary in quality and color. Detection of alterations sometimes involves comparative examination of the suspected areas of a coin (usually mintmarks and date digits) at magnification ranging from 10x to 40x.

CONDITIONS OF COINS

(Also see appendix D, pages 277–282)

Essential Elements of the Official ANA Grading System

Proof—A specially made coin distinguished by sharpness of detail and usually with a brilliant, mirrorlike surface. *Proof* refers to the method of manufacture and is not a condition, but normally the term implies nearly perfect condition unless otherwise noted.

> **Gem Proof (PF-65)**—Brilliant surfaces with no noticeable blemishes or flaws. A few scattered, barely noticeable marks or hairlines.

> **Choice Proof (PF-63)**—Reflective surfaces with only a few blemishes in secondary focal places. No major flaws.

> **Proof (PF-60)**—Surface may have several contact marks, hairlines, or light rubs. Luster may be dull and eye appeal lacking.

Mint State—The terms *Mint State (MS)* and *Uncirculated (Unc.)* are used interchangeably to describe coins showing no trace of wear. Such coins may vary to some degree because of blemishes, toning, or slight imperfections, as described in the following subdivisions:

> **Perfect Uncirculated (MS-70)**—Perfect new condition, showing no trace of wear. The finest quality possible, with no evidence of scratches, handling, or contact with other coins. Very few circulation-issue coins are ever found in this condition.

> **Gem Uncirculated (MS-65)**—An above average Uncirculated coin that may be brilliant or lightly toned and that has very few contact marks on the surface or rim. MS-67 through MS-62 indicate slightly higher or lower grades of preservation.

> **Choice Uncirculated (MS-63)**—Has some distracting contact marks or blemishes in prime focal areas. Luster may be impaired.

> **Uncirculated (MS-60)**—Has no trace of wear but may show a number of contact marks, and surface may be spotted or lack some luster.

Choice About Uncirculated (AU-55)—Evidence of friction on high points of design. Most of the mint luster remains.

About Uncirculated (AU-50)—Traces of light wear on many of the high points. At least half of the mint luster is still present.

Choice Extremely Fine (EF-45)—Light overall wear on highest points. All design details are very sharp. Some of the mint luster is evident.

Extremely Fine (EF-40)—Light wear on design throughout, but all features sharp and well defined. Traces of luster may show.

Choice Very Fine (VF-30)—Light, even wear on the surface and highest parts of the design. All lettering and major features are sharp.

Very Fine (VF-20)—Moderate wear on high points. All major details are clear.

Fine (F-12)—Moderate to considerable even wear. Entire design is bold with overall pleasing appearance.

Very Good (VG-8)—Well worn with main features clear and bold, although rather flat.

Good (G-4)—Heavily worn, with design visible but faint in areas. Many details are flat.

About Good (AG-3)—Very heavily worn with portions of lettering, date, and legend worn smooth. The date may be barely readable.

Important: Damaged coins, such as those that are bent, corroded, scratched, holed, nicked, stained, or mutilated, are worth less than those without defects. Flawless Uncirculated coins are generally worth more than values quoted in this book. Slightly worn coins ("sliders") that have been cleaned and conditioned ("buffed") to simulate Uncirculated luster are worth considerably less than perfect pieces.

Unlike damage inflicted after striking, manufacturing defects do not always lessen values. Examples include colonial coins with planchet flaws and weakly struck designs; early silver and gold with weight-adjustment "file marks" (parallel cuts made prior to striking); and coins with "lint marks" (surface marks due to the presence of dust or other foreign matter during striking).

Brief guides to grading are placed before each major coin type. Grading standards are not scientific and often vary among collectors, dealers, and certification services. For more on grading, consult the *Official ANA Grading Standards for United States Coins.*

PRESERVING AND CLEANING COINS

Most numismatists will tell you to "never clean a coin" and it is good advice! Cleaning coins almost always reduces their value. Collectors prefer coins in their original condition.

Some effort should be made to protect Uncirculated and Proof coins so they won't need cleaning. Tarnish on a coin is purely a chemical process caused by oxygen in the air acting on the metal, or by chemicals with which the coin comes in contact. One of the most common chemicals causing tarnish is sulphur; most paper, with the exception of specially manufactured "sulphur-free" kinds, contains sulphur due to the sulphuric acid that is used in paper manufacture; therefore do not wrap coins in ordinary paper. Also keep Uncirculated and Proof coins away from rubber bands (a rubber band placed on a silver coin for a few days will eventually produce a black stripe on the coin where the band touched). The utmost in protection is obtained by storing the coin in an airtight box, away from moisture and humidity, and by using holders made of inert materials.

Many coins become marred by careless handling. Always hold the coin by the edge. The accompanying illustration shows the right and wrong way to handle numismatic specimens. It is a breach of numismatic etiquette to handle another collector's coin except by the edge, even if it is not an Uncirculated or Proof piece.

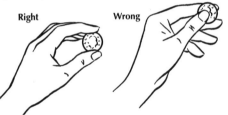

Right   **Wrong**

STARTING A COLLECTION

One may start a collection of United States coins with very little expense by systematically assembling the various dates and mintmarks of all the types and denominations that are now in general circulation, using Whitman's many different coin folders and albums, especially those for quarters and dollars with various designs.

With the exception of the price paid for the coin folder, collecting coins received in everyday business transactions entails no expense whatsoever; a Jefferson nickel taken out of circulation, for example, can always be spent for five cents if the occasion arises. Filling an album or two with coins found in circulation is probably the best method of determining whether coin collecting appeals to you. Not everyone can be a successful coin collector. It requires patience, intelligence of a high order, and a certain desire to know the meaning behind a lot of things that at first glance appear meaningless. You may not be cut out to be a collector but you'll never know until you look further into the subject, and if by the time an album or two of coins are collected you have no burning desire to acquire many more different coins, you will probably never be a collector. However, chances are that you will be, because if you have read this far in this book, it shows that you are interested in the subject.

High quality is the goal of every endeavor and coin collecting is no exception. After an album has been filled with circulated specimens, the next step will be to replace them with coins in Uncirculated condition, or perhaps to start collecting an obsolete series; in either case, it will be necessary to purchase some coins from dealers or other collectors. The most logical way to keep abreast of the market, or obtain the addresses of the country's leading dealers, is to subscribe to one or more of the trade publications. These magazines carry advertisements of various dealers listing coins for sale. Moreover, through these sources the beginner may obtain price lists and catalogs from the dealers.

There are several good reference books available at reasonable prices which will be helpful to the collector who wishes to know more about U.S. coins and paper money. R.S. Yeoman's *A Guide Book of United States Coins™* (the "Red Book") lists retail values of all regular U.S. coins and also lists all coins of the U.S. colonial period and private and territorial gold coins, plus tokens, pattern coins, errors, and other numismatic collectibles.

Most coin, book, and hobby dealers can supply the following titles:

The Official Red Book®: A Guide Book of United States Coins™—R.S. Yeoman, edited by Kenneth Bressett

The Official Red Book®: A Guide Book of United States Coins™, Deluxe Edition—R.S. Yeoman, edited by Kenneth Bressett

A Guide Book of Morgan Silver Dollars—Q. David Bowers

The Expert's Guide to Collecting and Investing in Rare Coins—Q. David Bowers

Coin Collecting: A Beginner's Guide to the World of Coins—Kenneth Bressett

History of the United States Mint and Its Coinage—David W. Lange

The Official ANA Grading Standards for United States Coins—Kenneth Bressett, et al.

A Guide Book of United States Type Coins—Q. David Bowers

Join a Coin Club

Beginners should join a "coin club" if they live in a city which has one. Associating with more experienced collectors will be of great benefit. Practically all larger cities have one or more clubs and they are being rapidly organized in smaller towns. Trade publications carry information about coin clubs and events such as coin shows and conventions.

The American Numismatic Association is a national organization that collectors can join. The ANA Web site (www.money.org) has a list of member coin clubs throughout the United States. Contact the ANA by mail at 818 North Cascade Avenue, Colorado Springs, CO 80903, or by phone at 800-367-9723.

SELLING YOUR COINS

Is it time to sell your coins? Perhaps you've inherited some of them; or maybe you've collected for years, and you want to explore a new pastime or you need to cash in on your investment. In any case, you have some decisions to make. Will you sell your collection privately, or at a public auction—or perhaps sell it yourself on the Internet? Will you sell locally or to dealers nationwide? What are the benefits of each path, and which will bring the greatest profits? To get started, ask yourself:

What Am I Selling?

Rolls of Modern Coins; Proof Sets; Modern Commemoratives; Bullion; Etc.
This includes bulk investment coins, such as American Eagle bullion pieces, bags of

common circulated coins, and so on. It also includes modern commemoratives and coin sets, not all of which have increased in value in the secondary market. Such accumulations are best sold privately to a coin dealer or to another collector. Auctioning them yourself, on the Internet, is another route. Consigning them to an auction house is not likely to be your best option; this venue is typically reserved for scarcer coins.

Coins With Sentimental—but Not Necessarily High-Dollar—Value. You might have inherited an accumulation (as opposed to a studiously compiled collection) of coins—for example, a coffee can full of Wheat cents. Your local coin dealer can make you an offer, either buying the entire lot or searching through them to "cherrypick" the better pieces. If you have the time, you might sell them yourself, through an Internet auction site. Also, you might donate them to a local Boy Scout troop or similar organization (this may be tax-deductible).

Rare and/or Significant Coins. For rare, valuable, and historically significant coins, public consigned auctions are often the best way to sell—dedicated collectors know they're good sources for scarce coins. A coin consigned to a well-established auction house with numismatic experience will be carefully studied, cataloged, and presented to a serious audience. You save the time and effort of searching for potential buyers. The auction firm makes money by collecting a commission on each sale.

Another option for selling your rare and significant coins is to approach a dealer nationally recognized as an expert in the field—for example, a specialist who focuses on colonial coins. You can also receive tax benefits from donating your coins to the American Numismatic Association (ANA), the American Numismatic Society, or a museum.

Selling to a Coin Shop

Your local coin shop has the advantage of the personal touch. Good coin-shop proprietors are happy to educate and advise their customers. An active coin dealer stays up to date on the hobby and the market, knows about tax and estate laws that might affect your sale, and can study your collection and make educated decisions. Many dealers have a wide audience for selling coins—which provides the leverage to offer you a good price.

A coin shop can be a venue for selling numismatic items of any value. The owner can often make you an offer and write you a check on the spot. Of course, very rare or specialized coins will likely fetch a higher price at public auction.

You should feel comfortable with the integrity of the shop's proprietor and staff. Talk to coin-collector friends, inquire at the local coin club, and check with the Better Business Bureau. Look at the shop's Web site, advertisements, and flyers or publications—do they project fairness and professionalism?

Coin shops can be found in a phone book or online business directory. Call to make sure the owner or a qualified assistant will be there to examine your coins. A busy dealer can schedule a convenient time to meet with you. Solicit at least two quotes before you decide to sell.

Selling Through the Mail

You can ship your coins to a dealer for their offer; again, trust is important. Does the dealer belong to the ANA or the Professional Numismatists Guild (www.pngdealers.com)? Does he advertise in hobby newspapers such as *Coin World* and *Numismatic News?* Search the dealer's name on the Internet: do you find satisfied customers, or complaints and concerns?

Inquire by mail, email, or phone before shipping any coins. The dealer might request a list beforehand, and should be able to give you a general idea of value without seeing the coins in person. Once you're comfortable and have decided to sell, ask the dealer for advice on shipping and insurance. Keep in mind that the dealer will need to examine your coins before making a firm offer.

Even if you live near a coin shop, you can broaden the playing field if you're open to selling your coins through the mail to established, respected dealers. This is a good option if you have the time. The entire transaction (finding dealers; packing and shipping; waiting for the check) will likely take longer than getting a local offer.

Selling to a Dealer at a Coin Show

Between the national coin shows and the hundreds of coin clubs that sponsor city and regional shows, chances are a show is held somewhere near you at least once a year. With dozens or even hundreds of dealers in one venue, you can shop your coins around before you sell; and, as at a coin shop, payment is immediate.

For best results, decide in advance which dealers would be best to appproach, especially if you'll have to travel a long way or you're interested in a narrow specialty.

Remember, a coin show is a public venue. Be alert; use common sense. Outside the show, do not publicize the fact that you're carrying valuable coins.

Most shows list participating dealers in their programs. Decide in advance the ones you want to approach (e.g., the silver-dollar specialists, if you have Morgan dollars to sell). Or simply stroll the aisles and introduce yourself to dealers who sell items similar to those in your collection. This is all part of the fun of a coin show.

Consigning at a Public Auction

Numismatic auction firms are often connected to larger retailers that also sell through the mail, online, etc. As always, reputation is important. Study a potential auctioneer's Web site; learn about their staff, past sales results, any media coverage they might receive. Look at their catalogs: are they professionally made? The effort and experience an auction firm brings to its work will affect how much your coins sell for.

Selling Online

Selling your coins yourself online can be fun, but it requires time and (usually) some skill with scanning or photography. Each auction site has its own rules, policies, and rates; read them carefully. Be security-conscious (e.g., rent a Post Office box instead of using your home address, and insist on full, guaranteed payment before you ship any coins). You can also use the Internet to sell your coins at a fixed price, through a bulletin-board posting or other announcement. Any online sale to the public requires you to take on responsibilities similar to those of a coin shop or auction firm. There is work involved, but the experience can be enjoyable and profitable.

Early American coins are rare in conditions better than those listed and consequently dealers pay much more for them.

BRITISH NEW WORLD ISSUES
Sommer Islands (Bermuda)

This coinage, issued around 1616, was the first struck for England's colonies in the New World. The coins were known as "Hogge Money" or "Hoggies."

The pieces were made of copper lightly silvered, in four denominations: shilling, sixpence, threepence, and twopence, indicated by Roman numerals. The hog is the main device and appears on the obverse side of each. SOMMER ISLANDS is inscribed within beaded circles. The reverse shows a full-rigged galleon with the flag of St. George on each of four masts.

Shilling

	AG	G	VG	F	VF	EF
Twopence	$2,000	$3,000	$4,500	$6,500	$17,500	$30,000
Threepence			65,000			
Sixpence	1,750	2,750	4,250	8,500	20,000	35,000
Shilling	2,500	3,750	5,500	18,000	40,000	50,000

Massachusetts
"New England" Coinage (1652)

In 1652 the General Court of Massachusetts ordered the first metallic currency to be struck in the British Americas, the New England silver threepence, sixpence, and shilling. These coins were made from silver bullion procured principally from the West Indies. Joseph Jenks made the punches for the first coins at his Iron Works in Saugus, Massachusetts, close to Boston where the mint was located. John Hull was appointed mintmaster; his assistant was Robert Sanderson.

NE Shilling (1652)

	G	VG	F	VF	EF
NE Threepence *(unique)*			—		
NE Sixpence *(8 known)*	$30,000	$50,000	$100,000	$150,000	$250,000
NE Shilling	26,000	45,000	80,000	120,000	225,000

Willow Tree Coinage (1653–1660)

The simplicity of the design on the N.E. coins invited counterfeiting and clipping of the edges. Therefore, they were soon replaced by the Willow Tree, Oak Tree, and Pine Tree series. The Willow Tree coins were struck from 1653 to 1660, the Oak Trees 1660 to 1667, and the Pine Trees 1667 to 1682. All of them (with the exception of the Oak Tree twopence) bore the date 1652. Many varieties of all of these coins exist. Values shown are for the most common types.

Sixpence

	Fair	G	VG	F	VF	EF
1652 Willow Tree Threepence *(3 known)*				—	—	—
1652 Willow Tree Sixpence *(14 known)*	$6,500	$14,000	$20,000	$40,000	$90,000	$150,000
1652 Willow Tree Shilling	6,500	14,000	20,000	30,000	75,000	125,000

Oak Tree Coinage (1660–1667)

Twopence

Threepence

	G	VG	F	VF	EF	AU	Unc.
1662 Oak Tree Twopence	$325	$500	$1,100	$1,800	$3,000	$4,200	$7,000
1652 Oak Tree Threepence	350	500	1,700	3,200	5,250	10,000	25,000
1652 Oak Tree Sixpence	400	700	1,800	3,750	6,000	10,000	20,000
1652 Oak Tree Shilling	450	750	1,850	4,000	6,000	7,500	15,000

Pine Tree Coinage (1667–1682)

The first Pine Tree coins were minted on the same size planchets as the Oak Tree pieces. Subsequent issues of the shilling were narrower and thicker, to conform to the size of English coins.

Shilling, Large Planchet (1667–1674)   Shilling, Small Planchet (1675–1682)

See next page for chart.

	G	VG	F	VF	EF	AU	Unc.
1652 Pine Tree Threepence..............	$350	$550	$1,000	$2,100	$3,300	$5,250	$10,000
1652 Pine Tree Sixpence..............	400	600	1,200	2,600	3,400	6,000	11,000
1652 Pine Tree Shilling, Large Planchet....	450	750	1,400	3,100	5,000	8,000	16,000
1652 Pine Tree Shilling, Small Planchet....	400	650	1,200	2,500	3,700	6,500	17,000

Maryland
Lord Baltimore Coinage

In 1659, Cecil Calvert, Lord Baltimore and Lord Proprietor of Maryland, had coinage struck in England for use in Maryland. There were four denominations: shilling, sixpence, fourpence (groat) in silver, and copper penny (denarium). The silver coins have the bust of Lord Baltimore on the obverse, and the Baltimore family arms with the denomination in Roman numerals on the reverse.

Fourpence (groat)

Lord Baltimore Shilling

	G	VG	F	VF	EF	AU
Penny copper *(9 known)*	—	—	$30,000	$50,000	$80,000	—
Fourpence...........................	$1,200	$2,500	4,000	12,000	17,500	$27,500
Sixpence...........................	800	1,300	2,500	5,000	8,000	12,000
Shilling	1,000	1,700	3,500	7,000	10,000	16,000

New Jersey
St. Patrick or Mark Newby Coinage

Mark Newby, who came to America from Dublin, Ireland, in November 1681, brought copper pieces believed by numismatists to have been struck in England circa 1663 to 1672. These are called St. Patrick coppers. The coin received wide circulation in the New Jersey Province, having been authorized to pass as legal tender by the General Assembly in May 1682. The smaller piece, known as a farthing, was never specifically authorized for circulation in the colonies.

St. Patrick Farthing

	G	VG	F	VF	EF	AU
St. Patrick "Farthing"....................	$90	$150	$450	$1,400	$3,500	$7,500
St. Patrick "Halfpenny"	150	350	600	1,500	5,250	

COINAGE AUTHORIZED BY BRITISH ROYAL PATENT

American Plantations Tokens

These pieces struck in nearly pure tin were the first royally authorized coinage for the British colonies in America. They were made under a franchise granted in 1688 to Richard Holt. Restrikes were made circa 1828 from original dies.

	G	VG	F	VF	EF	AU	Unc.
(1688) James II Plantation Token Farthing . .							
1/24 Part Real	$125	$150	$300	$550	$800	$1,850	$3,200
1/24 Part Real, Restrike	50	75	150	225	375	525	900

Coinage of William Wood

Rosa Americana Coins

William Wood, an Englishman, obtained a patent from King George I to make coins for Ireland and the American colonies. The Rosa Americana pieces were issued in three denominations—halfpenny, penny, and twopence—and were intended for use in America.

Penny

	VG	F	VF	EF	AU	Unc.
(No date) Twopence, Motto in Ribbon	$90	$170	$375	$700	$1,500	$2,800
1722 Halfpenny, DEI GRATIA REX UTILE DULCI . . .	55	125	210	425	750	1,750
1722 Penny	55	125	210	410	725	1,750
1722 Twopence	80	160	300	550	1,000	2,200

Halfpenny

	VG	F	VF	EF	AU	Unc.
1723 Halfpenny	$40	$100	$175	$450	$900	$1,800

Entry continued on next page.

Twopence

	VG	F	VF	EF	AU	Unc.
1723 Penny	$40	$110	$200	$400	$650	$1,400
1723 Twopence *(illustrated)*	80	130	250	475	850	1,500

Wood's Hibernia Coinage

The type intended for Ireland had a seated figure with a harp on the reverse side and the word HIBERNIA. Denominations struck were the halfpenny and the farthing with dates 1722, 1723, and 1724. Although these have no association with the Americas, because of the connection with William Wood many American collectors desire to obtain them.

1722, Hibernia
Halfpenny

First Type

Second Type

	G	VG	F	VF	EF	AU	Unc.
1722 Farthing, first type	$75	$200	$300	$850	$1,200	$2,500	$5,000
1722 Halfpenny (first or second type)	14	35	50	100	275	420	875

1723, Hibernia Farthing

1724, Hibernia Halfpenny

	G	VG	F	VF	EF	AU	Unc.
1723 Farthing	$10	$20	$35	$80	$150	$225	$425
1723 Halfpenny	10	20	30	75	140	225	400
1724 Farthing	15	40	90	250	350	600	1,200
1724 Halfpenny	12	32	75	170	325	500	950

Virginia Halfpennies

In 1773, coinage of a copper halfpenny was authorized for Virginia by the British Crown. The style is similar to the regular English coinage. These pieces did not arrive in Virginia until 1775, but after then they did circulate on a limited basis. Most examples known today are Uncirculated, by virtue of a hoard of several thousand pieces that came to light in the 19th century and was distributed in numismatic channels.

	G	VG	F	VF	EF	AU	Unc.
1773 Halfpenny...............	$10	$30	$50	$90	$200	$275	$550

EARLY AMERICAN AND RELATED TOKENS

Elephant Tokens

London Elephant Tokens

The London Elephant tokens were struck circa 1672 to 1694. Although they were undated, two examples are known to have been struck over 1672 British halfpennies. Most are struck in copper, but one is made of brass. The legend on this piece, GOD PRESERVE LONDON, is probably just a general plea for divine aid and not a specific reference to the outbreak of plague in 1665 or the great fire of 1666.

These pieces were not struck for the colonies, and probably did not circulate in America, although a few may have been carried there by colonists. They are associated with the 1694 Carolina and New England Elephant tokens, through a shared obverse die.

	VG	F	VF	EF	AU	Unc.
(1694) Halfpenny, GOD PRESERVE LONDON,						
Thick or Thin Planchet................	$160	$300	$500	$800	$1,500	$2,200

Carolina Elephant Tokens

Although no law is known authorizing coinage for Carolina, very interesting pieces known as Elephant tokens were made with the date 1694. These copper tokens were of halfpenny denomination. The reverse reads GOD PRESERVE CAROLINA AND THE LORDS PROPRIETERS 1694.

The Carolina pieces were probably struck in England and perhaps intended as advertising to heighten interest in the Carolina Plantation.

	VG	F	VF	EF	AU	Unc.
1694 CAROLINA.	$2,200	$4,250	$8,500	$18,000	$24,000	$45,000

New England Elephant Tokens

Like the Carolina Tokens, the New England Elephant tokens were believed to have been struck in England as promotional pieces to increase interest in the American colonies.

	F	VF	EF
1694 NEW ENGLAND.	$50,000	$85,000	$100,000

New Yorke in America Token

Little is known about the origin of this token. The design of a heraldic eagle on a regulated staff with oak leaf finials is identical to the crest found on the arms of William Lovelace, governor of New York, 1668 to 1673. It seems likely that this piece is a token farthing struck by Lovelace for use in New York.

	VG	F
(Undated) Brass or Copper.	$4,000	$10,000
(Undated) Pewter.	—	—

Gloucester Tokens

This token appears to have been a private coinage by a merchant of Gloucester (county), Virginia. The only specimens known are struck in brass. The exact origin and use of these pieces are unknown.

	F
1714 Shilling, brass *(2 known)*	$80,000

Higley or Granby Coppers

The Higley coppers were private issues. All the pieces were made of pure copper. There were seven obverse and four reverse dies. The first issue, in 1737, bore the legend THE VALUE OF THREEPENCE. After a time the quantity exceeded the local demand, and a protest arose against the stated value of the piece. The inscription was changed to VALUE ME AS YOU PLEASE.

	G	VG	F	VF
1737 THE VALVE OF THREE PENCE, CONNECTICVT, 3 Hammers..........	$6,000	$10,000	$17,000	$50,000
1737 THE VALVE OF THREE PENCE, I AM GOOD COPPER, 3 Hammers	6,500	11,000	19,000	65,000
1737 VALUE ME AS YOU PLEASE, I AM GOOD COPPER, 3 Hammers.......	6,500	10,500	17,500	50,000
(1737) VALUE ME AS YOU PLEASE, J CUT MY WAY THROUGH, Broad Axe...	6,500	10,500	17,500	50,000
1739 VALUE ME AS YOU PLEASE, J CUT MY WAY THROUGH, Broad Axe....	7,500	13,500	35,000	85,000

Hibernia–Voce Populi Coins

These coins, struck in the year 1760, were made in Dublin. Although these have no connection with America, they have been listed in numismatic publications in the United States for a long time and are collected by tradition.

Farthing (1760)   Halfpenny (1760)

	G	VG	F	VF	EF	AU	Unc.
1760 Farthing	$100	$160	$250	$650	$1,000	$1,750	$3,500
1760 Halfpenny................	35	60	100	160	300	600	1,000

25

Pitt Tokens

British politician William Pitt is the subject of these pieces, probably intended as commemorative medalets. He was a friend to the interests of America. The so-called halfpenny served as currency in England during a shortage of regular coinage.

	VG	F	VF	EF	AU	Unc.
1766 Farthing	$2,500	$4,500	$12,000	$20,000		
1766 Halfpenny	200	325	650	1,100	$2,000	$4,250

Rhode Island Ship Medals

Although this medal has a Dutch inscription, the spelling and design indicate an English or Anglo-American origin. It is believed that this token was struck in England circa 1779–1780 as propaganda to influence Dutch opinion against the American cause. Specimens are known in brass, copper, and pewter. As with many colonial issues, modern copies exist.

1778–1779, Rhode Island Ship Medal

Values shown are for brass or copper pieces. Those struck in pewter are rare and valued higher.

	VF	EF	AU	Unc.
Rhode Island Ship Medal	$450	$850	$1,400	$3,200

John Chalmers Issues

John Chalmers, a silversmith, struck a series of silver tokens at Annapolis in 1783. Certain of the dies were by Thomas Sparrow, who also engraved bank-note plates. As most examples show wear today, these pieces seem to have served well in commerce.

	VG	F	VF	EF	AU
1783 Threepence	$950	$1,800	$3,500	$7,500	$15,000

	VG	F	VF	EF	AU
1783 Sixpence	$1,200	$2,500	$5,000	$12,000	$20,000
1783 Shilling	700	1,300	2,200	5,000	9,500

FRENCH NEW WORLD ISSUES

None of the coins of the French regime is strictly American. They were all general issues for the French colonies of the New World. The copper of 1717 to 1722 was authorized by edicts of 1716 and 1721 for use in New France, Louisiana, and the French West Indies.

Copper Sou or Nine Deniers

	VG	F	VF	EF
1721-B (Rouen)	$200	$400	$1,750	$4,000
1721-H (La Rochelle)	50	110	350	1,200
1722-H	50	110	350	1,200

French Colonies in General

Coined for use in the French colonies, these circulated only unofficially in Louisiana, along with other foreign coins and tokens. Most were counterstamped RF (République Française) for use in the West Indies. The mintmark A signifies the Paris Mint.

	VG	VF	EF	AU
1767 French Colonies, Sou	$45	$125	$350	$700
1767 French Colonies, Sou, counterstamped RF	40	90	150	275

SPECULATIVE ISSUES, TOKENS, AND PATTERNS
Nova Constellatio Coppers

The Nova Constellatio pieces were struck supposedly by order of Gouverneur Morris. Evidence indicates that they were all struck in Birmingham, England, and imported for American circulation as a private business venture.

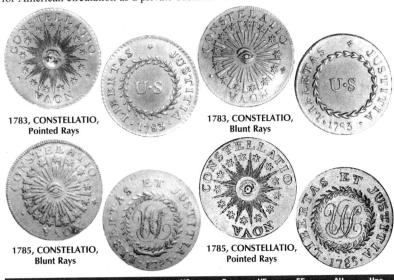

1783, CONSTELLATIO, Pointed Rays

1783, CONSTELATIO, Blunt Rays

1785, CONSTELATIO, Blunt Rays

1785, CONSTELLATIO, Pointed Rays

	VG	F	VF	EF	AU	Unc.
1783, CONSTELLATIO, Pointed Rays	$50	$100	$210	$450	$750	$1,500
1783, CONSTELLATIO, Blunt Rays	55	110	225	600	1,200	2,250
1785, CONSTELLATIO, Pointed Rays	50	100	210	450	750	1,500
1785, CONSTELLATIO, Blunt Rays	55	110	225	650	1,250	2,750

Immune Columbia Pieces

Nearly all of these are very rare. Many if not most seem to be unofficial, including pieces produced at the private Machin's Mills mint in Newburgh, New York.

1785, Copper, Star Reverse

1785, George III Obverse

	G	VG	F	VF	EF	AU
1785 Copper, Star Reverse			$8,000	$14,000	$20,000	
1785, George III Obverse	$2,500	$4,000	6,000	8,000		

1787, IMMUNIS COLUMBIA, Eagle Reverse

	G	VG	F	VF	EF	AU
1785, VERMON AUCTORI Obverse, IMMUNE COLUMBIA ..	$3,200	$5,500	$7,500	$19,000		
1787, IMMUNIS COLUMBIA, Eagle Reverse	150	375	800	1,800	$2,500	$4,000

Confederatio Coppers

Some Confederatio coppers may have been patterns, but others seem to have been used in limited numbers for general circulation. This will explain why the die with the CONFEDERATIO legend was combined with other designs such as a bust of George Washington, Libertas et Justitia of 1785, Immunis Columbia of 1786, the New York "Excelsiors," Inimica Tyrannis Americana, and others. In all there were 12 dies struck in 13 combinations. There are two types of the Confederatio reverse. In one instance the stars are contained in a small circle; in the other, larger stars are in a larger circle.

Typical Obverse	Small Circle Reverse	Large Circle Reverse

	VF
1785, Stars in Small Circle, various obverses	$29,000
1785, Stars in Large Circle, various obverses	35,000

Speculative Patterns

1786, IMMUNIS COLUMBIA	Eagle Reverse	Shield Reverse

	VF	EF
1786, IMMUNIS COLUMBIA, Eagle Reverse	$30,000	$37,500
1786, IMMUNIS COLUMBIA, Shield Reverse...................................	20,000	27,500

Chart continued on next page.   **29**

	VF	EF
(No date) (1786) Washington Obverse, Shield Reverse.............................	$40,000	
1786, Eagle Obverse, Shield Reverse...................................	30,000	
1786, Washington Obverse, Eagle Reverse (2 known).............................	—	

COINAGE OF THE STATES
New Hampshire

New Hampshire was the first of the states to consider the subject of coinage following the Declaration of Independence.

William Moulton was empowered to make a limited quantity of coins of pure copper, authorized by the State House of Representatives in 1776.

	G	VG
1776 New Hampshire Copper.....................................	$50,000	$75,000

Massachusetts

The coinage of Massachusetts copper cents and half cents in 1787 and 1788 was under the direction of Joshua Witherle. These were the first coins bearing the denomination *cent* as later established by Congress. Many varieties exist, the most valuable being the cent with arrows in the eagle's right talon (on the left side of the coin).

1787 Half Cent   1787 Cent

1788 Half Cent   1788 Cent

	G	F	VF	EF	AU	Unc.
1787 Half Cent.........................	$45	$120	$270	$400	$700	$1,500
1787 Cent, Arrows in Right Talon............	4,200	10,000	25,000			
1787 Cent, Arrows in Left Talon (illustrated)....	45	120	300	750	1,350	2,750

POST-COLONIAL ISSUES

	G	F	VF	EF	AU	Unc.
1788 Half Cent	$45	$130	$300	$500	$900	$1,700
1788 Cent	45	110	270	475	1,000	2,100

Connecticut

Authority for establishing a mint near New Haven was granted by the state to Samuel Bishop, Joseph Hopkins, James Hillhouse, and John Goodrich in 1785. Today, well over 300 different die varieties are known of Connecticut coppers dated from 1785 to 1788. These pieces circulated widely and effectively; most are seen with significant evidence of circulation.

1785, Bust
Facing Right

1785, Bust
Facing Left

1786–1787,
Mailed Bust
Facing Right

1786–1787,
Mailed Bust
Facing Left

1787, Draped
Bust Facing Left

1788, Mailed
Bust Facing Right

Entry continued on next page.

31

1788, Mailed
Bust Facing Left

1788, Draped
Bust Facing Left

	AG	G	VG	F	VF	EF	AU
1785, Bust Facing Left	$30	$75	$150	$275	$800	$1,500	$3,750
1785, Bust Facing Right	12	30	40	80	275	750	1,750
1786, Mailed Bust Facing Right	15	40	50	100	275	650	1,500
1786, Mailed Bust Facing Left	12	30	40	90	200	550	1,400
1787, Mailed Bust Facing Right	15	40	65	175	475	800	1,800
1787, Mailed Bust Facing Left	10	25	35	75	200	500	1,400
1787, Draped Bust Facing Left	10	25	35	75	200	500	1,200
1788, Mailed Bust Facing Right	10	25	50	100	300	700	1,400
1788, Mailed Bust Facing Left	10	25	32	80	210	550	1,350
1788, Draped Bust Facing Left	10	25	35	100	250	600	1,900

New York and Related Issues
Brasher Doubloons

Perhaps the most famous pieces coined before the establishment of the U.S. Mint at
Philadelphia were those produced by a well-known goldsmith and jeweler, Ephraim
Brasher of New York.

Brasher produced a gold piece weighing about 408 grains, approximately equal in
value to a Spanish doubloon (about $15.00 in New York currency).

The punch-mark EB appears in either of two positions as illustrated. This mark is
found on some foreign gold coins as well, and probably was so used by Brasher as
evidence of his testing of their value. Many modern forgeries exist.

	EF
1787 New York gold doubloon, EB on Breast	$2,000,000
1787 New York gold doubloon, EB on Wing	1,500,000

New York Copper Coinage

No coinage was authorized by the State of New York following the Revolutionary War, although several propositions were considered. The only coinage laws passed were those regulating coins already in use. Private mints struck several unauthorized coppers.

	G	VG	F	VF	EF
1786, NON VI VIRTUTE VICI	$2,500	$4,250	$8,000	$17,000	$26,000

	G	VG	F	VF	EF
1787 EXCELSIOR Copper, Eagle on Globe Facing Right	$1,000	$2,000	$4,000	$12,500	$25,000
1787 EXCELSIOR Copper, Eagle on Globe Facing Left	1,000	1,800	3,500	9,500	18,000

1787, George Clinton and
New York Arms

1787, Indian and
New York Arms

1787, Indian and Eagle on Globe

	G	VG	F	VF	EF
1787, George Clinton and New York Arms	$4,500	$10,000	$23,000	$45,000	$110,000
1787, Indian and New York Arms	4,000	6,000	12,000	20,000	50,000
1787, Indian and Eagle on Globe	4,000	6,000	12,000	18,000	35,000

Georgivs/Britannia
"Machin's Mills" Copper Halfpennies Made in America

During the era of American state coinage, James F. Atlee and other coiners minted unauthorized, lightweight, imitation British halfpence. These American-made false coins have the same devices, legends, and, in some cases, dates as genuine regal halfpence, but contain less copper. Overall quality of these pieces is similar to that of British-made imitations, but details are more often poorly rendered or missing. Identification of American-made imitations has been confirmed by identifying punch marks and matching them to those of known engravers.

Dates used on these pieces were often evasive, and are as follows: 1771, 1772, and 1774 through 1776 for the first group; 1747 and 1787 for the second group; and 1776, 1778, 1787, and 1788 for the third group. Pieces generally attributed to Atlee can be identified by a single outline in the crosses (British Union) of Britannia's shield and large triangular dentils along the coin circumference. The more-valuable American-made pieces are not to be confused with the similar English-made George III counterfeits (some of which have identical dates), or with genuine British half-pence dated 1770 to 1775.

Group I coins dated 1771, 1772, and 1774 through 1776 have distinctive bold designs but lack the fine details of the original coins. Planchets are generally of high quality. Group II coins dated 1747 and 1787 are generally poorly made. The 1 in the date is not J-shaped, and the dentils are of various sizes. There are no outlines to the stripes in the shield. Group III coins dated 1776, 1778, 1787, and 1788, struck at Machin's Mills in Newberg, New York, are similar to coins of Group II, with their triangular-shaped dentils. Most have wide dates and berries in the wreath.

	AG	G	VG	F	VF	EF	AU
1747, GEORGIVS II. Group II	$80	$125	$200	$450	$2,000	$4,000	—
1771, GEORGIVS III. Group I	30	50	110	200	750	1,200	$3,000
1772, GEORGIVS III. Group I	35	75	150	300	900	1,800	4,750
1772, GEORGIUS III. Group I	40	100	180	400	1,500	3,000	—
1774, GEORGIVS III. Group I	25	40	75	150	420	1,200	2,750
1774, GEORGIUS III. Group I	35	75	135	260	1,000	2,500	—
1775, GEORGIVS III. Group I	20	40	75	150	400	1,000	2,500
1776, GEORGIVS III. Group III	90	150	325	550	1,500	3,800	—
1776, GEORCIVS III, Small Date	650	1,200	3,000	5,000	10,000	—	—
1778, GEORGIVS III. Group III	25	50	85	200	450	1,250	2,000
1784, GEORGIVS III	100	200	500	900	1,800	2,750	4,000
1787, GEORGIVS III. Group II	20	40	75	120	350	800	1,750
1787, GEORGIVS III. Group III	20	40	75	120	350	800	1,750
1788, GEORGIVS III. Group III	20	40	85	150	375	900	1,800

Note: Values shown are what coin dealers pay for the most common varieties in each category. Rare pieces can be worth significantly more. Also see related George III combinations under Connecticut, Vermont, and New York.

Nova Eborac Coinage for New York

| | 1787, NOVA EBORAC Reverse, Seated Figure Facing Right | | 1787, NOVA EBORAC Reverse, Seated Figure Facing Left | |

	AG	G	F	VF	EF	AU
1787, NOVA EBORAC, Seated Figure Facing Right . . .	$27	$55	$120	$400	$900	$2,000
1787, NOVA EBORAC, Seated Figure Facing Left	27	45	100	300	600	1,250

New Jersey

On June 1, 1786, the New Jersey General Assembly granted to Thomas Goadsby, Albion Cox, and Walter Mould authority to coin some three million coppers no later than June 1788, on condition that they delivered to the treasurer of the state "one-tenth part of the full sum they shall strike and coin," in quarterly installments. These coppers were to pass current at 15 to the shilling. Produced in significant quantities, these coins are often seen in the market today and are widely collectible, although certain varieties can be rare and especially valuable.

Narrow Shield   Wide Shield

	AG	G	F	VF	EF	AU
1786, Narrow Shield	$12	$22	$85	$200	$375	$750
1786, Wide Shield	15	35	125	300	850	2,000

Small Planchet

	AG	G	F	VF	EF	AU
1787, Horse's Head Facing Right	$12	$22	$85	$200	$375	$750

Fox Before Legend

	AG	G	F	VF	EF	AU
1788, Horse's Head Facing Right............	$12	$27	$100	$275	$450	$800
1788, Similar, Fox in Legend	30	75	275	900	2,000	4,500
1788, Horse's Head Facing Left.............	85	200	800	2,250	6,000	—

Vermont

Reuben Harmon Jr. was granted permission to coin copper pieces beginning July 1, 1785. The franchise was extended for eight years in 1786. However, in 1787 production was shifted to Machin's Mills, Newburgh, New York, in which Harmon had a proprietary interest. Although the Vermont coins were legally issued there, most other products of Machin's Mills were counterfeits, some dies for which were combined with Vermont pieces, creating several illogical pieces below, including the 1785 Immune Columbia and the 1788 Georgivs III Rex.

1785, IMMUNE COLUMBIA   1785–1786, Plow Type   1786, Baby Head

	AG	G	VG	F	VF	EF
1785, IMMUNE COLUMBIA................	$1,900	$3,200	$5,500	$7,500	$19,000	—
1785, Plow Type, VERMONTS..............	80	150	300	425	1,400	$2,600
1786, Plow Type, VERMONTENSIUM	70	125	200	300	800	1,750
1786, Baby Head.......................	100	160	275	600	1,900	4,750

1786–1787, Bust Left | 1787, BRITANNIA | 1787, Bust Right

	AG	G	VG	F	VF	EF
1786, Bust Left	$25	$75	$180	$400	$1,200	$2,000
1787, Bust Left	1,200	2,500	5,500	12,500	22,000	—
1787, BRITANNIA	20	55	85	110	225	700
1787, Bust Right *(several varieties)*	20	70	135	245	600	1,250

1788, Bust Right | 1788, GEORGIVS III REX

	AG	G	VG	F	VF	EF
1788, Bust Right *(several varieties)*	$20	$60	$110	$225	$450	$900
1788, GEORGIVS III REX	100	250	450	1,200	2,400	6,000

Note: This piece should not be confused with the common British halfpence with similar design and reverse legend BRITANNIA.

PRIVATE TOKENS AFTER CONFEDERATION
North American Tokens

This piece was struck in Dublin, Ireland. The obverse shows the seated figure of Hibernia facing left. Although dated 1781, it is believed to have been struck early in the next century.

	VG	F	VF	EF
1781, Copper or brass	$25	$50	$100	$300

Bar Coppers

The Bar copper is undated and of uncertain origin. It has 13 parallel and unconnected bars on one side. On the other side is the large roman-letter USA monogram. The design was supposedly copied from a Continental Army uniform button.

	VG	F	VF	EF	AU
(Undated) (Circa 1785) Bar Copper	$925	$1,750	$3,000	$4,750	$6,750

Auctori Plebis Tokens

This token is sometimes included with the coins of Connecticut as it greatly resembles issues of that state. It was struck in England by an unknown maker.

	G	VG	F	VF	EF	AU	Unc.
1787, AUCTORI PLEBIS	$40	$75	$125	$250	$450	$900	$3,750

Mott Store Cards

This 19th century store card has long been considered an early token because of its date (1789). Most scholars believe it was most likely produced circa 1830 as a commemorative of the founding of the Mott Company, and probably served as a business card.

	VG	F	VF	EF	AU	Unc.
"1789," Mott Token	$45	$90	$175	$250	$320	$600

Standish Barry Threepence

Standish Barry, a Baltimore silversmith, circulated a silver threepence in 1790. The tokens were believed to have been an advertising venture at a time when small change was scarce.

	VG	F	VF	EF
1790 Threepence	$5,000	$11,000	$25,000	$45,000

Kentucky Tokens

These tokens were struck in England about 1795. Each star in the triangle represents a state, identified by its initial letter. These pieces are usually called *Kentucky cents* because the letter K (for Kentucky) happens to be at the top. In the 19th century these were often called *triangle tokens,* from the arrangement of the stars. Values are for the normal issue with plain edge; lettered-edge varieties exist and are scarcer.

	VG	VF	EF	AU	Unc.
(1792–1794) Copper, Plain Edge	$40	$80	$125	$275	$450

Franklin Press Tokens

This piece is an English tradesman's token, but, being associated with Benjamin Franklin, has accordingly been included in American collections.

	VG	VF	EF	AU	Unc.
1794, Franklin Press Token	$50	$100	$150	$300	$480

Talbot, Allum & Lee Cents

Talbot, Allum & Lee, engaged in the India trade and located in New York, placed a large quantity of English-made coppers in circulation during 1794 and 1795. ONE CENT appears on the 1794 issue and on the edge of the 1795 issue.

1794 Cent,
With NEW YORK

1795 Cent

	G	VG	VF	EF	AU	Unc.
1794 Cent, With NEW YORK...............	$25	$35	$120	$175	$300	$750
1794 Cent, Without NEW YORK	200	300	1,300	2,500	3,500	8,000
1795 Cent..........................	25	35	120	175	300	500

WASHINGTON PORTRAIT PIECES

An interesting series of coins and tokens dated from 1783 to 1795 bear the portrait of George Washington. The likenesses in most instances were faithfully reproduced and were designed to honor Washington. Many of these pieces were of English origin and made later than the dates indicate.

1783,
Military Bust

1783,
Draped Bust

	F	VF	EF	AU	Unc.
1783, Military Bust	$40	$90	$180	$375	$950
1783, Draped Bust	45	100	200	400	1,200

1783, UNITY STATES

	VG	F	VF	EF	AU	Unc.
1783, UNITY STATES	$30	$60	$100	$200	$300	$800

Undated Double-Head Cent

	VG	F	VF	EF	AU	Unc.
(Undated) Double-Head Cent	$30	$50	$100	$200	$400	$1,200

Obverse	Large Eagle Reverse	Small Eagle Reverse

	F	VF	EF	AU	Unc.
1791 Cent, Large Eagle (Date on Obverse)	$200	$250	$350	$600	$1,300
1791 Cent, Small Eagle (Date on Reverse).	225	300	400	650	1,500

	F	VF	EF	AU
1791 Liverpool Halfpenny, Lettered Edge.	$700	$850	$1,600	$2,500

1792, Eagle With Stars, copper	—
1792, Eagle With Stars, silver	—
1792, Eagle With Stars, gold *(unique)*	—

41

(1792) Undated Cent,
WASHINGTON BORN VIRGINIA

1792 Cent,
WASHINGTON PRESIDENT

	VG	F	VF
(1792) Undated Cent, WASHINGTON BORN VIRGINIA, copper	$550	$1,000	$2,200
1792 Cent, WASHINGTON PRESIDENT, Plain Edge	1,500	3,750	7,500

1792 Getz Pattern

1793 Ship Halfpenny

1795 Halfpenny, Grate Token

	VG	F	VF	EF	AU	Unc.
1792, Getz Pattern, copper	$3,500	$6,500	$14,000	$25,000		
1793 Ship Halfpenny, Lettered Edge	35	100	200	300	$450	$1,600
1795, Grate Token, Lettered Edge	40	80	150	360	750	1,100
1795, Grate Token, Reeded Edge	25	40	80	150	200	350

	F	VF	EF	AU	Unc.
1795, LIBERTY AND SECURITY Halfpenny, Plain Edge	$70	$150	$300	$600	$1,500
1795, LIBERTY AND SECURITY Halfpenny, Lettered Edge . . .	65	125	275	550	1,500
(1795) Undated, LIBERTY AND SECURITY Penny.	150	250	400	750	1,500

	G	F	VF	EF	AU
(1795) NORTH WALES Halfpenny	$50	$100	$250	$750	$1,500

	F	VF	EF	AU	Unc.
SUCCESS Medal, Large, Plain or Reeded Edge.	$100	$200	$350	$650	$1,400
SUCCESS Medal, Small, Plain or Reeded Edge.	125	250	425	700	1,500

CONTINENTAL CURRENCY

The Continental Currency pieces were made to circulate in lieu of paper dollars at their time of issue. The exact nature of their monetary role is uncertain; they might have been experimental, or they might have seen circulation. At any rate, this was the first dollar-sized coin proposed for the United States. They were probably struck in Philadelphia from dies engraved by Elisha Gallaudet. As with many early pieces, modern replicas exist.

	G	F	VF	EF	AU	Unc.
1776, CURENCY, pewter *(2 varieties)*	$4,000	$7,000	$14,000	$19,000	$27,500	$40,000
1776, CURENCY, silver *(2 known)*.		175,000				
1776, CURRENCY, pewter.	4,000	7,000	14,000	20,000	30,000	45,000
1776, CURRENCY, EG FECIT, pewter.	4,200	7,500	15,000	23,000	32,500	47,000

FUGIO COPPERS

The first coins issued by authority of the United States were the 1787 "Fugio" coppers. The legends have been credited to Benjamin Franklin by many, and the coins, as a consequence, have been referred to as *Franklin cents*.

1787, With
Pointed Rays

1787, With
Club Rays

	G	VG	F	VF	EF	AU	Unc.
Pointed Rays, STATES UNITED at Side of Circle *(illustrated)*	$60	$150	$275	$450	$900	$1,200	$2,250
Pointed Rays, UNITED STATES at Side of Circle	60	150	275	450	1,000	1,300	2,400
Club Rays, Rounded Ends	100	250	400	1,000	2,000	3,500	—

The half cent was authorized to be coined April 2, 1792. Originally the weight was to have been 132 grains, but this was changed to 104 grains by the Act of January 14, 1793, before coinage commenced. The weight was again changed to 84 grains January 26, 1796, by presidential proclamation in conformity with the Act of March 3, 1795. Coinage was discontinued by the Act of February 21, 1857. All were coined at the Philadelphia Mint.

LIBERTY CAP (1793–1797)

AG-3 About Good: Clear enough to identify.
G-4 Good: Outline of bust of Liberty clear, no details. Date readable. Reverse lettering incomplete.
VG-8 Very Good: Some hair details. Reverse lettering complete.
F-12 Fine: Most of hair detail visible. Leaves worn, but all visible.
VF-20 Very Fine: Hair near ear and forehead worn, other areas distinct. Some details in leaves visible.
EF-40 Extremely Fine: Light wear on highest parts of head and wreath.
AU-50 About Uncirculated: Only a trace of wear on Liberty's face.

Head Facing Left (1793)

	Mintage	AG-3	G-4	VG-8	F-12	VF-20	EF-40	AU-50
1793	35,334	$1,000	$2,000	$4,000	$5,000	$8,000	$17,000	$25,000

Head Facing Right (1794–1797)

Pole to Cap

Punctuated Date

No Pole to Cap

	Mintage	AG-3	G-4	VG-8	F-12	VF-20	EF-40	AU-50
1794	81,600	$125	$275	$370	$700	$1,500	$4,250	$7,000
1795, All kinds	139,690							
1795, Lettered Edge, With Pole		100	200	310	525	1,200	2,700	4,750
1795, Lettered Edge, Punctuated Date		100	200	310	525	1,250	2,900	5,000
1795, Plain Edge, Punctuated Date		90	160	260	425	1,000	2,700	4,200
1795, Plain Edge, No Pole		90	160	260	425	1,000	2,700	4,200
1796, With Pole	1,390	5,000	10,000	12,500	20,000	30,000	50,000	70,000
1796, No Pole	*	12,000	20,000	30,000	60,000	85,000	125,000	

* Included in number above.

1797, 1 Above 1, Plain Edge   **1797, Plain Edge**

	Mintage	AG-3	G-4	VG-8	F-12	VF-20	EF-40	AU-50
1797, All kinds.	127,840							
1797, 1 Above 1, Plain Edge		$100	$210	$300	$450	$900	$2,000	$3,500
1797, Plain Edge.		120	220	375	750	1,250	2,500	4,500
1797, Lettered Edge		210	700	1,200	2,750	10,000	17,500	32,000
1797, Gripped Edge.		6,500	15,000	30,000	40,000			

DRAPED BUST (1800–1808)

AG-3 About Good: Clear enough to identify.
G-4 Good: Outline of bust of Liberty clear, few details, date readable. Reverse lettering worn and incomplete.
VG-8 Very Good: Some drapery visible. Date and legends complete.
F-12 Fine: Shoulder drapery and hair over brow worn smooth.
VF-20 Very Fine: Only slight wear in previously mentioned areas. Slight wear on reverse.
EF-40 Extremely Fine: Light wear on highest parts of head and wreath.
AU-50 About Uncirculated: Wear slight on hair above forehead.

1st Reverse   **2nd Reverse**

	Mintage	AG-3	G-4	VG-8	F-12	VF-20	EF-40	AU-50
1800	202,908	$16	$35	$55	$75	$150	$300	$500
1802, 2 Over 0	20,266	150	400	850	2,000	6,000	15,000	
1803	92,000	20	40	60	85	200	550	1,000

Plain 4   **Crosslet 4**   **Stems to Wreath**   **Stemless Wreath**

	Mintage	AG-3	G-4	VG-8	F-12	VF-20	EF-40	AU-50
1804, All kinds.	1,055,312							
1804, Plain 4, Stems to Wreath		$18	$40	$60	$95	$200	$475	$1,200
1804, Plain 4, Stemless Wreath.		20	40	60	85	150	250	500
1804, Crosslet 4, Stemless Wreath . . .		20	40	60	85	150	250	500
1804, Crosslet 4, Stems to Wreath . . .		20	40	60	85	150	250	500

| 1804, "Spiked Chin" | Small 5 | Large 5 |

Mintage	AG-3	G-4	VG-8	F-12	VF-20	EF-40	AU-50
1804, "Spiked Chin" . . . .*	$20	$50	$70	$100	$150	$250	$850
1805, All kinds. 814,464							
1805, Medium 5, Stemless Wreath . . .	20	40	60	85	150	250	500
1805, Small 5, Stems to Wreath	115	400	750	1,800	3,500	8,500	20,000
1805, Large 5, Stems to Wreath	20	40	60	85	165	250	500

* Included in "1804, All kinds" mintage (previous page).

| Small 6 | Large 6 | 1808, 8 Over 7 | Normal Date |

Mintage	AG-3	G-4	VG-8	F-12	VF-20	EF-40	AU-50
1806, All kinds. 356,000							
1806, Small 6, Stems to Wreath	$40	$110	$185	$325	$800	$1,500	$4,000
1806, Small 6, Stemless Wreath	20	40	60	85	150	250	500
1806, Large 6, Stems to Wreath	20	40	60	85	150	250	500
1807 476,000	20	40	60	85	150	300	550
1808, Normal Date 400,000	20	40	60	85	150	300	500
1808, 8 Over 7 . . . .*	45	70	125	300	1,000	2,250	6,000

* Included in number below.

CLASSIC HEAD (1809–1836)

G-4 Good: LIBERTY only partly visible on hair band. Lettering, date, and stars worn but visible.
VG-8 Very Good: LIBERTY entirely visible on hair band. Lower curls worn.
F-12 Fine: Only partial wear on LIBERTY, and hair at top worn in spots.
VF-20 Very Fine: Lettering clear-cut. Hair only slightly worn.
EF-40 Extremely Fine: Light wear on highest points of hair and leaves.
AU-50 About Uncirculated: Sharp hair detail with only a trace of wear on higher points.
MS-60 Uncirculated: Typical brown to red surface. No trace of wear.
MS-63 Choice Uncirculated: Well-defined color, brown to red. No traces of wear.

| 1828, 13 Stars | 1828, 12 Stars |

Dealers often pay more than the prices shown for brilliant or red Uncirculated coins, and less for spotted, cleaned, or discolored pieces.

Mintage	AG-3	G-4	VG-8	F-12	VF-20	EF-40	AU-50	MS-60	MS-63
1809 1,154,572	$15	$30	$50	$60	$75	$90	$150	$400	$750
1810 215,000	15	30	50	65	110	250	475	1,000	1,600
1811 63,140	100	200	400	800	1,500	3,500	6,500	15,000	35,000

Chart continued on next page.

	Mintage	G-4	VG-8	F-12	VF-20	EF-40	AU-50	MS-60	MS-63	PF-63
1825 63,000		$25	$30	$50	$75	$100	$200	$500	$1,250	
1826 234,000		25	30	50	60	85	125	275	475	
1828, 13 Stars 606,000		25	30	50	60	75	120	190	325	
1828, 12 Stars . . . . *		25	35	65	85	125	175	650	1,100	
1829 487,000		25	30	50	60	85	125	225	350	
1831 2,200										—
1832 51,000		25	30	50	60	75	100	175	300	$8,500
1833 103,000		25	30	50	60	75	100	175	300	4,500
1834 141,000		25	30	50	60	75	100	175	300	3,000
1835 398,000		25	30	50	60	75	100	175	300	3,000
1836										7,500

* Included in number above.

BRAIDED HAIR (1840–1857)

VG-8 Very Good: Beads in hair uniformly distinct. Hair lines visible in spots.
F-12 Fine: Hair lines above ear worn. Beads sharp.
VF-20 Very Fine: Lowest curl worn; hair otherwise distinct.
EF-40 Extremely Fine: Light wear on highest points of hair and on leaves.
AU-50 About Uncirculated: Very slight trace of wear on hair above Liberty's ear.
MS-60 Uncirculated: No trace of wear. Clear luster.
MS-63 Choice Uncirculated: No trace of wear.
PF-63 Choice Proof: Nearly perfect; only light blemishes.

Dealers often pay more than the prices shown for brilliant or red Uncirculated coins, and less for spotted, cleaned, or discolored pieces.

	Mintage	PF-63
1840, Original		$5,250
1840, Restrike		4,500
1841, Original		4,500
1841, Restrike		4,000
1842, Original		4,500
1842, Restrike		4,000
1843, Original		4,500
1843, Restrike		4,000
1844, Original		5,250
1844, Restrike		4,500

	Mintage	PF-63
1845, Original		$5,250
1845, Restrike		4,500
1846, Original		5,250
1846, Restrike		4,500
1847, Original		4,500
1847, Restrike		4,000
1848, Original		5,000
1848, Restrike		4,500
1849, Original, Small Date		4,500
1849, Restrike, Small Date		4,000

Small Date   **Large Date**

	Mintage	G-4	VG-8	F-12	VF-20	EF-40	AU-50	MS-60	MS-63	PF-63
1849, Large Date 39,864		$25	$30	$40	$50	$75	$110	$225	$300	—
1850 39,812		25	30	40	50	75	110	225	350	$4,500
1851 147,672		25	30	40	50	65	85	135	250	3,000
1852										3,500
1853 129,694		25	30	40	50	65	85	135	250	
1854 55,358		25	30	40	50	65	85	135	250	4,500
1855 56,500		25	30	40	50	65	85	135	250	3,000
1856 40,430		25	30	40	50	65	90	150	275	3,000
1857 35,180		25	30	45	70	85	130	195	320	3,000

Cents and half cents were the first coins struck at the United States Mint. Coinage began in 1793 with laws stating that the cent should weigh exactly twice as much as the half cent. Large cents are dated every year from 1793 to 1857 with the exception of 1815, when a lack of copper prevented production. All were coined at the Philadelphia Mint. Varieties listed are those most significant to collectors. Numerous other die varieties may be found, as each of the early dies was individually made.

FLOWING HAIR (1793)

AG-3 About Good: Date and devices clear enough to identify.
G-4 Good: Lettering worn but readable. No detail on bust.
VG-8 Very Good: Date and lettering distinct, some details of head visible.
F-12 Fine: About half of hair and other details visible.
VF-20 Very Fine: Ear visible, most details visible.
EF-40 Extremely Fine: Wear evident on highest points of hair and back of temple.

Chain Reverse (1793)

AMERI. Reverse   AMERICA Reverse

	Mintage	AG-3	G-4	VG-8	F-12	VF-20	EF-40
1793, Chain, All kinds 36,103							
1793, AMERI. in Legend		$2,500	$5,000	$10,000	$18,000	$30,000	$55,000
1793, AMERICA		2,000	3,800	7,500	12,000	23,000	50,000

Wreath Reverse (1793)

Strawberry Leaf Variety

	Mintage	AG-3	G-4	VG-8	F-12	VF-20	EF-40
1793, Wreath, All kinds 63,353							
1793, Vine and Bars Edge		$500	$2,000	$3,000	$5,000	$8,500	$16,000
1793, Lettered Edge		500	2,000	3,000	5,000	8,500	16,000
1793, Strawberry Leaf. . . . . *(4 known)*		—	—	—			

LIBERTY CAP (1793–1796)

1793, Vine and Bars Edge   **Lettered Edge (1793–1795)**
Chain and Wreath types only.   **ONE HUNDRED FOR A DOLLAR**

Entry continued on next page.   **49**

Beaded Border (1793)

Head of 1793 (1793–1794)
Head in high, rounded relief.

Head of 1794 (1794)
*Well-defined hair;
hook on lowest curl.*

Head of 1795 (1794–1796)
*Head in low relief;
no hook on lowest curl.*

	Mintage	AG-3	G-4	VG-8	F-12	VF-20	EF-40
1793, Liberty Cap 11,056		$1,500	$3,000	$5,500	$10,000	$27,000	$45,000
1794, All kinds. 918,521							
1794, "Head of 1793"		225	725	1,500	2,000	4,500	10,000
1794, "Head of 1794"		50	125	200	750	1,000	3,000
1794, "Head of 1795"		50	125	200	750	1,000	2,500
1795, Lettered Edge 37,000		50	130	200	750	1,200	2,400
1795, Plain Edge 501,500		50	115	225	600	1,000	2,000
1796, Liberty Cap 109,825		75	180	275	700	1,250	2,800

DRAPED BUST (1796–1807)

AG-3 About Good: Clear enough to identify.
G-4 Good: Lettering worn, but clear; date clear. Bust lacking in detail.
VG-8 Very Good: Drapery on Liberty partly visible. Less wear in date and lettering.
F-12 Fine: Hair over brow smooth; some detail showing in other parts of hair.
VF-20 Very Fine: Hair lines slightly worn. Hair over brow better defined.
EF-40 Extremely Fine: Hair above forehead and left of eye outlined and detailed. Only slight wear on olive leaves.

LIHERTY Error

	Mintage	AG-3	G-4	VG-8	F-12	VF-20	EF-40
1796, Draped Bust 363,375		$40	$100	$200	$400	$1,500	$4,500
1796, LIHERTY Error . . . . *		80	135	325	800	1,900	6,000

* Included in number above.

	Gripped Edge		With Stems		Stemless	
Mintage	**AG-3**	**G-4**	**VG-8**	**F-12**	**VF-20**	**EF-40**
1797, All kinds. 897,510						
1797, Gripped Edge, 1795-Style Reverse . . .	$40	$75	$150	$250	$850	$2,500
1797, Plain Edge, 1795-Style Reverse.	30	65	125	230	750	3,000
1797, 1797 Reverse, With Stems.	30	50	100	200	750	1,500
1797, 1797 Reverse, Stemless	30	65	125	250	750	2,300

1798, 8 Over 7 **1799, 9 Over 8** **1800 Over 1798** **1800, 80 Over 79**

	Mintage	AG-3	G-4	VG-8	F-12	VF-20	EF-40
1798, All kinds. 1,841,745							
1798, 8 Over 7		$25	$65	$135	$225	$1,000	$3,000
1798		20	35	50	125	300	1,350
1799, 9 Over 8	*	750	1,850	3,000	6,500	20,000	50,000
1799, Normal Date	*	750	1,850	3,000	6,500	22,000	60,000
1800, All kinds. 2,822,175							
1800, 1800 Over 1798		20	30	55	115	500	1,750
1800, 80 Over 79		20	30	50	100	250	1,100
1800, Normal Date		20	30	50	100	225	1,000

* Included in "1798, All kinds," mintage.

Fraction 1/000 **Corrected Fraction** **1801 Reverse, 3 Errors**

	Mintage	AG-3	G-4	VG-8	F-12	VF-20	EF-40
1801, All kinds. 1,362,837							
1801, Normal Reverse.		$20	$25	$30	$75	$200	$750
1801, 3 Errors: 1/000, One Stem, and IINITED		25	65	120	325	1,000	3,250
1801, Fraction 1/000.		20	30	40	120	250	825
1801, 1/100 Over 1/000		20	30	50	125	300	950
1802, All kinds. 3,435,100							
1802, Normal Reverse.		20	30	40	90	200	750
1802, Fraction 1/000.		20	35	50	120	250	1,500
1802, Stemless Wreath		20	30	40	90	200	750

1803, Small Date, Blunt 1 **1803, Large Date, Pointed 1** **Small Fraction** **Large Fraction**

See next page for chart.

	Mintage	AG-3	G-4	VG-8	F-12	VF-20	EF-40
1803, All kinds. 3,131,691							
1803, Small Date, Small Fraction.		$20	$30	$40	$80	$200	$750
1803, Small Date, Large Fraction		20	30	40	80	200	750
1803, Large Date, Small Fraction		1,000	2,500	5,000	10,000	20,000	
1803, Large Date, Large Fraction		25	40	80	150	500	1,500
1803, 1/100 Over 1/000		20	35	50	100	250	800
1803, Stemless Wreath		20	35	50	100	250	800

Broken Dies

All genuine 1804 cents have crosslet 4 in date and a large fraction.
The 0 in date is in line with O in OF on reverse.

	Mintage	AG-3	G-4	VG-8	F-12	VF-20	EF-40
1804 (a) 96,500		$350	$1,000	$1,250	$2,500	$5,000	$10,000
1805 941,116		20	30	40	80	200	750
1806 348,000		20	35	55	100	235	950

a. Values shown are for coins with normal or broken dies.

Small 1807, 7 Over 6
(Blunt 1)

Large 1807, 7 Over 6
(Pointed 1)

	Mintage	AG-3	G-4	VG-8	F-12	VF-20	EF-40
1807, All kinds. 829,221							
1807, Small 7 Over 6, Blunt 1		$450	$1,200	$2,500	$5,000	$10,000	$25,000
1807, Large 7 Over 6		20	30	35	70	200	750
1807, Small Fraction		20	30	35	70	225	800
1807, Large Fraction		20	30	35	70	200	750

CLASSIC HEAD (1808–1814)

AG-3 About Good: Details clear enough to identify.

G-4 Good: Legends, stars, and date worn, but plain.

VG-8 Very Good: LIBERTY all readable. Liberty's ear visible. Details worn but plain.

F-12 Fine: Hair on forehead and before ear nearly smooth. Ear and hair under ear sharp.

VF-20 Very Fine: Some detail in all hair lines. Slight wear on leaves on reverse.

EF-40 Extremely Fine: All hair lines sharp. Very slight wear on high points.

	Mintage	AG-3	G-4	VG-8	F-12	VF-20	EF-40
1808	1,007,000	$25	$50	$100	$250	$650	$1,500
1809	222,867	25	50	110	225	650	1,600

| 1810, 10 Over 09 | 1810, Normal Date | 1811, Last 1 Over 0 | 1811, Normal Date |

	Mintage	AG-3	G-4	VG-8	F-12	VF-20	EF-40
1810, All kinds.	1,458,500						
1810, 10 Over 09		$20	$50	$100	$250	$650	$1,400
1810, Normal Date		20	50	100	250	650	1,400
1811, All kinds.	218,025						
1811, Last 1 Over 0.		20	50	100	250	1,000	3,000
1811, Normal Date		20	50	100	250	650	1,500
1812	1,075,500	20	50	100	250	650	1,400
1813	418,000	20	50	100	250	650	1,500
1814	357,830	20	50	100	250	650	1,400

MODIFIED LIBERTY HEAD (1816–1857)

G-4 Good: Details on Liberty's head partly visible. Even wear in date and legends.
VG-8 Very Good: LIBERTY, date, stars, and legends clear. Part of hair cord visible.
F-12 Fine: All hair lines visible. Hair cords uniformly visible.
VF-20 Very Fine: Hair cords only slightly worn. Hair lines only partly worn, all well defined.
EF-40 Extremely Fine: Both hair cords stand out sharply. All hair lines sharp.
AU-50 About Uncirculated: Only traces of wear on hair and highest points on leaves and bow.
MS-60 Uncirculated: Typical brown surface. No trace of wear.
MS-63 Choice Uncirculated: Some distracting contact marks or blemishes in prime focal areas. Impaired luster possible.

Matron Head (1816–1835)

1817, 13 Stars 1817, 15 Stars

Dealers often pay more than the prices shown for brilliant or red Uncirculated coins, and less for spotted, cleaned, or discolored pieces.

	Mintage	G-4	VG-8	F-12	VF-20	EF-40	AU-50	MS-60	MS-63
1816	2,820,982	$15	$20	$25	$55	$125	$175	$250	$500
1817, 13 Stars.	3,948,400	15	20	25	45	75	145	240	500
1817, 15 Stars.	*	15	20	30	100	300	500	1,200	—
1818	3,167,000	15	20	25	45	75	145	240	500

* Included in number above.

1819, 9 Over 8   **1820, 20 Over 19**

	Mintage	G-4	VG-8	F-12	VF-20	EF-40	AU-50	MS-60	MS-63
1819 2,671,000		$15	$20	$25	$40	$65	$125	$200	$450
1819, 9 Over 8 . . . . *		20	25	30	40	150	175	300	550
1820 4,407,550		15	20	25	40	60	100	200	350
1820, 20 Over 19 . . . . *		20	25	30	55	150	225	500	700
1821 (a) 389,000		20	25	60	185	650	1,500	4,500	—
1822 2,072,339		15	20	25	50	100	275	475	775

* Included in number above. **a.** Wide and closely spaced AMER varieties are valued the same.

1823, 3 Over 2   **1824, 4 Over 2**   **1826, 6 Over 5**

	Mintage	G-4	VG-8	F-12	VF-20	EF-40	AU-50	MS-60	MS-63
1823, 3 Over 2 . . . . *		$27	$50	$150	$300	$1,000	$1,900	$10,000	—
1823, Normal Date . . . . *		30	55	175	425	1,500	3,000	10,000	—
1824, 4 Over 2 . . . . *		20	30	50	200	750	1,500	3,500	$7,500
1824, Normal Date . 1,262,000		15	20	25	75	210	350	950	1,650
1825 1,461,100		15	20	25	45	150	250	800	1,500
1826, 6 Over 5 1,517,425		20	25	40	110	425	600	1,500	3,500
1826, Normal Date . . . . **		15	20	25	45	110	190	500	1,000
1827 2,357,732		15	20	25	40	80	150	400	1,000

* Included in number below. ** Included in number above.

Date Size, Through 1828   **Date Size, 1828 and Later**

	Mintage	G-4	VG-8	F-12	VF-20	EF-40	AU-50	MS-60	MS-63
1828, Large Narrow Date 2,260,624		$15	$20	$25	$40	$70	$150	$400	$700
1828, Small Wide Date . . . . *		15	20	30	50	100	200	550	1,200
1829 1,414,500		15	20	25	40	70	110	250	525
1830 1,711,500		15	20	25	40	60	100	200	400
1831 3,359,260		15	20	25	40	50	100	200	350
1832 2,362,000		15	20	25	40	50	80	175	325
1833 2,739,000		15	20	25	40	50	80	175	325
1834 1,855,100		15	20	25	40	70	100	200	350
1835 3,878,400		15	20	25	40	65	90	200	350

* Included in number above.

Matron Head Modified (1835–1839) and Braided Hair (1837–1857)

G-4 Good: Considerably worn. LIBERTY readable.

VG-8 Very Good: Hairlines smooth but visible; outline of ear clearly defined.

F-12 Fine: Hairlines at top of head and behind ear worn but visible. Braid over brow plain; ear clear.

VF-20 Very Fine: All details sharper than for F-12. Only slight wear on hair over brow.

EF-40 Extremely Fine: Hair above ear detailed, but slightly worn.

AU-50 About Uncirculated: Trace of wear on high points of hair above ear and eye and on highest points on leaves and bow.

MS-60 Uncirculated: Typical brown surface. No trace of wear.

MS-63 Choice Uncirculated: Some distracting contact marks or blemishes in prime focal areas. Impaired luster possible.

1839, 1839 Over 1836

Dealers often pay more than the prices shown for brilliant or red Uncirculated coins, and less for spotted, cleaned, or discolored pieces.

	Mintage	G-4	VG-8	F-12	VF-20	EF-40	AU-50	MS-60	MS-63
1836 2,111,000		$15	$20	$25	$40	$55	$85	$160	$300
1837 5,558,300		15	20	25	40	65	90	160	275
1838 6,370,200		15	20	25	40	50	85	150	275
1839 3,128,661		15	20	25	40	45	80	150	275
1839, 1839 Over 1836, Plain Cords . . . . . .*		110	275	550	1,250	3,500	7,000	—	—
1840 2,462,700		15	20	25	30	40	75	150	300
1841 1,597,367		15	20	25	30	40	75	150	300
1842 2,383,390		15	20	25	30	40	75	150	300

* Included in number above.

Small Letters

"Head of 1840"
Petite Head (1839–1843)

"Head of 1844"
Mature Head (1843–1857)

Large Letters

	Mintage	G-4	VG-8	F-12	VF-20	EF-40	AU-50	MS-60	MS-63
1843, Petite, Small Letters 2,425,342		$15	$20	$25	$28	$30	$60	$145	$185
1843, Petite, Large Letters . . . .*		15	20	30	35	70	125	325	600
1843, Mature, Large Letters . . . .*		15	20	25	30	50	90	160	400
1844, Normal Date 2,398,752		15	20	25	30	40	65	120	200
1844, 44 Over 81 . . . .*		20	25	30	45	115	235	550	1,250
1845 3,894,804		15	20	25	30	40	70	125	200
1846 4,120,800		15	20	25	30	40	70	125	200
1847 6,183,669		15	20	25	30	40	70	125	200
1847, 7 Over "Small 7" . . . .*		15	20	25	40	75	185	525	900

* Included in number above.

	Mintage	G-4	VG-8	F-12	VF-20	EF-40	AU-50	MS-60	MS-63
1848	6,415,799	$15	$20	$25	$30	$40	$70	$110	$150
1849	4,178,500	15	20	25	30	40	70	125	225
1850	4,426,844	15	20	25	30	40	70	100	200

1844, 44 Over 81

1851, 51 Over 81

1847, 7 Over "Small" 7

Dealers often pay more than the prices shown for brilliant or red Uncirculated coins, and less for spotted, cleaned, or discolored pieces.

	Mintage	G-4	VG-8	F-12	VF-20	EF-40	AU-50	MS-60	MS-63
1851, Normal Date	9,889,707	$15	$20	$25	$30	$40	$70	$100	$150
1851, 51 Over 81	*	15	20	25	30	75	110	250	450
1852	5,063,094	15	20	25	30	40	70	100	200
1853	6,641,131	15	20	25	30	40	70	100	200
1854	4,236,156	15	20	25	30	40	70	100	200

* Included in number above.

1855, Upright 5's   **1855, Slanting 5's**   **1855, Knob on Ear**

	Mintage	G-4	VG-8	F-12	VF-20	EF-40	AU-50	MS-60	MS-63
1855, All kinds.	1,574,829								
1855, Upright 5's.		$15	$20	$25	$30	$40	$70	$100	$125
1855, Slanting 5's		15	20	25	30	40	70	115	200
1855, Slanting 5's, Knob on Ear.		15	20	25	30	45	90	160	300
1856, Upright 5	2,690,463	15	20	25	30	35	70	100	200
1856, Slanting 5	*	15	20	25	30	35	70	100	200

* Included in number above.

1857, Large Date   **1857, Small Date**

	Mintage	G-4	VG-8	F-12	VF-20	EF-40	AU-50	MS-60	MS-63
1857, Large Date	333,546	$15	$25	$30	$35	$50	$120	$200	$325
1857, Small Date	*	15	27	35	40	55	130	220	350

* Included in number above.

FLYING EAGLE (1856–1858)

The Act of February 21, 1857, provided for the coinage of the new copper-nickel small cent. The 1856 Flying Eagle cent was not an authorized Mint issue, as the law governing the new-size coin was enacted after the date of issue. It is believed that nearly 1,000 original strikings and 1,500 or more restrikes were made of the 1856. They are properly referred to as *patterns*.

G-4 Good: All details worn, but readable.

VG-8 Very Good: Details in eagle's feathers and eye evident, but worn.

F-12 Fine: Eagle-head details and feather tips sharp.

VF-20 Very Fine: Considerable detail visible in feathers in right wing and tail.

EF-40 Extremely Fine: Slight wear, all details sharp.

AU-50 About Uncirculated: Slight wear on eagle's left wing and breast.

MS-60 Uncirculated: No trace of wear. Light blemishes.

MS-63 Choice Uncirculated: Some distracting contact marks or blemishes in prime focal areas. Some impairment of luster possible.

PF-63 Choice Proof: Nearly perfect.

| 1858, 8 Over 7 | 1856–1858, Large Letters | 1858, Small Letters |

Dealers often pay more than the prices shown for brilliant Uncirculated and Proof coins, and less for spotted, cleaned, or discolored pieces.

	Mintage	G-4	VG-8	F-12	VF-20	EF-40	AU-50	MS-60	MS-63	PF-63
1856	2,000	$5,000	$6,000	$7,500	$8,500	$9,500	$10,000	$12,000	$15,000	$15,000
1857	17,450,000	15	25	30	35	80	100	350	650	
	(100)									5,000
1858, Large Letters	24,600,000	15	25	30	35	80	100	350	650	
	(100)									5,000
1858, 8 Over 7	*	25	50	115	210	450	735	2,000	5,500	
1858, Small Letters	*	15	25	30	35	80	100	350	650	
	(200)									4,000

* Included in mintage for 1858, Large Letters.

INDIAN HEAD (1859–1909)

The small cent was redesigned in 1859, and a representation of Miss Liberty wearing an Indian war bonnet was adopted as the obverse device. The 1859 reverse was also changed to represent a laurel wreath. In 1860 the reverse was modified to display an oak wreath with a small shield at the top. From 1859 into 1864, cents were struck in copper-nickel. In 1864 the composition was changed to bronze, although copper-nickel cents were also struck during that year.

G-4 Good: No LIBERTY visible.
VG-8 Very Good: At least some letters of LIBERTY readable on head band.
F-12 Fine: LIBERTY mostly visible.
VF-20 Very Fine: Slight but even wear on LIBERTY.
EF-40 Extremely Fine: LIBERTY sharp. All other details sharp. Only slight wear on ribbon end.
AU-50 About Uncirculated: Very slight trace of wear above the ear and the lowest curl of hair.
MS-60 Uncirculated: No trace of wear. Light blemishes.
MS-63 Choice Uncirculated: Some distracting contact marks or blemishes in prime focal areas. Impaired luster possible.
PF-63 Choice Proof: Nearly perfect.

Without Shield at Top of Wreath (1859 Only)

With Shield on Reverse (1860–1909)

Variety 1 – Copper-Nickel, Laurel Wreath Reverse (1859)

Dealers often pay more than the prices shown for brilliant Uncirculated coins, and less for spotted, cleaned, or discolored pieces.

	Mintage	G-4	VG-8	F-12	VF-20	EF-40	AU-50	MS-60	MS-63	PF-63
1859 . . . . . . *(800)* . . 36,400,000		$7	$8	$10	$27	$55	$100	$140	$500	$850

Variety 2 – Copper-Nickel, Oak Wreath With Shield (1860–1864)

	Mintage	G-4	VG-8	F-12	VF-20	EF-40	AU-50	MS-60	MS-63	PF-63
1860 . . . . . . *(1,000)*	20,566,000	$6.00	$7	$8	$12	$32	$65	$90	$200	$575
1861 . . . . . . *(1,000)*	10,100,000	11.00	13	18	32	65	85	125	225	650
1862 *(1,500–2,000)*	28,075,000	5.50	6	10	15	30	45	85	140	500
1863 . . *(800–1,000)*	49,840,000	5.50	6	10	15	30	45	85	140	500
1864 . . *(800–1,000)*	13,740,000	8.00	10	15	25	40	70	125	225	550

Variety 3 – Bronze (1864–1909)

1864, Indian Head Cent With "L"

	Mintage	G-4	VG-8	F-12	VF-20	EF-40	AU-50	MS-60	MS-63	PF-63
1864, All kinds. 39,233,714										
1864, No L *(150)*.		$5	$7	$10	$22	$32	$42	$55	$85	$300
1864, With L *(20)*.		27	45	70	100	170	190	225	375	—
1865 . . *(750–1,000)*. . 35,429,286		5	6	9	12	20	35	50	100	200
1866 . . *(725–1,000)*. . . 9,826,500		22	25	35	65	100	150	175	275	220
1867 . . *(850–1,100)*. . . 9,821,000		22	25	35	65	100	150	175	275	220
1868 . . *(750–1,000)*. . 10,266,500		22	25	35	65	100	150	175	275	200
1869 . . *(850–1,100)*. . . 6,420,000		35	40	90	150	225	275	300	450	210
1870 . . . . . . *(1,000)*. . . 5,275,000		28	35	85	135	200	275	300	400	175
1871 . . . . . . *(960)*. . . 3,929,500		35	45	125	185	225	300	365	500	175
1872 . . *(850–1,100)*. . . 4,042,000		45	65	160	225	300	400	450	700	220
1873 *(1,500–2,000)*. . 11,676,500		11	15	24	38	80	100	120	250	160
1874 *(1,000–1,200)*. . 14,187,500		10	10	18	30	50	75	110	175	150
1875 *(1,000–1,250)*. . 13,528,000		10	14	20	35	55	85	115	175	150
1876 *(1,500–2,000)*. . . 7,944,000		15	18	30	60	100	145	185	275	150
1877 *(1,250–1,500)*. 852,500		400	500	750	1,200	1,600	1,900	2,200	3,000	1,500

Dealers often pay more than the prices shown for brilliant or red Uncirculated coins, and less for spotted, cleaned, or discolored pieces.

	Mintage	G-4	VG-8	F-12	VF-20	EF-40	AU-50	MS-60	MS-63	PF-63
1878 .... (2,350).... 5,797,500		$14.00	$18.00	$25.00	$65.00	$100	$145	$165	$250	$150
1879 .... (3,200)... 16,228,000		4.00	6.00	8.00	18.00	40	45	50	80	135
1880 .... (3,955)... 38,961,000		1.75	2.00	3.00	6.00	15	25	40	70	125
1881 .... (3,575)... 39,208,000		1.75	2.00	3.00	5.00	10	16	26	37	125
1882 .... (3,100)... 38,578,000		1.75	2.00	3.00	5.00	10	16	26	37	125
1883 .... (6,609)... 45,591,500		1.75	2.00	3.00	5.00	10	16	26	37	125
1884 .... (3,942)... 23,257,800		2.25	2.50	3.50	6.00	14	20	30	60	125
1885 .... (3,790)... 11,761,594		3.00	4.00	6.00	14.00	35	45	60	95	125
1886 .... (4,290)... 17,650,000		1.75	3.00	8.00	24.00	65	85	100	125	125
1887 .... (2,960)... 45,223,523		1.25	1.50	1.75	2.25	8	14	25	35	125
1888 .... (4,582)... 37,489,832		0.85	1.10	1.80	2.75	8	14	25	40	125
1889 .... (3,336)... 48,866,025		0.85	1.10	1.80	2.75	6	12	25	35	125
1890 .... (2,740)... 57,180,114		0.85	1.10	1.80	2.75	6	12	25	35	125
1891 .... (2,350)... 47,070,000		0.85	1.10	1.80	2.75	6	12	25	35	125
1892 .... (2,745)... 37,647,087		0.85	1.10	1.80	2.75	6	12	25	35	125
1893 .... (2,195)... 46,640,000		0.85	1.10	1.80	2.75	6	12	25	35	125
1894 .... (2,632)... 16,749,500		2.00	3.00	4.75	8.50	25	30	40	50	125
1895 .... (2,062)... 38,341,574		0.85	1.10	1.30	2.00	6	11	25	28	125
1896 .... (1,862)... 39,055,431		0.85	1.10	1.30	2.00	6	11	25	28	125
1897 .... (1,938)... 50,464,392		0.85	1.10	1.30	2.00	6	11	25	28	125
1898 .... (1,795)... 49,821,284		0.85	1.10	1.30	2.00	6	11	25	28	125
1899 .... (2,031)... 53,598,000		0.85	1.10	1.30	2.00	6	11	25	28	125
1900 .... (2,262)... 66,831,502		0.80	1.00	1.10	1.50	5	10	18	25	125
1901 .... (1,985)... 79,609,158		0.80	1.00	1.10	1.50	5	10	18	25	125
1902 .... (2,018)... 87,374,704		0.80	1.00	1.10	1.50	5	10	18	25	125
1903 .... (1,790)... 85,092,703		0.80	1.00	1.10	1.50	5	10	18	25	125
1904 .... (1,817)... 61,326,198		0.80	1.00	1.10	1.50	5	10	18	25	125
1905 .... (2,152)... 80,717,011		0.80	1.00	1.10	1.50	5	10	18	25	125
1906 .... (1,725)... 96,020,530		0.80	1.00	1.10	1.50	5	10	18	25	125
1907 .... (1,475).. 108,137,143		0.80	1.00	1.10	1.50	5	10	18	25	125

Location of Mintmark S on Reverse of Indian Head Cent (1908 and 1909 Only)

	Mintage	G-4	VG-8	F-12	VF-20	EF-40	AU-50	MS-60	MS-63	PF-63
1908 .... (1,620)... 32,326,367		$0.80	$1.10	$1.25	$1.50	$5	$10	$18	$25	$125
1908S 1,115,000		40.00	50.00	55.00	65.00	95	120	175	250	
1909 .... (2,175)... 14,368,470		5.00	6.00	8.00	10.00	12	16	25	35	150
1909S 309,000		275.00	300.00	325.00	350.00	425	475	600	750	

LINCOLN, WHEAT EARS REVERSE (1909–1958)

Victor D. Brenner designed this cent, which was issued to commemorate the 100th anniversary of Abraham Lincoln's birth. The designer's initials (V.D.B.) appear on the reverse of a limited quantity of cents of 1909. Later in the year they were removed from the dies but restored in 1918 as very small incuse letters beneath the shoulder. The Lincoln type was the first cent to have the motto IN GOD WE TRUST.

G-4 Good: Date worn but apparent. Lines in wheat heads missing. Full rims.
VG-8 Very Good: Half of lines visible in upper wheat heads.
F-12 Fine: Wheat lines worn but visible.
VF-20 Very Fine: Lincoln's cheekbone and jawbone worn but separated. No worn spots on wheat heads.
EF-40 Extremely Fine: Slight wear. All details sharp.
AU-50 About Uncirculated: Slight wear on cheek and jaw and on wheat stalks.
MS-60 Uncirculated: No trace of wear. Light blemishes. Brown or red-brown color.
MS-63 Choice Uncirculated: No trace of wear. Slight blemishes. Red-brown color.
MS-65 Gem Uncirculated: No trace of wear. Barely noticeable blemishes. Nearly full red color.
PF-63 Choice Proof: Reflective surfaces with only a few blemishes in secondary focal places. No major flaws.

Location of mintmark S or D on obverse of Lincoln cent.

**Designer's Initials
V.D.B. (1909 Only)**

**No V.D.B.
on Reverse
(1909–1958)**

Dealers often pay more than the prices shown for brilliant Uncirculated coins, and less for spotted, cleaned, or discolored pieces.

	Mintage	G-4	VG-8	F-12	VF-20	EF-40	AU-50	MS-60	MS-63	MATTE PF-63
1909, V.D.B. .... (1,194)...27,995,000		$6.00	$6.50	$7.00	$8.00	$9.00	$10.00	$13.00	$20	$1,450
1909S, V.D.B. 484,000		400	425	500	550	600	750	900.00	1,100	
1909 .... (2,618)...72,702,618		1.00	1.25	1.60	2.00	2.50	6.00	8.50	15	300
1909S 1,825,000		50.00	60.00	70.00	95.00	150.00	165.00	200.00	250	
1910 .... (4,083)..146,801,218		0.10	0.12	0.15	0.30	1.00	2.50	9.00	15	270
1910S 6,045,000		8.00	10.00	12.00	14.00	25.00	40.00	55.00	70	
1911 .... (1,725)..101,177,787		0.10	0.15	0.30	0.50	1.50	3.50	11.00	25	275
1911D 12,672,000		2.40	3.00	4.50	9.00	21.00	35.00	50.00	70	
1911S 4,026,000		20.00	25.00	30.00	35.00	50.00	65.00	110.00	150	
1912 .... (2,172)...68,153,060		0.15	0.25	0.70	2.00	2.50	8.00	17.00	25	275
1912D 10,411,000		2.75	3.50	4.25	10.00	25.00	40.00	75.00	120	
1912S 4,431,000		11.00	13.00	15.00	18.00	35.00	47.00	90.00	125	
1913 .... (2,983)...76,532,352		0.15	0.20	0.50	1.50	8.00	12.00	16.00	25	275
1913D 15,804,000		0.75	1.00	1.50	3.50	20.00	26.00	50.00	100	
1913S 6,101,000		5.50	6.75	9.00	12.00	27.00	50.00	85.00	135	
1914 .... (1,365)...75,238,432		0.20	0.30	0.75	2.00	6.50	17.00	25.00	37	275
1914D (a) 1,193,000		110.00	130.00	175.00	250.00	450.00	1,000.00	1,400.00	2,500	
1914S 4,137,000		11.00	14.00	16.00	19.00	40.00	90.00	175.00	350	
1915 .... (1,150)...29,092,120		0.40	1.00	2.00	8.00	26.00	35.00	46.00	65	300
1915D 22,050,000		0.50	1.00	1.50	2.25	9.00	22.00	45.00	60	
1915S 4,833,000		9.00	11.00	15.00	18.00	35.00	65.00	110.00	150	
1916 .... (1,050)..131,833,677		0.10	0.15	0.25	0.50	2.00	5.00	10.00	15	700
1916D 35,956,000		0.30	0.50	0.85	2.00	5.50	12.00	35.00	65	
1916S 22,510,000		0.50	0.75	1.50	3.00	10.00	20.00	45.00	90	
1917 196,429,785		0.05	0.07	0.10	0.25	0.60	3.00	10.00	15	
1917D 55,120,000		0.25	0.40	0.75	1.50	14.00	19.00	39.00	70	
1917S 32,620,000		0.10	0.15	0.25	0.50	2.75	12.00	35.00	65	

a. Beware of altered date or mintmark. No V.D.B. on shoulder of genuine 1914-D cent.

Designer's initials placed on Lincoln's shoulder next to rim, starting in 1918.

For brilliant Unc. coins before 1934, dealers usually pay more than the prices shown. They pay less for spotted, cleaned, or discolored pieces.

Mintage	G-4	VG-8	F-12	VF-20	EF-40	AU-50	MS-60	MS-63
1918 288,104,634	$0.04	$0.05	$0.10	$0.20	$1.00	$3.00	$6.00	$15.00
1918D 47,830,000	0.20	0.25	0.60	1.25	6.00	12.00	33.00	68.00
1918S 34,680,000	0.15	0.20	0.50	1.00	4.00	15.00	35.00	75.00
1919 392,021,000	0.04	0.05	0.07	0.15	0.75	1.50	5.00	14.00
1919D 57,154,000	0.10	0.12	0.15	0.40	2.50	15.00	28.00	55.00
1919S 139,760,000	0.05	0.06	0.10	0.30	1.35	7.00	18.00	60.00
1920 310,165,000	0.03	0.05	0.07	0.15	0.50	1.50	6.00	12.00
1920D 49,280,000	0.20	0.40	0.80	2.00	6.00	15.00	35.00	55.00
1920S 46,220,000	0.10	0.20	0.30	0.70	3.50	17.00	45.00	90.00
1921 39,157,000	0.06	0.08	0.15	0.35	1.50	6.00	22.00	40.00
1921S 15,274,000	0.35	0.50	0.70	1.50	15.00	35.00	55.00	100.00
1922D 7,160,000	7.00	8.00	9.00	11.00	17.00	28.00	45.00	75.00
1922, No D (b) . . . . . . *	325.00	385.00	575.00	700.00	1,450.00	2,500.00	6,500.00	15,000.00
1923 74,723,000	0.04	0.05	0.07	0.15	1.00	2.50	7.00	14.00
1923S 8,700,000	1.25	1.50	2.00	3.00	15.00	35.00	100.00	225.00
1924 75,178,000	0.04	0.05	0.07	0.15	1.50	3.50	15.00	25.00
1924D 2,520,000	18.00	20.00	25.00	30.00	55.00	95.00	150.00	210.00
1924S 11,696,000	0.40	0.50	0.80	1.10	9.00	30.00	55.00	100.00
1925 139,949,000	0.03	0.04	0.05	0.15	0.50	2.00	5.00	10.00
1925D 22,580,000	0.10	0.15	0.50	1.00	4.50	11.00	27.00	38.00
1925S 26,380,000	0.05	0.06	0.10	0.25	3.00	14.00	40.00	95.00
1926 157,088,000	0.03	0.04	0.05	0.15	0.50	2.00	5.00	8.00
1926D 28,020,000	0.25	0.35	0.70	1.10	3.00	10.00	35.00	50.00
1926S 4,550,000	3.00	3.50	4.50	6.00	14.00	32.00	65.00	145.00
1927 144,440,000	0.03	0.04	0.05	0.20	0.50	1.00	5.00	10.00
1927D 27,170,000	0.10	0.15	0.50	1.00	2.00	6.00	26.00	42.00
1927S 14,276,000	0.25	0.30	0.50	1.25	4.00	11.00	35.00	70.00
1928 134,116,000	0.03	0.04	0.05	0.15	0.50	1.00	4.50	10.00
1928D 31,170,000	0.05	0.10	0.15	0.25	0.85	4.00	15.00	34.00
1928S 17,266,000	0.10	0.12	0.25	0.50	1.50	5.00	34.00	55.00
1929 185,262,000	0.03	0.04	0.05	0.15	0.35	1.50	4.00	6.00
1929D 41,730,000	0.04	0.06	0.10	0.25	1.00	2.00	12.00	15.00
1929S 50,148,000	0.03	0.05	0.10	0.20	0.60	1.75	7.00	11.00
1930 157,415,000	0.03	0.04	0.05	0.15	0.25	0.75	2.00	3.50
1930D 40,100,000	0.04	0.06	0.10	0.25	0.60	1.00	5.00	10.00
1930S 24,286,000	0.03	0.05	0.10	0.15	0.40	2.00	3.50	5.00
1931 19,396,000	0.15	0.20	0.30	0.40	0.60	2.00	10.00	15.00
1931D 4,480,000	2.00	2.25	3.00	3.50	5.00	14.00	30.00	42.00
1931S 866,000	45.00	50.00	60.00	70.00	75.00	85.00	100.00	125.00
1932 9,062,000	0.40	0.50	0.60	1.00	1.25	3.75	10.00	13.00
1932D 10,500,000	0.25	0.35	0.40	0.50	1.00	3.25	10.00	15.00
1933 14,360,000	0.30	0.40	0.50	0.70	1.25	3.75	10.00	15.00
1933D 6,200,000	1.00	1.25	1.50	2.50	4.25	7.00	13.00	16.00

* Included in number above. **b.** 1922 cents with a weak or missing mintmark were made from extremely worn dies that originally struck normal 1922-D cents. Three different die pairs were involved; two of them produced "Weak D" coins. One die pair (no. 2, identified by a "strong reverse") is acknowledged as striking "No D" coins. Weak D cents are worth considerably less. Beware of removed mintmark.

Chart continued on next page.

SMALL CENTS

	Mintage	G-4	VG-8	F-12	VF-20	EF-40	AU-50	MS-60	MS-63	PF-63
1934	219,080,000	$0.03	$0.03	$0.03	$0.03	$0.10	$1.00	$3.00	$4.50	
1934D	28,446,000	0.04	0.06	0.08	0.15	0.50	2.00	9.00	15.00	
1935	245,388,000	0.03	0.03	0.03	0.04	0.06	0.20	2.00	3.00	
1935D	47,000,000	0.03	0.03	0.03	0.04	0.20	0.50	3.00	4.00	
1935S	38,702,000	0.03	0.04	0.04	0.04	0.12	1.25	4.00	6.00	
1936 .... (5,569)	309,632,000	0.03	0.03	0.03	0.04	0.06	0.25	1.00	3.00	$100
1936D	40,620,000	0.03	0.03	0.03	0.04	0.08	0.20	1.00	3.00	
1936S	29,130,000	0.03	0.03	0.03	0.04	0.10	0.20	1.00	3.00	
1937 .... (9,320)	309,170,000	0.02	0.03	0.03	0.03	0.05	0.20	0.50	3.00	35
1937D	50,430,000	0.02	0.03	0.03	0.03	0.06	0.30	0.80	4.00	
1937S	34,500,000	0.03	0.03	0.03	0.04	0.06	0.30	0.80	4.00	
1938 ... (14,734)	156,682,000	0.02	0.03	0.03	0.03	0.05	0.30	0.75	2.00	25
1938D	20,010,000	0.02	0.03	0.05	0.06	0.15	0.50	1.00	5.00	
1938S	15,180,000	0.06	0.08	0.10	0.12	0.15	0.30	1.00	4.00	
1939 ... (13,520)	316,466,000	0.02	0.03	0.03	0.03	0.03	0.20	0.30	2.50	23
1939D	15,160,000	0.06	0.08	0.10	0.12	0.15	0.35	1.00	4.00	
1939S	52,070,000	0.03	0.03	0.05	0.08	0.10	0.30	1.00	4.00	
1940 ... (15,872)	586,810,000	0.02	0.03	0.03	0.03	0.03	0.20	0.30	2.00	15
1940D	81,390,000	0.02	0.03	0.03	0.03	0.03	0.20	0.40	2.00	
1940S	112,940,000	0.02	0.03	0.03	0.03	0.04	0.20	0.40	2.75	
1941 ... (21,100)	887,018,000	0.02	0.03	0.03	0.03	0.03	0.20	0.30	2.00	15
1941D	128,700,000	0.02	0.03	0.03	0.03	0.03	0.40	0.80	3.00	
1941S	92,360,000	0.02	0.03	0.03	0.03	0.04	0.35	1.00	4.00	
1942 ... (32,600)	657,796,000	0.02	0.03	0.03	0.03	0.03	0.10	0.15	1.00	15
1942D	206,698,000	0.02	0.03	0.03	0.03	0.03	0.10	0.25	1.50	
1942S	85,590,000	0.02	0.03	0.03	0.03	0.10	1.00	2.25	6.00	

Variety 2 – Zinc-Coated Steel (1943)

	Mintage	F-12	VF-20	EF-40	MS-60	MS-63	MS-65
1943	684,628,670	$0.05	$0.10	$0.15	$0.70	$1.25	$3.25
1943D	217,660,000	0.05	0.10	0.15	0.90	2.00	4.50
1943S	191,550,000	0.06	0.12	0.20	1.20	2.75	9.00

Variety 1 (Bronze) Resumed (1944–1958)

1944-D, D Over S   1955, Doubled-Die Obverse

	Mintage	VF-20	EF-40	MS-63	MS-65	PF-65
1944	1,435,400,000	$0.03	$0.03	$0.25	$1.60	
1944D	430,578,000	0.03	0.03	0.20	1.50	
1944D, D Over S	*	60.00	80.00	200.00	350.00	
1944S	282,760,000	0.03	0.03	0.20	1.50	

* Included in number above.

	Mintage	VF-20	EF-40	MS-63	MS-65	PF-65
1945	1,040,515,000	$0.03	$0.03	$0.20	$0.50	
1945D	266,268,000	0.03	0.03	0.15	0.50	
1945S	181,770,000	0.03	0.03	0.10	1.00	
1946	991,655,000	0.03	0.03	0.10	0.50	
1946D	315,690,000	0.03	0.03	0.15	1.00	
1946S	198,100,000	0.03	0.03	0.15	1.25	
1947	190,555,000	0.03	0.03	0.25	0.75	
1947D	194,750,000	0.03	0.03	0.12	0.50	
1947S	99,000,000	0.03	0.03	0.15	1.50	
1948	317,570,000	0.03	0.03	0.15	0.50	
1948D	172,637,500	0.03	0.03	0.12	0.60	
1948S	81,735,000	0.03	0.03	0.20	1.50	
1949	217,775,000	0.03	0.03	0.30	0.75	
1949D	153,132,500	0.03	0.03	0.20	0.75	
1949S	64,290,000	0.04	0.05	0.50	2.00	
1950 (51,386)	272,635,000	0.03	0.03	0.25	0.50	$37
1950D	334,950,000	0.03	0.03	0.10	0.50	
1950S	118,505,000	0.03	0.03	0.25	0.80	
1951 (57,500)	284,576,000	0.03	0.03	0.25	0.80	35
1951D	625,355,000	0.03	0.03	0.10	0.50	
1951S	136,010,000	0.03	0.03	0.25	0.60	
1952 (81,980)	186,775,000	0.03	0.03	0.15	0.60	25
1952D	746,130,000	0.03	0.03	0.15	0.60	
1952S	137,800,004	0.03	0.03	0.50	1.50	
1953 (128,800)	256,755,000	0.03	0.03	0.10	0.50	18
1953D	700,515,000	0.03	0.03	0.10	0.50	
1953S	181,835,000	0.03	0.04	0.12	0.75	
1954 (233,300)	71,640,050	0.03	0.06	0.15	0.85	10
1954D	251,552,500	0.03	0.03	0.05	0.30	
1954S	96,190,000	0.03	0.03	0.05	0.30	
1955 (378,200)	330,958,200	0.03	0.03	0.06	0.30	9
1955, Doubled-Die Obverse	*	950.00	1,100.00 (a)	1,800.00	7,500.00	
1955D	563,257,500	0.03	0.03	0.05	0.25	
1955S	44,610,000	0.10	0.15	0.15	0.50	
1956 (669,384)	420,745,000	0.03	0.03	0.05	0.25	3
1956D	1,098,201,100	0.03	0.03	0.05	0.30	
1957 (1,247,952)	282,540,000	0.03	0.03	0.05	0.30	3
1957D	1,051,342,000	0.03	0.03	0.05	0.30	
1958 (875,652)	252,525,000	0.03	0.03	0.05	0.30	3
1958D	800,953,300	0.03	0.03	0.05	0.30	

* Included in number above. **a.** For MS-60 Uncirculated coins, dealers usually pay $1,400.

LINCOLN, MEMORIAL REVERSE (1959–2008)

Small Date

Large Date

	Mintage	MS-63	MS-65	PF-65
1959 (1,149,291)	609,715,000	$0.02	$0.10	$1.00

Entry continued on next page.

| 1969-S, Doubled-Die Obverse | Small Date, Numbers Aligned at Top | Large Date, Low 7 in Date | Enlarged Detail of 1972 Doubled-Die Obverse |

	Mintage	MS-63	MS-65	PF-63
1959D	1,279,760,000	$0.02	$0.10	
1960, Lg Dt	586,405,000	0.02	0.10	
	(1,691,602)			$0.75
1960, Sm Dt	*	1.00	2.70	
	*			9.50
1960D,				
Lg Dt	1,580,884,000	0.02	0.10	
1960D, Sm Dt	*	0.02	0.10	
1961	753,345,000	0.02	0.10	
	(3,028,244)			0.50
1961D	1,753,266,700	0.02	0.10	
1962	606,045,000	0.02	0.10	
	(3,218,019)			0.50
1962D	1,793,148,140	0.02	0.10	
1963	754,110,000	0.02	0.10	
	(3,075,645)			0.50
1963D	1,774,020,400	0.02	0.10	
1964	2,648,575,000	0.02	0.10	
	(3,950,762)			0.50
1964D	3,799,071,500	0.02	0.10	
1965	1,497,224,900	0.03	0.12	
1966	2,188,147,783	0.04	0.12	
1967	3,048,667,100	0.03	0.12	
1968	1,707,880,970	0.03	0.12	
1968D	2,886,269,600	0.02	0.12	
1968S	258,270,001	0.02	0.15	
	(3,041,506)			0.35
1969	1,136,910,000	0.05	0.20	
1969D	4,002,832,200	0.03	0.15	
1969S	544,375,000	0.03	0.15	
	(2,934,631)			0.35
1969S, DDO	*	—	—	
1970	1,898,315,000	0.05	0.20	
1970D	2,891,438,900	0.02	0.10	
1970S, Sm Dt				
(High 7)	**	20.00	30.00	
	**			20.00
1970S, Lg Dt				
(Low 7)	690,560,004	0.03	0.20	
	(2,632,810)			0.25

	Mintage	MS-63	MS-65	PF-63
1971	1,919,490,000	$0.05	$0.20	
1971D	2,911,045,600	0.03	0.20	
1971S	525,133,459	0.03	0.20	
	(3,220,733)			$0.25
1972, DDO	**	200.00	350.00	
1972	2,933,255,000	0.02	0.10	
1972D	2,665,071,400	0.02	0.10	
1972S	376,939,108	0.02	0.10	
	(3,260,996)			0.25
1973	3,728,245,000	0.02	0.10	
1973D	3,549,576,588	0.02	0.10	
1973S	317,177,295	0.02	0.15	
	(2,760,339)			0.25
1974	4,232,140,523	0.02	0.10	
1974D	4,235,098,000	0.02	0.10	
1974S	409,426,660	0.03	0.20	
	(2,612,568)			0.25
1975	5,451,476,142	0.02	0.10	
1975D	4,505,275,300	0.02	0.10	
1975S	(2,845,450)			1.60
1976	4,674,292,426	0.02	0.10	
1976D	4,221,592,455	0.02	0.10	
1976S	(4,149,730)			1.25
1977	4,469,930,000	0.02	0.10	
1977D	4,194,062,300	0.02	0.10	
1977S	(3,251,152)			1.00
1978	5,558,605,000	0.02	0.10	
1978D	4,280,233,400	0.02	0.10	
1978S	(3,127,781)			1.00
1979	6,018,515,000	0.02	0.10	
1979D	4,139,357,254	0.02	0.10	
1979S, Type 1	(3,677,175)			1.75
1979S, Type 2	*			2.00
1980	7,414,705,000	0.02	0.10	
1980D	5,140,098,660	0.02	0.10	
1980S	(3,554,806)			1.00
1981	7,491,750,000	0.02	0.10	
1981D	5,373,235,677	0.02	0.10	
1981S, Type 1	(4,063,083)			1.50
1981S, Type 2	*			14.00

* Included in number above. ** Included in number below.

Large Date

Small Date

	Mintage	MS-63	MS-65	PF-63
1982,...............				
Lg Dt. .10,712,525,000		$0.02	$0.10	
1982, Sm Dt ....*		0.03	0.12	

* Included in number above.

	Mintage	MS-63	MS-65	PF-63
1982D, ...				
Lg Dt. . .6,012,979,368		$0.02	$0.10	
1982S .... (3,857,479)				$1.60

Copper-Plated Zinc (1982–2008)

Close AM

Wide AM

1995, Doubled Die showing strong doubling on word LIBERTY.

	Mintage	MS-63	MS-65	PF-63
1982, Lg Dt ....*		$0.02	$0.25	
1982, Sm Dt ....*		0.02	0.30	
1982D, Lg Dt ....*		0.05	0.20	
1982D, Sm Dt ....*		0.01	0.10	
1983 7,752,355,000		0.01	0.10	
1983D......6,467,199,428		0.01	0.10	
1983S .... (3,279,126)		0.01	0.05	$1.10
1984 8,151,079,000		0.01	0.05	
1984, Dbl Ear ....**		50.00	100.00	
1984D......5,569,238,906		0.01	0.10	
1984S .... (3,065,110)				1.10
1985 5,648,489,887		0.01	0.05	
1985D......5,287,339,926		0.01	0.05	
1985S .... (3,362,821)				1.25
1986 4,491,395,493		0.01	0.06	
1986D......4,442,866,698		0.01	0.05	
1986S .... (3,010,497)				2.00
1987 4,682,466,931		0.01	0.05	
1987D......4,879,389,514		0.01	0.05	
1987S .... (4,227,728)				1.10
1988 6,092,810,000		0.01	0.05	
1988D......5,253,740,443		0.01	0.05	
1988S .... (3,262,948)				2.00
1989 7,261,535,000		0.01	0.05	
1989D......5,345,467,111		0.01	0.05	
1989S .... (3,220,194)				2.00
1990 6,851,765,000		0.01	0.05	
1990D......4,922,894,533		0.01	0.05	
1990S .... (3,299,559)				2.00
1990, Pf, No S ....**				—

	Mintage	MS-63	MS-65	PF-63
1991 5,165,940,000		$0.01	$0.05	
1991D......4,158,446,076		0.01	0.05	
1991S .... (2,867,787)				$6.75
1992 4,648,905,000		0.01	0.05	
1992, Close AM (a) ......**		—	—	
1992D......4,448,673,300		0.01	0.05	
1992D, Close AM (a).....**		—	—	
1992S .... (4,176,560)				1.10
1993 5,684,705,000		0.01	0.05	
1993D......6,426,650,571		0.01	0.05	
1993S .... (3,394,792)				3.00
1994 6,500,850,000		0.01	0.05	
1994D......7,131,765,000		0.01	0.05	
1994S .... (3,269,923)				3.00
1995 6,411,440,000		0.01	0.05	
1995, DblDie Obv ....**		5.00	20.00	
1995D......7,128,560,000		0.01	0.05	
1995S .... (2,797,481)				3.00
1996 6,612,465,000		0.01	0.05	
1996D......6,510,795,000		0.01	0.05	
1996S .... (2,525,265)				1.25
1997 4,622,800,000		0.01	0.05	
1997D......4,576,555,000		0.01	0.05	
1997S .... (2,796,678)				4.00
1998 5,032,155,000		0.01	0.05	
1998, Wide AM (b)........**		2.00	10.00	
1998D......5,225,353,500		0.01	0.05	
1998S .... (2,086,507)				3.00
1998S, Close AM (a) .....**				150.00
1999 5,237,600,000		0.01	0.05	

* Included in previous section's mintages. ** Included in number above. **a.** The circulation-strike hub adopted in 1993, with AM almost touching, was accidentally used on these cents. **b.** Varieties were made using Proof dies that have a wide space between AM in AMERICA. The letters nearly touch on other Uncirculated cents.

Chart continued on next page.

	Mintage	MS-63	MS-65	PF-63
1999, Wide AM (b)	**		—	
1999D	6,360,065,000	$0.01	$0.05	
1999S	(3,347,966)			$2.00
1999S, Close AM (a)	**			30.00
2000	5,503,200,000	0.01	0.05	
2000, Wide AM (b)	**	2.00	5.00	
2000D	8,774,220,000	0.01	0.05	
2000S	(4,047,993)			1.20
2001	4,959,600,000	0.01	0.05	
2001D	5,374,990,000	0.01	0.05	
2001S	(3,184,606)			1.20
2002	3,260,800,000	0.01	0.05	
2002D	4,028,055,000	0.01	0.05	
2002S	(3,211,995)			1.20
2003	3,300,000,000	0.01	0.05	
2003D	3,548,000,000	0.01	0.05	

	Mintage	MS-63	MS-65	PF-63
2003S	(3,298,439)			$1.20
2004	3,379,600,000	$0.01	$0.05	
2004D	3,456,400,000	0.01	0.05	
2004S	(2,965,422)			1.20
2005	3,935,600,000	0.01	0.05	
2005D	3,764,450,500	0.01	0.05	
2005S	(3,344,679)			1.20
2006	4,290,000,000	0.01	0.05	
2006D	3,944,000,000	0.01	0.05	
2006S	(3,054,436)			1.20
2007	3,762,400,000	0.01	0.05	
2007D	3,638,800,000	0.01	0.05	
2007S	(2,577,166)			1.20
2008	2,558,800,000	0.01	0.05	
2008D	2,849,600,000	0.01	0.05	
2008S	(2,169,561)			1.20

** Included in number above. **a.** The circulation-strike hub adopted in 1993, with AM almost touching, was accidentally used on these cents. **b.** Varieties were made using Proof dies that have a wide space between AM in AMERICA. The letters nearly touch on other Uncirculated cents.

LINCOLN, BICENTENNIAL (2009)

One-cent coins issued during 2009 are a unique tribute to President Abraham Lincoln, recognizing the bicentennial of his birth and the 100th anniversary of the first issuance of the Lincoln cent. These coins use four different design themes on the reverse to represent the four major aspects of President Lincoln's life. The obverse of each of these coins carries the traditional portrait of Lincoln that has been in use since 1909.

The special reverse designs, released as quarterly issues throughout 2009, are described as: Birth and Early Childhood in Kentucky (designer, Richard Masters; sculptor, Jim Licaretz); Formative Years in Indiana (designer and sculptor, Charles Vickers); Professional Life in Illinois (designer, Joel Iskowitz; sculptor, Don Everhart); and Presidency in Washington (designer, Susan Gamble; sculptor, Joseph Menna). Those issued for commercial circulation are made of the exact same copper-plated composition used since 1982. Special versions included in collector sets are made of the same metallic composition as was used for the original 1909 cents (95% copper, 5% tin and zinc).

2009 Lincoln cent reverse designs

	Mintage	MS-63	MS-65	PF-65
2009, Birth and Early Childhood	284,400,000	$0.05	$0.10	
2009, Birth and Early Childhood, copper, Satin finish	784,614		4.00	
2009D, Birth and Early Childhood	350,400,000	0.05	0.10	
2009D, Birth and Early Childhood, copper, Satin finish	784,614		4.00	
2009S, Birth and Early Childhood	(2,995,615)			$2
2009, Formative Years	376,000,000	0.05	0.10	
2009, Formative Years, copper, Satin finish	784,614		4.00	
2009D, Formative Years	363,600,000	0.05	0.10	

	Mintage	MS-63	MS-65	PF-65
2009D, Formative Years, copper, Satin finish	784,614		$4.00	
2009S, Formative Years	(2,995,615)			$2
2009, Professional Life	316,000,000	$0.05	0.10	
2009, Professional Life, copper, Satin finish	784,614		4.00	
2009D, Professional Life	336,000,000	0.05	0.10	
2009D, Professional Life, copper, Satin finish	784,614		4.00	
2009S, Professional Life	(2,995,615)			2
2009, Presidency	129,600,000	0.05	0.10	
2009, Presidency, copper, Satin finish	784,614		4.00	
2009D, Presidency	198,000,000	0.05	0.10	
2009D, Presidency, copper, Satin finish	784,614		4.00	
2009S, Presidency	(2,995,615)			2

LINCOLN, SHIELD REVERSE (2010 TO DATE)

Since the conclusion of the 2009 Bicentennial One-Cent Program, one-cent coins feature a reverse that has "an image emblematic of President Lincoln's preservation of the United States of America as a single and united country."

	Mintage	MS-65	PF-63
2010	1,963,630,000	$0.01	
2010D	2,047,200,000	0.01	
2010S	(1,689,216)		$2.00
2011	2,402,400,000	0.01	
2011D	2,536,140,000	0.01	
2011S	(1,673,010)		
2012	3,132,000,000	0.01	
2012D	2,883,200,000	0.01	
2012S	(1,239,148)		1.20
2013	3,750,400,000	0.01	
2013D	3,319,600,000	0.01	

	Mintage	MS-65	PF-63
2013S	(1,274,505)		$2
2014	3,677,600,000	$0.01	
2014D	3,832,400,000	0.01	
2014S	(1,190,369)		2
2015	4,691,300,000	0.01	
2015D	4,674,000,000	0.01	
2015S	(1,022,410)		2
2016		0.01	
2016D		0.01	
2016S			2

TWO-CENT PIECE (1864–1873)

The Act of April 22, 1864, which changed the copper-nickel cent to a lighter-weight bronze composition, included a provision for a new coin, the two-cent piece. Its weight was specified as 96 grains, and its bronze alloy the same as for the cent. The two-cent piece was the nation's first circulating coin to bear the motto IN GOD WE TRUST.

There are two varieties for 1864, the first year of issue: the scarcer Small Motto, and the Large Motto. The differences are illustrated in the close-ups below. On the Small Motto variety, the stem to the cluster of leaves below TRUST is plainly visible, the D in GOD is wide, the first T in TRUST is close to the ribbon crease, and the U in TRUST is squat. On the Large Motto variety there is no stem, the D is narrow, the first T is farther from the crease, and the U is tall and narrow.

1864, Small Motto

1864, Large Motto

G-4 Good: At least part of IN GOD visible.
VG-8 Very Good: WE weakly visible.
F-12 Fine: Complete motto visible. The word WE weak.
VF-20 Very Fine: WE is clear, but not strong.
EF-40 Extremely Fine: The word WE bold.
AU-50 About Uncirculated: Traces of wear visible on leaf tips, arrow points, and the word WE.
MS-60 Uncirculated: No trace of wear. Light blemishes.
MS-63 Choice Uncirculated: Some distracting contact marks or blemishes in prime focal areas. Some impairment of luster possible.
PF-63 Choice Proof: Reflective surfaces with only a few blemishes in secondary focal places. No major flaws.

Dealers often pay more than the prices shown for brilliant red choice Uncirculated and Proof coins, and less for cleaned or discolored pieces.

	Mintage	G-4	VG-8	F-12	VF-20	EF-40	AU-50	MS-60	MS-63	PF-63
1864, Small Motto	*	$125	$175	$200	$300	$500	$650	$1,000	$1,200	$12,500
1864, Large Motto *(100+)*. .	19,822,500	10	12	15	20	30	45	70	100	450
1865 . . . . *(500+)*. .	13,640,000	10	12	15	20	30	45	70	100	300
1866 . . . . *(725+)*. .	3,177,000	10	12	15	20	30	45	70	100	300
1867 . . . . *(625+)*. .	2,938,750	10	12	15	20	30	45	70	100	300
1868 . . . . *(600+)*. .	2,803,750	10	12	15	25	35	50	75	110	300
1869 . . . . *(600+)*. .	1,546,500	15	20	25	30	45	75	100	110	300
1870 . . . . *(1,000+)*. .	861,250	17	25	30	35	50	85	125	150	300
1871 . . . . *(960+)*. .	721,250	20	30	35	40	75	100	165	190	350
1872 . . . . *(950+)*. .	65,000	250	300	400	500	650	1,000	1,500	2,250	600
1873 . . . . *(600)*										2,000

* Included in number below.

SILVER THREE-CENT PIECES (TRIMES) (1851–1873)

This smallest of United States silver coins was authorized by Congress March 3, 1851. The first three-cent silver pieces had no lines bordering the six-pointed star. From 1854 through 1858 there were two lines, while issues of the last 15 years show only one line. Issues from 1854 through 1873 have an olive sprig over the III and a bundle of three arrows beneath.

G-4 Good: Star worn smooth. Legend and date readable.
VG-8 Very Good: Outline of shield defined. Legend and date clear.
F-12 Fine: Only star points worn smooth.
VF-20 Very Fine: Only partial wear on star ridges.
EF-40 Extremely Fine: Ridges on star points visible.
AU-50 About Uncirculated: Trace of wear visible at each star point. Center of shield possibly weak.
MS-60 Uncirculated: No trace of wear. Light blemishes.
MS-63 Choice Uncirculated: Some distracting contact marks or blemishes in prime focal areas. Some impairment of luster possible.
PF-63 Choice Proof: Reflective surfaces with only a few blemishes in secondary focal places. No major flaws.

Mintmark location.

No Outline Around Star (1851–1853)   Three Outlines to Star, Large Date (1854–1858)   Two Outlines to Star, Small Date (1859–1873)   1862, 2 Over 1

Dealers usually pay higher prices for well-struck examples.

	Mintage	G-4	VG-8	F-12	VF-20	EF-40	AU-50	MS-60	MS-63	PF-63
1851	5,447,400	$18	$25	$30	$40	$45	$100	$125	$200	—
1851O	720,000	20	30	35	50	100	125	300	500	
1852	18,663,500	18	25	30	40	45	100	125	200	—
1853	11,400,000	18	25	30	40	45	100	125	200	
1854	671,000	20	35	40	50	75	125	175	400	$6,000
1855	139,000	20	35	40	60	100	135	325	650	2,500
1856	1,458,000	20	35	40	50	75	125	150	400	1,800
1857	1,042,000	20	35	40	50	75	125	150	400	1,800
1858 (210)	1,603,700	20	35	40	50	75	125	150	400	1,200
1859 (800)	364,200	20	35	40	50	65	100	125	200	275
1860 (1,000)	286,000	20	35	40	50	65	100	125	200	275
1861 (1,000)	497,000	20	35	40	50	65	100	125	200	275
1862, 2/1	*	20	35	40	50	70	125	110	250	
1862 (550)	343,000	20	35	40	50	65	100	125	200	285
1863 (460)	21,000				250	300	350	500	750	350
1864 (470)	12,000				250	300	350	500	750	350

	Mintage	VF-20	EF-40	AU-50	MS-60	MS-63	PF-63
1865	(500) 8,000	$300	$325	$350	$500	$875	$350
1866	(725) 22,000	300	325	350	500	800	350
1867	(625) 4,000	300	325	350	550	1,000	350
1868	(600) 3,500	300	325	500	550	1,100	350
1869	(600) 4,500	300	325	450	560	1,100	350
1870	(1,000) 3,000	300	325	350	500	750	350
1871	(960) 3,400	300	325	350	550	850	350
1872	(950) 1,000	300	325	450	800	1,500	350
1873, Proof only	(600)						850

* Included in number below.

NICKEL THREE-CENT PIECES (1865–1889)

Three-cent pieces struck in a nickel alloy were intended to replace the earlier silver three-cent coins, which were hoarded by the public during the Civil War. The Mint struck more than 11 million three-cent coins of the new composition (75% copper and 25% nickel) in 1865, their first year of issue, compared to only 8,000 silver pieces. The nickel coins were all made at the Philadelphia Mint. They have a plain (non-reeded) edge.

G-4 Good: Date and legends complete though worn. III smooth.
VG-8 Very Good: III half worn. Rims complete.
VF-20 Very Fine: Three-quarters of hair details visible.
EF-40 Extremely Fine: Slight, even wear.
AU-50 About Uncirculated: Slight wear on hair curls, above forehead, and on wreath and numeral III.
MS-60 Uncirculated: No trace of wear. Light blemishes.
MS-63 Choice Uncirculated: Some distracting contact marks or blemishes in prime focal areas. Some impairment of luster possible.
PF-63 Choice Proof: Reflective surfaces with only a few blemishes in secondary focal places. No major flaws.

Dealers often pay more than the prices shown for brilliant choice Unc. and Proof coins, and less for spotted, cleaned, or discolored pieces.

	Mintage	G-4	VG-8	F-12	VF-20	EF-40	AU-50	MS-60	MS-63	PF-63
1865 . . . .(500+). .11,382,000		$10	$12	$14	$16	$25	$35	$65	$100	$650
1866 . . . .(725+). . 4,801,000		10	12	14	16	25	35	65	100	225
1867 . . . .(625+). . 3,915,000		10	12	14	16	25	35	65	100	225
1868 . . . .(600+). . 3,252,000		10	12	14	16	25	35	65	100	225
1869 . . . .(600+). . 1,604,000		10	12	14	16	25	35	65	100	225
1870 . . . . . (1,000+). . 1,335,000		10	12	14	16	25	35	65	100	225
1871 . . . .(960+). . . .604,000		10	12	14	16	25	35	65	125	225
1872 . . . .(950+). . . .862,000		10	12	14	16	25	35	65	145	225
1873 . . . . . (1,100+). . . .390,000		10	12	14	16	25	35	65	100	225
1874 . . . .(700+). . . .790,000		10	12	14	16	25	35	65	100	225
1875 . . . .(700+). . . .228,000		10	12	14	16	25	35	80	120	225
1876 . . . . . (1,150+). . . .162,000		10	12	14	16	25	35	110	150	250
1877, Pf only . .(900).					575	650				950
1878, Pf only (2,350).					250	375				475
1879 . . . . . . (3,200). 38,000		20	25	30	40	60	75	150	250	250
1880 . . . . . . (3,955). 21,000		40	45	50	60	70	85	175	250	250
1881 . . . . . . (3,575). . 1,077,000		10	12	14	16	25	35	65	125	225
1882 . . . . . . (3,100). 22,200		35	45	50	75	85	125	225	400	225
1883 . . . . . . (6,609). 4,000		75	85	100	135	175	250	750	1,500	235
1884 . . . . . . (3,942). 1,700		155	175	190	250	450	500	1,250	3,500	275
1885 . . . . . . (3,790). 1,000		175	200	225	275	450	600	1,250	4,000	275
1886, Pf only (4,290).					175	200				250
1887 . . . . . . (2,960). 5,001		120	140	150	160	175	250	300	350	250
1887, 7/6 . . . .*.					180	225				350
1888 . . . . . . (4,582). 36,501		20	23	27	35	45	60	175	250	225
1889 . . . . . . (3,436). 18,125		35	45	60	75	100	125	175	275	200

* Included in number above.

SHIELD (1866–1883)

The Shield type nickel was made possible by the Act of May 16, 1866. Its weight was set at 77-16/100 grains with the same composition as the nickel three-cent piece.

G-4 Good: All letters in motto readable.
VG-8 Very Good: Motto clear and stands out. Rims slightly worn but even. Part of shield lines visible.
F-12 Fine: Half of each olive leaf worn smooth.
EF-40 Extremely Fine: Slight wear to leaf tips and cross over shield.
AU-50 About Uncirculated: Traces of light wear on only the high design points. Half of mint luster present.
MS-60 Uncirculated: No trace of wear. Light blemishes.
MS-63 Choice Uncirculated: Some distracting blemishes in prime focal areas. Impaired luster possible.
PF-63 Choice Proof: Reflective surfaces. Only a few blemishes in secondary focal areas. No major flaws.

With Rays (1866–1867)   **Without Rays (1867–1883)**

1873, Close 3   1873, Open 3   **Typical Example of 1883, 3 Over 2**
Other varieties exist.

Dealers often pay more than the prices shown for brilliant choice Unc. and Proof coins, and less for spotted, cleaned, or discolored pieces.

	Mintage	G-4	VG-8	F-12	VF-20	EF-40	AU-50	MS-60	MS-63	PF-63
1866, Rays	(600+) ..14,742,500	$15	$25	$30	$40	$85	$135	$200	$275	$1,200
1867, Rays	(25+) ...2,019,000	15	25	30	50	90	150	250	325	20,000
1867, Without Rays	(600+) ..28,890,500	10	12	15	20	25	50	100	145	275
1868	(600+) ..28,817,000	10	12	15	20	25	50	100	145	225
1869	(600+) ..16,395,000	10	12	15	20	25	50	100	145	225
1870	(1,000+) ...4,806,000	10	12	15	20	25	50	100	145	225
1871	(960+) 561,000	28	32	55	70	110	140	190	250	225
1872	(950+) ...6,036,000	10	12	15	20	25	75	200	225	225
1873, Close 3	(1,100+) 436,050	10	12	15	25	30	60	100	150	225
1873, Open 3	4,113,950	10	12	15	25	35	75	125	150	
1874	(700+) ...3,538,000	10	12	15	25	35	75	150	175	225
1875	(700+) ...2,097,000	15	20	25	30	50	80	165	185	225
1876	(1,150+) ...2,530,000	12	15	20	27	40	55	125	175	200
1877, Pf only	(900)			1,000	1,100	1,250				2,250
1878, Pf only	(2,350)			500	600	700				1,000
1879	(3,200)....... 25,900	180	225	275	300	325	350	400	475	300
1880	(3,955)....... 16,000	375	450	550	775	1,000	3,200	5,250	8,000	275
1881	(3,575)....... 68,800	125	150	175	200	250	275	350	450	275
1882	(3,100)....11,472,900	10	11	12	16	22	25	65	100	225
1883	(5,419).....1,451,500	10	11	12	16	22	25	65	100	225
1883, 3 Over 2	*	75	140	210	250	350	450	850	1,000	

* Included in number above.

LIBERTY HEAD (1883–1913)

In 1883 the design was changed to the "Liberty head." This type first appeared without the word CENTS on the coin, merely a large letter V. These "CENTS-less" coins were goldplated by fraudsters and passed as $5 pieces. Later in that year the word CENTS was added.

G-4 Good: No details in head. LIBERTY obliterated.
VG-8 Very Good: Some letters in LIBERTY legible.
F-12 Fine: All letters in LIBERTY legible.
VF-20 Very Fine: LIBERTY bold, including letter L.
EF-40 Extremely Fine: LIBERTY sharp. Corn grains at bottom of wreath visible on reverse.
AU-50 About Uncirculated: Traces of light wear on only high points of design. Half of mint luster present.
MS-60 Uncirculated: No trace of wear. Contact marks possible. Surface may be spotted, or luster faded.
MS-63 Choice Uncirculated: No trace of wear. Light blemishes.
PF-63 Choice Proof: Reflective surfaces. Only a few blemishes in secondary focal areas. No major flaws.

Variety 1, Without CENTS (1883 Only)   **Variety 2, With CENTS (1883–1913)**   **Mintmark Location**

Dealers often pay more than the prices shown for brilliant choice Unc. and Proof coins, and less for spotted, cleaned, or discolored pieces.

	Mintage	G-4	VG-8	F-12	VF-20	EF-40	AU-50	MS-60	MS-63	PF-63
1883, Without CENTS ..(5,219) ...5,474,300		$2.75	$3.25	$3.75	$6	$6.50	$9	$18	$26	$200
1883, CENTS (6,783) ..16,026,200		7.00	10.00	13.00	21	35.00	45	75	100	150
1884......(3,942) ..11,270,000		8.00	12.00	14.00	22	38.00	50	100	130	150
1885......(3,790) ...1,472,700		250.00	300.00	350.00	500	750.00	1,000	1,200	2,000	800
1886......(4,290) ...3,326,000		100.00	125.00	200.00	250	310.00	395	475	1,100	400
1887......(2,960) ..15,260,692		4.00	7.00	11.00	20	40.00	45	75	110	150
1888......(4,582) ..10,167,901		10.00	15.00	25.00	50	65.00	90	135	180	150
1889......(3,336) ..15,878,025		4.00	5.00	11.00	20	35.00	50	75	125	150
1890......(2,740) ..16,256,532		2.50	4.00	10.00	15	25.00	30	75	125	150
1891......(2,350) ..16,832,000		2.50	4.00	10.00	15	25.00	30	75	125	150
1892......(2,745) ..11,696,897		2.50	4.00	10.00	15	25.00	30	75	125	150
1893......(2,195) ..13,368,000		2.50	4.00	10.00	15	30.00	35	80	135	150
1894......(2,632) ...5,410,500		6.00	10.00	40.00	75	115.00	150	180	210	165
1895......(2,062) ...9,977,822		1.50	2.50	7.00	10	25.00	30	75	130	150
1896......(1,862) ...8,841,058		2.00	5.00	15.00	20	35.00	50	90	140	150
1897......(1,938) ..20,426,797		2.00	5.00	9.00	12	22.00	30	50	125	150
1898......(1,795) ..12,530,292		2.00	5.00	9.00	12	22.00	30	50	125	150
1899......(2,031) ..26,027,000		0.75	1.00	2.50	6	15.00	30	50	100	150
1900......(2,262) ..27,253,733		0.75	1.00	2.50	6	15.00	30	45	100	150
1901......(1,985) ..26,478,228		0.75	1.00	2.50	6	15.00	30	45	100	150
1902......(2,018) ..31,487,561		0.75	1.00	2.50	6	15.00	30	45	100	150
1903......(1,790) ..28,004,935		0.75	1.00	2.50	6	15.00	30	45	100	150
1904......(1,817) ..21,403,167		0.75	1.00	2.50	6	15.00	30	45	100	150
1905......(2,152) ..29,825,124		0.75	1.00	2.50	6	15.00	30	45	100	150
1906......(1,725) ..38,612,000		0.75	1.00	2.50	6	15.00	30	45	100	150
1907......(1,475) ..39,213,325		0.75	1.00	2.50	6	15.00	30	45	100	150
1908......(1,620) ..22,684,557		0.75	1.00	2.50	6	15.00	30	45	100	150

	Mintage	G-4	VG-8	F-12	VF-20	EF-40	AU-50	MS-60	MS-63	PF-63
1909 .... (4,763)... 11,585,763		$0.75	$1.25	$2.50	$8	$18	$35	$50	$95	$150
1910 .... (2,405)... 30,166,948		0.75	1.00	2.25	4	15	30	45	80	150
1911 .... (1,733)... 39,557,639		0.75	1.00	2.25	4	15	30	45	80	150
1912 .... (2,145)... 26,234,569		0.75	1.00	2.25	4	15	30	45	80	150
1912D 8,474,000		1.00	1.50	4.00	13	35	85	140	175	
1912S 238,000		65.00	100.00	125.00	225	425	750	850	1,250	
1913 Liberty Head (5 known). ...									2,750,000	

INDIAN HEAD OR BUFFALO (1913–1938)

The Buffalo nickel was designed by James E. Fraser, whose initial F is below the date. He modeled the bison after Black Diamond in the New York Central Park Zoo.

G-4 Good: Legends and date readable. Buffalo's horn does not show.
VG-8 Very Good: Horn worn nearly flat.
F-12 Fine: Horn and tail smooth but partially visible. Obverse rim intact.
VF-20 Very Fine: Much of horn visible. Indian's cheekbone worn.
EF-40 Extremely Fine: Horn lightly worn. Slight wear on Indian's hair ribbon.
AU-50 About Uncirculated: Traces of light wear on high points of design. Half of mint luster present.
MS-60 Uncirculated: No trace of wear. May have several blemishes.
MS-63 Choice Uncirculated: No trace of wear. Light blemishes.
Matte PF-63 Choice Proof: Crisp surfaces. Only a few blemishes in secondary focal areas. No major flaws.

Variety 1 – FIVE CENTS on Raised Ground (1913)

Dealers often pay more than the prices shown for brilliant choice Unc. coins, and less for spotted, cleaned, weakly struck, or discolored pieces.

	Mintage	G-4	VG-8	F-12	VF-20	EF-40	AU-50	MS-60	MS-63	MATTE PF-63
1913, Variety 1 .. (1,520) .. 30,992,000		$4	$5	$6	$8	$12	$14	$22	$35	$1,000
1913D, Variety 1 5,337,000		6	8	10	15	20	25	35	45	
1913S, Variety 1 2,105,000		17	22	24	30	42	55	75	100	

Variety 2 – FIVE CENTS in Recess (1913–1938)

Mintmark Below FIVE CENTS   **1916, Doubled-Die Obverse**   **1918-D, 8 Over 7**

	Mintage	G-4	VG-8	F-12	VF-20	EF-40	AU-50	MS-60	MS-63	MATTE PF-63
1913, Variety 2 29,857,186		$4.25	$5.50	$6.50	$7.50	$11	$15	$22	$32	
................(1,514)										$750
1913D, Variety 2 4,156,000		50.00	60.00	75.00	90.00	120	140	150	175	
1913S, Variety 2 1,209,000		150.00	165.00	210.00	240.00	325	375	500	700	
1914 20,664,463		10.00	11.00	12.00	14.00	16	22	35	50	
................(1,275)										750

Chart continued on next page.

Dealers often pay more than the prices shown for brilliant choice Unc. coins, and less for spotted, cleaned, weakly struck, or discolored pieces.

	Mintage	G-4	VG-8	F-12	VF-20	EF-40	AU-50	MS-60	MS-63	MATTE PF-63
1914D	3,912,000	$35.00	$50.00	$75.00	$110.00	$150	$200	$235	$325	
1914S	3,470,000	12.00	14.00	18.00	35.00	50	80	100	240	
1915	20,986,220	2.50	3.00	4.00	5.00	12	30	45	50	
	(1,050)									$750
1915D	7,569,000	8.00	11.00	18.00	35.00	75	85	140	175	
1915S	1,505,000	19.00	25.00	40.00	72.00	150	185	275	425	
1916	63,497,466	2.00	2.50	3.00	3.50	5	10	28	35	
	(600)									850
1916, DblDie Obv	* 2,000.00	3,000.00	5,000.00	7,500.00	11,000	22,500	40,000	100,000	
1916D	13,333,000	7.00	10.00	11.00	22.00	45	60	90	135	
1916S	11,860,000	5.00	6.00	9.00	22.00	45	65	100	165	
1917	51,424,019	2.00	2.50	3.00	4.00	7	16	30	60	
1917D	9,910,000	7.00	12.00	18.00	42.00	75	110	175	350	
1917S	4,193,000	9.00	13.00	20.00	50.00	85	135	225	600	
1918	32,086,314	1.50	2.00	2.50	6.00	16	22	60	135	

* Included in number above.

	Mintage	G-4	VG-8	F-12	VF-20	EF-40	AU-50	MS-60	MS-63
1918D, 8 Over 7	** $650.00	$1,000.00	$2,000.00	$3,500.00	$5,500.00	$8,500	$25,000	$35,000
1918D	8,362,000	8.50	14.00	18.00	70.00	130.00	175	235	600
1918S	4,882,000	5.00	12.00	16.00	45.00	90.00	150	250	1,300
1919	60,868,000	0.50	0.55	0.80	2.00	7.00	15	35	60
1919D (a)	8,006,000	6.00	10.00	30.00	70.00	130.00	160	325	750
1919S (a)	7,521,000	4.00	8.00	17.00	60.00	130.00	160	325	900
1920	63,093,000	0.45	0.60	1.25	2.50	6.00	15	35	70
1920D (a)	9,418,000	3.00	6.00	12.00	65.00	150.00	175	275	800
1920S	9,689,000	1.50	4.00	10.00	50.00	120.00	150	275	900
1921	10,663,000	0.80	2.00	3.00	10.00	25.00	35	70	140
1921S	1,557,000	35.00	55.00	90.00	300.00	465.00	550	865	1,100
1923	35,715,000	0.45	0.60	0.80	4.00	7.50	18	35	80
1923S (a)	6,142,000	3.00	3.50	9.00	60.00	150.00	180	235	450
1924	21,620,000	0.40	0.60	0.80	4.00	9.00	25	40	80
1924D	5,258,000	3.50	4.00	10.00	40.00	120.00	140	190	400
1924S	1,437,000	8.00	18.00	40.00	200.00	600.00	800	1,000	1,900
1925	35,565,100	0.75	1.25	2.00	4.00	8.00	16	25	47
1925D (a)	4,450,000	4.00	8.00	18.00	45.00	85.00	125	210	325
1925S	6,256,000	2.00	5.00	10.00	45.00	90.00	125	230	1,000
1926	44,693,000	0.35	0.45	0.60	3.00	5.00	12	22	35
1926D (a)	5,638,000	3.00	6.00	10.00	50.00	90.00	140	160	235
1926S	970,000	10.00	20.00	45.00	225.00	550.00	1,400	2,750	6,000
1927	37,981,000	0.50	0.45	0.60	1.50	6.00	10	25	40
1927D	5,730,000	0.85	2.00	2.50	15.00	40.00	55	85	160
1927S	3,430,000	0.60	0.90	1.75	18.00	45.00	75	250	1,400
1928	23,411,000	0.40	0.45	0.60	2.00	5.00	10	22	30
1928D	6,436,000	0.45	0.85	1.75	6.00	20.00	25	30	50
1928S	6,936,000	0.60	0.75	1.25	5.00	15.00	50	125	300
1929	36,446,000	0.35	0.40	0.60	2.00	5.00	10	16	35
1929D	8,370,000	0.45	0.60	0.80	3.00	15.00	20	35	65
1929S	7,754,000	0.40	0.60	0.75	0.90	5.50	12	25	45

** Included in number below. **a.** Dealers pay considerably more for Uncirculated pieces with full, sharp details.

1937-D, "3-Legged" Variety   **1938-D, D Over S**

Dealers often pay more than the prices shown for brilliant choice Unc. coins, and less for spotted, cleaned, weakly struck, or discolored pieces.

	Mintage	G-4	VG-8	F-12	VF-20	EF-40	AU-50	MS-60	MS-63	PF-63
1930	22,849,000	$0.40	$0.50	$0.70	$0.80	$5.00	$11.00	$16	$35	
1930S	5,435,000	0.40	0.50	0.70	0.80	6.00	15.00	25	60	
1931S	1,200,000	7.00	8.00	8.80	9.25	15.00	25.00	30	45	
1934	20,213,003	0.35	0.45	0.55	0.75	3.00	9.00	16	30	
1934D	7,480,000	0.50	0.75	1.25	3.00	9.00	21.00	35	55	
1935	58,264,000	0.35	0.45	0.55	0.75	1.25	4.25	10	25	
1935D	12,092,000	0.35	0.50	1.00	3.00	6.00	20.00	30	40	
1935S	10,300,000	0.35	0.45	0.55	0.75	2.00	7.50	15	36	
1936 .... (4,420)	118,997,000	0.35	0.45	0.55	0.75	1.25	4.00	10	25	$600
1936D	24,814,000	0.45	0.60	0.75	0.95	1.75	4.50	15	20	
1936S	14,930,000	0.35	0.45	0.55	0.75	1.25	4.50	10	15	
1937 .... (5,769)	79,480,000	0.35	0.45	0.55	0.75	1.25	3.00	15	15	625
1937D	17,826,000	0.35	0.45	0.55	0.75	1.25	4.00	10	15	
1937D, 3-Legged	*	250.00	350.00	450.00	550.00	650.00	750.00	1,250	3,000	
1937S	5,635,000	0.35	0.45	0.55	0.75	1.25	4.00	11	20	
1938D	7,020,000	1.00	1.10	1.50	1.75	2.00	4.00	11	15	
1938D, D Over S	*	1.50	2.00	4.00	5.00	8.00	12.00	25	36	

* Included in number above.

JEFFERSON (1938–2003)

This nickel was originally designed by Felix Schlag. He won an award of $1,000 in a competition with some 390 artists. It established the definite public approval of portrait and pictorial rather than symbolic devices on our coinage. On October 8, 1942, the wartime five-cent piece composed of copper (56%), silver (35%), and manganese (9%) was introduced to eliminate nickel, a critical war material. A larger mintmark was placed above the dome. The letter P (Philadelphia) was used for the first time, indicating the change of alloy. The designer's initials FS were added below the bust starting in 1966. The mintmark position was moved to the obverse starting in 1968.

VG-8 Very Good: Second porch pillar from right nearly gone, other three still visible but weak.

F-12 Fine: Jefferson's cheekbone worn flat. Hair lines and eyebrow faint. Second pillar weak, especially at bottom.

VF-20 Very Fine: Second pillar plain and complete on both sides.

EF-40 Extremely Fine: Cheekbone, hair lines, eyebrow slightly worn but well defined. Base of triangle above pillars visible but weak.

MS-63 Select Uncirculated: No trace of wear. Slight blemishes.

MS-65 Choice Uncirculated: No trace of wear. Barely noticeable blemishes.

PF-65 Gem Proof: Brilliant surfaces. No noticeable blemishes or flaws. May have a few barely noticeable marks or hairlines.

Mintmark located at right of building.   *Mintmark, starting in 1968.*

Entry continued on next page.

75

Coin dealers usually pay more than the Mint State prices shown for Uncirculated Jefferson nickels with fully struck steps visible in Monticello.

	Mintage	VG-8	F-12	VF-20	EF-40	MS-63	MS-65	PF-65
1938 . . . . . (19,365) . . . 19,496,000		$0.10	$0.12	$0.20	$0.25	$1.10	$6.00	$55
1938D 5,376,000		0.25	0.35	0.75	1.00	2.25	7.00	
1938S 4,105,000		0.40	0.60	0.85	1.50	2.75	8.00	
1939 . . . . . (12,535) . . 120,615,000		0.08	0.10	0.12	0.25	1.00	2.00	55
1939D 3,514,000		1.20	1.60	3.00	5.00	37.00	55.00	
1939S 6,630,000		0.25	0.30	0.50	1.50	14.00	30.00	
1940 . . . . . (14,158) . . 176,485,000		0.05	0.05	0.05	0.10	1.00	2.00	55
1940D 43,540,000		0.05	0.05	0.05	0.10	1.25	3.50	
1940S 39,690,000		0.05	0.05	0.05	0.10	1.25	3.50	
1941 . . . . . (18,720) . . 203,265,000		0.05	0.05	0.05	0.10	0.50	2.00	45
1941D 53,432,000		0.05	0.05	0.05	0.10	1.25	3.00	
1941S 43,445,000		0.05	0.05	0.05	0.10	1.50	3.50	
1942 . . . . . (29,600) . . . 49,789,000		0.05	0.05	0.05	0.10	1.25	4.00	45
1942D 13,938,000		0.10	0.15	0.25	1.00	16.00	23.00	

Wartime Silver Alloy (1942–1945)

Mintmark Location   **1943-P, 3 Over 2**

	Mintage	VG-8	F-12	VF-20	EF-40	MS-63	MS-65	PF-65
1942P . . . . (27,600) . . . 57,873,000		$1	$1.10	$1.20	$1.40	$4	$8	$100
1942S 32,900,000		1	1.10	1.20	1.40	4	9	
1943P, 3 Over 2 . . . . *			15.00	20.00	38.00	130	320	
1943P 271,165,000		1	1.10	1.20	1.40	3	8	
1943D 15,294,000		1	1.10	1.20	1.40	5	8	
1943S 104,060,000		1	1.10	1.20	1.40	3	8	
1944P 119,150,000		1	1.10	1.20	1.40	5	9	
1944D 32,309,000		1	1.10	1.20	1.40	5	9	
1944S 21,640,000		1	1.10	1.20	1.40	4	8	
1945P 119,408,100		1	1.10	1.20	1.40	3	8	
1945D 37,158,000		1	1.10	1.20	1.40	3	8	
1945S 58,939,000		1	1.10	1.20	1.40	3	8	

* Included in number below.

Prewar Composition, Mintmark Style Resumed (1946–1967)

1954-S, S Over D   **1955-D, D Over S**

	Mintage	VF-20	EF-40	MS-63	MS-65	PF-65
1946 161,116,000		$0.05	$0.05	$0.60	$5	
1946D 45,292,200		0.05	0.05	0.60	4	
1946S 13,560,000		0.05	0.06	0.35	4	

NICKEL FIVE-CENT PIECES

	Mintage	VF-20	EF-40	MS-63	MS-65	PF-65
1947	95,000,000	$0.05	$0.05	$0.35	$4.00	
1947D	37,822,000	0.05	0.05	0.35	4.00	
1947S	24,720,000	0.05	0.06	0.35	5.00	
1948	89,348,000	0.05	0.05	0.35	3.00	
1948D	44,734,000	0.05	0.06	0.75	2.00	
1948S	11,300,000	0.05	0.06	0.50	2.00	
1949	60,652,000	0.05	0.10	2.00	5.00	
1949D	36,498,000	0.05	0.05	0.75	3.00	
1949D, D Over S	*	18.00	30.00	100.00	175.00	
1949S	9,716,000	0.05	0.10	0.50	3.00	
1950	(51,386) 9,796,000	0.05	0.10	0.50	2.50	$30.00
1950D	2,630,030	3.00	3.50	8.50	12.50	
1951	(57,500) 28,552,000	0.05	0.06	1.25	5.00	25.00
1951D	20,460,000	0.05	0.06	1.50	4.00	
1951S	7,776,000	0.05	0.10	1.50	4.00	
1952	(81,980) 63,988,000	0.05	0.05	0.35	3.00	18.00
1952D	30,638,000	0.05	0.05	2.00	5.00	
1952S	20,572,000	0.05	0.05	0.55	4.00	
1953	(128,800) 46,644,000	0.05	0.05	0.25	2.50	18.00
1953D	59,878,600	0.05	0.05	0.25	2.75	
1953S	19,210,900	0.05	0.05	0.30	3.00	
1954	(233,300) 47,684,050	0.05	0.05	0.50	4.00	9.00
1954D	117,183,060	0.05	0.05	0.40	10.00	
1954S	29,384,000	0.05	0.05	0.50	5.00	
1954S, S Over D	*	2.50	5.00	18.00	35.00	
1955	(378,200) 7,888,000	0.06	0.08	0.40	5.00	6.00
1955D	74,464,100	0.05	0.05	0.25	7.00	
1955D, D Over S (a)	*	3.00	5.00	23.00	40.00	
1956	(669,384) 35,216,000	0.05	0.05	0.25	7.00	1.00
1956D	67,222,940	0.05	0.05	0.25	7.00	
1957	(1,247,952) 38,408,000	0.05	0.05	0.25	5.00	1.00
1957D	136,828,900	0.05	0.05	0.25	5.00	
1958	(875,652) 17,088,000	0.05	0.05	0.20	4.00	1.50
1958D	168,249,120	0.05	0.05	0.15	4.00	
1959	(1,149,291) 27,248,000	0.05	0.05	0.15	3.00	0.85
1959D	160,738,240	0.05	0.05	0.15	2.50	
1960	(1,691,602) 55,416,000	0.05	0.05	0.15	2.50	0.85
1960D	192,582,180	0.05	0.05	0.15	3.00	
1961	(3,028,144) 73,640,100	0.05	0.05	0.15	4.00	0.85
1961D	229,342,760	0.05	0.05	0.15	4.00	
1962	(3,218,019) 97,384,000	0.05	0.05	0.15	3.00	0.85
1962D	280,195,720	0.05	0.05	0.15	7.00	
1963	(3,075,645) 175,776,000	0.05	0.05	0.15	3.00	0.85
1963D	276,829,460	0.05	0.05	0.15	8.00	
1964	(3,950,762) 1,024,672,000	0.05	0.05	0.15	2.50	0.85
1964D	1,787,297,160	0.05	0.05	0.15	1.00	
1965	136,131,380	0.05	0.05	0.15	1.00	

* Included in number above. **a.** Varieties exist. Values are for the variety illustrated on previous page.

1966 Through 2003

	Mintage	MS-63	MS-65	PF-65
1966	156,208,283	$0.10	$1	
1967	107,325,800	0.10	1	

	Mintage	MS-63	MS-65	PF-65
1968D	91,227,880	$0.10	$1	
1968S	100,396,004	0.10	1	

	Mintage	MS-63	MS-65	PF-65
1968S, Proof . . .	(3,041,506)			$0.75
1969D	202,807,500	$0.10	$1.00	
1969S	120,165,000	0.10	0.80	
. . . .	(2,934,631)			0.75
1970D	515,485,380	0.10	3.00	
1970S	238,832,004	0.10	2.00	
. . . .	(2,632,810)			0.75
1971	106,884,000	0.25	0.80	
1971D	316,144,800	0.10	0.80	
1971S	(3,220,733)			0.75

	Mintage	MS-63	MS-65	PF-65
1972	202,036,000	$0.10	$0.80	
1972D	351,694,600	0.10	0.80	
1972S	(3,260,996)			$1.00
1973	384,396,000	0.10	0.80	
1973D	261,405,000	0.10	0.80	
1973S	(2,760,339)			0.75
1974	601,752,000	0.10	0.80	
1974D	277,373,000	0.10	0.80	
1974S	(2,612,568)			1.00

	Mintage	MS-65	PF-65
1975	181,772,000	$0.75	
1975D	401,875,300	0.75	
1975S	(2,845,450)		$0.85
1976	367,124,000	0.75	
1976D	563,964,147	0.75	
1976S	(4,149,730)		0.85
1977	585,376,000	0.75	
1977D	297,313,422	0.75	
1977S	(3,251,152)		0.75
1978	391,308,000	0.75	
1978D	313,092,780	0.75	
1978S	(3,127,781)		0.75
1979	463,188,000	0.75	
1979D	325,867,672	1.00	
1979S, Type 1	(3,677,175)		0.75
1979S, Type 2	*		1.00
1980P	593,004,000	0.50	
1980D	502,323,448	0.50	
1980S	(3,554,806)		0.75
1981P	657,504,000	0.50	
1981D	364,801,843	0.50	
1981S, Type 1	(4,063,083)		1.00
1981S, Type 2	*		2.00
1982P	292,355,000	3.00	
1982D	373,726,544	2.00	
1982S	(3,857,479)		1.00
1983P	561,615,000	3.00	
1983D	536,726,276	1.50	
1983S	(3,279,126)		1.00
1984P	746,769,000	1.25	
1984D	517,675,146	0.75	
1984S	(3,065,110)		1.50
1985P	647,114,962	0.50	
1985D	459,747,446	0.50	
1985S	(3,362,821)		1.25
1986P	536,883,483	0.50	
1986D	361,819,140	0.50	
1986S	(3,010,497)		2.75
1987P	371,499,481	0.70	
1987D	410,590,604	0.75	

	Mintage	MS-65	PF-65
1987S	(4,227,728)		$1.00
1988P	771,360,000	$0.60	
1988D	663,771,652	0.60	
1988S	(3,262,948)		2.00
1989P	898,812,000	0.50	
1989D	570,842,474	0.50	
1989S	(3,220,194)		1.75
1990P	661,636,000	0.50	
1990D	663,938,503	0.50	
1990S	(3,299,559)		1.75
1991P	614,104,000	0.50	
1991D	436,496,678	0.50	
1991S	(2,867,787)		2.00
1992P	399,552,000	0.75	
1992D	450,565,113	0.50	
1992S	(4,176,560)		1.25
1993P	412,076,000	0.30	
1993D	406,084,135	0.30	
1993S	(3,394,792)		1.50
1994P	722,160,000	0.50	
1994D	715,762,110	0.30	
1994S	(3,269,923)		1.25
1995P	774,156,000	0.30	
1995D	888,112,000	0.30	
1995S	(2,797,481)		2.00
1996P	829,332,000	0.30	
1996D	817,736,000	0.30	
1996S	(2,525,265)		1.00
1997P	470,972,000	0.30	
1997D	466,640,000	0.50	
1997S	(2,796,678)		1.75
1998P	688,272,000	0.30	
1998D	635,360,000	0.30	
1998S	(2,086,507)		1.75
1999P	1,212,000,000	0.30	
1999D	1,066,720,000	0.30	
1999S	(3,347,966)		2.00
2000P	846,240,000	0.30	
2000D	1,509,520,000	0.30	
2000S	(4,047,993)		1.75

* Included in number above.

	Mintage	MS-65	PF-65
2001P	675,704,000	$0.20	
2001D	627,680,000	0.20	
2001S	(3,184,606)		$1.75
2002P	539,280,000	0.20	
2002D	691,200,000	0.20	

	Mintage	MS-65	PF-65
2002S	(3,211,995)		$1.50
2003P	441,840,000	$0.20	
2003D	383,040,000	0.20	
2003S	(3,298,439)		1.50

WESTWARD JOURNEY (2004–2005)

The Westward Journey Nickel Series™ commemorates the bicentennial of the Louisiana Purchase and the journey of Meriwether Lewis and William Clark to explore that vast territory. **2004**—*Obverse:* traditional portrait of Jefferson. *Reverses:* Louisiana Purchase / Peace Medal reverse, by Mint sculptor Norman E. Nemeth. Keelboat reverse, by Mint sculptor Al Maletsky. **2005**—*Obverse:* new portrait of Jefferson, designed by Joe Fitzgerald after a 1789 marble bust by Jean-Antoine Houdon, and rendered by Mint sculptor Don Everhart. *Reverses:* American Bison reverse, designed by Jamie Franki and produced by Norman E. Nemeth. "Ocean in View" reverse, designed by Joe Fitzgerald and produced by Mint sculptor Donna Weaver.

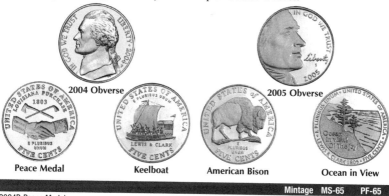

2004 Obverse · 2005 Obverse

Peace Medal · Keelboat · American Bison · Ocean in View

	Mintage	MS-65	PF-65
2004P, Peace Medal	361,440,000	$0.25	
2004D, Peace Medal	372,000,000	0.25	
2004S, Peace Medal	(2,992,069)		$1.25
2004P, Keelboat	366,720,000	0.25	
2004D, Keelboat	344,880,000	0.25	
2004S, Keelboat	(2,965,422)		1.25
2005P, American Bison	448,320,000	0.30	
2005D, American Bison	487,680,000	0.30	
2005S, American Bison	(3,344,679)		1.35
2005P, Ocean in View	394,080,000	0.25	
2005D, Ocean in View	411,120,000	0.25	
2005S, Ocean in View	(3,344,679)		1.25

JEFFERSON MODIFIED (2006 TO DATE)

In 2006 the Monticello design of 1938 to 2003 was returned to the reverse of the nickel five-cent coin. A new obverse motif featured a facing portrait of Thomas Jefferson, designed by Jamie Franki and sculpted by Donna Weaver. These designs have continued in use to date.

Felix Schlag's initials moved to reverse

	Mintage	MS-65	PF-63
2006P, Monticello	693,120,000	$0.25	
2006D, Monticello	809,280,000	0.25	
2006S, Monticello	(3,054,436)		$1.25
2007P	571,680,000	0.20	
2007D	626,160,000	0.20	
2007S	(2,577,166)		1.10
2008P	279,840,000	0.20	
2008D	345,600,000	0.20	
2008S	(2,169,561)		1.10
2009P	39,840,000	0.50	
2009D	46,800,000	0.50	
2009S	(2,179,867)		1.10
2010P	260,640,000	0.20	
2010D	229,920,000	0.20	
2010S	(1,689,216)		1.10
2011P	450,000,000	0.20	
2011D	540,240,000	0.20	

	Mintage	MS-65	PF-63
2011S	(1,673,010)		$1.10
2012P	464,640,000	$0.20	
2012D	558,960,000	0.20	
2012S	(1,239,148)		1.10
2013P	607,440,000	0.20	
2013D	615,600,000	0.20	
2013S	(1,274,505)		1.10
2014P	632,520,000	0.20	
2014D	570,720,000	0.20	
2014S	(1,190,369)		1.10
2015P	752,880,000	0.20	
2015D	846,720,000	0.20	
2015S	(1,022,410)		1.10
2016		0.20	
2016D		0.20	
2016S			1.10

Learn More About Nickel Five-Cent Pieces

Q. David Bowers has written two helpful references: *A Guide Book of Shield and Liberty Head Nickels,* and *A Guide Book of Buffalo and Jefferson Nickels.* Illustrated in full color, with photographs of every coin, these books include fascinating history, behind-the-scenes looks at the U.S. Mint, information on rare varieties, market values, grading tips, and more. Visit your local bookstore, call 1-800-546-2995, or order your copy online at Whitman.com. $19.95 each.

Mention code B7 for free shipping until May 1, 2017.

The half dime types present the same general characteristics as larger United States silver coins. Authorized by the Act of April 2, 1792, they were not coined until February 1795, although dated 1794. At first the weight was 20.8 grains, and fineness .8924. By the Act of January 18, 1837, the weight was slightly reduced to 20-5/8 grains and the fineness changed to .900. Finally, the weight was reduced to 19.2 grains by the Act of February 21, 1853.

FLOWING HAIR (1794–1795)

AG-3 About Good: Details clear enough to identify.
G-4 Good: Eagle, wreath, bust outlined but lack details.
VG-8 Very Good: Some details on face. All lettering legible.
F-12 Fine: Hair ends visible. Hair at top smooth.
VF-20 Very Fine: Hair lines at top visible. Hair about ear defined.
EF-40 Extremely Fine: Hair above forehead and at neck well defined but shows some wear.

AU-50 About Uncirculated: Slight wear on high waves of hair, near ear and face, and on head and tips of eagle's wings.
MS-60 Uncirculated: No trace of wear. Light blemishes.
MS-63 Choice Uncirculated: Some distracting marks or blemishes in prime focal areas. Some impairment of luster possible.

For Uncirculated examples, coin dealers usually pay less than the prices shown for pieces that are weakly struck.

	Mintage	AG-3	G-4	VG-8	F-12	VF-20	EF-40	AU-50	MS-60	MS-63
1794 86,416		$500	$950	$1,050	$1,450	$3,000	$5,500	$7,500	$11,000	$20,000
1795 . . . .*	350	800	1,000	1,350	2,100	4,250	5,500		8,000	11,000

* Included in number above.

DRAPED BUST (1796–1805)

AG-3 About Good: Details clear enough to identify.
G-4 Good: Date, stars, LIBERTY readable. Bust of Liberty outlined, but no details.
VG-8 Very Good: Some details visible.
F-12 Fine: Hair and drapery lines worn, but visible.
VF-20 Very Fine: Only left side of drapery indistinct.
EF-40 Extremely Fine: Details visible in all hair lines.
AU-50 About Uncirculated: Slight wear on bust, shoulder, and hair; wear on eagle's head and top of wings.
MS-60 Uncirculated: No trace of wear. Light blemishes.
MS-63 Choice Uncirculated: Some distracting marks or blemishes in prime focal areas. Impaired luster possible.

Small Eagle Reverse (1796–1797)

	Mintage	AG-3	G-4	VG-8	F-12	VF-20	EF-40	AU-50	MS-60	MS-63
1796, 6 Over 5 10,230		$550	$1,000	$1,250	$2,300	$3,250	$6,000	$9,500	$17,500	$25,000
1796, LIKERTY . . . .*	500	950	1,250	2,250	3,250	6,000	8,000	13,500	22,500
1797, 15 Stars 44,527	500	950	1,250	2,250	3,250	6,000	7,000	10,000	14,000
1797, 16 Stars . . . .*	500	950	1,250	2,250	3,250	5,250	7,500	10,000	14,500
1797, 13 Stars . . . .*	750	1,500	1,600	2,750	4,250	8,000	15,000	27,500	35,000

* Included in number above.

Heraldic Eagle Reverse (1800–1805)

1800 LIBEKTY

	Mintage	AG-3	G-4	VG-8	F-12	VF-20	EF-40	AU-50	MS-60	MS-63
1800	24,000	$350	$800	$950	$1,300	$1,750	$4,000	$5,000	$8,500	$13,000
1800, LIBEKTY	16,000	350	800	950	1,300	1,750	4,500	5,750	9,000	14,000
1801	27,760	350	800	950	1,450	2,000	5,000	6,500	11,500	16,500
1802	3,060	10,000	20,000	30,000	37,500	50,000	120,000	—	—	—
1803	37,850	400	950	950	1,300	1,750	4,500	6,250	9,000	12,500
1805	15,600	400	900	1,000	1,450	2,250	7,000	11,000	—	—

CAPPED BUST (1829–1837)

G-4 Good: Bust of Liberty outlined, no detail. Date and legend legible.
VG-8 Very Good: Complete legend and date plain. At least three letters
of LIBERTY on edge of cap show clearly.
F-12 Fine: All letters in LIBERTY visible.
VF-20 Very Fine: Full rims. Ear and shoulder clasp show plainly.
EF-40 Extremely Fine: Ear very distinct; eyebrow and hair well defined.
AU-50 About Uncirculated: Traces of light wear on many of the high points. At least half of mint luster
still present.
MS-60 Uncirculated: No trace of wear. Light blemishes.
MS-63 Choice Uncirculated: No trace of wear. Light blemishes. Attractive mint luster.

	Mintage	G-4	VG-8	F-12	VF-20	EF-40	AU-50	MS-60	MS-63
1829	1,230,000	$35	$55	$60	$80	$120	$175	$250	$650
1830	1,240,000	35	50	55	70	110	150	225	650
1831	1,242,700	35	50	55	70	110	150	225	650
1832	965,000	35	50	55	70	110	150	225	650
1833	1,370,000	35	50	55	70	110	150	225	650
1834	1,480,000	35	50	55	70	110	150	225	650
1835	2,760,000	35	50	55	70	110	150	225	650
1836	1,900,000	35	50	55	70	110	150	225	650
1837, Small 5 C.	871,000	35	55	65	100	150	300	650	1,250
1837, Large 5 C.	*	35	45	55	80	110	175	250	650

* Included in number above.

LIBERTY SEATED (1837–1873)

G-4 Good: LIBERTY on shield smooth. Date and letters legible.
VG-8 Very Good: At least three letters in LIBERTY visible.
F-12 Fine: Entire LIBERTY visible, weak spots.
VF-20 Very Fine: Entire LIBERTY strong and even.
EF-40 Extremely Fine: LIBERTY and scroll edges distinct.
AU-50 About Uncirculated: Traces of light wear on many of the high points. At least half of mint luster
still present.
MS-60 Uncirculated: No trace of wear. Light blemishes.
MS-63 Choice Uncirculated: No trace of wear. Light blemishes. Attractive mint luster.

Variety 1 – No Stars on Obverse (1837–1838)

	Mintage	G-4	VG-8	F-12	VF-20	EF-40	AU-50	MS-60	MS-63
1837	1,405,000	$25	$30	$55	$100	$150	$275	$425	$625
18380, No Stars	70,000	50	75	120	240	625	800	1,500	5,250

Variety 2 – Stars on Obverse (1838–1853)

From 1838 through 1859 the mintmark was located above the bow on the reverse. Large, medium, or small mintmark varieties occur for several dates.

	Mintage	G-4	VG-8	F-12	VF-20	EF-40	AU-50	MS-60	MS-63
1838	2,255,000	$10	$12	$15	$20	$50	$125	$150	$275
18390	1,291,600	12	15	20	25	60	125	325	1,000
1840	1,344,085	10	12	15	40	50	125	125	275
18400	935,000	12	15	20	25	55	180	475	1,400
1841	1,150,000	10	12	15	20	30	85	110	175
18410	815,000	12	12	20	25	65	115	450	750
1842	815,000	10	12	15	20	40	85	110	175
18420	350,000	15	20	35	100	300	450	650	1,400
1843	815,000	10	12	15	20	40	85	110	175
1844	430,000	10	12	15	20	40	85	110	175
18440	220,000	45	65	120	325	725	1,500	3,250	6,250
1845	1,564,000	10	12	15	20	40	85	110	175
1846	27,000	300	650	1,400	1,600	2,250	3,000	7,000	10,000
1847	1,274,000	10	12	15	20	40	85	110	200
1848	668,000	10	12	15	20	40	85	125	275
18480	600,000	12	15	20	30	65	125	225	400
1849, 9 Over 6	*	13	15	20	35	65	150	375	750
1849, 9 Over Widely Placed 6	*	18	22	30	40	75	150	375	750
1849, Normal Date	1,309,000	10	12	15	30	40	85	110	240
18490	140,000	14	22	50	125	275	625	1,200	2,500
1850	955,000	10	12	16	20	40	85	110	175
18500	690,000	12	15	20	35	80	175	450	1,000
1851	781,000	10	12	16	20	40	85	110	175
18510	860,000	12	15	20	25	75	140	300	500
1852	1,000,500	10	12	16	20	40	85	110	175
18520	260,000	16	20	40	75	150	300	450	1,250
1853, No Arrows	135,000	25	40	60	130	200	375	450	700
18530, No Arrows	160,000	140	225	325	500	1,400	2,500	3,750	7,500

* Included in number below.

Variety 3 – Arrows at Date (1853–1855)

As on the dimes, quarters, and halves, arrows were placed at the sides of the date for a short period starting in 1853 to denote the reduction of weight.

	Mintage	G-4	VG-8	F-12	VF-20	EF-40	AU-50	MS-60	MS-63	PF-63
1853	13,210,020	$10	$12	$15	$20	$40	$100	$140	$225	—
18530	2,200,000	12	14	16	22	40	85	175	575	
1854	5,740,000	10	12	15	20	35	80	135	200	$4,000

Chart continued on next page.

Mintage	G-4	VG-8	F-12	VF-20	EF-40	AU-50	MS-60	MS-63	PF-63
18540 1,560,000	$12	$14	$16	$20	$40	$90	$140	$400	
1855 1,750,000	10	12	15	20	35	80	135	200	$4,000
18550 600,000	12	14	16	35	85	120	400	675	

Variety 2 Resumed, with Weight Standard of 1853 (1856–1859)

1858 Over Inverted Date

Mintage	G-4	VG-8	F-12	VF-20	EF-40	AU-50	MS-60	MS-63	PF-63
1856 4,880,000	$10	$12	$15	$20	$35	$80	$100	$175	$2,000
18560 1,100,000	10	12	15	30	50	140	325	625	
1857 7,280,000	10	12	15	20	35	80	100	175	1,500
18570 1,380,000	10	12	15	22	35	100	200	225	
1858 . . . . . . (300) 3,500,000	10	12	15	20	35	80	100	175	500
1858, Over Inverted Date . . . .*	18	25	40	55	110	175	400	750	
18580 1,660,000	10	12	15	25	40	80	125	225	
1859 . . . . . . (800) 340,000	10	12	15	20	40	80	125	200	500
18590 560,000	10	12	17	25	65	110	150	225	

* Included in number above.

Variety 4 – Legend on Obverse (1860–1873)

Mintage	G-4	VG-8	F-12	VF-20	EF-40	AU-50	MS-60	MS-63	PF-63
1860 . . . . . . (1,000) 799,000	$10	$12	$15	$17	$30	$45	$100	$150	$250
18600 1,060,000	10	12	15	17	30	50	110	175	
1861 . . . . . . (1,000) . . 3,360,000	10	12	15	17	30	45	100	150	250
1862 . . . . (550) . . 1,492,000	10	20	25	35	40	50	110	200	250
1863 . . . . (460) 18,000	100	125	175	225	325	375	450	525	250
1863S 100,000	15	30	65	80	125	200	425	625	
1864 . . . . (470) 48,000	225	300	400	675	775	800	1,000	1,050	250
1864S 90,000	30	50	90	125	200	325	475	750	
1865 . . . . (500) 13,000	200	250	450	525	600	675	725	800	250
1865S 120,000	15	25	35	50	125	325	625	1,250	
1866 . . . . (725) 10,000	200	225	475	500	600	675	700	750	250
1866S 120,000	15	25	35	50	120	225	275	550	
1867 . . . . (625) 8,000	275	325	575	700	775	825	875	1,000	250
1867S 120,000	10	20	30	50	100	200	375	625	
1868 . . . . (600) 88,600	30	40	80	125	180	300	400	525	250
1868S 280,000	10	12	16	20	35	70	175	325	
1869 . . . . (600) 208,000	10	12	16	20	35	70	125	200	250
1869S 230,000	10	12	16	20	30	70	175	450	
1870 . . . . . . (1,000) 535,000	10	12	15	17	30	45	100	150	250
1870S (unique)								400,000	
1871 . . . . (960) . . 1,873,000	10	12	15	17	30	45	100	150	250
1871S 161,000	10	15	20	35	45	100	150	250	
1872 . . . . (950) . . 2,947,000	10	12	15	17	30	45	100	150	250
1872S 837,000	10	12	15	17	30	45	100	150	
1873 . . . . (600) . . 7,126,000	10	12	15	17	30	45	100	150	250
1873S 324,000	10	12	15	17	30	45	100	150	

The designs of the dimes, first coined in 1796, follow closely those of the half dimes up through the Liberty Seated type. The dimes in each instance weigh twice as much as the half dimes.

DRAPED BUST (1796–1807)
Small Eagle Reverse (1796–1797)

AG-3 About Good: Details clear enough to identify.
G-4 Good: Date legible. Bust outlined, but no detail.
VG-8 Very Good: All but deepest drapery folds worn smooth. Hair lines nearly gone and curls lacking in detail.
F-12 Fine: All drapery lines visible. Hair partly worn.
VF-20 Very Fine: Only left side of drapery indistinct.
EF-40 Extremely Fine: Hair well outlined with details visible.
AU-50 About Uncirculated: Traces of light wear on many of the high points. At least half of mint luster still present.
MS-60 Uncirculated: No trace of wear. Light blemishes.
MS-63 Choice Uncirculated: Some distracting marks or blemishes in prime focal areas. Impaired luster possible.

1797, 16 Stars   **1797, 13 Stars**

	Mintage	AG-3	G-4	VG-8	F-12	VF-20	EF-40	AU-50	MS-60	MS-63
1796	22,135	$800	$1,800	$2,400	$3,500	$5,000	$8,000	$10,000	$15,000	$25,000
1797, All kinds	25,261									
1797, 16 Stars		800	1,900	2,600	3,750	5,000	8,500	11,000	20,000	30,000
1797, 13 Stars		900	2,000	2,750	3,850	5,750	9,000	12,000	32,500	50,000

Heraldic Eagle Reverse (1798–1807)

	Mintage	AG-3	G-4	VG-8	F-12	VF-20	EF-40	AU-50	MS-60	MS-63
1798, All kinds	27,550									
1798, 8 Over 7, 16 Stars on Reverse		$250	$450	$650	$950	$1,250	$2,000	$3,750	$5,000	$10,500
1798, 8 Over 7, 13 Stars on Reverse		300	800	1,750	2,500	4,000	6,000	8,000		
1798		200	450	650	750	1,100	1,750	3,000	5,000	10,000
1800	21,760	200	450	650	750	1,100	2,000	4,000	17,500	30,000
1801	34,640	200	450	650	950	1,750	3,250	7,000	27,500	30,000
1802	10,975	450	750	1,000	1,500	2,250	4,250	9,000	20,000	
1803	33,040	200	475	700	900	1,100	3,000	6,500	30,000	
1804	8,265	700	1,200	2,250	5,250	10,000	20,000	37,500	—	
1805	120,780	200	450	625	725	1,100	1,750	2,600	4,250	7,250
1807	165,000	200	400	625	725	1,100	1,750	2,600	4,250	7,250

CAPPED BUST (1809–1837)

G-4 Good: Date, letters, and stars discernible. Bust outlined, no details.
VG-8 Very Good: Legends and date plain. Some letters in LIBERTY visible.
F-12 Fine: Clear LIBERTY. Ear and shoulder clasp visible. Part of rim visible on both sides.
VF-20 Very Fine: LIBERTY distinct. Full rim. Ear and clasp plain and distinct.
EF-40 Extremely Fine: LIBERTY sharp. Ear distinct. Hair above eye well defined.
AU-50 About Uncirculated: Traces of light wear on only the high points of the design. Half of mint luster present.
MS-60 Uncirculated: No trace of wear. Light blemishes.
MS-63 Choice Uncirculated: Some distracting marks or blemishes in prime focal areas. Impaired luster possible.

Variety 1 – Wide Border (1809–1828)

1823, 3 Over 2	1824, 4 Over 2	1828, Large Date	1828, Small Date

	Mintage	G-4	VG-8	F-12	VF-20	EF-40	AU-50	MS-60	MS-63
1809	51,065	$80	$150	$275	$575	$1,000	$1,400	$2,250	$4,500
1811, 11 Over 09	65,180	70	100	200	500	800	1,100	2,000	4,250
1814	421,500	35	50	90	165	400	500	1,000	2,000
1820	942,587	30	50	80	140	375	450	900	1,800
1821	1,186,512	30	50	80	140	375	450	900	1,800
1822	100,000	1,000	1,750	2,250	3,000	5,500	7,500	10,000	17,500
1823, 3 Over 2, All kinds	440,000								
1823, 3 Over 2, Small E's		30	50	80	140	375	450	900	1,800
1823, 3 Over 2, Large E's		30	50	80	140	375	450	900	1,800
1824, 4 Over 2	510,000	50	80	125	325	625	700	1,000	2,250
1825	*	30	50	80	140	375	450	900	1,800
1827	1,215,000	30	50	80	140	375	450	950	1,800
1828, Large Date, Curl Base 2	125,000	30	50	80	150	450	650	1,200	2,750

* Included in number above.

Variety 2 – Modified Design (1828–1837)

1829, Small 10 C.	1829, Large 10 C.	1830, 30 Over 29

	Mintage	G-4	VG-8	F-12	VF-20	EF-40	AU-50	MS-60	MS-63
1828, Small Date, Square Base 2	*	$25	$35	$50	$75	$220	$350	$650	$1,400
1829, Small 10 C.	770,000	20	30	40	65	175	275	600	1,400
1829, Medium 10 C.	*	20	30	40	65	175	275	600	1,400
1829, Large 10 C.	*	20	30	40	65	175	275	600	1,400
1830, 30 Over 29	510,000	20	30	50	90	225	375	675	1,750

* Included in number above.

	Mintage	G-4	VG-8	F-12	VF-20	EF-40	AU-50	MS-60	MS-63
1830, Large 10 C. ... *		$20	$30	$40	$65	$175	$275	$600	$1,400
1830, Small 10 C. ... *		20	30	40	65	175	275	600	1,400
1831	771,350	20	30	40	65	175	275	600	1,400
1832	522,500	20	30	40	65	175	275	600	1,400
1833	485,000	20	30	40	65	175	275	600	1,400
1834	635,000	20	30	40	65	175	275	600	1,400
1835	1,410,000	20	30	40	65	175	275	600	1,400
1836	1,190,000	20	30	40	65	175	275	600	1,400
1837	359,500	20	30	40	65	175	275	600	1,400

* Included in mintage for 1830, 30 Over 29 (previous page).

LIBERTY SEATED (1837–1891)
Variety 1 – No Stars on Obverse (1837–1838)

G-4 Good: LIBERTY on shield not readable. Date and letters legible.
F-12 Fine: LIBERTY visible, weak spots.
VF-20 Very Fine: LIBERTY strong and even.
EF-40 Extremely Fine: LIBERTY and scroll edges distinct.
AU-50 About Uncirculated: Wear on Liberty's shoulder and hair high points.
MS-60 Uncirculated: No trace of wear. Light blemishes.
MS-63 Choice Uncirculated: Some distracting marks or blemishes in focal areas. Impaired luster possible.

No Drapery From Elbow
No Stars on Obverse

Mintmarks on Liberty Seated dimes on reverse, within or below the wreath. Size of mintmark varies on many dates.

	Mintage	G-4	F-12	VF-20	EF-40	AU-50	MS-60	MS-63
1837	682,500	$20	$55	$160	$275	$450	$700	$1,200
1838O	489,034	25	75	175	325	700	1,750	3,500

Variety 2 – Stars on Obverse (1838–1853)

No Drapery From Elbow, Tilted Shield (1838–1840)

Drapery From Elbow, Upright Shield (1840–1891)

1838, Small Stars   1838, Large Stars

	Mintage	G-4	F-12	VF-20	EF-40	AU-50	MS-60	MS-63
1838, All kinds	1,992,500							
1838, Small Stars		$10	$25	$50	$100	$225	$400	$700
1838, Large Stars		8	12	25	80	175	275	550
1838, Partial Drapery		9	18	35	75	210	425	1,000
1839	1,053,115	8	15	25	80	175	275	550
1839O	1,291,600	10	20	25	90	185	325	750
1840, No Drapery	981,500	8	15	25	80	185	275	550
1840O, No Drapery	1,175,000	10	15	30	135	550	1,750	4,000
1840, Drapery	377,500	15	45	100	135	250	750	3,500

Chart continued on next page.

	Mintage	G-4	F-12	VF-20	EF-40	AU-50	MS-60	MS-63
1841	1,622,500	$8	$12	$18	$25	$80	$175	$400
18410	2,007,500	10	20	35	80	125	525	1,000
1842	1,887,500	8	12	18	25	80	175	375
18420	2,020,000	10	18	40	200	700	1,450	2,750
1843	1,370,000	8	12	18	25	80	175	475
18430	150,000	75	325	600	1,250	4,500	11,000	
1844	72,500	100	225	400	650	1,000	2,500	5,750
1845	1,755,000	8	12	18	25	80	175	450
18450	230,000	10	45	125	425	750	1,500	—
1846	31,300	100	300	625	1,500	5,500	9,000	22,500
1847	245,000	9	16	35	100	200	550	1,400
1848	451,500	8	12	30	45	85	325	475
1849	839,000	8	12	20	30	80	175	550
18490	300,000	10	20	70	150	425	1,250	3,250
1850	1,931,500	8	12	18	30	90	200	375
18500	510,000	10	15	35	60	125	550	1,200
1851	1,026,500	8	12	18	25	80	200	500
18510	400,000	10	20	45	100	275	1,100	1,750
1852	1,535,500	8	12	18	25	80	175	375
18520	430,000	12	25	75	150	250	825	1,450
1853, No Arrows	95,000	60	200	325	450	525	625	1,000

Variety 3 – Arrows at Date (1853–1855)

	Mintage	G-4	F-12	VF-20	EF-40	AU-50	MS-60	MS-63	PF-63
1853, With Arrows	12,173,000	$7	$10	$18	$25	$90	$175	$400	$15,000
18530	1,100,000	8	20	75	200	325	1,100	1,750	
1854	4,470,000	7	10	18	25	90	200	400	5,500
18540	1,770,000	8	10	18	25	90	175	600	
1855	2,075,000	7	10	18	25	90	200	550	5,500

Variety 2 Resumed, With Weight Standard of Variety 3 (1856–1860)

Small Date, Arrows Removed (1856–1860)

	Mintage	G-4	F-12	VF-20	EF-40	AU-50	MS-60	MS-63	PF-63
1856, All kinds	5,780,000								
1856, Large Date		$7	$10	$18	$25	$80	$175	$375	
1856, Small Date		7	10	15	20	80	175	350	$2,000
18560	1,180,000	8	10	18	35	125	500	825	
1856S	70,000	55	200	375	750	1,000	2,250	7,500	

	Mintage	G-4	F-12	VF-20	EF-40	AU-50	MS-60	MS-63	PF-63
1857	5,580,000	$7	$10	$15	$25	$80	$175	$375	$1,800
1857O	1,540,000	8	10	15	25	100	225	400	
1858 . . . . . . *(300+)*. . .	1,540,000	7	10	15	25	80	175	375	900
1858O	200,000	8	15	40	90	175	325	600	
1858S	60,000	60	125	275	625	1,000	2,250	10,000	
1859 . . . . . . *(800+)*. . . .	429,200	7	10	15	25	80	175	375	700
1859O	480,000	8	10	20	45	125	200	375	
1859S	60,000	45	200	400	750	1,750	6,500	14,000	
1860S	140,000	20	40	100	275	400	1,350	2,750	

Variety 4 – Legend on Obverse (1860–1873)

	Mintage	G-4	F-12	VF-20	EF-40	AU-50	MS-60	MS-63	PF-63
1860 . . . . . .(1,000). . . .	606,000	$7	$10	$18	$20	$50	$125	$175	$350
1860O	40,000	200	575	1,500	3,000	4,000	8,250	—	
1861 . . . . . .(1,000). . .	1,883,000	7	10	15	20	40	100	175	350
1861S	172,500	20	75	125	250	375	1,400	3,000	
1862 . . . . (550). . . .	847,000	7	10	15	20	50	120	175	350
1862S	180,750	25	50	150	475	675	775	2,250	
1863 . . . . (460).	14,000	175	425	600	650	700	775	750	350
1863S	157,500	20	40	100	250	500	950	3,000	
1864 . . . . (470).	11,000	125	300	500	600	700	775	900	425
1864S	230,000	40	85	160	250	425	1,000	1,250	
1865 . . . . (500).	10,000	150	350	525	525	600	800	1,100	350
1865S	175,000	35	175	350	500	1,500	4,500	7,000	
1866 . . . . (725).	8,000	325	1,000	1,300	1,450	1,550	1,600	1,750	350
1866S	135,000	20	50	80	275	425	750	3,250	
1867 . . . . (625).	6,000	300	500	700	725	750	750	1,100	350
1867S	140,000	20	75	125	325	550	750	1,500	
1868 . . . . (600). . . .	464,000	10	15	25	40	90	175	425	350
1868S	260,000	10	15	60	325	375	450	600	
1869 . . . . (600). . . .	256,000	10	15	55	65	100	225	450	350
1869S	450,000	10	15	20	150	200	300	500	
1870 . . . . . .(1,000). . . .	470,500	10	12	15	20	55	150	250	350
1870S	50,000	150	400	500	600	700	825	1,350	
1871 . . . . (960). . .	906,750	10	12	15	20	80	150	225	350
1871CC	20,100	1,500	3,500	5,250	7,500	15,000	—	—	
1871S	320,000	15	60	90	150	200	400	750	
1872 . . . . (950). . .	2,395,500	10	12	15	20	45	100	175	350
1872CC	35,480	300	1,250	2,000	4,500	12,000	—	—	
1872S	190,000	15	55	80	150	275	700	1,400	
1873, Close 3 (600). . .	*1,507,400*	10	12	15	20	45	100	175	350
1873, Open 3	*60,000*	10	30	45	80	110	325	750	
1873CC *(unique)*	12,400							—	

Variety 5 – Arrows at Date (1873–1874)

In 1873, the dime was increased in weight from 2.49 grams to 2.50 grams. Arrows at the date in 1873 and 1874 indicate this change.

	Mintage	G-4	F-12	VF-20	EF-40	AU-50	MS-60	MS-63	PF-63
1873 . . . . . . (500) . . .	2,377,700	$10	$18	$30	$100	$175	$275	$575	$600
1873CC	18,791	2,000	2,500	6,000	11,500	25,000	—	—	
1873S	455,000	10	20	35	110	275	525	1,100	
1874 . . . . . . (700) . . .	2,940,000	10	16	30	100	175	285	575	600
1874CC	10,817	2,000	6,500	12,000	20,000	32,500	—	—	
1874S	240,000	11	40	65	125	275	500	1,100	

Variety 4 Resumed, With Weight Standard of Variety 5 (1875–1891)

	Mintage	G-4	F-12	VF-20	EF-40	AU-50	MS-60	MS-63	PF-63
1875 . . . . . . (700) . .	10,350,000	$7	$10	$12	$20	$45	$100	$150	$325
1875CC	4,645,000	12	25	30	50	80	150	300	
1875S	9,070,000	7	10	12	20	45	100	150	
1876 . . . . . .(1,250) . .	11,460,000	7	10	12	20	45	100	150	325
1876CC	8,270,000	12	25	30	45	80	150	245	
1876S	10,420,000	7	10	12	20	45	100	175	
1877 . . . . . . (510) . . .	7,310,000	7	10	12	20	45	100	150	325
1877CC	7,700,000	12	25	30	55	80	125	325	
1877S	2,340,000	7	10	12	20	45	100	175	
1878 . . . . . . (800) . . .	1,677,200	7	10	12	20	45	100	175	325
1878CC	200,000	100	200	250	300	475	750	1,400	
1879 . . . . . .(1,100)	14,000	100	175	225	400	400	450	500	325
1880 . . . . . .(1,355)	36,000	80	160	200	250	275	375	450	325
1881 . . . . . . (975)	24,000	95	175	225	250	300	325	400	325
1882 . . . . .(1,100) . . .	3,910,000	7	10	12	20	45	100	150	325
1883 . . . . .(1,039) . .	7,674,673	7	10	12	20	45	100	150	325
1884 . . . . . . (875) . . .	3,365,505	7	10	12	20	45	100	150	325
1884S	564,969	10	15	30	60	175	400	625	
1885 . . . . (930) . .	2,532,497	7	10	12	20	45	110	150	325
1885S	43,690	225	500	750	1,250	2,000	3,000	4,500	
1886 . . . . . . (886) . . .	6,376,684	7	10	12	20	45	100	150	325
1886S	206,524	12	25	40	65	95	300	625	
1887 . . . . . . (710) . .	11,283,229	7	10	12	20	45	100	150	325
1887S	4,454,450	7	10	12	20	45	100	150	
1888 . . . . . . (832) . . .	5,495,655	7	10	12	20	45	100	150	325
1888S	1,720,000	7	10	12	25	45	125	375	
1889 . . . . . . (711) . . .	7,380,000	7	10	12	20	45	100	150	325
1889S	972,678	10	15	25	40	75	225	525	
1890 . . . . . . (590) . . .	9,910,951	7	10	12	20	45	100	150	325
1890S	1,423,076	7	12	20	40	75	180	375	
1891 . . . . . . (600) . .	15,310,000	7	10	12	20	45	100	150	325
18910	4,540,000	7	15	18	20	45	125	165	
1891S	3,196,116	7	10	12	20	45	100	150	

BARBER OR LIBERTY HEAD (1892–1916)

This type was designed by Charles E. Barber, chief engraver of the Mint. His initial B is at the truncation of the neck. He also designed the quarters and half dollars of the same period.

G-4 Good: Date and letters plain. LIBERTY obliterated.
VG-8 Very Good: Some letters visible in LIBERTY.
F-12 Fine: Letters in LIBERTY visible, though some weak.
VF-20 Very Fine: Letters of LIBERTY evenly plain.
EF-40 Extremely Fine: All letters in LIBERTY sharp, distinct. Headband edges distinct.
AU-50 About Uncirculated: Slight traces of wear on hair cheekbone and on leaf tips in wreath.
MS-60 Uncirculated: No trace of wear. Light blemishes.
MS-63 Choice Uncirculated: Some distracting blemishes in prime focal areas. Impaired luster possible.

Mintmark location is on reverse, below wreath.

	Mintage	G-4	VG-8	F-12	VF-20	EF-40	AU-50	MS-60	MS-63	PF-63
1892 .... (1,245)...	12,120,000	$3.00	$4.00	$8	$12	$15	$35	$75	$145	$300
1892O	3,841,700	4.00	6.00	15	25	35	45	90	175	
1892S	990,710	30.00	50.00	110	125	160	180	240	450	
1893, 3/2	*	45.00	65.00	85	100	120	175	425	1,000	—
1893 ......(792)....	3,339,940	3.00	5.00	10	15	24	35	95	145	300
1893O	1,760,000	12.00	25.00	75	85	100	125	175	350	
1893S (a)	2,491,401	6.00	12.00	18	25	40	75	150	375	
1894 ......(972)....	1,330,000	10.00	20.00	65	85	100	125	175	275	300
1894O	720,000	30.00	45.00	110	160	250	400	925	1,500	
1894S	24 (b)								750,000	
1895 ......(880)......	690,000	35.00	75.00	180	275	325	400	475	675	300
1895O	440,000	185.00	275.00	525	800	1,600	2,250	3,750	7,500	
1895S	1,120,000	20.00	30.00	75	100	125	175	300	625	
1896 ......(762)....	2,000,000	4.50	10.00	28	36	50	55	95	225	300
1896O	610,000	40.00	85.00	175	225	280	400	750	1,500	
1896S	575,056	40.00	70.00	160	200	275	310	500	900	
1897 ......(731)...	10,868,533	2.00	2.50	3	6	12	35	75	145	300
1897O	666,000	35.00	50.00	160	200	250	350	575	900	
1897S	1,342,844	8.00	16.00	50	75	90	140	250	625	
1898 ......(735)...	16,320,000	2.00	2.50	3	5	12	35	75	145	300
1898O	2,130,000	5.00	10.00	38	75	80	150	275	650	
1898S	1,702,507	2.00	5.00	16	25	35	75	200	650	
1899 ......(846)...	19,580,000	2.00	2.50	3	5	12	35	75	145	300
1899O	2,650,000	4.00	7.00	35	45	70	125	225	600	
1899S	1,867,493	2.00	5.00	12	16	20	55	175	375	
1900 ......(912)...	17,600,000	1.75	2.00	3	5	12	35	75	145	300

* Included in number below. **a.** Boldy doubled mintmark is valued slightly higher. **b.** Five of these were reserved for assay.

Chart continued on next page.

	Mintage	G-4	VG-8	F-12	VF-20	EF-40	AU-50	MS-60	MS-63	PF-63
1900O	2,010,000	$7.00	$18.00	$55.00	$75.00	$130	$200	$350	$600	
1900S	5,168,270	1.75	2.00	5.00	7.00	14	35	95	225	
1901 ......(813)	18,859,665	1.75	2.00	2.50	5.00	12	35	75	145	$300
1901O	5,620,000	1.75	2.00	6.00	10.00	30	85	275	500	
1901S	593,022	45.00	70.00	185.00	250.00	300	400	675	1,100	
1902 ......(777)	21,380,000	1.75	2.00	2.50	4.00	12	35	75	145	300
1902O	4,500,000	1.75	2.00	6.00	12.00	30	70	250	525	
1902S	2,070,000	3.00	8.00	25.00	40.00	60	100	225	525	
1903 ......(755)	19,500,000	1.75	2.00	2.50	4.00	12	35	75	145	300
1903O	8,180,000	1.75	2.00	7.00	10.00	20	40	150	325	
1903S	613,300	42.00	65.00	200.00	275.00	400	500	725	1,000	
1904 ......(670)	14,600,357	1.75	2.00	2.50	4.00	12	35	75	145	300
1904S	800,000	20.00	35.00	75.00	125.00	160	275	475	925	
1905 ......(727)	14,551,623	1.75	2.00	2.50	4.00	12	35	75	145	300
1905O	3,400,000	1.75	4.00	16.00	25.00	50	75	150	225	
1905S	6,855,199	1.75	2.00	3.00	7.00	18	40	125	175	
1906 ......(675)	19,957,731	1.75	2.00	2.50	4.00	12	35	75	145	300
1906D	4,060,000	1.75	2.00	2.50	6.00	15	35	95	200	
1906O	2,610,000	2.00	5.00	22.00	35.00	47	65	125	185	
1906S	3,136,640	1.75	2.00	5.00	10.00	18	55	135	250	
1907 ......(575)	22,220,000	1.75	2.00	2.50	4.00	12	35	75	145	300
1907D	4,080,000	1.75	2.00	4.00	6.00	18	55	150	500	
1907O	5,058,000	1.75	3.00	15.00	22.00	24	50	100	185	
1907S	3,178,470	1.75	2.00	6.00	10.00	25	65	225	425	
1908 ......(545)	10,600,000	1.75	2.00	2.50	4.00	12	35	75	145	300
1908D	7,490,000	1.75	2.00	2.50	4.00	14	35	75	150	
1908O	1,789,000	2.00	4.00	22.00	30.00	45	65	160	325	
1908S	3,220,000	1.75	2.00	4.00	8.00	18	75	175	400	
1909 ......(650)	10,240,000	1.75	2.00	2.50	3.50	12	35	75	145	300
1909D	954,000	3.00	7.00	35.00	50.00	75	125	275	600	
1909O	2,287,000	1.75	3.00	5.00	8.00	25	85	175	375	
1909S	1,000,000	3.00	8.00	40.00	60.00	90	175	300	675	
1910 ......(551)	11,520,000	1.75	2.00	2.50	3.50	12	35	75	145	300
1910D	3,490,000	1.75	2.00	3.00	6.00	20	45	125	250	
1910S	1,240,000	2.00	3.00	25.00	35.00	50	100	250	400	
1911 ......(543)	18,870,000	1.75	2.00	2.50	3.50	12	35	75	145	300
1911D	11,209,000	1.75	2.00	2.50	3.50	12	35	75	145	
1911S	3,520,000	1.75	2.00	3.00	8.50	16	45	120	200	
1912 ......(700)	19,349,300	1.75	2.00	2.50	3.50	12	35	75	145	300
1912D	11,760,000	1.75	2.00	2.50	3.50	12	35	75	145	
1912S	3,420,000	1.75	2.00	2.50	3.50	16	45	95	165	
1913 ......(622)	19,760,000	1.75	2.00	2.50	3.50	12	35	75	145	300
1913S	510,000	15.00	25.00	55.00	90.00	125	190	325	575	
1914 ......(425)	17,360,230	1.75	2.00	2.50	3.50	12	35	75	145	300
1914D	11,908,000	1.75	2.00	2.50	3.50	12	35	75	145	
1914S	2,100,000	1.75	2.00	3.00	7.00	15	35	85	145	
1915 ......(450)	5,620,000	1.75	2.00	2.50	3.50	12	35	75	145	300
1915S	960,000	2.00	4.00	15.00	20.00	32	70	140	275	
1916	18,490,000	1.75	2.00	2.50	3.50	12	35	75	145	
1916S	5,820,000	1.75	2.00	2.50	3.50	12	35	75	145	

WINGED LIBERTY HEAD
OR "MERCURY" (1916–1945)

Although this coin is commonly called the *Mercury* dime, the main device is in fact a representation of Liberty. The wings crowning her cap are intended to symbolize liberty of thought. Designer Adolph Weinman's monogram, AW, is at the right of the neck.

G-4 Good: Letters and date clear. Lines and bands in fasces obliterated.
VG-8 Very Good: Half of sticks discernible in fasces.
F-12 Fine: All sticks in fasces defined. Diagonal bands worn nearly flat.
VF-20 Very Fine: Diagonal bands definitely visible.
EF-40 Extremely Fine: Only slight wear on diagonal bands. Braids and hair before ear clearly visible.
AU-50 About Uncirculated: Slight trace of wear. Most mint luster present.
MS-63 Choice Uncirculated: No trace of wear. Light blemishes. Attractive mint luster.
MS-65 Gem Uncirculated: Only light, scattered, non-distracting marks. Strong luster, good eye appeal.

Mintmark location is on reverse,
left of fasces.

The Mint State prices shown are what coin dealers pay for average Uncirculated pieces with minimum blemishes. For coins with sharp strikes and split horizontal bands on the reverse, they usually pay much more.

	Mintage	G-4	VG-8	F-12	VF-20	EF-40	MS-60	MS-63	MS-65
1916	22,180,080	$2.00	$2.50	$3.00	$4.00	$5.00	$18	$24	$55
1916D	264,000	475.00	850.00	1,400.00	2,500.00	4,500.00	8,000	10,000	16,000
1916S	10,450,000	2.00	2.50	4.00	6.00	10.00	20	35	120
1917	55,230,000	1.50	1.50	2.00	2.50	4.00	15	26	85
1917D	9,402,000	2.00	3.00	5.00	10.00	22.00	65	180	700
1917S	27,330,000	1.50	1.50	2.00	3.00	6.00	30	100	275
1918	26,680,000	1.50	1.50	3.00	5.00	13.00	40	75	225
1918D	22,674,800	1.50	1.50	3.00	5.00	12.00	55	140	400
1918S	19,300,000	1.50	1.50	2.00	4.00	9.00	60	125	525
1919	35,740,000	1.50	1.50	2.00	2.50	6.00	20	100	200
1919D	9,939,000	1.50	1.50	5.00	12.00	22.00	105	250	900
1919S	8,850,000	1.50	1.50	4.00	8.00	20.00	105	270	1,000
1920	59,030,000	1.50	1.50	2.00	2.50	5.00	16	35	150
1920D	19,171,000	1.50	1.50	2.00	3.00	11.00	65	200	475
1920S	13,820,000	1.50	1.50	3.00	3.00	10.00	65	175	800
1921	1,230,000	25.00	40.00	60.00	150.00	325.00	650	1,250	2,000
1921D	1,080,000	30.00	65.00	100.00	200.00	425.00	700	1,350	2,000
1923	50,130,000	1.50	1.50	2.00	2.50	3.00	16	24	65
1923S	6,440,000	1.50	1.50	4.00	8.00	32.00	90	220	750
1924	24,010,000	1.50	1.50	2.00	2.50	6.00	23	45	105
1924D	6,810,000	1.50	1.50	3.00	9.00	26.00	95	280	600
1924S	7,120,000	1.50	1.50	2.00	5.00	24.00	120	300	775
1925	25,610,000	1.50	1.50	2.00	2.50	4.00	16	40	140
1925D	5,117,000	2.00	2.50	5.00	22.00	60.00	200	425	1,000
1925S	5,850,000	1.50	1.50	3.00	7.00	35.00	90	275	800
1926	32,160,000	1.50	1.50	2.00	2.50	3.00	15	30	130
1926D	6,828,000	1.50	1.50	2.00	6.00	16.00	60	150	350
1926S	1,520,000	4.00	6.00	12.00	32.00	140.00	550	950	2,250
1927	28,080,000	1.50	1.50	2.00	2.50	3.00	15	32	80
1927D	4,812,000	1.50	1.50	2.00	12.00	35.00	100	225	725

Chart continued on next page.

	Mintage	G-4	VG-8	F-12	VF-20	EF-40	MS-60	MS-63	MS-65
1927S	4,770,000	$1.50	$1.50	$2.00	$4.00	$15.00	$150	$300	$800
1928	19,480,000	1.50	1.50	2.00	2.50	3.00	15	30	75
1928D	4,161,000	1.50	1.50	4.00	10.00	24.00	100	225	500
1928S	7,400,000	1.50	1.50	2.00	3.00	8.00	75	175	265
1929	25,970,000	1.50	1.50	2.00	2.50	3.00	13	20	40
1929D	5,034,000	1.50	1.50	2.00	3.00	8.00	16	17	40
1929S	4,730,000	1.50	1.50	2.00	2.50	3.00	18	20	60
1930	6,770,000	1.50	1.50	2.00	2.50	3.00	15	25	60
1930S	1,843,000	1.50	1.50	3.00	2.50	8.00	35	75	110
1931	3,150,000	1.50	1.50	2.00	2.50	5.00	20	40	80
1931D	1,260,000	3.00	4.00	6.00	8.00	18.00	46	75	160
1931S	1,800,000	2.00	3.00	3.00	4.00	9.00	40	75	160

	Mintage	VG-8	F-12	VF-20	EF-40	MS-60	MS-63	MS-65	PF-63
1934	24,080,000	$1.50	$1.50	$1.60	$1.60	$10.00	$15	$25	
1934D	6,772,000	1.50	1.50	1.60	1.60	20.00	30	45	
1935	58,830,000	1.50	1.50	1.60	1.60	5.00	8	15	
1935D	10,477,000	1.50	1.50	1.60	1.60	16.00	25	50	
1935S	15,840,000	1.50	1.50	1.60	1.60	10.00	16	20	
1936 (4,130)	87,500,000	1.50	1.50	1.60	1.60	5.00	8	15	$500
1936D	16,132,000	1.50	1.50	1.60	1.60	14.00	20	30	
1936S	9,210,000	1.50	1.50	1.60	1.60	12.00	15	20	
1937 (5,756)	56,860,000	1.50	1.50	1.60	1.60	4.00	7	15	250
1937D	14,146,000	1.50	1.50	1.60	1.60	12.00	16	24	
1937S	9,740,000	1.50	1.50	1.60	1.60	12.00	15	20	
1938 (8,728)	22,190,000	1.50	1.50	1.60	1.60	6.00	7	15	125
1938D	5,537,000	1.50	1.50	1.60	1.60	9.00	10	16	
1938S	8,090,000	1.50	1.50	1.60	1.60	8.00	9	20	
1939 (9,321)	67,740,000	1.50	1.50	1.60	1.60	4.00	6	15	125
1939D	24,394,000	1.50	1.50	1.60	1.60	4.00	6	15	
1939S	10,540,000	1.50	1.50	1.60	1.60	12.00	15	20	
1940 (11,827)	65,350,000	1.50	1.50	1.60	1.60	4.00	6	15	100
1940D	21,198,000	1.50	1.50	1.60	1.60	4.00	6	16	
1940S	21,560,000	1.50	1.50	1.60	1.60	4.00	6	16	
1941 (16,557)	175,090,000	1.50	1.50	1.60	1.60	4.00	6	15	100
1941D	45,634,000	1.50	1.50	1.60	1.60	4.00	6	16	
1941S	43,090,000	1.50	1.50	1.60	1.60	4.00	6	16	
1942, 42 Over 41	*	285.00	290.00	300.00	400.00	1,500.00	2,750	8,000	
1942 (22,329)	205,410,000	1.50	1.50	1.60	1.60	4.00	6	15	100
1942D, 42 Over 41	*	275.00	280.00	290.00	375.00	1,500.00	3,000	8,000	
1942D	60,740,000	1.50	1.50	1.60	1.60	5.00	7	16	
1942S	49,300,000	1.50	1.50	1.60	1.60	6.00	7	16	
1943	191,710,000	1.50	1.50	1.60	1.60	4.00	6	15	
1943D	71,949,000	1.50	1.50	1.60	1.60	5.00	7	16	
1943S	60,400,000	1.50	1.50	1.60	1.60	5.00	7	15	
1944	231,410,000	1.50	1.50	1.60	1.60	4.00	6	15	
1944D	62,224,000	1.50	1.50	1.60	1.60	5.00	7	15	
1944S	49,490,000	1.50	1.50	1.60	1.60	5.00	7	15	
1945	159,130,000	1.50	1.50	1.60	1.60	4.00	6	15	
1945D	40,245,000	1.50	1.50	1.60	1.60	4.00	6	16	
1945S	41,920,000	1.50	1.50	1.60	1.60	5.00	7	16	
1945S, Micro S	*	1.50	1.50	1.60	2.00	12.50	18	45	

* Included in number above.

ROOSEVELT (1946 TO DATE)

John R. Sinnock (whose initials, JS, are at the truncation of the neck) designed this dime showing a portrait of Franklin D. Roosevelt. The design has heavier lettering and a more modernistic character than preceding types.

VF-20 Very Fine: Moderate wear on high points of design. All major details are clear.
EF-40 Extremely Fine: All lines of torch, flame, and hair very plain.
MS-63 Choice Uncirculated: Some distracting contact marks or blemishes in prime focal areas. Impaired luster possible.
MS-65 Gem Uncirculated: Only light, non-distracting scattered marks. Strong luster, good eye appeal.
PF-65 Gem Proof: Nearly perfect.

Mintmark on reverse,
1946–1964.

Silver Coinage (1946–1964)

	Mintage	VF-20	EF-40	MS-63	MS-65	PF-65
1946	255,250,000	$1.50	$1.50	$2.50	$6.00	
1946D	61,043,500	1.50	1.50	2.50	7.00	
1946S	27,900,000	1.50	1.50	4.00	10.00	
1947	121,520,000	1.50	1.50	2.50	6.00	
1947D	46,835,000	1.50	1.50	2.50	6.00	
1947S	34,840,000	1.50	1.50	2.50	6.00	
1948	74,950,000	1.50	1.50	2.50	6.00	
1948D	52,841,000	1.50	1.50	2.50	6.00	
1948S	35,520,000	1.50	1.50	2.50	6.00	
1949	30,940,000	1.50	1.50	14.00	19.00	
1949D	26,034,000	1.50	1.50	5.00	9.00	
1949S	13,510,000	1.50	1.50	22.00	32.50	
1950	(51,386)	50,130,114	1.50	1.50	6.50	8.00	$25
1950D	46,803,000	1.50	1.50	2.50	6.00	
1950S	20,440,000	1.50	1.50	20.00	30.00	
1951	(57,500)	103,880,102	1.50	1.50	2.00	5.00	25
1951D	56,529,000	1.50	1.50	2.00	5.00	
1951S	31,630,000	1.50	1.50	7.50	14.00	
1952	(81,980)	99,040,093	1.50	1.50	2.00	5.00	18
1952D	122,100,000	1.50	1.50	2.00	4.00	
1952S	44,419,500	1.50	1.50	3.75	6.25	
1953	(128,800)	53,490,120	1.50	1.50	2.50	4.50	20
1953D	136,433,000	1.50	1.50	2.50	4.50	
1953S	39,180,000	1.50	1.50	2.50	4.50	
1954	(233,300)	114,010,203	1.50	1.50	2.00	4.00	10
1954D	106,397,000	1.50	1.50	2.00	4.00	
1954S	22,860,000	1.50	1.50	2.00	4.00	

Chart continued on next page.

	Mintage	VF-20	EF-40	MS-63	MS-65	PF-65
1955 . . . . (378,200) 12,450,181		$1.50	$1.50	$1.75	$5.00	$8
1955D 13,959,000		1.50	1.50	1.75	4.00	
1955S 18,510,000		1.50	1.50	1.75	4.00	
1956 . . . . (669,384) 108,640,000		1.50	1.50	1.75	4.00	4
1956D 108,015,100		1.50	1.50	1.75	3.50	
1957 . . . . (1,247,952) 160,160,000		1.50	1.50	1.75	3.50	3
1957D 113,354,330		1.50	1.50	1.75	3.25	
1958 . . . . (875,652) 31,910,000		1.50	1.50	1.75	4.00	3
1958D 136,564,600		1.50	1.50	1.75	4.00	
1959 . . . . (1,149,291) 85,780,000		1.50	1.50	1.75	3.50	3
1959D 164,919,790		1.50	1.50	1.75	3.50	
1960 . . . . (1,691,602) . . . 70,390,000		1.50	1.50	1.75	3.50	3
1960D 200,160,400		1.50	1.50	1.75	3.00	
1961 . . . . (3,028,244) 93,730,000		1.50	1.50	1.75	3.00	3
1961D 209,146,550		1.50	1.50	1.75	3.00	
1962 . . . . (3,218,019) 72,450,000		1.50	1.50	1.75	3.00	3
1962D 334,948,380		1.50	1.50	1.75	3.00	
1963 . . . . (3,075,645) 123,650,000		1.50	1.50	1.75	3.00	3
1963D 421,476,530		1.50	1.50	1.75	3.00	
1964 . . . . (3,950,762) 929,360,000		1.50	1.50	1.75	3.00	3
1964D 1,357,517,180		1.50	1.50	1.75	3.00	

Clad Coinage and Silver Proofs (1965 to Date)

Mintmark on obverse,
starting in 1968.

	Mintage	MS-63	MS-65	PF-65		Mintage	MS-63	MS-65	PF-65
1965	1,652,140,570	$0.15	$1.00		1973	315,670,000	$0.15	$0.50	
1966	1,382,734,540	0.15	0.90		1973D	455,032,426	0.15	0.50	
1967	2,244,007,320	0.15	0.80		1973S	(2,760,339)			$0.80
1968	424,470,400	0.15	0.80		1974	470,248,000	0.15	0.50	
1968D	480,748,280	0.15	0.80		1974D	571,083,000	0.15	0.50	
1968S	(3,041,506)			$0.80	1974S	(2,612,568)			0.80
1969	145,790,000	0.25	1.00		1975	585,673,900	0.15	0.50	
1969D	563,323,870	0.15	0.75		1975D	313,705,300	0.15	0.50	
1969S	(2,394,631)			0.80	1975S	(2,845,450)			1.00
1970	345,570,000	0.15	0.50		1976	568,760,000	0.15	0.50	
1970D	754,942,100	0.15	0.50		1976D	695,222,774	0.15	0.50	
1970S	(2,632,810)			0.80	1976S	(4,149,730)			1.00
1971	162,690,000	0.18	0.75		1977	796,930,000	0.15	0.50	
1971D	377,914,240	0.16	0.65		1977D	376,607,228	0.15	0.50	
1971S	(3,220,733)			0.80	1977S	(3,251,152)			0.80
1972	431,540,000	0.15	0.50		1978	663,980,000	0.15	0.50	
1972D	330,290,000	0.15	0.50		1978D	282,847,540	0.15	0.50	
1972S	(3,260,996)			0.80	1978S	(3,127,781)			0.80

	Mintage	MS-63	MS-65	PF-65
1979	315,440,000	$0.15	$0.50	
1979D	390,921,184	0.15	0.50	
1979S, Type 1	(3,677,175)			$2.75
1979S, Type 2	*			4.00
1980P	735,170,000	0.15	0.50	
1980D	719,354,321	0.15	0.50	
1980S	(3,554,806)			0.80
1981P	676,650,000	0.15	0.50	
1981D	712,284,143	0.15	0.50	
1981S, Type 1	(4,063,083)			2.75
1981S, Type 2	*			14.00
1982, No Mmk.		30.00	50.00	
1982P	519,475,000	1.50	2.75	
1982D	542,713,584	0.60	1.50	
1982S	(3,857,479)			1.50
1983P	647,025,000	1.25	2.75	
1983D	730,129,224	0.50	1.75	
1983S	(3,279,126)			1.00
1984P	856,669,000	0.15	0.60	
1984D	704,803,976	0.20	0.75	
1984S	(3,065,110)			1.00
1985P	705,200,962	0.15	0.60	
1985D	587,979,970	0.15	0.60	
1985S	(3,362,821)			1.00
1986P	682,649,693	0.25	0.75	
1986D	473,326,970	0.25	0.75	
1986S	(3,010,497)			1.75
1987P	762,709,481	0.15	0.60	
1987D	653,203,402	0.15	0.60	
1987S	(4,227,728)			1.25
1988P	1,030,550,000	0.12	0.50	
1988D	962,385,489	0.12	0.50	
1988S	(3,262,948)			1.75
1989P	1,298,400,000	0.10	0.50	
1989D	896,535,597	0.10	0.50	
1989S	(3,220,194)			1.75
1990P	1,034,340,000	0.10	0.50	
1990D	839,995,824	0.10	0.50	
1990S	(3,299,559)			1.00
1991P	927,220,000	0.10	0.50	
1991D	601,241,114	0.12	0.50	
1991S	(2,867,787)			1.70
1992P	593,500,000	0.10	0.50	
1992D	616,273,932	0.10	0.50	
1992S	(2,858,981)			1.50
1992S, Silver	(1,317,579)			3.00
1993P	766,180,000	0.10	0.50	
1993D	750,110,166	0.10	0.50	
1993S	(2,633,439)			2.25
1993S, Silver	(761,353)			3.50
1994P	1,189,000,000	$0.10	$0.50	
1994D	1,303,268,110	0.10	0.50	
1994S	(2,484,594)			$2.25
1994S, Silver	(785,329)			3.75
1995P	1,125,500,000	0.10	0.50	
1995D	1,274,890,000	0.15	0.50	
1995S	(2,117,496)			5.50
1995S, Silver	(679,985)			7.50
1996P	1,421,163,000	0.10	0.50	
1996D	1,400,300,000	0.10	0.50	
1996W	1,457,000	6.00	11.00	
1996S	(1,750,244)			1.25
1996S, Silver	(775,021)			3.50
1997P	991,640,000	0.10	0.50	
1997D	979,810,000	0.10	0.50	
1997S	(2,055,000)			3.50
1997S, Silver	(741,678)			7.00
1998P	1,163,000,000	0.10	0.50	
1998D	1,172,250,000	0.10	0.50	
1998S	(2,086,507)			1.75
1998S, Silver	(878,792)			3.00
1999P	2,164,000,000	0.10	0.50	
1999D	1,397,750,000	0.10	0.50	
1999S	(2,543,401)			1.75
1999S, Silver	(804,565)			3.50
2000P	1,842,500,000	0.10	0.50	
2000D	1,818,700,000	0.10	0.50	
2000S	(3,082,572)			1.00
2000S, Silver	(965,421)			3.00
2001P	1,369,590,000	0.10	0.50	
2001D	1,412,800,000	0.10	0.50	
2001S	(2,294,909)			0.75
2001S, Silver	(889,697)			3.00
2002P	1,187,500,000	0.10	0.50	
2002D	1,379,500,000	0.10	0.50	
2002S	(2,319,766)			0.75
2002S, Silver	(892,229)			3.00
2003P	1,085,500,000	0.10	0.50	
2003D	986,500,000	0.10	0.50	
2003S	(2,172,684)			0.75
2003S, Silver	(1,125,755)			3.00
2004P	1,328,000,000	0.10	0.50	
2004D	1,159,500,000	0.10	0.50	
2004S	(1,789,488)			0.75
2004S, Silver	(1,175,934)			3.00
2005P	1,412,000,000	0.10	0.50	
2005D	1,423,500,000	0.10	0.50	
2005S	(2,275,000)			0.75
2005S, Silver	(1,069,679)			3.00
2006P	1,381,000,000	0.10	0.50	

* Included in number above.

97

	Mintage	MS-63	MS-65	PF-65
2006D	1,447,000,000	$0.10	$0.50	
2006S	(2,000,428)			$0.75
2006S, Silver	(1,054,008)			3.00
2007P	1,047,500,000	0.10	0.50	
2007D	1,042,000,000	0.10	0.50	
2007S	(1,702,116)			0.75
2007S, Silver	(875,050)			3.00
2008P	391,000,000	0.10	0.50	
2008D	624,500,000	0.10	0.50	
2008S	(1,405,674)			0.75
2008S, Silver	(763,887)			3.00
2009P	96,500,000	0.20	0.50	
2009D	49,500,000	0.20	0.50	
2009S	(1,482,502)			0.75
2009S, Silver	(697,365)			3.00
2010P	557,000,000	0.10	0.50	
2010D	562,000,000	0.10	0.50	
2010S	(1,103,815)			0.75
2010S, Silver	(585,401)			3.00
2011P	748,000,000	0.10	0.50	
2011D	754,000,000	0.10	0.50	
2011S	(1,098,835)			0.75
2011S, Silver	(574,175)			3.00

	Mintage	MS-63	MS-65	PF-65
2012P	808,000,000	$0.10	$0.50	
2012D	868,000,000	0.10	0.50	
2012S	(794,002)			$0.75
2012S, Silver	(495,315)			12.00
2013P	1,086,500,000	0.10	0.50	
2013D	1,025,500,000	0.10	0.50	
2013S	(854,785)			0.75
2013S, Silver	(467,691)			3.00
2014P	1,125,500,000	0.10	0.50	
2014D	1,177,000,000	0.10	0.50	
2014S	(760,876)			0.75
2014S, Silver	(491,157)			3.00
2015P	1,497,510,000	0.10	0.50	
2015D	1,543,500,000	0.10	0.50	
2015P, Rev Pf	(74,430)			20.00
2015S	(669,960)			0.75
2015S, Silver	(352,450)			3.00
2015W	74,430			15.00
2016P		0.10	0.50	
2016D		0.10	0.50	
2016S				0.75
2016S, Silver				3.00

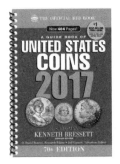

LIBERTY SEATED (1875–1878)

The twenty-cent piece was a short-lived coin authorized by the Act of March 3, 1875. The edge of the coin is plain. Most of the 1876-CC coins were melted at the Mint and never released. The mintmark is on the reverse below the eagle.

G-4 Good: LIBERTY on shield obliterated. Letters and date legible.
VG-8 Very Good: One or two letters in LIBERTY barely visible. Other details bold.
F-12 Fine: Some letters of LIBERTY possibly visible.
VF-20 Very Fine: LIBERTY readable, but partly weak.
EF-40 Extremely Fine: LIBERTY mostly sharp. Only slight wear on high points of coin.
AU-50 About Uncirculated: Slight trace of wear on breast, head, and knees.
MS-60 Uncirculated: No trace of wear. Light blemishes.
MS-63 Choice Uncirculated: Some distracting blemishes in prime focal areas. Some impairment of luster possible.
PF-63 Choice Proof: Reflective surfaces with only a few blemishes in secondary focal places. No major flaws.

	Mintage	G-4	VG-8	F-12	VF-20	EF-40	AU-50	MS-60	MS-63	PF-63
1875 .... (1,200)	38,500	$125	$150	$175	$200	$250	$350	$550	$950	$1,850
1875CC	133,290	200	250	300	350	700	1,000	1,400	2,500	
1875S	1,155,000	75	85	105	140	175	225	475	950	
1876 .... (1,150)	14,750	125	150	175	200	300	350	550	1,100	1,850
1876CC	10,000						100,000	125,000	200,000	
1877 ...... (510)					1,750	2,500				4,000
1878 ...... (600)					1,200	2,000				3,250

A NOTE ON COUNTERFEIT COINS

Many colonial and United States coins have been extensively counterfeited, including very deceptive issues produced in China in recent years. These include issues from half cents to $20 gold, some rarities, and many issues that are not necessarily rare, but sell for significant premiums. There is no effective policing of offerings on Internet mail bid sales or other sales. A coin thought to be rare or expensive, if not bought from a recognized professional numismatist, should be certified by a professional third-party coin grading service.

Authorized in 1792, this denomination was not issued until four years later. The first type weighed 104 grains, the standard until modified to 103-1/8 grains by the Act of January 18, 1837. As with the dime and half dime, the weight was reduced and arrows placed at the date in 1853. Rays were placed in the field of the reverse during that year only.

DRAPED BUST (1796–1807)

AG-3 About Good: Details clear enough to identify.
G-4 Good: Date readable. Bust outlined, but no detail.
VG-8 Very Good: All but deepest drapery folds worn smooth. Hairlines nearly gone and curls lacking in detail.
F-12 Fine: All drapery lines visible. Hair partly worn.
VF-20 Very Fine: Only left side of drapery indistinct.
EF-40 Extremely Fine: Hair well outlined and detailed.
AU-50 About Uncirculated: Slight trace of wear on shoulder and highest waves of hair.
MS-60 Uncirculated: No trace of wear. Light blemishes.
MS-63 Choice Uncirculated: Some distracting marks or blemishes in focal areas. Impaired luster possible.

Small Eagle Reverse (1796)

	Mintage	AG-3	G-4	VG-8	F-12	VF-20	EF-40	AU-50	MS-60	MS-63
1796	6,146	$3,500	$7,500	$10,000	$15,000	$20,000	$37,500	$47,500	$50,000	$115,000

Heraldic Eagle Reverse (1804–1807)

	Mintage	AG-3	G-4	VG-8	F-12	VF-20	EF-40	AU-50	MS-60	MS-63
1804	6,738	$1,250	$2,750	$4,250	$5,500	$8,000	$17,500	$30,000	$65,000	$110,000
1805	121,394*	125	300	450	650	1,100	2,500	3,750	7,500	12,500
1806, 6 Over 5	......*	125	300	450	700	1,050	2,500	3,750	7,500	16,000
1806	206,124	125	300	450	650	1,100	2,750	3,750	7,500	12,500
1807	220,643	125	300	450	650	1,000	2,500	3,750	7,500	12,500

* Included in number below.

CAPPED BUST (1815–1838)
Variety 1 – Large Diameter (1815–1828)

AG-3 About Good: Details clear enough to identify.
G-4 Good: Date, letters, stars legible. Hair under Liberty's headband smooth. Cap lines worn smooth.
VG-8 Very Good: Rim well defined. Main details visible. Full LIBERTY on cap. Hair above eye nearly smooth.
F-12 Fine: All hair lines visible, but only partial detail visible in drapery. Shoulder clasp distinct.
VF-20 Very Fine: All details visible, but some wear evident. Clasp and ear sharp.
EF-40 Extremely Fine: All details distinct. Hair well outlined.
AU-50 About Uncirculated: Slight trace of wear on tips of curls and above the eye, and on the wing and claw tips.
MS-60 Uncirculated: No trace of wear. Light blemishes.
MS-63 Choice Uncirculated: Some distracting marks or blemishes in focal areas. Impaired luster possible.

	Mintage	AG-3	G-4	VG-8	F-12	VF-20	EF-40	AU-50	MS-60	MS-63
1815	89,235	$75	$125	$250	$400	$550	$1,500	$2,250	$3,000	$5,500
1818, 8 Over 5	*	35	60	100	275	500	1,000	1,350	2,500	4,500
1818, Normal Date	361,174	35	60	100	175	325	1,000	1,350	2,500	4,500
1819	144,000	35	60	100	175	325	1,000	1,500	2,750	4,750
1820	127,444	35	60	100	175	325	1,000	1,500	2,750	4,250
1821	216,851	35	60	100	175	325	1,000	1,350	2,500	4,500
1822	64,080	75	125	200	350	600	1,150	1,750	2,750	5,500
1822, 25 Over 50 C.	*	650	1,700	3,750	4,750	6,750	12,000	19,000	35,000	
1823, 3 Over 2	17,800	15,000	25,000	30,000	40,000	52,500	67,500	80,000	—	
1824, 4 Over 2	**	250	500	700	1,200	1,600	3,500	4,750	7,500	
1825	168,000	35	60	100	175	325	1,000	1,500	2,500	4,250
1827, Original (Curl Base 2 in 25 C.) **(a)**	4,000									100,000
1827, Restrike (Square Base 2 in 25 C.) **(a)**	*									35,000
1828	102,000	35	60	100	175	325	1,000	1,500	2,500	4,250
1828, 25 Over 50 C.	*	80	160	280	560	1,250	2,400	3,200	10,000	50,000

* Included in regular mintage. ** Included in 1825 mintage. **a.** The 7 is punched over a 3, which is punched over an earlier 2.

Variety 2 – Reduced Diameter (1831–1838), Motto Removed

G-4 Good: Bust of Liberty well defined. Hair under headband smooth. Date, letters, stars legible. Scant rims.
VG-8 Very Good: Details apparent but worn on high spots. Rims strong. Full LIBERTY.
F-12 Fine: All hair lines visible. Drapery partly worn. Shoulder clasp distinct.
VF-20 Very Fine: Only top spots worn. Clasp sharp. Ear distinct.
EF-40 Extremely Fine: Hair details and clasp bold and clear.

AU-50 About Uncirculated: Slight trace of wear on hair around forehead, on cheek, and at top and bottom tips of eagle's wings and left claw.
MS-60 Uncirculated: No trace of wear. Light blemishes.
MS-63 Choice Uncirculated: Some distracting contact marks or blemishes in prime focal areas. Impaired luster possible.

	Mintage	G-4	VG-8	F-12	VF-20	EF-40	AU-50	MS-60	MS-63
1831	398,000	$40	$60	$75	$110	$275	$500	$1,200	$3,000
1832	320,000	40	60	75	100	275	500	1,200	3,000
1833	156,000	40	60	75	110	275	500	1,250	3,000
1834	286,000	40	60	75	100	275	500	1,200	3,000
1835	1,952,000	40	60	75	100	275	500	1,200	3,000
1836	472,000	40	60	75	100	275	500	1,200	3,250
1837	252,400	40	60	75	100	275	500	1,200	3,000
1838	366,000	40	60	75	100	275	500	1,200	3,000

LIBERTY SEATED (1838–1891)

G-4 Good: Scant rim. LIBERTY on shield worn off. Date and letters legible.
VG-8 Very Good: Rim fairly defined, at least three letters in LIBERTY evident.
F-12 Fine: LIBERTY complete, but partly weak.
VF-20 Very Fine: LIBERTY strong.
EF-40 Extremely Fine: Complete LIBERTY and edges of scroll. Shoulder clasp clear on Liberty's gown.
AU-50 About Uncirculated: Slight wear on Liberty's knees and breast and on eagle's neck, wing tips, and claws.
MS-60 Uncirculated: No trace of wear. Light blemishes.
MS-63 Choice Uncirculated: Some distracting marks or blemishes in focal areas. Impaired luster possible.

Variety 1 – No Motto Above Eagle (1838–1853)

Small Date

Large Date

Mintmark location is on reverse, below eagle.

	Mintage	G-4	VG-8	F-12	VF-20	EF-40	AU-50	MS-60	MS-63
1838	466,000	$15	$22	$30	$80	$275	$600	$1,100	$2,750
1839	491,146	15	20	30	80	275	600	1,100	2,750
1840	188,127	15	22	30	65	110	200	575	2,000
1840O	425,200	20	22	40	70	125	300	650	2,250
1841	120,000	25	35	50	75	150	275	475	900
1841O	452,000	20	25	30	75	200	225	425	1,000
1842, Small Date (Proof only)									28,000
1842, Large Date	88,000	35	50	90	150	200	425	800	1,500
1842O, Small Date	*	150	275	475	1,200	2,750	4,500	10,000	
1842O, Large Date	769,000	18	25	30	35	100	200	650	2,500
1843	645,600	15	20	25	30	55	125	275	650
1843O	968,000	18	25	50	225	325	525	1,050	2,750
1844	421,200	15	20	25	30	50	125	300	700
1844O	740,000	18	25	30	50	100	200	575	1,750
1845	922,000	15	20	25	30	60	125	300	625
1846	510,000	15	20	25	30	75	150	300	700
1847	734,000	15	20	25	30	55	125	300	650
1847O	368,000	18	25	40	90	650	1,200	2,750	5,000
1848	146,000	15	22	40	65	125	225	600	1,750
1849	340,000	15	22	25	45	80	150	450	900
1849O	(a)	225	325	625	1,500	4,500	5,250	11,000	12,500
1850	190,800	22	36	50	70	115	180	600	1,450
1850O	412,000	27	35	45	70	175	400	1,200	2,600
1851	160,000	27	42	60	100	215	320	600	1,300
1851O	88,000	115	225	425	750	1,200	2,600	4,000	
1852	177,060	35	45	75	110	180	240	540	1,200
1852O	96,000	115	175	275	750	1,750	3,250	5,000	25,000
1853, Recut Date, No Arrows or Rays	44,200	240	320	500	640	1,200	2,000	2,800	4,400

* Included in number below. **a.** Mintage for 1849-O included with 1850-O.

Variety 2 – Arrows at Date, Rays Around Eagle (1853)

1853, 3 Over 4

QUARTER DOLLARS

	Mintage	G-4	VG-8	F-12	VF-20	EF-40	AU-50	MS-60	MS-63
1853 15,210,020		$15	$18	$20	$30	$115	$250	$700	$1,300
1853, 3 Over 4 . . . . . . *		20	45	65	125	225	375	1,100	2,500
1853O 1,332,000		20	25	35	40	200	750	1,750	4,750

* Included in number above.

Variety 3 – Arrows at Date, No Rays (1854–1855)

	Mintage	G-4	VG-8	F-12	VF-20	EF-40	AU-50	MS-60	MS-63
1854 12,380,000		$10	$15	$18	$25	$50	$160	$400	$950
1854O 1,484,000		20	25	30	30	70	200	625	1,000
1855 2,857,000		10	15	20	25	50	160	400	850
1855O 176,000		32	50	90	220	320	1,250	2,000	5,500
1855S 396,400		30	40	50	100	325	500	1,300	4,000

Variety 1 Resumed, With Weight Standard of Variety 2 (1856–1865)

	Mintage	G-4	VG-8	F-12	VF-20	EF-40	AU-50	MS-60	MS-63	PF-63
1856 7,264,000		$10	$11	$15	$25	$40	$120	$225	$400	$2,500
1856O 968,000		20	25	30	35	80	160	575	1,100	
1856S 286,000		25	35	50	125	950	1,600	3,000	12,500	
1857 9,644,000		10	11	15	25	40	120	225	400	2,000
1857O 1,180,000		20	25	30	35	125	275	575	1,500	
1857S 82,000		30	80	140	250	475	800	1,750	3,750	
1858 . . . . . (300+). . . 7,368,000		10	11	15	25	40	120	225	400	1,000
1858O 520,000		20	25	30	35	75	225	800	2,750	
1858S 121,000		30	45	140	425	1,350	2,250	5,000	—	
1859 . . . . . (800). . . . 1,343,200		10	11	15	25	40	120	225	525	700
1859O 260,000		20	25	30	35	100	225	700	1,750	
1859S 80,000		55	90	125	550	1,500	9,000	—	—	
1860 . . . . (1,000). 804,400		10	11	15	25	40	120	225	400	700
1860O 388,000		20	25	30	35	55	225	650	1,100	
1860S 56,000		400	800	1,500	4,000	9,000	13,500	—	—	
1861 . . . . (1,000). . . . 4,853,600		10	11	15	25	40	120	225	400	700
1861S 96,000		110	225	450	1,150	2,500	6,000	17,500	—	
1862 . . . .(550). 932,000		10	20	25	25	45	120	225	400	700
1862S 67,000		30	45	90	250	500	850	2,000	4,500	
1863 . . . . . (460). 191,600		25	30	45	90	125	200	325	550	700
1864 . . . . . (470). 93,600		45	60	80	140	250	300	375	800	700
1864S 20,000		175	275	425	700	1,500	2,750	—	—	
1865 . . . . . (500). 58,800		50	60	140	250	300	350	450	800	700
1865S 41,000		50	60	110	225	600	800	1,500	2,500	

Variety 4 – Motto Above Eagle (1866–1873)

	Mintage	G-4	VG-8	F-12	VF-20	EF-40	AU-50	MS-60	MS-63	PF-63
1866 . . . . . .(725). 16,800		$225	$325	$375	$600	$800	$1,000	$1,400	$1,500	$500
1866S 28,000		125	200	375	675	1,100	1,500	2,250	3,500	

Chart continued on next page.

	Mintage	G-4	VG-8	F-12	VF-20	EF-40	AU-50	MS-60	MS-63	PF-63
1867 . . . .(625). . . .20,000		$125	$200	$325	$400	$800	$1,000	$1,100	$2,500	$500
1867S 48,000		90	175	300	525	1,500	3,750	7,500	—	
1868 . . . .(600). . . .29,400		70	90	130	175	350	450	600	900	500
1868S 96,000		50	65	100	200	525	650	1,500	3,250	
1869 . . . .(600). . . .16,000		175	225	300	400	600	700	800	2,000	500
1869S 76,000		55	85	140	275	525	725	1,750	2,750	
1870 . . . . . . (1,000). . .86,400		30	35	75	120	150	225	500	800	500
1870CC 8,340	5,500	10,000	12,500	16,000	17,500	30,000	—		
1871 . . . .(960). . .118,200		15	20	30	60	225	275	475	875	500
1871CC 10,890	1,500	4,000	6,000	10,000	15,000	20,000	—	—	
1871S 30,900		300	450	1,000	1,250	2,250	3,250	4,500	5,500	
1872 . . . .(950). . .182,000		15	20	40	55	200	275	700	1,200	500
1872CC 22,850		750	1,100	1,750	2,750	7,500	12,500	25,000		
1872S 83,000	1,000	1,000	1,200	1,750	2,750	3,750	4,750		
1873 . . . .(600). . .212,600		15	25	30	45	80	100	225	500	500
1873CC 4,000				—	50,000	—	—		

Variety 5 – Arrows at Date (1873–1874)

	Mintage	G-4	VG-8	F-12	VF-20	EF-40	AU-50	MS-60	MS-63	PF-63
1873 . . . .(500). . 1,271,200		$15	$18	$20	$40	$125	$250	$550	$1,000	$800
1873CC 12,462	3,000	5,500	7,500	11,000	16,000	27,500	55,000	75,000	
1873S 156,000		20	25	35	80	225	375	800	1,500	
1874 . . . .(700). . . .471,200		15	20	20	40	125	275	550	1,000	800
1874S 392,000		15	20	35	60	150	300	550	1,000	

Variety 4 Resumed, With Weight Standard of Variety 5 (1875–1891)

1877-S, S Over Horizontal S

	Mintage	G-4	VG-8	F-12	VF-20	EF-40	AU-50	MS-60	MS-63	PF-63
1875 . . . . . .(700). . . .4,292,800		$15	$18	$20	$25	$40	$100	$175	$400	$450
1875CC 140,000		40	85	140	275	550	650	2,250	4,500	
1875S 680,000		15	18	25	40	80	160	375	600	
1876 . . . . (1,150). . . 17,816,000		15	18	20	25	40	100	175	400	450
1876CC 4,944,000		25	40	50	60	100	125	275	600	
1876S 8,596,000		15	18	20	25	40	100	175	400	
1877 . . . . . .(510). . . 10,911,200		15	18	20	25	40	100	175	400	450
1877CC 4,192,000		30	40	50	60	100	125	250	400	
1877S 8,996,000		15	18	20	25	40	100	175	400	

	Mintage	G-4	VG-8	F-12	VF-20	EF-40	AU-50	MS-60	MS-63	PF-63
1877S, S Over Horizontal S . . . . .*		$15	$25	$40	$75	$125	$200	$400	$1,100	
1878 . . . . . (800). . 2,260,000		15	18	20	25	40	100	200	400	$450
1878CC 996,000		35	45	55	75	100	150	300	625	
1878S 140,000		90	175	275	350	600	800	1,000	2,000	
1879 . . . . . . (1,100). 13,600		90	110	150	175	250	400	450	550	450
1880 . . . . . . (1,355). 13,600		90	110	150	175	250	300	390	520	450
1881 . . . . (975). 12,000		115	135	200	225	250	325	420	575	450
1882 . . . . . . (1,100). 15,200		100	125	165	225	275	350	425	625	450
1883 . . . . . . (1,039). 14,400		100	125	175	200	300	350	425	625	450
1884 . . . . (875). 8,000		175	200	275	300	400	450	550	700	450
1885 . . . . (930). 13,600		100	125	175	200	250	300	415	725	450
1886 . . . . (886). 5,000		225	275	375	450	600	750	850	1,050	450
1887 . . . . (710). 10,000		150	200	250	325	375	425	485	675	450
1888 . . . . (832). 10,001		150	200	235	300	350	400	475	515	450
1888S 1,216,000		15	18	29	25	40	100	175	400	
1889 . . . . (711). 12,000		125	140	175	200	250	325	400	525	450
1890 . . . . 590). 80,000		40	50	75	100	140	225	335	515	450
1891 . . . . (600). . 3,920,000		20	18	20	25	40	130	175	400	450
18910 68,000		175	300	550	800	1,500	2,250	3,000	5,500	
1891S 2,216,000		20	18	20	25	40	100	175	400	

* Included in 1877-S regular mintage (previous page).

BARBER OR LIBERTY HEAD (1892–1916)

Like other silver coins of this type, the quarter dollars minted from 1892 to 1916 were designed by U.S. Mint chief engraver Charles E. Barber. His initial B is found at the truncation of the neck of Miss Liberty.

G-4 Good: Date and legends legible. LIBERTY worn off headband.
VG-8 Very Good: Some letters in LIBERTY legible.
F-12 Fine: LIBERTY completely legible but not sharp.
VF-20 Very Fine: All letters in LIBERTY evenly plain.
EF-40 Extremely Fine: LIBERTY bold, its ribbon distinct.
AU-50 About Uncirculated: Slight trace of wear above forehead, on cheek, and on eagle's head, wings, and tail.
MS-60 Uncirculated: No trace of wear. Light blemishes.
MS-63 Choice Uncirculated: Some distracting marks or blemishes in focal areas. Impaired luster possible.

PF-63 Choice Proof: Reflective surfaces with only a few blemishes in secondary focal places. No major flaws.

	Mintage	G-4	VG-8	F-12	VF-20	EF-40	AU-50	MS-60	MS-63	PF-63
1892 . . . . . . (1,245). . 8,236,000		$6	$7	$12	$20	$30	$75	$150	$250	$400
18920 2,460,000		8	9	15	25	40	85	200	260	
1892S 964,079		15	25	40	60	85	150	325	525	
1893 . . . . (792). . 5,444,023		6	7	12	15	30	75	150	250	400
18930 3,396,000		6	7	12	25	45	85	150	275	
1893S 1,454,535		9	12	30	60	80	150	275	600	
1894 . . . . (972). . 3,432,000		6	7	12	15	35	75	150	250	400
18940 2,852,000		6	7	15	30	60	125	175	400	
1894S 2,648,821		6	7	12	25	55	100	175	425	
1895 . . . . (880). . 4,440,000		6	7	12	15	30	75	150	250	400
18950 2,816,000		6	8	15	30	60	125	225	575	
1895S 1,764,681		9	13	35	60	75	175	250	600	
1896 . . . . (762). . 3,874,000		6	7	10	15	35	75	150	250	400
18960 1,484,000		30	40	100	160	275	450	675	1,100	

Chart continued on next page.

	Mintage	G-4	VG-8	F-12	VF-20	EF-40	AU-50	MS-60	MS-63	PF-63
1896S	188,039	$450	$950	$1,350	$2,250	$3,000	$4,250	$6,750	$11,000	
1897	(731) 8,140,000	6	7	8	15	30	75	150	250	$400
1897O	1,414,800	12	30	100	160	200	275	500	1,100	
1897S	542,229	50	75	175	275	400	475	1,100	1,100	
1898	(735) 11,100,000	6	7	8	15	30	75	150	250	400
1898O	1,868,000	8	12	35	65	125	175	400	1,000	
1898S	1,020,592	6	7	20	30	45	125	250	900	
1899	(846) 12,624,000	6	7	8	15	30	75	150	250	400
1899O	2,644,000	7	8	15	30	60	150	250	475	
1899S	708,000	10	20	45	55	65	200	350	900	
1900	(912) 10,016,000	6	7	8	15	30	75	150	250	400
1900O	3,416,000	8	10	30	50	70	200	350	500	
1900S	1,858,585	6	7	12	20	30	75	200	650	
1901	(813) 8,892,000	8	12	15	30	35	75	150	250	400
1901O	1,612,000	25	40	120	175	275	350	650	1,100	
1901S	72,664	2,500	5,250	10,000	12,500	15,000	20,000	25,000	32,500	
1902	(777) 12,196,967	5	6	8	15	30	75	150	250	400
1902O	4,748,000	6	7	20	30	60	125	275	800	
1902S	1,524,612	7	9	20	35	70	125	300	550	
1903	(755) 9,759,309	5	6	8	15	30	75	150	250	400
1903O	3,500,000	5	6	15	25	50	125	250	675	
1903S	1,036,000	8	9	15	35	65	150	250	500	
1904	(670) 9,588,143	5	6	8	15	30	75	150	250	400
1904O	2,456,000	10	16	35	75	125	250	525	750	
1905	(727) 4,967,523	10	12	20	30	30	75	150	250	400
1905O	1,230,000	20	25	55	100	125	200	300	950	
1905S	1,884,000	12	18	30	45	55	110	200	600	
1906	(675) 3,655,760	4	5	8	15	30	75	150	250	400
1906D	3,280,000	4	6	8	15	30	75	150	275	
1906O	2,056,000	4	5	12	20	45	100	160	325	
1907	(575) 7,132,000	4	5	8	15	30	75	150	250	400
1907D	2,484,000	4	5	10	15	30	80	150	400	
1907O	4,560,000	5	5	8	15	30	75	150	250	
1907S	1,360,000	5	6	15	30	55	150	300	800	
1908	(545) 4,232,000	4	5	8	15	30	75	150	250	400
1908D	5,788,000	4	5	8	15	30	75	150	250	
1908O	6,244,000	5	5	8	15	30	75	150	250	
1908S	784,000	10	25	65	70	150	275	425	650	
1909	(650) 9,268,000	4	5	8	15	30	75	150	250	400
1909D	5,114,000	4	5	8	15	30	85	150	250	
1909O	712,000	18	45	275	500	1,200	1,500	2,000	2,500	
1909S	1,348,000	5	5	12	20	40	100	175	425	
1910	(551) 2,244,000	4	5	10	15	30	75	150	250	400
1910D	1,500,000	4	5	15	30	50	125	200	500	
1911	(543) 3,720,000	4	5	8	15	30	75	150	250	400
1911D	933,600	12	18	75	150	225	400	575	700	
1911S	988,000	5	6	20	35	70	125	225	425	
1912	(700) 4,400,000	4	5	8	15	30	75	150	250	400
1912S	708,000	8	12	25	40	55	125	250	525	
1913	(613) 484,000	10	14	40	75	185	300	550	700	400
1913D	1,450,800	5	6	12	20	35	90	150	250	
1913S	40,000	800	1,200	2,500	4,500	5,500	6,500	8,000	11,500	

	Mintage	G-4	VG-8	F-12	VF-20	EF-40	AU-50	MS-60	MS-63	PF-63
1914 . . . . . . (380)	6,244,230	$4	$5	$7	$15	$30	$75	$150	$250	$400
1914D	3,046,000	4	5	7	15	30	75	150	250	
1914S	264,000	55	90	225	275	400	750	1,100	1,000	
1915 . . . . . . (450)	3,480,000	4	5	7	15	30	75	150	250	400
1915D	3,694,000	4	5	7	15	30	75	150	250	
1915S	704,000	10	20	30	45	45	125	175	275	
1916	1,788,000	4	5	7	15	30	75	150	250	
1916D	6,540,800	4	5	7	15	30	75	150	250	

STANDING LIBERTY (1916–1930)

This design is by Hermon A. MacNeil, whose initial M is above and to the right of the date. Liberty bears a shield of protection in her left arm, while the right hand holds the olive branch of peace. There was a modification in 1917. The reverse had a new arrangement of stars and the eagle was higher. After 1924 the date was "recessed," thereby giving it greater protection from the effects of circulation.

G-4 Good: Date and lettering legible. Top of date worn. Liberty's right leg and toes worn off. Much wear evident on left leg and drapery lines.

VG-8 Very Good: Distinct date. Toes faintly visible. Drapery lines visible above Liberty's left leg.

F-12 Fine: High curve of right leg flat from thigh to ankle. Only slight wear evident on left leg. Drapery lines over right thigh seen only at sides of leg.

VF-20 Very Fine: Garment line across right leg worn, but visible at sides.

EF-40 Extremely Fine: Flattened only at high spots. Liberty's toes are sharp. Drapery lines across right leg evident.

AU-50 About Uncirculated: Slight trace of wear on head, kneecap, shield's center, and highest point on eagle's body.

MS-60 Uncirculated: No trace of wear, but contact marks, surface spots, or faded luster possible.

MS-63 Choice Uncirculated: No trace of wear. Light blemishes. Attractive mint luster.

Variety 1 – No Stars Below Eagle (1916–1917)

Mintmark location is on obverse, to left of date.

	Mintage	G-4	VG-8	F-12	VF-20	EF-40	AU-50	MS-60	MS-63
1916	52,000	$1,750	$3,500	$4,500	$5,500	$6,500	$7,750	$10,000	$11,500
1917, Variety 1	8,740,000	12	20	30	40	60	110	150	210
1917D, Variety 1 . . .	1,509,200	14	25	35	55	80	125	210	250
1917S, Variety 1 . . .	1,952,000	16	30	40	65	105	150	240	290

Variety 2 – Stars Below Eagle (1917–1930)
Pedestal Date (1917–1924)

See next page for chart.

1918-S, 8 Over 7

	Mintage	G-4	VG-8	F-12	VF-20	EF-40	AU-50	MS-60	MS-63
1917, Variety 2	13,880,000	$11	$20	$25	$30	$45	$75	$120	$165
1917D, Variety 2	6,224,400	18	25	35	45	65	100	160	225
1917S, Variety 2	5,552,000	18	25	35	45	70	95	150	225
1918	14,240,000	8	10	15	17	25	45	90	150
1918D	7,380,000	13	18	30	35	65	100	175	250
1918S, Normal Date	11,072,000	9	10	15	20	30	50	110	160
1918S, 8 Over 7	*	1,000	1,250	2,500	3,250	5,250	7,250	12,000	20,000
1919	11,324,000	18	25	30	35	40	60	100	150
1919D	1,944,000	45	50	110	225	350	500	600	1,100
1919S	1,836,000	40	50	100	200	325	475	725	1,200
1920	27,860,000	7	9	12	20	25	50	100	125
1920D	3,586,400	30	35	45	65	90	100	300	525
1920S	6,380,000	8	12	15	20	30	85	125	450
1921	1,916,000	90	110	220	375	500	675	1,000	1,250
1923	9,716,000	7	9	15	20	25	50	100	160
1923S	1,360,000	160	250	375	550	900	1,200	1,500	2,250
1924	10,920,000	7	9	12	20	20	55	110	160
1924D	3,112,000	25	35	50	75	100	125	175	225
1924S	2,860,000	12	15	20	30	60	125	175	525

* Included in number above.

Recessed Date (1925–1930)

	Mintage	G-4	VG-8	F-12	VF-20	EF-40	AU-50	MS-60	MS-63
1925	12,280,000	$4	$5	$6	$7	$16	$40	$80	$140
1926	11,316,000	4	5	6	7	16	40	80	125
1926D	1,716,000	4	6	10	20	45	75	100	140
1926S	2,700,000	4	5	6	10	50	125	200	475
1927	11,912,000	4	5	6	7	16	40	80	125
1927D	976,000	6	10	15	35	80	125	160	200
1927S	396,000	20	25	50	175	600	1,500	3,000	4,500
1928	6,336,000	4	5	6	7	16	40	80	125
1928D	1,627,600	4	5	6	7	16	40	80	125
1928S	2,644,000	4	5	6	7	16	40	80	125
1929	11,140,000	4	5	6	7	16	40	80	125
1929D	1,358,000	4	5	6	7	16	40	80	125
1929S	1,764,000	4	5	6	7	16	40	80	125
1930	5,632,000	4	5	6	7	16	40	80	125
1930S	1,556,000	4	5	6	7	16	40	80	125

WASHINGTON (1932 TO DATE)

This type was intended to be a commemorative issue marking the 200th anniversary of President Washington's birth. John Flanagan, a New York sculptor, was the designer. The initials JF are found at the base of the neck. The mintmark is on the reverse below the wreath for coins from 1932 to 1964. Starting in 1968, the mintmark was moved to the obverse at the right of the ribbon.

F-12 Fine: Hair lines about Washington's ear visible. Tiny feathers on eagle's breast faintly visible.
VF-20 Very Fine: Most hair details visible. Wing feathers clear.
EF-40 Extremely Fine: Hair lines sharp. Wear spots confined to top of eagle's legs and center of breast.
MS-60 Uncirculated: No trace of wear, but many contact marks, surface spotting, or faded luster possible.
MS-63 Choice Uncirculated: No trace of wear. Light blemishes. Attractive mint luster.
MS-64 Uncirculated: A few scattered contact marks. Good eye appeal and attractive luster.
MS-65 Gem Uncirculated: Only light, scattered, non-distracting marks. Strong luster, good eye appeal.
PF-65 Gem Proof: Hardly any blemishes, and no flaws.

QUARTER DOLLARS

Silver Coinage (1932–1964)

	Mintage	VG-8	F-12	VF-20	EF-40	MS-60	MS-63	MS-65	PF-63
1932	5,404,000	$4	$4.50	$5	$5.50	$13	$25	$145	
1932D	436,800	50	60.00	75	90.00	675	1,050	7,500	
1932S	408,000	50	60.00	75	90.00	275	475	2,500	
1934	31,912,052	3	3.50	4	5.00	10	18	50	
1934D	3,527,200	3	3.50	5	8.00	100	175	350	
1935	32,484,000	3	3.50	4	5.00	8	15	35	
1935D	5,780,000	3	3.50	4	8.00	100	140	275	
1935S	5,660,000	3	3.50	4	6.00	45	60	145	
1936 (3,837)	41,300,000	3	3.50	4	5.00	10	16	45	$850
1936D	5,374,000	3	3.50	4	15.00	225	350	575	
1936S	3,828,000	3	3.50	4	6.00	45	65	175	
1937 (5,542)	19,696,000	3	3.50	4	5.00	10	15	45	250
1937D	7,189,600	3	3.50	4	6.00	25	40	75	
1937S	1,652,000	3	3.50	4	8.00	70	110	180	
1938 (8,045)	9,472,000	3	3.50	4	6.00	45	50	120	140
1938S	2,832,000	3	3.50	4	6.00	45	60	110	
1939 (8,795)	33,540,000	3	3.50	4	5.00	6	11	25	120
1939D	7,092,000	3	3.50	4	5.00	16	20	45	
1939S	2,628,000	3	3.50	4	7.00	45	65	150	

	Mintage	F-12	VF-20	EF-40	MS-60	MS-63	MS-65	PF-65
1940 (11,246)	35,704,000	$3	$3.50	$4	$7	$12	$25	$70
1940D	2,797,600	3	3.50	6	50	80	125	
1940S	8,244,000	3	3.50	4	10	13	20	
1941 (15,287)	79,032,000	3	3.50	4	5	7	18	60
1941D	16,714,800	3	3.50	5	12	22	25	
1941S	16,080,000	3	3.50	4	9	18	25	
1942 (21,123)	102,096,000	3	3.50	4	5	6	10	50
1942D	17,487,200	3	3.50	4	7	11	15	
1942S	19,384,000	3	3.50	5	30	45	70	
1943	99,700,000	3	3.50	4	5	6	18	
1943D	16,095,600	3	3.50	4	10	15	20	
1943S	21,700,000	3	3.50	4	9	20	22	
1944	104,956,000	3	3.50	4	5	6	13	
1944D	14,600,800	3	3.50	4	8	9	15	
1944S	12,560,000	3	3.50	4	7	8	12	
1945	74,372,000	3	3.50	4	5	6	17	
1945D	12,341,600	3	3.50	4	8	10	17	
1945S	17,004,001	3	3.50	4	5	6	12	
1946	53,436,000	3	3.50	4	5	6	15	
1946D	9,072,800	3	3.50	4	5	6	12	
1946S	4,204,000	3	3.50	4	5	6	12	
1947	22,556,000	3	3.50	4	5	7	12	

Chart continued on next page.

	Mintage	F-12	VF-20	EF-40	MS-60	MS-63	MS-65	PF-65
1947D	15,338,400	$3	$3.50	$4.00	$5.00	$7.00	$14	
1947S	5,532,000	3	3.50	4.00	5.00	7.00	10	
1948	35,196,000	3	3.50	4.00	5.00	6.00	10	
1948D	16,766,800	3	3.50	4.00	5.00	7.00	20	
1948S	15,960,000	3	3.50	4.00	5.00	6.00	15	
1949	9,312,000	3	3.50	5.00	12.00	20.00	30	
1949D	10,068,400	3	3.50	4.00	7.00	12.00	15	
1950 (51,386)	24,920,126	3	3.50	4.00	5.00	6.00	10	$25.00
1950D	21,075,600	3	3.50	4.00	5.00	6.00	10	
1950D, D Over S	*	10	25.00	75.00	125.00	425.00	2,750	
1950S	10,284,004	3	3.50	4.50	5.00	6.00	10	
1950S, S Over D	*	10	27.00	80.00	200.00	250.00	800	
1951 (57,500)	43,448,102	3	3.50	4.00	4.50	6.00	10	25.00
1951D	35,354,800	3	3.50	4.00	4.50	6.00	10	
1951S	9,048,000	3	3.50	4.50	5.00	12.00	15	
1952 (81,980)	38,780,093	3	3.50	4.00	4.50	6.00	10	25.00
1952D	49,795,200	3	3.50	4.00	4.50	6.00	15	
1952S	13,707,800	3	3.50	4.50	5.00	10.00	15	
1953 (128,800)	18,536,120	3	3.50	4.00	4.50	6.00	15	20.00
1953D	56,112,400	3	3.50	4.00	4.50	6.00	14	
1953S	14,016,000	3	3.50	4.00	4.50	6.00	13	
1954 (233,300)	54,412,203	3	3.50	4.00	4.50	6.00	10	8.00
1954D	42,305,500	3	3.50	4.00	4.50	6.00	15	
1954S	11,834,722	3	3.50	4.00	4.50	6.00	13	
1955 (378,200)	18,180,181	3	3.50	4.00	4.50	6.00	10	10.00
1955D	3,182,400	3	3.50	4.00	4.50	6.00	18	
1956 (669,384)	44,144,000	3	3.50	4.00	4.50	6.00	9	7.50
1956D	32,334,500	3	3.50	4.00	4.50	6.00	10	
1957 (1,247,952)	46,532,000	3	3.50	4.00	4.50	6.00	10	6.00
1957D	77,924,160	3	3.50	4.00	4.50	6.00	9	
1958 (875,652)	6,360,000	3	3.50	4.00	4.50	6.00	8	6.00
1958D	78,124,900	3	3.50	4.00	4.50	6.00	8	
1959 (1,149,291)	24,384,000	3	3.50	4.00	4.50	6.00	8	5.00
1959D	62,054,232	3	3.50	4.00	4.50	6.00	8	
1960 (1,691,602)	29,164,000	3	3.50	4.00	4.25	5.50	6	5.00
1960D	63,000,324	3	3.50	4.00	4.25	5.50	6	
1961 (3,028,244)	37,036,000	3	3.50	4.00	4.25	5.50	6	5.00
1961D	83,656,928	3	3.50	4.00	4.25	5.50	6	
1962 (3,218,019)	36,156,000	3	3.50	4.00	4.25	5.50	6	5.00
1962D	127,554,756	3	3.50	4.00	4.25	5.50	6	
1963 (3,075,645)	74,316,000	3	3.50	4.00	4.25	5.50	6	5.00
1963D	135,288,184	3	3.50	4.00	4.25	5.50	6	
1964 (3,950,762)	560,390,585	3	3.50	4.00	4.25	5.50	6	5.00
1964D	704,135,528	3	3.50	4.00	4.25	5.50	6	

* Included in number above.

Clad Coinage and Silver Proofs (1965 to Date)

	Mintage	MS-63	MS-65	PF-65		Mintage	MS-63	MS-65	PF-65
1965	1,819,717,540	$0.30	$4.00		1968D	101,534,000	$0.30	$3.00	
1966	821,101,500	0.30	3.00		1968S	(3,041,506)			$1
1967	1,524,031,848	0.30	3.00		1969	176,212,000	0.75	3.50	
1968	220,731,500	0.50	3.50		1969D	114,372,000	0.50	4.00	

	Mintage	MS-63	MS-65	PF-65
1969S	(2,934,631)			$1
1970	136,420,000	$0.25	$3	
1970D	417,341,364	0.25	2	
1970S	(2,632,810)			1
1971	109,284,000	0.30	2	
1971D	258,634,428	0.30	2	
1971S	(3,220,733)			1
1972	215,048,000	0.30	2	

	Mintage	MS-63	MS-65	PF-65
1972D	311,067,732	$0.30	$2	
1972S	(3,260,996)			$1
1973	346,924,000	0.30	2	
1973D	232,977,400	0.30	2	
1973S	(2,760,339)			1
1974	801,456,000	0.30	2	
1974D	353,160,300	0.30	3	
1974S	(2,612,568)			1

Bicentennial (1776–1976)

	Mintage	MS-63	MS-65	PF-65
1776–1976, Copper-Nickel Clad	809,784,016	$0.30	$2	
1776–1976D, Copper-Nickel Clad	860,118,839	0.30	2	
1776–1976S, Copper-Nickel Clad	(7,059,099)			$1
1776–1976S, Silver Clad	11,000,000	2.50	3	
1776–1976S, Silver Clad	(4,000,000)			3

Note: Mintage figures for 1976-S silver clad coins are approximate; many were melted in 1982.

Eagle Reverse Resumed (1977–1998)
(Dies Slightly Modified to Lower Relief)

	Mintage	MS-63	MS-65	PF-65
1977	468,556,000	$0.27		
1977D	256,524,978	0.27	$1.00	
1977S	(3,251,152)			$1
1978	521,452,000	0.27	1.50	
1978D	287,373,152	0.27	1.50	
1978S	(3,127,781)			1
1979	515,708,000	0.28	1.50	
1979D	489,789,780	0.27	1.25	
1979S	(3,677,175)			
Type 1				1
Type 2				2
1980P	635,832,000	0.27	1.50	
1980D	518,327,487	0.27	1.25	
1980S	(3,554,806)			1
1981P	601,716,000	0.27	1.50	
1981D	575,722,833	0.27	1.00	
1981S	(4,063,083)			
Type 1				3
Type 2				6
1982P	500,931,000	1.00	10.00	
1982D	480,042,788	1.00	8.00	
1982S	(3,857,479)			1
1983P	673,535,000	8.00	25.00	

	Mintage	MS-63	MS-65	PF-65
1983D	617,806,446	$3.00	$20	
1983S	(3,279,126)			$1
1984P	676,545,000	0.30	3	
1984D	546,483,064	0.30	3	
1984S	(3,065,110)			1
1985P	775,818,962	0.50	5	
1985D	519,962,888	0.35	3	
1985S	(3,362,821)			1
1986P	551,199,333	1.00	4	
1986D	504,298,660	2.00	9	
1986S	(3,010,497)			1
1987P	582,499,481	0.27	3	
1987D	655,594,696	0.27	1	
1987S	(4,227,728)			1
1988P	562,052,000	0.50	5	
1988D	596,810,688	0.50	4	
1988S	(3,262,948)			1
1989P	512,868,000	0.30	5	
1989D	896,535,597	0.27	1	
1989S	(3,220,194)			1
1990P	613,792,000	0.27	4	
1990D	927,638,181	0.28	4	
1990S	(3,299,559)			1

Chart continued on next page.

	Mintage	MS-63	MS-65	PF-65
1991P	570,968,000	$0.30	$4	
1991D	630,966,693	0.30	4	
1991S	(2,867,787)			$1.25
1992P	384,764,000	0.35	5	
1992D	389,777,107	0.35	5	
1992S	(2,858,981)			1.25
1992S, Silver	(1,317,579)			5.00
1993P	639,276,000	0.30	2	
1993D	645,476,128	0.30	2	
1993S	(2,633,439)			1.25
1993S, Silver	(761,353)			5.00
1994P	825,600,000	0.30	4	
1994D	880,034,110	0.30	4	
1994S	(2,484,594)			1.25
1994S, Silver	(785,329)			5.00
1995P	1,004,336,000	0.30	4	

	Mintage	MS-63	MS-65	PF-65
1995D	1,103,216,000	$0.30	$3	
1995S	(2,117,496)			$3.00
1995S, Silver	(679,985)			5.00
1996P	925,040,000	0.25	3	
1996D	906,868,000	0.25	3	
1996S	(1,750,244)			2.00
1996S, Silver	(775,021)			5.00
1997P	595,740,000	0.25	3	
1997D	599,680,000	0.25	3	
1997S	(2,055,000)			2.00
1997S, Silver	(741,678)			5.00
1998P	896,268,000	0.25	2	
1998D	821,000,000	0.25	2	
1998S	(2,086,507)			2.50
1998S, Silver	(878,792)			5.00

State Quarters (1999–2008)

The United States Mint 50 State Quarters® Program, which began in 1999, produced a series of 50 quarter dollar coins with special designs honoring each state. Five different designs were issued each year during the period 1999 through 2008. States were commemorated in the order of their entrance into statehood.

These are all legal-tender coins of standard weight and composition. The obverse side depicting President George Washington was modified to include some of the wording previously used on the reverse. The modification was authorized by special legislation, and carried out by Mint sculptor-engraver William Cousins, whose initials were added to the truncation of Washington's neck adjacent to those of the original designer, John Flanagan.

Each state theme was proposed, and the design approved, by the governor of the state. Final designs were created by Mint personnel.

Circulation coins were made at the Philadelphia and Denver mints. Proof coins were made in San Francisco. Both copper-nickel and silver Proof coins were made each year.

	Mintage	AU-50	MS-63	PF-65
Delaware				
1999P	373,400,000	$0.25	$0.50	
1999D	401,424,000	0.25	0.50	
1999S	(3,713,359)			$1.75
1999S, Silver	(804,565)			14.00
Pennsylvania				
1999P	349,000,000	0.25	0.50	
1999D	358,332,000	0.25	0.50	
1999S	(3,713,359)			1.75
1999S, Silver	(804,565)			14.00

	Mintage	AU-50	MS-63	PF-65
New Jersey				
1999P	363,200,000	$0.25	$0.30	
1999D	299,028,000	0.25	0.35	
1999S	(3,713,359)			$1.75
1999S, Silver	(804,565)			14.00
Georgia				
1999P	451,188,000	0.25	0.30	
1999D	488,744,000	0.25	0.30	
1999S	(3,713,359)			1.75
1999S, Silver	(804,565)			14.00

	Mintage	AU-50	MS-63	PF-65
Connecticut				
1999P.....	688,744,000	$0.25	$0.30	
1999D.....	657,880,000	0.25	0.30	

	Mintage	AU-50	MS-63	PF-65
Connecticut				
1999S......	(3,713,359)			$1.75
1999S, Silver..	(804,565)			14.00

	Mintage	AU-50	MS-63	PF-65
Massachusetts				
2000P.....	628,600,000	$0.25	$0.30	
2000D.....	535,184,000	0.25	0.30	
2000S......	(4,020,172)			$1.50
2000S, Silver.	(965,421)			6.00
Maryland				
2000P.....	678,200,000	0.25	0.30	
2000D.....	556,532,000	0.25	0.30	
2000S......	(4,020,172)			1.50
2000S, Silver.	(965,421)			6.00
South Carolina				
2000P.....	742,576,000	0.25	0.32	
2000D.....	566,208,000	0.25	0.32	

	Mintage	AU-50	MS-63	PF-65
South Carolina				
2000S......	(4,020,172)			$1.50
2000S, Silver...	(965,421)			6.00
New Hampshire				
2000P.....	673,040,000	$0.25	$0.30	
2000D.....	495,976,000	0.25	0.30	
2000S......	(4,020,172)			1.50
2000S, Silver...	(965,421)			6.00
Virginia				
2000P.....	943,000,000	0.25	0.30	
2000D.....	651,616,000	0.25	0.30	
2000S......	(4,020,172)			1.50
2000S, Silver...	(965,421)			6.00

	Mintage	AU-50	MS-63	PF-65
New York				
2001P.....	655,400,000	$0.25	$0.30	
2001D.....	619,640,000	0.25	0.30	
2001S......	(3,094,140)			$1.50
2001S, Silver...	(889,697)			8.00
North Carolina				
2001P.....	627,600,000	0.25	0.30	
2001D.....	427,876,000	0.25	0.30	
2001S......	(3,094,140)			1.50
2001S, Silver...	(889,697)			8.00
Rhode Island				
2001P.....	423,000,000	0.25	0.30	
2001D.....	447,100,000	0.25	0.30	

	Mintage	AU-50	MS-63	PF-65
Rhode Island				
2001S......	(3,094,140)			$1.50
2001S, Silver...	(889,697)			8.00
Vermont				
2001P.....	423,400,000	$0.25	$0.30	
2001D.....	459,404,000	0.25	0.30	
2001S......	(3,094,140)			1.50
2001S, Silver...	(889,697)			8.00
Kentucky				
2001P....	353,000,000	0.25	0.30	
2001D.....	370,564,000	0.25	0.30	
2001S......	(3,094,140)			1.50
2001S, Silver...	(889,697)			8.00

	Mintage	AU-50	MS-63	PF-65
Tennessee				
2002P	361,600,000	$0.30	$0.40	
2002D	286,468,000	0.30	0.40	
2002S	(3,084,245)			$1.50
2002S, Silver	(892,229)			6.00
Ohio				
2002P	217,200,000	0.25	0.30	
2002D	414,832,000	0.25	0.30	
2002S	(3,084,245)			1.50
2002S, Silver	(892,229)			6.00
Louisiana				
2002P	362,000,000	0.25	0.30	
2002D	402,204,000	0.25	0.30	
2002S	(3,084,245)			1.50
2002S, Silver	(892,229)			6.00
Indiana				
2002P	362,600,000	0.25	0.30	
2002D	327,200,000	0.25	0.30	
2002S	(3,084,245)			1.50
2002S, Silver	(892,229)			6.00
Mississippi				
2002P	290,000,000	0.25	0.30	
2002D	289,600,000	0.25	0.30	
2002S	(3,084,245)			1.50
2002S, Silver	(892,229)			6.00
Illinois				
2003P	225,800,000	$0.25	$0.30	
2003D	237,400,000	0.25	0.30	
2003S	(3,408,516)			$1.50
2003S, Silver	(1,125,755)			6.00
Alabama				
2003P	225,000,000	0.25	0.30	
2003D	232,400,000	0.25	0.30	
2003S	(3,408,516)			1.50
2003S, Silver	(1,125,755)			6.00
Maine				
2003P	217,400,000	0.25	0.30	
2003D	231,400,000	0.25	0.30	
2003S	(3,408,516)			1.50
2003S, Silver	(1,125,755)			6.00
Missouri				
2003P	225,000,000	0.25	0.30	
2003D	228,200,000	0.25	0.30	
2003S	(3,408,516)			1.50
2003S, Silver	(1,125,755)			6.00
Arkansas				
2003P	228,000,000	0.25	0.30	
2003D	229,800,000	0.25	0.30	
2003S	(3,408,516)			1.50
2003S, Silver	(1,125,755)			6.00

	Mintage	AU-50	MS-63	PF-65
Michigan				
2004P	233,800,000	$0.25	$0.30	
2004D	225,800,000	0.25	0.30	
2004S	(2,740,684)			$1.50
2004S, Silver.	(1,769,786)			6.00
Florida				
2004P	240,200,000	0.25	0.30	
2004D	241,600,000	0.25	0.30	
2004S	(2,740,684)			1.50
2004S, Silver.	(1,769,786)			6.00
Texas				
2004P	278,800,000	0.25	0.30	
2004D	263,000,000	0.25	0.30	
2004S	(2,740,684)			1.50
2004S, Silver.	(1,769,786)			6.00
Iowa				
2004P	213,800,000	0.25	0.30	
2004D	251,400,000	0.25	0.30	
2004S	(2,740,684)			1.50
2004S, Silver.	(1,769,786)			6.00
Wisconsin				
2004P	226,400,000	0.25	0.30	
2004D	226,800,000	0.25	0.30	
2004S	(2,740,684)			1.50
2004S, Silver.	(1,769,786)			6.00

	Mintage	AU-50	MS-63	PF-65
California				
2005P	257,200,000	$0.25	$0.30	
2005D	263,200,000	0.25	0.30	
2005S	(3,262,960)			$1.50
2005S, Silver.	(1,678,649)			6.00
Minnesota				
2005P	239,600,000	0.25	0.30	
2005D	248,400,000	0.25	0.30	
2005S	(3,262,960)			1.50
2005S, Silver.	(1,678,649)			6.00
Oregon				
2005P	316,200,000	0.25	0.30	
2005D	404,000,000	0.25	0.30	
2005S	(3,262,960)			1.50
2005S, Silver.	(1,678,649)			6.00
Kansas				
2005P	263,400,000	0.25	0.30	
2005D	300,000,000	0.25	0.30	
2005S	(3,262,960)			1.50
2005S, Silver.	(1,678,649)			6.00
West Virginia				
2005P	365,400,000	0.25	0.30	
2005D	356,200,000	0.25	0.30	
2005S	(3,262,960)			1.50
2005S, Silver.	(1,678,649)			6.00

	Mintage	AU-50	MS-63	PF-65
Nevada				
2006P	277,000,000	$0.25	$0.30	
2006D	312,800,000	0.25	0.30	
2006S	(2,882,428)			$1.50
2006S, Silver.	(1,585,008)			6.00
Nebraska				
2006P	318,000,000	0.25	0.30	
2006D	273,000,000	0.25	0.30	
2006S	(2,882,428)			1.50
2006S, Silver.	(1,585,008)			6.00
Colorado				
2006P	274,800,000	0.25	0.30	
2006D	294,200,000	0.25	0.30	
2006S	(2,882,428)			1.50
2006S, Silver.	(1,585,008)			6.00
North Dakota				
2006P	305,800,000	0.25	0.30	
2006D	359,000,000	0.25	0.30	
2006S	(2,882,428)			1.50
2006S, Silver.	(1,585,008)			6.00
South Dakota				
2006P	245,000,000	0.25	0.30	
2006D	265,800,000	0.25	0.30	
2006S	(2,882,428)			1.50
2006S, Silver.	(1,585,008)			6.00

	Mintage	AU-50	MS-63	PF-65
Montana				
2007P	257,000,000	$0.25	$0.30	
2007D	256,240,000	0.25	0.30	
2007S	(2,374,778)			$1.50
2007S, Silver.	(1,313,481)			6.00
Washington				
2007P	265,200,000	0.25	0.30	
2007D	280,000,000	0.25	0.30	
2007S	(2,374,778)			1.50
2007S, Silver.	(1,313,481)			6.00
Idaho				
2007P	294,600,000	0.25	0.30	
2007D	286,800,000	0.25	0.30	
2007S	(2,374,778)			1.50
2007S, Silver.	(1,313,481)			6.00
Wyoming				
2007P	243,600,000	0.25	0.30	
2007D	320,800,000	0.25	0.30	
2007S	(2,374,778)			1.50
2007S, Silver.	(1,313,481)			6.00
Utah				
2007P	255,000,000	0.25	0.30	
2007D	253,200,000	0.25	0.30	
2007S	(2,374,778)			1.50
2007S, Silver.	(1,313,481)			6.00

	Mintage	AU-50	MS-63	PF-65
Oklahoma				
2008P	222,000,000	$0.25	$0.30	
2008D	194,600,000	0.25	0.30	
2008S	(2,078,112)			$1.50
2008S, Silver.	(1,192,908)			6.00
New Mexico				
2008P	244,200,000	0.25	0.30	
2008D	244,400,000	0.25	0.30	
2008S	(2,078,112)			1.50
2008S, Silver.	(1,192,908)			6.00
Arizona				
2008P	244,600,000	0.25	0.30	
2008D	265,000,000	0.25	0.30	

	Mintage	AU-50	MS-63	PF-65
Arizona				
2008S	(2,078,112)			$1.50
2008S, Silver.	(1,192,908)			6.00
Alaska				
2008P	251,800,000	$0.25	$0.30	
2008D	254,000,000	0.25	0.30	
2008S	(2,078,112)			1.50
2008S, Silver.	(1,192,908)			6.00
Hawaii				
2008P	254,000,000	0.25	0.30	
2008D	263,600,00	0.25	0.30	
2008S	(2,078,112)			3.00
2008S, Silver.	(1,192,908)			6.00

Some State quarters were accidentally made with misaligned dies and are valued higher than ordinary pieces. Normal United States coins have dies oriented in "coin alignment," such that the reverse appears upside down when the coin is rotated from right to left. Values for the rotated-die quarters vary according to the amount of shifting. The most valuable are those that are shifted 180 degrees, so that both sides appear upright when the coin is turned over (called *medal alignment*).

Manufacturing varieties showing die doubling or other minor, unintentional characteristics are of interest to collectors and are often worth premium prices.

District of Columbia and U.S. Territories Quarters (2009)

At the ending of the U.S. Mint 50 State Quarters® Program a new series of quarter-dollar reverse designs was authorized to recognize the District of Columbia and the five U.S. territories: the Commonwealth of Puerto Rico, Guam, American Samoa, the U.S. Virgin Islands, and the Commonwealth of the Northern Mariana Islands. Each of these coins, issued sequentially during 2009, has the portrait of George Washington, as in the past, and is made of the same weight and composition. Each coin commemorates the history, geography, or traditions of the place it represents.

	Mintage	AU-50	MS-63	PF-65
District of Columbia				
2009P	83,600,000	$0.25	$0.30	
2009D	88,800,000	0.25	0.30	
2009S	(2,113,478)			$1.50
2009S, Silver	(996,548)			6.00
Puerto Rico				
2009P	53,200,000	0.25	0.30	
2009D	86,000,000	0.25	0.30	
2009S	(2,113,478)			1.50
2009S, Silver	(996,548)			6.00
Guam				
2009P	45,000,000	0.25	0.30	
2009D	42,600,000	0.25	0.30	
2009S	(2,113,478)			1.50
2009S, Silver	(996,548)			6.00

	Mintage	AU-50	MS-63	PF-65
American Samoa				
2009P	42,600,000	$0.25	$0.30	
2009D	39,600,000	0.25	0.30	
2009S	(2,113,478)			$1.50
2009S, Silver	(996,548)			6.00
U.S. Virgin Islands				
2009P	41,000,000	0.25	0.40	
2009D	41,000,000	0.25	0.40	
2009S	(2,113,478)			1.50
2009S, Silver	(996,548)			6.00
Northern Mariana Islands				
2009P	35,200,000	0.25	0.30	
2009D	37,600,000	0.25	0.30	
2009S	(2,113,478)			1.50
2009S, Silver	(996,548)			6.00

America the Beautiful™ Quarters Program (2010–2021)

Following up on the popularity of the 50 State Quarters® Program, Congress has authorized the production of new circulating commemorative quarters from 2010 to 2021. The coins honor a site of "natural or historic significance" from each of the 50 states, five U.S. territories, and the District of Columbia. They continue to bear George Washington's portrait on the obverse.

Five designs will be released each year through 2020, with the final coin issued in 2021, in the order the coins' featured locations were designated national parks or national sites. At the discretion of the secretary of the Treasury, this series could be extended an additional 11 years by featuring a second national park or site from each state, district, and territory.

In addition to the circulating quarters, a series of five-ounce silver bullion pieces are being coined each year with designs nearly identical to those of the America the Beautiful™ quarters, with two main exceptions: the size, which is three inches in diameter; and the edge, which is marked .999 FINE SILVER 5.0 OUNCE, rather than reeded as on the standard quarters.

	Mintage	AU-50	MS-63	PF-65
Hot Springs National Park (Arkansas)				
2010P	35,600,000	$0.25	$0.30	
2010D	34,000,000	0.25	0.30	
2010S	(1,402,889)			$1.50
2010S, Silver	(859,417)			6.00
Yellowstone National Park (Wyoming)				
2010P	33,600,000	0.25	0.30	
2010D	34,800,000	0.25	0.30	
2010S	(1,404,259)			1.50
2010S, Silver	(859,417)			6.00
Yosemite National Park (California)				
2010P	35,200,000	0.25	0.30	
2010D	34,800,000	0.25	0.30	
2010S	(1,401,522)			1.50
2010S, Silver	(859,417)			6.00
Grand Canyon National Park (Arizona)				
2010P	34,800,000	0.25	0.30	
2010D	35,400,000	0.25	0.30	
2010S	(1,401,462)			1.50
2010S, Silver	(859,417)			6.00
Mount Hood National Forest (Oregon)				
2010P	34,400,000	0.25	0.30	
2010D	34,400,000	0.25	0.30	
2010S	(1,398,106)			1.50
2010S, Silver	(859,417)			6.00

	Mintage	AU-50	MS-63	PF-65
Gettysburg National Military Park (Pennsylvania)				
2011P	30,800,000	$0.25	$0.30	
2011D	30,400,000	0.25	0.30	
2011S	(1,273,068)			$1.50
2011S, Silver	(722,076)			6.00
Glacier National Park (Montana)				
2011P	30,400,000	0.25	0.30	
2011D	31,200,000	0.25	0.30	
2011S	(1,273,068)			1.50
2011S, Silver	(722,076)			6.00
Olympic National Park (Washington)				
2011P	30,400,000	0.25	0.30	
2011D	30,600,000	0.25	0.30	
2011S	(1,268,231)			1.50
2011S, Silver	(722,076)			6.00
Vicksburg National Military Park (Mississippi)				
2011P	30,800,000	0.25	0.30	
2011D	33,400,000	0.25	0.30	
2011S	(1,268,623)			1.50
2011S, Silver	(722,076)			6.00
Chickasaw National Recreation Area (Oklahoma)				
2011P	73,800,000	0.25	0.30	
2011D	69,400,000	0.25	0.30	
2011S	(1,266,825)			1.50
2011S, Silver	(722,076)			6.00

	Mintage	AU-50	MS-63	PF-65
El Yunque National Forest (Puerto Rico)				
2012P	25,800,000	$0.25	$0.30	
2012D	25,000,000	0.25	0.30	
2012S	1,680,140		0.50 **(a)**	
2012S	(1,012,094)			$1.50
2012S, Silver	(608,060)			6.00
Chaco Culture National Historical Park (New Mexico)				
2012P	22,000,000	0.25	0.30	
2012D	22,000,000	0.25	0.30	
2012S	1,389,020		0.50 **(a)**	
2012S	(961,464)			1.50
2012S, Silver	(608,060)			6.00
Acadia National Park (Maine)				
2012P	24,800,000	0.25	0.30	
2012D	21,606,000	0.25	0.30	
2012S	1,409,120		0.50 **(a)**	
2012S	(962,038)			1.50
2012S, Silver	(608,060)			6.00
Hawai'i Volcanoes National Park (Hawaii)				
2012P	46,200,000	0.25	0.30	
2012D	78,600,000	0.25	0.30	
2012S	1,409,120		0.50 **(a)**	
2012S	(962,447)			1.50
2012S, Silver	(608,060)			6.00
Denali National Park and Preserve (Alaska)				
2012P	135,400,000	0.25	0.30	
2012D	166,600,000	0.25	0.30	
2012S	1,409,220		0.50 **(a)**	
2012S	(959,602)			1.50
2012S, Silver	(608,060)			6.00

	Mintage	AU-50	MS-63	PF-65
White Mountain National Forest (New Hampshire)				
2013P	68,800,000	$0.25	$0.30	
2013D	107,600,000	0.25	0.30	
2013S	1,606,900		0.50 **(a)**	
2013S	(989,803)			$1.50
2013S, Silver	(467,691)			6.00
Perry's Victory and International Peace Memorial (Ohio)				
2013P	107,800,000	0.25	0.30	
2013D	131,600,000	0.25	0.30	
2013S	1,425,860		0.50 **(a)**	
2013S	(947,815)			1.50
2013S, Silver	(467,691)			6.00
Great Basin National Park (Nevada)				
2013P	122,400,000	0.25	0.30	
2013D	141,400,000	0.25	0.30	
2013S	1,316,500		0.50 **(a)**	
2013S	(945,777)			1.50
2013S, Silver	(467,691)			6.00
Ft. McHenry Nat'l Monument and Historic Shrine (Maryland)				
2013P	120,000,000	0.25	0.30	
2013D	151,400,000	0.25	0.30	
2013S	1,313,680		0.50 **(a)**	
2013S	(946,380)			1.50
2013S, Silver	(467,691)			6.00
Mount Rushmore National Memorial (South Dakota)				
2013P	231,800,000	0.25	0.30	
2013D	272,400,000	0.25	0.30	
2013S	1,373,260		0.50 **(a)**	
2013S	(958,853)			1.50
2013S, Silver	(467,691)			6.00

a. Not issued for circulation.

	Mintage	AU-50	MS-63	PF-65
Great Smoky Mountains National Park (Tennessee)				
2014P	73,200,000	$0.25	$0.30	
2014D	99,400,000	0.25	0.30	
2014S	1,360,780		0.50	(a)
2014S	(881,896)			$1.50
2014S, Silver . . .	(472,107)			6.00
Shenandoah National Park (Virginia)				
2014P	112,800,000	0.25	0.30	
2014D	197,800,000	0.25	0.30	
2014S	1,260,700		0.50	(a)
2014S	(846,441)			1.50
2014S, Silver . . .	(472,107)			6.00
Arches National Park (Utah)				
2014P	214,200,000	0.25	0.30	
2014D	251,400,000	0.25	0.30	
2014S	1,226,220		0.50	(a)
2014S	(844,775)			$1.50
2014S, Silver . . .	(472,107)			6.00
Great Sand Dunes National Park (Colorado)				
2014P	159,600,000	$0.25	0.30	
2014D	171,800,000	0.25	0.30	
2014S	1,170,500		0.50	(a)
2014S	(843,238)			1.50
2014S, Silver . . .	(472,107)			6.00
Everglades National Park (Florida)				
2014P	157,601,200	0.25	0.30	
2014D	142,400,000	0.25	0.30	
2014S	1,173,720		0.50	(a)
2014S	(856,139)			1.50
2014S, Silver . . .	(472,107)			6.00

	Mintage	AU-50	MS-63	PF-65
Homestead National Monument of America (Nebraska)				
2015P	214,400,000	$0.25	$0.30	
2015D	248,600,000	0.25	0.30	
2015S	1,135,460		0.50	(a)
2015S	(764,611)			$1.50
2015S, Silver . . .	(447,489)			6.00
Kisatchie National Forest (Louisiana)				
2015P	397,200,000	0.25	0.30	
2015D	379,600,000	0.25	0.30	
2015S	1,081,560		0.50	(a)
2015S	(730,469)			1.50
2015S, Silver . . .	(447,489)			6.00
Blue Ridge Parkway (North Carolina)				
2015P	325,616,000	0.25	0.30	
2015D	505,200,000	0.25	0.30	
2015S	1,049,500		0.50	(a)
2015S	(731,823)			1.50
2015S, Silver . . .	(447,489)			6.00
Bombay Hook National Wildlife Refuge (Delaware)				
2015P	275,000,000	0.25	0.30	
2015D	206,400,000	0.25	0.30	
2015S	923,960		0.50	(a)
2015S	(728,412)			1.50
2015S, Silver . . .	(447,489)			6.00
Saratoga National Historical Park (New York)				
2015P	223,000,000	0.25	0.30	
2015D	215,800,000	0.25	0.30	
2015S	888,380		0.50	(a)
2015S	(743,133)			1.50
2015S, Silver . . .	(447,489)			6.00

a. Not issued for circulation.

	Mintage	AU-50	MS-63	PF-65
Shawnee National Forest (Illinois)				
2016P		$0.25	$0.30	
2016D		0.25	0.30	
2016S				$1.50
2016S, Silver.				6.00
Cumberland Gap National Historical Park (Kentucky)				
2016P		0.25	0.30	
2016D		0.25	0.30	
2016S				1.50
2016S, Silver.				6.00
Harpers Ferry National Historical Park (West Virginia)				
2016P		0.25	0.30	
2016D		0.25	0.30	

	Mintage	AU-50	MS-63	PF-65
Harpers Ferry National Historical Park (West Virginia)				
2016S				$1.50
2016S, Silver.				6.00
Theodore Roosevelt National Park (North Dakota)				
2016P		$0.25	$0.30	
2016D		0.25	0.30	
2016S				1.50
2016S, Silver.				6.00
Ft. Moultrie at Ft. Sumter Nat'l Monument (South Carolina)				
2016P		0.25	0.30	
2016D		0.25	0.30	
2016S				1.50
2016S, Silver.				6.00

The half dollar, authorized by the Act of April 2, 1792, was not minted until December 1794. The weight of the half dollar was 208 grains and its fineness .8924 when first issued. This standard was not changed until 1837 when the Act of January 18, 1837, specified 206-1/4 grains, .900 fine. This fineness continued in use until 1965.

Arrows at the date in 1853 indicate the reduction of weight to 192 grains. During that year only, rays were added to the reverse. Arrows remained in 1854 and 1855. In 1873 the weight was raised by .9 grains and arrows were again placed at the date.

FLOWING HAIR (1794–1795)

AG-3 About Good: Clear enough to identify.
G-4 Good: Date and letters sufficient to be legible. Main devices outlined, but lacking in detail.
VG-8 Very Good: Major details discernible. Letters well formed but worn.
F-12 Fine: Hair ends distinguishable. Top hair lines visible, but otherwise worn smooth.
VF-20 Very Fine: Some detail visible in hair in center; other details more bold.
EF-40 Extremely Fine: Hair above head and down neck detailed, with slight wear.
AU-50 About Uncirculated: All hair visible; slight wear on bust of Liberty and on top edges of eagle's wings, head, and breast.

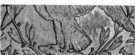

1795, 2 Leaves Under Each Wing

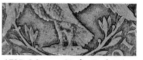

1795, 3 Leaves Under Each Wing

	Mintage	AG-3	G-4	VG-8	F-12	VF-20	EF-40	AU-50
1794	23,464	$1,500	$3,250	$4,500	$7,500	$15,000	$27,500	$45,000
1795	299,680	350	600	900	1,500	2,750	7,000	12,000
1795, Recut Date	*	350	600	900	1,500	3,500	7,500	14,000
1795, 3 Leaves Under Each Wing	*	800	1,600	2,000	3,250	5,000	12,000	25,000

* Included in number above.

DRAPED BUST (1796–1807)

AG-3 About Good: Clear enough to identify.
G-4 Good: Date and letters sufficiently clear to be legible. Main devices outlined, but lacking in detail.
VG-8 Very Good: Major details discernible. Letters well formed but worn.
F-12 Fine: Hair ends distinguishable. Top hair lines visible, but otherwise worn smooth.
VF-20 Very Fine: Right side of drapery slightly worn. Left side to curls smooth.
EF-40 Extremely Fine: All lines in drapery on bust distinctly visible around to hair curls.
AU-50 About Uncirculated: Slight trace of wear on cheek, hair, and shoulder.

Small Eagle Reverse (1796–1797)

1796, 16 Stars

1797, 15 Stars

See next page for chart.

	Mintage	AG-3	G-4	VG-8	F-12	VF-20	EF-40	AU-50
1796, All kinds.	3,918							
1796, 15 Stars		$10,000	$22,500	$28,000	$35,000	$50,000	$75,000	$120,000
1796, 16 Stars		10,000	22,500	27,500	35,000	50,000	75,000	120,000
1797, 15 Stars		10,000	25,000	30,000	40,000	55,000	77,500	120,000

Heraldic Eagle Reverse (1801–1807)

1805, 5 Over 4

1806, 6 Over 5

	Mintage	G-4	VG-8	F-12	VF-20	EF-40	AU-50	MS-60
1801	30,289	$600	$900	$1,500	$2,250	$3,750	$10,000	$30,000
1802	29,890	600	950	1,600	2,300	4,500	8,500	27,500
1803	188,234	150	225	325	550	1,300	2,750	8,500
1805, All kinds.	211,722							
1805, 5 Over 4		175	400	700	1,100	2,000	4,000	13,500
1805, Normal Date		125	160	225	450	1,250	3,250	12,000
1806, All kinds.	839,576							
1806, Normal Date		125	160	200	450	1,250	3,250	7,500
1806, 6 Over 5		125	160	200	450	1,250	3,250	9,500
1806, 6 Over Inverted 6.		225	325	650	1,000	2,250	4,500	9,000
1807	301,076	125	160	200	450	1,250	3,250	6,000

CAPPED BUST, LETTERED EDGE (1807–1836)

John Reich designed this capped-head concept of Liberty. Reich's design of Liberty facing left was used on all U.S. silver denominations for the next 30 years.

G-4 Good: Date and letters legible. Bust worn smooth with outline distinct.

VG-8 Very Good: LIBERTY faint. Legends distinguishable. Clasp at shoulder visible; curl above it nearly smooth.

F-12 Fine: Clasp and adjacent curl clearly outlined with slight details.

VF-20 Very Fine: Clasp at shoulder clear. Wear visible on highest point of curl. Hair over brow distinguishable.

EF-40 Extremely Fine: Clasp and adjacent curl fairly sharp. Brow and hair above distinct. Curls well defined.

AU-50 About Uncirculated: Trace of wear on hair over eye and over ear.

MS-60 Uncirculated: No trace of wear. Light blemishes. Possible slide marks from storage handling.

MS-63 Choice Uncirculated: Some distracting contact marks or blemishes in prime focal areas. Impaired luster possible.

First Style (1807–1808)

	Mintage	G-4	VG-8	F-12	VF-20	EF-40	AU-50	MS-60	MS-63
1807	750,500	$85	$125	$400	$500	$800	$1,600	$3,500	$6,500
1808, 8 Over 7	*	50	65	85	125	425	800	1,750	3,750
1808	1,368,600	40	50	55	85	225	750	1,400	2,500

* Included in number below.

Remodeled Portrait and Eagle (1809–1836)

	Mintage	G-4	VG-8	F-12	VF-20	EF-40	AU-50	MS-60	MS-63
1809	1,405,810	$40	$50	$55	$80	$250	$425	$1,100	$2,500
1810	1,276,276	40	55	65	85	250	400	1,000	2,750
1811	1,203,644	40	55	55	70	225	325	1,000	2,000

1812, 2 Over 1	1813, 50 C. Over UNI	1814, 4 Over 3

	Mintage	G-4	VG-8	F-12	VF-20	EF-40	AU-50	MS-60	MS-63
1812, All kinds	1,628,059								
1812, 2 Over 1		$45	$60	$80	$125	$225	$475	$1,500	$4,500
1812		40	50	65	80	225	525	1,000	1,900
1813	1,241,903	40	50	55	75	275	450	1,750	2,750
1813, 50 C. Over UNI	*	50	65	80	110	225	600	1,200	3,250
1814, All kinds	1,039,075								
1814, 4 Over 3		60	80	100	135	550	650	1,400	3,500
1814		40	50	60	100	550	650	1,000	2,000

* Included in number above.

1817, 7 Over 3	1817, 7 Over 4	1817, "Punctuated" Date

	Mintage	G-4	VG-8	F-12	VF-20	EF-40	AU-50	MS-60	MS-63
1815, 5 Over 2	47,150	$750	$1,000	$2,250	$2,500	$4,000	$7,000	$10,000	$25,000
1817, All kinds	1,215,567								
1817, 7 Over 3		65	100	225	25	475	1,000	2,250	5,500
1817, 7 Over 4 (8 known)				80,000	110,000	150,000			
1817, Dated 181.7		40	50	55	70	150	550	850	1,750
1817		40	50	55	70	150	550	850	1,750

1818, 2nd 8 Over 7   1819, 9 Over 8   1820, 20 Over 19

	Mintage	G-4	VG-8	F-12	VF-20	EF-40	AU-50	MS-60	MS-63
1818, 2nd 8 Over 7	*	$55	$65	$70	$90	$160	$475	$1,000	$3,250
1818	1,960,322	40	50	55	70	175	250	825	1,750
1819, 9 Over 8	*	40	55	60	120	175	375	900	2,200
1819	2,208,000	40	50	55	120	200	325	825	1,600
1820, 20 Over 19	*	55	70	80	125	225	600	1,350	3,000
1820	751,122	40	55	60	85	200	350	825	2,000
1821	1,305,797	40	55	55	70	225	375	1,000	2,000
1822	1,559,573	40	50	55	70	175	325	825	1,650
1823	1,694,200	40	50	55	65	175	750	925	1,750

* Included in number below.

"Various Dates" Probably 4 Over 2 Over 0.   1824, 4 Over 1   1828, Curl Base, Knob 2   1828, Square Base 2

	Mintage	G-4	VG-8	F-12	VF-20	EF-40	AU-50	MS-60	MS-63
1824, All kinds	3,504,954								
1824, 4 Over Various Dates		$40	$50	$55	$60	$110	$275	$825	$1,500
1824, 4 Over 1		45	55	60	70	125	275	825	2,000
1824		40	50	55	60	110	275	825	1,500
1825	2,943,166	35	50	55	60	110	250	825	1,500
1826	4,004,180	35	50	55	60	110	250	825	1,500
1827, All kinds	5,493,400								
1827, 7 Over 6		55	60	70	80	130	250	825	1,600
1827		35	50	55	60	150	225	825	1,500
1828, All kinds	3,075,200								
1828, Curl Base No Knob 2		40	50	55	65	110	250	825	1,550
1828, Curl Base Knob 2		40	50	55	65	110	250	825	1,550
1828, Square Base 2		40	50	55	65	125	250	825	1,550
1829, 9 Over 7	*	40	55	60	70	125	250	825	2,250
1829	3,712,156	35	45	50	60	110	225	800	1,350
1830	4,764,800	35	45	50	60	110	225	800	1,350
1831	5,873,660	35	45	50	60	110	225	800	1,350
1832	4,797,000	35	45	50	60	110	225	800	1,350
1833	5,206,000	35	45	50	60	110	225	800	1,350
1834	6,412,004	35	45	50	60	110	225	800	1,350
1835	5,352,006	35	45	50	60	110	225	800	1,350
1836	6,545,000	35	45	50	60	110	225	800	1,350
1836, 50 Over 00	**	50	55	65	90	175	450	1,100	2,250

* Included in number below. ** Included in number above.

CAPPED BUST, REEDED EDGE (1836–1839)

G-4 Good: LIBERTY barely discernible on headband.
VG-8 Very Good: Some letters in LIBERTY clear.
F-12 Fine: LIBERTY complete but faint.
VF-20 Very Fine: LIBERTY sharp. Shoulder clasp clear.
EF-40 Extremely Fine: LIBERTY sharp and strong. Hair details visible.
AU-50 About Uncirculated: Slight trace of wear on cap, cheek, and hair above forehead, and on eagle's claws, wing tops, and head.
MS-60 Uncirculated: No trace of wear. Light blemishes.
MS-63 Choice Uncirculated: Some distracting marks or blemishes in focal areas. Impaired luster possible.

Reverse 50 CENTS (1836–1837)

	Mintage	G-4	VG-8	F-12	VF-20	EF-40	AU-50	MS-60	MS-63
1836	1,200+	$650	$750	$1,250	$1,500	$2,500	$3,750	$6,500	$12,500
1837	3,629,820	35	45	55	75	135	275	825	1,750

Reverse HALF DOL. (1838–1839)

On half dollars of 1838 and 1839, the mintmark appears on the obverse; on those thereafter, through 1915, it is on the reverse.

	Mintage	G-4	VG-8	F-12	VF-20	EF-40	AU-50	MS-60	MS-63
1838	3,546,000	$35	$45	$55	$75	$135	$275	$825	$1,750
1838O	20						200,000	300,000	
1839	1,392,976	35	45	55	75	135	275	825	1,750
1839O	116,000	175	300	600	800	1,250	1,500	3,250	6,000

LIBERTY SEATED (1839–1891)

G-4 Good: Scant rim. LIBERTY on shield worn off. Date and letters legible.
VG-8 Very Good: Rim fairly defined. Some letters in LIBERTY evident.
F-12 Fine: LIBERTY complete, but weak.
VF-20 Very Fine: LIBERTY mostly sharp.
EF-40 Extremely Fine: LIBERTY entirely sharp. Scroll edges and clasp distinct.
AU-50 About Uncirculated: Slight wear on Liberty's breast and knees; eagle's head, claws, and wing tops.
MS-60 Uncirculated: No trace of wear. Light blemishes.
MS-63 Choice Uncirculated: Some distracting blemishes in prime focal areas. Impaired luster possible.
PF-63 Choice Proof: Reflective surfaces with only a few blemishes in secondary focal places. No major flaws.

Variety 1 – No Motto Above Eagle (1839–1853)

1842, Small Date

1842, Medium Date

No Drapery From Elbow

Drapery From Elbow (Starting 1839)

	Mintage	G-4	VG-8	F-12	VF-20	EF-40	AU-50	MS-60	MS-63
1839, No Drapery From Elbow . . . . . *		$35	$80	$225	$375	$800	$2,000	$4,500	$16,500
1839, Drapery	1,972,400	25	40	45	65	150	300	800	1,500
1840	1,435,008	30	40	40	65	175	250	500	1,050
18400	855,100	30	40	60	95	150	300	800	2,650
1841	310,000	25	35	55	85	200	450	875	1,750
18410	401,000	25	40	70	95	175	450	750	2,250
1842, Small Date	2,012,764	25	40	45	60	100	250	1,000	1,750
1842, Medium Date . . . . **		25	40	40	75	120	225	500	1,000
18420, Small Date	754,000	550	650	900	1,400	3,000	4,500	10,500	22,000
18420, Medium Date . . . . **		25	40	45	50	150	275	875	3,250
1843	3,844,000	30	35	40	60	80	150	375	1,000
18430	2,268,000	35	40	45	50	100	225	550	2,250
1844	1,766,000	30	35	40	50	100	150	375	950
18440	2,005,000	25	35	45	55	120	200	400	1,250
1845	589,000	30	45	50	70	110	175	575	2,000
18450	2,094,000	25	40	40	60	100	180	400	1,000
1846	2,210,000	25	40	45	50	100	225	600	900
1846, 6 Over Horizontal 6 . . . . **		80	110	165	325	500	950	3,000	5,750
18460	2,304,000	25	40	45	50	120	180	850	1,050
1847	1,156,000	25	35	40	50	110	150	300	1,000
18470	2,584,000	30	45	45	50	100	190	375	1,750
1848	580,000	30	40	55	95	150	300	600	1,250
18480	3,180,000	25	35	40	50	120	225	475	1,750
1849	1,252,000	25	45	50	50	100	200	600	1,500
18490	2,310,000	35	40	45	60	100	180	600	1,500
1850	227,000	150	225	350	425	525	750	1,310	2,500
18500	2,456,000	30	35	45	55	110	210	650	1,000
1851	200,750	650	700	725	775	1,100	1,350	2,500	3,500
18510	402,000	35	45	100	115	160	275	800	1,750
1852	77,130	275	400	475	625	850	1,100	1,650	1,850
18520	144,000	175	250	400	600	850	1,300	3,000	5,000
18530 (4 known)		125,000	175,000	250,000					

* Included in number below. **Included in number above.

Variety 2 – Arrows at Date, Rays Around Eagle (1853)

	Mintage	G-4	VG-8	F-12	VF-20	EF-40	AU-50	MS-60	MS-63
1853	3,532,708	$25	$30	$45	$65	$160	$375	$1,100	$2,000
1853O	1,328,000	30	40	55	70	175	475	1,650	2,750

Variety 3 – Arrows at Date, No Rays (1854–1855)

	Mintage	G-4	VG-8	F-12	VF-20	EF-40	AU-50	MS-60	MS-63
1854	2,982,000	$25	$30	$45	$50	$80	$200	$375	$900
1854O	5,240,000	25	30	40	50	80	200	375	900
1855, Over 1854	*	40	50	110	200	225	375	1,250	2,000
1855	759,500	25	30	40	50	90	200	400	1,100
1855O	3,688,000	25	30	40	50	90	200	375	900
1855S	129,950	275	600	825	1,100	2,250	4,500	22,500	27,500

* Included in number below.

Variety 1 Resumed, With Weight Standard of Variety 2 (1856–1866)

	Mintage	G-4	VG-8	F-12	VF-20	EF-40	AU-50	MS-60	MS-63	PF-63
1856	938,000	$25	$40	$40	$55	$75	$150	$350	$700	
1856O	2,658,000	25	40	45	60	75	150	325	700	
1856S	211,000	30	45	80	125	400	700	2,250	6,750	
1857	1,988,000	25	35	40	55	75	150	325	700	
1857O	818,000	25	35	40	50	75	150	600	2,000	
1857S	158,000	40	50	100	150	475	700	2,250	6,750	
1858 (300+)	4,225,700	25	35	40	50	75	150	325	700	$1,250
1858O	7,294,000	25	35	40	50	75	150	325	700	
1858S	476,000	25	35	45	70	175	225	625	2,250	
1859 (800)	747,200	25	35	40	50	75	150	325	700	1,200
1859O	2,834,000	25	35	40	60	75	150	325	700	
1859S	566,000	25	40	45	65	125	125	525	2,000	
1860 (1,000)	302,700	30	35	45	50	80	150	450	700	1,200
1860O	1,290,000	25	35	40	55	75	150	325	700	
1860S	472,000	25	45	50	65	120	175	500	2,000	
1861 (1,000)	2,887,400	25	40	50	65	100	200	325	700	1,200
1861O	2,532,633	40	45	55	65	100	175	400	700	
1861S	939,500	30	40	50	65	100	175	450	1,350	
1862 (550)	253,000	25	45	55	70	100	175	350	700	1,200
1862S	1,352,000	30	50	60	60	100	150	500	1,100	
1863 (460)	503,200	25	45	55	80	140	200	350	700	1,200
1863S	916,000	25	45	55	60	120	175	400	1,050	
1864 (470)	379,100	25	40	85	200	275	400	700	1,050	1,200
1864S	658,000	30	40	50	60	150	200	550	1,750	
1865 (500)	511,400	25	45	55	55	140	225	600	1,000	1,200
1865S	675,000	30	45	55	60	130	200	1,200	2,250	
1866S, No Motto	60,000	300	400	625	800	1,500	2,250	4,000	12,500	

Variety 4 – Motto Above Eagle (1866–1873)

	Mintage	G-4	VG-8	F-12	VF-20	EF-40	AU-50	MS-60	MS-63	PF-63
1866 . . . . . . (725)	744,900	$30	$45	$50	$60	$85	$150	$325	$1,150	$850
1866S	994,000	25	40	45	55	120	150	375	1,150	
1867 . . . . . . (625)	449,300	25	35	50	100	120	175	325	800	850
1867S	1,196,000	25	35	55	60	100	175	375	1,150	
1868 . . . . . . (600)	417,600	25	35	55	80	125	175	350	700	850
1868S	1,160,000	25	35	40	55	100	175	350	1,250	
1869 . . . . . . (600)	795,300	25	35	40	60	80	175	325	700	850
1869S	656,000	25	35	40	60	100	175	525	1,500	
1870 . . . . (1,000)	633,900	25	35	45	60	110	150	375	700	850
1870CC	54,617	850	1,750	3,250	4,500	7,500	20,000	—	—	
1870S	1,004,000	25	35	55	55	125	250	750	2,250	
1871 . . . . . . (960) . . .	1,203,600	25	30	45	55	100	175	350	700	850
1871CC	153,950	275	450	700	475	2,250	3,750	12,000	30,000	
1871S	2,178,000	25	35	45	55	100	175	350	1,000	
1872 . . . . . . (950)	880,600	25	30	40	55	100	200	350	850	850
1872CC	257,000	150	250	400	675	1,500	2,750	10,500	42,500	
1872S	580,000	25	35	45	65	120	200	675	1,500	
1873 . . . . . . (600) . . .	801,200	25	30	45	50	80	175	325	1,050	850
1873CC	122,500	225	400	525	750	2,250	3,750	6,250	30,000	

Variety 5 – Arrows at Date (1873–1874)

	Mintage	G-4	VG-8	F-12	VF-20	EF-40	AU-50	MS-60	MS-63	PF-63
1873 . . . . . . (800) . . .	1,815,200	$25	$30	$45	$55	$160	$300	$600	$1,250	$1,500
1873CC	214,560	160	325	500	800	1,350	2,250	6,000	11,500	
1873S	228,000	40	75	120	140	250	500	1,500	5,250	
1874 . . . . . . (700) . . .	2,359,600	25	30	45	55	160	300	600	1,250	1,500
1874CC	59,000	650	900	1,200	1,750	3,750	5,750	10,000	17,500	
1874S	394,000	35	110	120	130	200	400	1,100	2,250	

Variety 4 Resumed, With Weight Standard of Variety 5 (1875–1891)

	Mintage	G-4	VG-8	F-12	VF-20	EF-40	AU-50	MS-60	MS-63	PF-63
1875 . . . . . . (700)	6,026,800	$25	$30	$40	$50	$75	$140	$300	$600	$750
1875CC	1,008,000	35	55	80	100	120	225	625	1,450	
1875S	3,200,000	25	30	45	50	75	140	300	600	
1876 . . . . (1,150) . .	8,418,000	25	35	45	50	75	140	300	600	750
1876CC	1,956,000	35	50	65	80	110	200	450	900	
1876S	4,528,000	25	35	40	50	75	140	275	600	
1877 . . . . . . (510)	8,304,000	25	30	40	50	75	140	275	600	750
1877CC	1,420,000	35	50	65	110	130	175	425	900	
1877S	5,356,000	25	30	40	50	75	140	275	600	
1878 . . . . . . (800)	1,377,600	25	50	80	85	90	160	300	600	750
1878CC	62,000	500	800	1,500	1,750	2,500	3,750	5,500	14,000	
1878S	12,000	20,000	27,500	30,000	31,000	47,500	52,500	62,500	115,000	
1879 . . . . (1,100)	4,800	200	250	300	350	450	525	600	1,000	750
1880 . . . . (1,355)	8,400	175	200	275	325	450	500	575	1,000	750
1881 . . . . . . (975)	10,000	175	200	275	350	450	500	550	975	750
1882 . . . . (1,100)	4,400	225	265	300	350	450	500	600	1,000	750
1883 . . . . (1,039)	8,000	225	250	300	350	450	500	575	1,000	750
1884 . . . . . . (875)	4,400	265	300	325	350	450	500	575	1,000	750
1885 . . . . . . (930)	5,200	275	300	325	350	450	500	600	1,000	750
1886 . . . . . . (886)	5,000	300	375	400	425	475	525	600	1,000	750
1887 . . . . . . (710)	5,000	375	425	475	525	575	650	675	1,000	750
1888 . . . . . . (832)	12,001	185	225	275	300	450	500	600	1,000	750
1889 . . . . . . (711)	12,000	200	250	275	325	450	550	650	1,000	750
1890 . . . . . . (590)	12,000	200	250	275	300	400	450	600	1,000	750
1891 . . . . . . (600)	200,000	40	50	75	85	110	140	350	900	750

BARBER OR LIBERTY HEAD (1892–1915)

Like the dime and quarter dollar, this type was designed by U.S. Mint chief engraver Charles E. Barber, whose initial B is on the truncation of the neck.

G-4 Good: Date and legends legible. LIBERTY worn off headband.

VG-8 Very Good: Some letters legible in LIBERTY.

F-12 Fine: LIBERTY nearly completely legible, but worn.

VF-20 Very Fine: All letters in LIBERTY evenly plain.

EF-40 Extremely Fine: LIBERTY bold, and its ribbon distinct.

AU-50 About Uncirculated: Slight trace of wear above forehead, leaf tips, and cheek, and on eagle's head, tail, and wing tips.

MS-60 Uncirculated: No trace of wear. Light blemishes.

MS-63 Choice Uncirculated: Some distracting contact marks or blemishes in prime focal areas. Impaired luster possible.

PF-63 Choice Proof: Reflective surfaces with only a few blemishes in secondary focal places. No major flaws.

Mintmark location on reverse, below eagle.

See next page for chart.

	Mintage	G-4	VG-8	F-12	VF-20	EF-40	AU-50	MS-60	MS-63	PF-63
1892 . . . . (1,245)	934,000	$15	$18	$40	$75	$125	$225	$400	$700	$800
1892O	390,000	190	225	300	375	375	450	525	1,250	
1892S	1,029,028	140	180	235	350	340	475	625	1,250	
1893 . . . . . . (792)	1,826,000	13	18	45	80	125	225	400	850	800
1893O	1,389,000	18	35	70	120	200	275	500	950	
1893S	740,000	75	125	325	450	775	950	1,350	2,750	
1894 . . . . . . (972)	1,148,000	15	25	60	120	160	225	400	700	800
1894O	2,138,000	13	18	45	100	180	225	400	700	
1894S	4,048,690	13	18	40	75	135	225	400	950	
1895 . . . . . . (880)	1,834,338	13	15	40	75	125	225	400	700	800
1895O	1,766,000	20	35	70	100	150	225	425	1,000	
1895S	1,108,086	15	25	70	125	180	225	425	800	
1896 . . . . . . (762)	950,000	20	25	55	100	150	225	425	700	800
1896O	924,000	20	25	100	300	440	650	2,800	6,250	
1896S	1,140,948	45	60	115	200	500	750	1,500	2,250	
1897 . . . . . . (731)	2,480,000	13	15	30	70	125	225	400	700	800
1897O	632,000	70	110	300	500	650	825	1,100	2,250	
1897S	933,900	70	110	225	350	450	800	1,500	2,500	
1898 . . . . . . (735)	2,956,000	13	11	30	70	125	225	400	700	800
1898O	874,000	18	45	125	225	350	375	750	2,000	
1898S	2,358,550	13	20	45	90	200	300	650	2,500	
1899 . . . . . . (846)	5,538,000	13	11	30	70	140	225	400	700	800
1899O	1,724,000	13	20	40	90	175	300	450	900	
1899S	1,686,411	13	20	50	90	125	225	400	1,300	
1900 . . . . . . (912)	4,762,000	8	11	30	70	125	225	400	700	800
1900O	2,744,000	8	11	30	90	175	225	550	2,000	
1900S	2,560,322	8	11	30	70	150	225	400	1,500	
1901 . . . . . . (813)	4,268,000	8	11	30	70	125	225	400	700	800
1901O	1,124,000	8	12	40	125	600	850	1,500	3,000	
1901S	847,044	8	30	100	225	750	1,000	2,000	6,000	
1902 . . . . . . (777)	4,922,000	8	11	30	70	125	225	400	700	800
1902O	2,526,000	8	11	30	70	125	225	500	2,250	
1902S	1,460,670	8	11	30	90	175	225	500	1,500	
1903 . . . . . . (755)	2,278,000	8	11	30	70	125	225	400	1,000	800
1903O	2,100,000	8	11	30	70	125	225	400	1,000	
1903S	1,920,772	8	11	30	75	150	275	400	1,100	
1904 . . . . . . (670)	2,992,000	8	11	30	70	125	225	400	700	800
1904O	1,117,600	8	12	45	125	250	350	850	2,500	
1904S	553,038	20	50	175	450	1,750	3,500	7,500	12,500	
1905 . . . . . . (727)	662,000	10	12	50	110	150	225	400	1,000	800
1905O	505,000	10	20	60	125	200	225	450	1,000	
1905S	2,494,000	8	11	30	75	125	225	400	1,100	
1906 . . . . . . (675)	2,638,000	8	11	30	70	125	225	400	700	800
1906D	4,028,000	8	11	30	70	125	225	400	700	
1906O	2,446,000	8	11	30	70	125	225	400	900	
1906S	1,740,154	8	11	30	70	125	225	400	800	
1907 . . . . . . (575)	2,598,000	8	11	30	70	125	225	400	700	800
1907D	3,856,000	8	11	30	70	125	225	400	700	
1907O	3,946,600	8	11	30	70	125	225	400	700	
1907S	1,250,000	8	20	40	100	225	425	750	3,750	
1908 . . . . . . (545)	1,354,000	8	11	30	70	125	225	400	700	800
1908D	3,280,000	8	11	30	70	125	225	400	700	

	Mintage	G-4	VG-8	F-12	VF-20	EF-40	AU-50	MS-60	MS-63	PF-63
1908O	5,360,000	$8	$11	$30	$70	$125	$225	$400	$700	
1908S	1,644,828	8	11	40	100	175	225	500	1,250	
1909 . . . . . (650)	2,368,000	8	11	30	70	125	225	400	700	$800
1909O	925,400	8	11	40	110	250	475	900	1,000	
1909S	1,764,000	8	11	35	70	125	225	400	700	
1910 . . . . . (551)	418,000	10	15	45	110	200	225	400	700	800
1910S	1,948,000	8	12	30	70	125	225	400	1,250	
1911 . . . . . (543)	1,406,000	8	11	30	70	125	225	400	700	800
1911D	695,080	8	11	30	70	125	225	400	700	
1911S	1,272,000	8	11	30	70	125	225	400	850	
1912 . . . . . (700)	1,550,000	8	11	30	70	125	225	400	700	800
1912D	2,300,800	8	11	30	70	125	225	400	700	
1912S	1,370,000	8	11	30	70	125	225	400	700	
1913 . . . . . (627)	188,000	40	50	125	275	400	525	900	1,200	800
1913D	534,000	8	15	30	70	125	225	400	700	
1913S	604,000	8	15	30	70	125	225	400	850	
1914 . . . . . (380)	124,230	65	100	175	325	475	650	1,150	1,350	800
1914S	992,000	8	11	30	70	125	225	400	700	
1915 . . . . . (450)	138,000	50	75	165	225	350	550	850	1,250	800
1915D	1,170,400	8	11	30	70	125	225	400	700	
1915S	1,604,000	8	11	30	70	125	225	400	700	

LIBERTY WALKING (1916–1947)

This type was designed by American sculptor Adolph A. Weinman, whose monogram, AW, appears under the tip of the tail feathers. On the 1916 coins and some of the 1917 coins, the mintmark is located on the obverse below the motto.

G-4 Good: Rims defined. Motto IN GOD WE TRUST legible.

VG-8 Very Good: Motto distinct. About half of skirt lines at left clear.

F-12 Fine: All skirt lines evident, but worn in spots. Clear details in sandal below motto.

VF-20 Very Fine: Skirt lines sharp, including leg area. Little wear on breast and right arm.

EF-40 Extremely Fine: All skirt lines bold.

AU-50 About Uncirculated: Slight trace of wear on Liberty's head, knee, and breast tips and on eagle's claws and head.

MS-60 Uncirculated: No trace of wear. Light blemishes.

MS-63 Choice Uncirculated: Some distracting contact marks or blemishes in prime focal areas. Impaired luster possible.

PF-63 Choice Proof: Reflective surfaces with only a few blemishes in secondary focal places. No major flaws.

PF-65 Gem Proof: Brilliant surfaces with no noticeable blemishes or flaws. A few scattered, barely noticeable marks or hairlines possible.

1916–1917

1917–1947

Mintmark Locations

See next page for chart.

Coin dealers often pay more than the Mint State prices shown for choice Uncirculated examples that are well struck.

	Mintage	G-4	VG-8	F-12	VF-20	EF-40	AU-50	MS-60	MS-63
1916	608,000	$25	$30	$45	$90	$125	$175	$250	$450
1916D, Obverse Mintmark	1,014,400	25	30	40	70	115	145	250	475
1916S, Obverse Mintmark	508,000	50	65	125	250	375	450	750	1,400
1917	12,292,000	10	10	10	12	20	40	75	125
1917D, Obverse Mintmark	765,400	12	16	40	80	125	175	425	800
1917D, Reverse Mintmark	1,940,000	10	10	25	65	175	325	650	1,500
1917S, Obverse Mintmark	952,000	15	22	75	200	400	700	1,750	3,750
1917S, Reverse Mintmark	5,554,000	10	10	10	17	38	125	375	1,250
1918	6,634,000	10	10	10	35	70	175	375	850
1918D	3,853,040	10	13	20	50	125	300	850	2,750
1918S	10,282,000	10	10	10	20	45	100	325	1,300
1919	962,000	15	18	40	150	300	675	1,500	2,500
1919D	1,165,000	15	20	50	175	450	1,250	3,250	9,500
1919S	1,552,000	10	18	35	175	475	900	2,750	6,250
1920	6,372,000	10	10	10	25	45	85	275	500
1920D	1,551,000	10	10	35	125	275	550	1,600	3,250
1920S	4,624,000	10	10	10	50	125	375	700	2,000
1921	246,000	75	100	200	475	1,250	2,000	4,250	5,500
1921D	208,000	125	200	350	575	1,750	3,500	6,250	10,000
1921S	548,000	20	30	125	550	2,750	5,500	15,000	25,000
1923S	2,178,000	10	10	15	60	300	750	1,250	3,250
1927S	2,392,000	8	8	10	25	100	300	750	1,500
1928S	1,940,000	8	8	10	35	115	350	800	2,250
1929D	1,001,200	8	8	10	20	50	110	275	600
1929S	1,902,000	8	8	10	15	60	125	300	750
1933S	1,786,000	8	8	10	15	40	160	450	1,000
1934	6,964,000	6	6	7	8	9	12	40	50
1934D	2,361,000	6	6	7	8	15	45	80	175
1934S	3,652,000	6	6	7	8	16	55	200	550
1935	9,162,000	6	6	7	8	9	15	25	40
1935D	3,003,800	6	6	7	8	15	30	75	175
1935S	3,854,000	6	6	7	8	25	55	150	275

	Mintage	G-4	VG-8	F-12	VF-20	EF-40	AU-50	MS-60	MS-63	PF-63	PF-65
1936 ... (3,901)	12,614,000	$6	$6	$7	$8	$9	$12	$25	$40	$1,000	$2,000
1936D	4,252,400	6	6	7	8	10	25	45	60		
1936S	3,884,000	6	6	7	8	15	30	80	125		
1937 ... (5,728)	9,522,000	6	6	7	8	10	12	25	35	325	600
1937D	1,676,000	6	6	7	8	15	50	120	175		
1937S	2,090,000	6	6	7	8	10	30	85	125		
1938 ... (8,152)	4,110,000	6	6	7	8	9	20	35	90	275	400
1938D	491,600	30	50	55	60	80	140	300	375		
1939 ... (8,808)	6,812,000	6	6	7	8	9	15	25	35	300	400
1939D	4,267,800	6	6	7	8	9	12	25	40		
1939S	2,552,000	6	6	7	8	10	40	90	100		

	Mintage	VG-8	F-12	VF-20	EF-40	AU-50	MS-60	MS-63	PF-63	PF-65
1940 ... (11,279)	9,156,000	$6	$6	$7	$8	$12	$20	$30	$250	$350
1940S	4,550,000	6	6	7	8	12	25	35		
1941 ... (15,412)	24,192,000	6	6	7	8	12	20	30	250	350
1941D	11,248,400	6	6	7	8	12	20	35		
1941S	8,098,000	6	6	7	8	12	40	55		
1942 ... (21,120)	47,818,000	6	6	7	8	12	20	30	250	350

	Mintage	VG-8	F-12	VF-20	EF-40	AU-50	MS-60	MS-63
1942D	10,973,800	$6	$6	$7	$8	$12	$20	$45
1942S	12,708,000	6	6	7	8	12	20	35
1943	53,190,000	6	6	7	8	12	20	30
1943D	11,346,000	6	6	7	8	12	22	35
1943S	13,450,000	6	6	7	8	12	22	30
1944	28,206,000	6	6	7	8	12	20	30
1944D	9,769,000	6	6	7	8	12	20	35
1944S	8,904,000	6	6	7	8	12	22	30
1945	31,502,000	6	6	7	8	12	20	30
1945D	9,966,800	6	6	7	8	12	20	30
1945S	10,156,000	6	6	7	8	12	22	30
1946	12,118,000	6	6	7	8	12	20	30
1946D	2,151,000	6	6	7	8	12	25	30
1946S	3,724,000	6	6	7	8	12	30	35
1947	4,094,000	6	6	7	8	12	25	30
1947D	3,900,600	6	6	7	8	12	25	30

FRANKLIN (1948–1963)

The Benjamin Franklin half dollar and the Roosevelt dime were both designed by U.S. Mint chief engraver John R. Sinnock. His initials appear below the shoulder.

VF-20 Very Fine: At least half of the lower and upper incused lines on rim of Liberty Bell on reverse visible.

EF-40 Extremely Fine: Wear spots at top of end of Franklin's curls and hair at back of ears. Wear evident at top and on lettering of Liberty Bell.

MS-60 Uncirculated: No trace of wear. Light blemishes.

MS-63 Choice Uncirculated: Some distracting contact marks or blemishes in prime focal areas. Impaired luster possible.

MS-65 Gem Uncirculated: Only light, scattered contact marks that are not distracting. Strong luster, good eye appeal.

PF-63 Choice Proof: Reflective surfaces with only a few blemishes in secondary focal places. No major flaws.

PF-65 Gem Proof: Brilliant surfaces with no noticeable blemishes or flaws. A few scattered, barely noticeable marks or hairlines possible.

Mintmark Location

Coin dealers usually pay more than the Mint State prices shown for well-struck Uncirculated halves with full bell lines.

	Mintage	VF-20	EF-40	MS-60	MS-63	MS-65	PF-63	PF-65
1948	3,006,814	$6	$6	$10	$12	$35		
1948D	4,028,600	6	6	10	12	60		
1949	5,614,000	6	6	20	30	65		
1949D	4,120,600	6	6	25	30	250		
1949S	3,744,000	6	6	40	45	75		
1950	(51,386)	7,742,123	6	6	12	18	50	$200	$250
1950D	8,031,600	6	6	10	23	110		
1951	(57,500)	16,802,102	6	6	10	10	30	175	200
1951D	9,475,200	6	6	15	18	85		
1951S	13,696,000	6	6	12	15	30		
1952	(81,980)	21,192,093	6	6	9	10	30	80	100
1952D	25,395,600	6	6	9	10	60		
1952S	5,526,000	6	6	35	40	50		

Chart continued on next page.

	Mintage	VF-20	EF-40	MS-60	MS-63	MS-65	PF-63	PF-65
1953 .... (128,800).... 2,668,120		$6	$6	$12	$11	$35	$65	$85
1953D 20,900,400		6	6	10	10	55		
1953S 4,148,000		6	6	15	20	25		
1954 .... (233,300)... 13,188,202		6	6	9	10	20	25	45
1954D 25,445,580		6	6	9	10	40		
1954S 4,993,400		6	6	9	10	20		
1955 .... (378,200).... 2,498,181		6	6	9	13	25	25	40
1956 .... (669,384).... 4,032,000		6	6	9	10	15	15	20
1957 ...(1,247,952).... 5,114,000		6	6	9	10	15	12	15
1957D 19,966,850		6	6	9	10	20		
1958 .... (875,652).... 4,042,000		6	6	9	10	15	12	17
1958D 23,962,412		6	6	9	10	15		
1959 ...(1,149,291).... 6,200,000		6	6	9	10	25	12	14
1959D 13,053,750		6	6	9	10	40		
1960 ...(1,691,602).... 6,024,000		6	6	9	10	45	12	14
1960D 18,215,812		6	6	9	10	100		
1961 ...(3,028,244).... 8,290,000		6	6	9	10	20	12	14
1961D 20,276,442		6	6	9	10	60		
1962 ...(3,218,019).... 9,714,000		6	6	9	10	40	12	14
1962D 35,473,281		6	6	9	10	35		
1963 ...(3,075,645)... 22,164,000		6	6	9	10	15	12	14
1963D 67,069,292		6	6	9	10	15		

KENNEDY (1964 TO DATE)

Gilroy Roberts, chief engraver of the U.S. Mint from 1948 to 1964, designed the obverse of this coin, a tribute to President John F. Kennedy, who was assassinated in November 1963. Roberts's stylized initials are on the truncation of the forceful bust of Kennedy. The reverse, which uses as its motif the eagle from the Seal of the President of the United States, is the work of assistant engraver Frank Gasparro. The Kennedy half dollar was minted in 90% silver in its first year of issue, 1964. From 1965 to 1970 its fineness was reduced to 40% silver. Since 1971 the coin has been struck in copper-nickel (except for certain silver Proofs, 1992 to date). Dates after 2001 have not been released into general circulation, instead being made available in 20-coin rolls, 200-coin bags, and coin sets sold by the Mint. In 2014 a .999 fine gold version was made for collectors, dual-dated 1964–2014 to mark the coin's 50th anniversary.

In the early 1970s an open contest was held to select a new reverse design for the Kennedy half dollar, to celebrate the nation's bicentennial. Seth G. Huntington's winning entry featured a view of Independence Hall in Philadelphia. The Bicentennial half dollars bear the dual date 1776–1976.

Mintmark Location (1964)

Mintmark Location (1968 to Date)

Silver Coinage (1964)

	Mintage	MS-63	PF-63	PF-65
1964 . . . . (3,950,762) 273,304,004		$8	$11	$13
1964D 156,205,446		8		

Silver Clad Coinage (1965–1970)

	Mintage	MS-63	PF-63	PF-65		Mintage	MS-63	PF-63	PF-65
1965	65,879,366	$3			1969D	129,881,800	$3		
1966	108,984,932	3			1969S	(2,934,631)		$3.50	$5
1967	295,046,978	3			1970D	2,150,000	10		
1968D	246,951,930	3			1970S	(2,632,810)		4.00	8
1968S	(3,041,506)		$3.50	$5					

Clad Coinage and Silver Proofs (1971 to Date)

	Mintage	MS-63	PF-63	PF-65		Mintage	MS-63	PF-63	PF-65
1971	155,164,000	$0.55			1973	64,964,000	$0.55		
1971D	302,097,424	0.55			1973D	83,171,400	0.55		
1971S	(3,220,733)		$1.50	$3	1973S	(2,760,339)		$1.50	$2.50
1972	153,180,000	0.60			1974	201,596,000	0.55		
1972D	141,890,000	0.60			1974D	79,066,300	0.55		
1972S	(3,260,996)		1.50	3	1974S	(2,612,568)		1.50	3.00

Bicentennial (1776–1976)

	Mintage	MS-63	PF-63	PF-65
1776–1976, Clad 234,308,000		$0.55		
1776–1976D, Clad 287,565,248		0.55		
1776–1976S, Clad . . . . (7,059,099)			$0.75	$2.50
1776–1976S, Silver 11,000,000		3.00		
1776–1976S, Silver . . . . (4,000,000)			3.50	5.00

Note: Mintage figures for 1976-S silver coins are approximate; many were melted in 1982.

Eagle Reverse Resumed (1977 to Date)

	Mintage	MS-63	PF-63	PF-65		Mintage	MS-63	PF-63	PF-65
1977	43,598,000	$0.60			1979S	(3,677,175)			
1977D	31,449,106	0.60			Type 1			$1.00	$2.00
1977S	(3,251,152)		$1.00	$1.25	Type 2			3.00	6.00
1978	14,350,000	0.60			1980P	44,134,000	$0.55		
1978D	13,765,799	1.00			1980D	33,456,449	0.55		
1978S	(3,127,781)		1.00	1.50	1980S	(3,554,806)		1.00	1.50
1979	68,312,000	0.55			1981P	29,544,000	0.75		
1979D	15,815,422	0.55			1981D	27,839,533	0.55		

Chart continued on next page.

Eagle Reverse Resumed (1977 to Date)

	Mintage	MS-63	PF-63	PF-65
1981S	(4,063,083)			
Type 1			$1.00	$2.00
Type 2			5.00	10.00
1982P	10,819,000	$2.50		
1982D	13,140,102	2.50		
1982S	(3,857,479)		1.00	1.50
1983P	34,139,000	3.00		
1983D	32,472,244	3.50		
1983S	(3,279,126)		1.00	1.75
1984P	26,029,000	0.75		
1984D	26,262,158	0.75		
1984S	(3,065,110)		1.00	2.00
1985P	18,706,962	2.00		
1985D	19,814,034	1.50		
1985S	(3,362,821)		1.00	1.75
1986P	13,107,633	3.00		
1986D	15,336,145	2.50		
1986S	(3,010,497)		3.00	4.50
1987P (a)	2,890,758	2.50		
1987D (a)	2,890,758	2.50		
1987S	(4,227,728)		1.00	1.75
1988P	13,626,000	1.50		
1988D	12,000,096	1.35		
1988S	(3,262,948)		2.00	2.50
1989P	24,542,000	1.00		
1989D	23,000,216	1.10		
1989S	(3,220,194)		1.50	3.00
1990P	22,278,000	1.00		
1990D	20,096,242	1.10		
1990S	(3,299,559)		1.50	2.00
1991P	14,874,000	0.70		
1991D	15,054,678	1.25		
1991S	(2,867,787)		4.00	4.00
1992P	17,628,000	0.50		
1992D	17,000,106	1.10		
1992S	(2,858,981)		2.00	3.00
1992S, Silver	(1,317,579)		10.00	12.00
1993P	15,510,000	0.50		
1993D	15,000,006	0.50		
1993S	(2,633,439)		3.00	5.00
1993S, Silver	(761,353)		10.00	12.00
1994P	23,718,000	0.50		
1994D	23,828,110	0.50		
1994S	(2,484,594)		3.00	4.00
1994S, Silver	(785,329)		10.00	12.00
1995P	26,496,000	0.50		
1995D	26,288,000	0.50		
1995S	(2,117,496)		6.00	8.00
1995S, Silver	(679,985)		15.00	20.00
1996P	24,442,000	0.50		

	Mintage	MS-63	PF-63	PF-65
1996D	24,744,000	$0.50		
1996S	(1,750,244)		$3.00	$5
1996S, Silver	(775,021)		11.00	16
1997P	20,882,000	0.50		
1997D	19,876,000	0.50		
1997S	(2,055,000)		3.00	6
1997S, Silver	(741,678)		20.00	25
1998P	15,646,000	0.50		
1998D	15,064,000	0.50		
1998S	(2,086,507)		3.00	6
1998S, Silver	(878,792)		10.00	11
1998S, Silver, Matte Finish	(62,000)		75.00	85
1999P	8,900,000	0.55		
1999D	10,682,000	0.55		
1999S	(2,543,401)		3.00	5
1999S, Silver	(804,565)		10.00	12
2000P	22,600,000	0.60		
2000D	19,466,000	0.60		
2000S	(3,082,483)		2.00	3
2000S, Silver	(965,421)		8.00	11
2001P	21,200,000	0.55		
2001D	19,504,000	0.55		
2001S	(2,294,909)		3.25	4
2001S, Silver	(889,697)		8.00	11
2002P (a)	3,100,000	0.65		
2002D (a)	2,500,000	0.65		
2002S	(2,319,766)		2.00	3
2002S, Silver	(892,229)		8.00	11
2003P (a)	2,500,000	0.65		
2003D (a)	2,500,000	0.65		
2003S	(2,172,684)		2.00	3
2003S, Silver	(1,125,755)		8.00	11
2004P (a)	2,900,000	0.65		
2004D (a)	2,900,000	0.65		
2004S	(1,789,488)		3.00	7
2004S, Silver	(1,175,934)		8.00	11
2005P	3,800,000	0.65		
2005D	3,500,000	0.65		
2005S	(2,275,000)		2.00	3
2005S, Silver	(1,069,679)		8.00	11
2006P (a)	2,400,000	0.65		
2006D (a)	2,000,000	0.65		
2006S	(2,000,428)		2.00	3
2006S, Silver	(1,054,008)		8.00	11
2007P (a)	2,400,000	0.65		
2007D (a)	2,400,000	0.65		
2007S	(1,702,116)		2.00	3
2007S, Silver	(875,050)		8.00	11
2008P (a)	1,700,000	0.65		

a. Not issued for circulation.

	Mintage	MS-63	PF-63	PF-65
2008D **(a)**	1,700,000	$0.65		
2008S	(1,405,674)		$4	$6
2008S, Silver	(763,887)		8	11
2009P **(a)**	1,900,000	0.65		
2009D **(a)**	1,900,000	0.65		
2009S	(1,482,502)		2	3
2009S, Silver	(697,365)		8	11
2010P **(a)**	1,800,000	0.65		
2010D **(a)**	1,700,000	0.65		
2010S	(1,103,815)		4	6
2010S, Silver	(585,401)		10	12
2011P **(a)**	1,750,000	0.65		
2011D **(a)**	1,700,000	0.65		
2011S	(1,098,835)		4	6
2011S, Silver	(574,175)		12	14
2012P **(a)**	1,800,000	0.65		
2012D **(a)**	1,700,000	0.65		
2012S	(843,705)		12	15
2012S, Silver	(445,612)		75	85
2013P **(a)**	5,000,000	0.65		
2013D **(a)**	4,600,000	0.65		
2013S	(854,785)		3	4

	Mintage	MS-63	PF-63	PF-65
2013S, Silver	(467,691)		$14	$16
2014P **(a,b)**	2,500,000	$0.65		
2014P, Silver **(c)**	(219,173)		18	20
2014D **(a,b)**	2,100,000	0.65		
2014D, Silver **(c)**	(219,173)	18.00		
2014S	(767,977)		2	3
2014S, Silver	(472,107)		10	12
2014S, Silver Enhanced **(c)**	219,173	20.00		
2014W, Reverse Proof, Silver **(c)**	(219,173)		20	22
2014W, 50th Anniversary, Gold **(d)**	(73,722)		950	1,000
2015P **(a)**	2,300,000	0.65		
2015D **(a)**	2,300,000	0.65		
2015S	(669,960)		2	3
2015S, Silver	(352,450)		10	12
2016P **(a)**		0.65		
2016D **(a)**		0.65		
2016S			2	3
2016S, Silver			10	12

a. Not issued for circulation. b. To celebrate the 50th anniversary of the Kennedy half dollar, the U.S. Mint issued an Uncirculated two-coin set featuring a Kennedy half dollar from Philadelphia and one from Denver. c. Featured in the 2014 half dollar silver-coin collection released by the U.S. Mint to commemorate the 50th anniversary of the Kennedy half dollar. d. First gold half dollar offered by the U.S. Mint. It commemorates the 50th anniversary of the first release of the Kennedy half dollar in 1964.

The silver dollar was authorized by Congress April 2, 1792. Its weight was specified at 416 grains and its fineness at .8924. The first issues appeared in 1794, and until 1804 all silver dollars had the value stamped on the edge: HUNDRED CENTS, ONE DOLLAR OR UNIT. After a lapse in coinage of the silver dollar during the period 1804 to 1835, coins were made with either plain (1836 only) or reeded edges and the value was placed on the reverse side.

Mintages shown here are as reported by the Mint for calendar years and do not necessarily refer to the dates on the coins.

The weight was changed by the law of January 18, 1837, to 412-1/2 grains, fineness .900. The coinage was discontinued by the Act of February 12, 1873, and reauthorized by the Act of February 28, 1878. The silver dollar was again discontinued after 1935, and since then copper-nickel and other base-metal pieces have been coined for circulation. (See also Silver Bullion, page 238.)

FLOWING HAIR (1794–1795)

AG-3 About Good: Clear enough to identify.
G-4 Good: Date and letters legible. Main devices outlined, but lacking in detail.
VG-8 Very Good: Major details discernible. Letters well formed but worn.
F-12 Fine: Hair ends distinguishable. Top hair lines visible, but otherwise worn smooth.
VF-20 Very Fine: Some detail visible in hair in center. Other details more bold.
EF-40 Extremely Fine: Hair well defined but with some wear.
AU-50 About Uncirculated: Slight trace of wear on tips of highest curls; breast feathers usually weak.
MS-60 Uncirculated: No trace of wear. Light blemishes.

	Mintage	AG-3	G-4	VG-8	F-12	VF-20	EF-40	AU-50	MS-60
1794	1,758	$25,000	$50,000	$75,000	$88,000	$120,000	$230,000	$360,000	—
1795	160,295	750	1,300	1,600	2,800	4,250	9,000	14,000	$42,500

DRAPED BUST (1795–1804)
Small Eagle Reverse (1795–1798)

AG-3 About Good: Clear enough to identify.
G-4 Good: Bust outlined, no detail. Date legible, some leaves evident.
VG-8 Very Good: Drapery worn except deepest folds. Hair lines smooth.
F-12 Fine: All drapery lines distinguishable. Some detail visible in hair lines near cheek and neck.
VF-20 Very Fine: Left side of drapery worn smooth.
EF-40 Extremely Fine: Drapery distinctly visible. Hair well outlined and detailed.
AU-50 About Uncirculated: Slight trace of wear on the bust shoulder and hair to left of forehead, as well as on eagle's breast and top edges of wings.
MS-60 Uncirculated: No trace of wear. Light blemishes.

	Mintage	AG-3	G-4	VG-8	F-12	VF-20	EF-40	AU-50	MS-60
1795, Bust Type. . *42,738*	$500	$1,250	$1,550	$2,750	$3,750	$7,000	$10,500	$35,000
1796 79,920	500	1,250	1,500	2,750	3,750	7,000	10,500	36,000
1797 7,776	500	1,250	1,500	2,750	3,750	7,000	10,500	42,000
1798 327,536	550	1,350	1,600	2,850	3,950	7,500	12,500	65,000

Heraldic Eagle Reverse (1798–1804)

G-4 Good: Letters and date legible. E PLURIBUS UNUM illegible.
VG-8 Very Good: Motto partially legible. Only deepest drapery details visible. All other lines smooth.
F-12 Fine: All drapery lines distinguishable. Some detail visible in hair lines near cheek and neck.
VF-20 Very Fine: Left side of drapery worn smooth.
EF-40 Extremely Fine: Drapery distinct. Hair well detailed.
AU-50 About Uncirculated: Slight trace of wear on the bust shoulder and hair to left of forehead, as well as on eagle's breast and top edges of wings.
MS-60 Uncirculated: No trace of wear. Light blemishes.

	Mintage	G-4	VG-8	F-12	VF-20	EF-40	AU-50	MS-60
1798, Heraldic Eagle . . . .*	$650	$850	$1,200	$1,850	$3,500	$6,000	$15,000
1799 423,515	650	850	1,200	1,850	3,500	6,000	15,000
1800 220,920	650	850	1,200	1,850	3,500	6,000	15,000
1801 54,454	650	900	1,300	2,000	3,750	6,000	17,500
1802 41,650	650	850	1,250	1,850	3,500	6,000	15,000
1803 85,634	750	950	1,350	1,900	3,750	7,000	17,500
1804, Variety 1, 0 Above Cloud **(a)**			*Proof: $3,500,000*				
1804, Variety 2, 0 Above Space Between Clouds **(a)**			*Proof: $2,500,000*				

* Included in number above. **a.** Numerous counterfeits exist.

GOBRECHT (1836–1839)

Silver dollars of 1836, 1838, and 1839 were mostly made as patterns and restrikes, but some dated 1836 were made for general circulation.

	VF-20	EF-40	AU-50	PF-60
1836, C. GOBRECHT F. on base. Reverse eagle flying upward amid stars. Plain edge. Although scarce, this is the most common variety and was issued for circulation as regular coinage....................	$7,000	$8,500	$10,000	$15,000
1838, Similar obverse, designer's name omitted, stars added around border. Reverse eagle flying left in plain field. Reeded edge..............	9,500	15,000	15,000	20,000
1839, Obverse as above. Reverse eagle in plain field. Reeded edge. Issued for circulation as regular coinage...........	8,500	12,000	12,500	15,000

LIBERTY SEATED (1840–1873)

Starting again in 1840, silver dollars were issued for general circulation, continuing to about 1850, after which their main use was in the export trade to China. The seated figure of Liberty was adopted for the obverse, and a heraldic eagle for the reverse.

VG-8 Very Good: Any three letters of LIBERTY at least two-thirds complete.

F-12 Fine: All seven letters of LIBERTY visible, though weak.

VF-20 Very Fine: LIBERTY strong, but slight wear visible on its ribbon.

EF-40 Extremely Fine: Horizontal lines of shield complete. Eagle's eye plain.

AU-50 About Uncirculated: Traces of light wear on only the high points of the design. Half of mint luster present.

MS-60 Uncirculated: No trace of wear. Light marks or blemishes.

PF-60 Proof: Several contact marks, hairlines, or light rubs possible on surface. Luster possibly dull and eye appeal lacking.

PF-63 Choice Proof: Reflective surfaces with only a few blemishes in secondary focal places. No major flaws.

No Motto (1840–1865)

Location of mintmark, when present, is on reverse, below eagle.

SILVER AND RELATED DOLLARS

	Mintage	VG-8	F-12	VF-20	EF-40	AU-50	MS-60	PF-60	PF-63
1840	61,005	$200	$225	$325	$500	$1,000	$2,400	$8,250	$17,000
1841	173,000	200	225	250	425	750	2,000	17,500	35,000
1842	184,618	200	225	250	450	700	1,850	10,000	22,500
1843	165,100	200	225	250	425	750	1,850	8,500	20,000
1844	20,000	250	300	375	600	1,100	4,000	7,000	20,000
1845	24,500	250	300	375	650	1,100	7,500	8,000	19,000
1846	110,600	225	250	275	425	750	1,800	6,500	18,000
1846O	59,000	200	225	250	500	1,000	5,000		
1847	140,750	200	225	250	400	650	2,250	8,250	16,500
1848	15,000	325	400	500	900	1,200	4,750	8,250	19,000
1849	62,600	250	300	375	450	700	1,850	9,500	21,000
1850	7,500	450	575	700	1,300	1,900	4,500	8,750	16,000
1850O	40,000	250	325	550	1,150	2,500	8,000		
1851	1,300	5,500	7,500	8,750	12,500	18,000	25,000	16,000	22,000
1852	1,100	3,250	4,500	6,500	11,500	18,500	25,000	17,500	23,000
1853	46,110	350	425	500	750	950	2,500	15,000	23,000
1854	33,140	1,200	1,650	2,250	3,250	4,300	6,250	7,500	12,000
1855	26,000	900	1,300	1,800	2,750	3,800	6,750	7,500	11,500
1856	63,500	425	600	850	1,250	1,800	2,500	3,750	8,500
1857	94,000	425	600	850	1,250	2,250	3,000	3,250	8,000
1858	(210)	2,250	3,000	3,500	4,500	6,000		6,000	8,000
1859	(800) 255,700	225	350	450	600	850	1,900	1,500	2,750
1859O	360,000	200	225	250	375	650	1,500		
1859S	20,000	375	500	800	1,200	2,500	9,000		
1860	(1,330) 217,600	200	225	325	450	650	1,800	1,500	2,750
1860O	515,000	200	215	250	425	650	1,400		
1861	(1,000) 77,500	475	600	800	1,600	2,000	2,500	1,500	2,750
1862	(550) 11,540	400	600	1,100	1,900	2,500	5,000	1,500	2,750
1863	(460) 27,200	600	900	100	1,250	1,850	2,750	1,500	2,750
1864	(470) 30,700	325	400	500	850	1,500	2,500	1,500	2,750
1865	(500) 46,500	400	475	600	1,400	1,850	3,500	1,500	2,750

With Motto IN GOD WE TRUST (1866–1873)

Motto IN GOD WE TRUST on Reverse (1866–1873)

	Mintage	VG-8	F-12	VF-20	EF-40	AU-50	MS-60	PF-60	PF-63
1866	(725) 48,900	$225	$275	$450	$500	$875	$1,650	$1,250	$2,250
1867	(625) 46,900	225	275	400	550	725	1,650	1,250	2,250
1868	(600) 162,100	225	275	400	550	725	2,000	1,250	2,250
1869	(600) 423,700	225	275	375	500	725	1,650	1,250	2,250

Chart continued on next page.

143

	Mintage	VG-8	F-12	VF-20	EF-40	AU-50	MS-60	PF-60	PF-63
1870 . . . (1,000). . . 415,000		$200	$225	$300	$600	$650	$1,500	$1,250	$2,250
1870CC 11,758		650	800	1,250	3,500	6,000	20,000		
1870S 175,000		200,000	350,000	450,000	640,000	1,000,000			
1871 . . . . . (960). .1,073,800		200	225	275	400	600	1,500	1,250	2,250
1871CC 1,376		2,750	3,750	5,000	10,000	17,500	52,500		
1872 . . . . . (950). .1,105,500		200	225	275	400	600	1,500	1,250	2,250
1872CC 3,150		1,500	2,000	3,000	5,500	8,000	20,000		
1872S 9,000		450	600	700	1,250	2,250	6,500		
1873 . . . . . (600). . . 293,000		200	225	300	400	600	1,500	1,250	2,250
1873CC 2,300		8,000	12,500	15,000	20,000	37,500	100,000		

TRADE DOLLARS (1873–1885)

This trade dollar was issued for circulation in the Orient to compete with dollar-size coins of other countries. It weighed 420 grains compared to 412-1/2 grains, the weight of the regular silver dollar.

VG-8 Very Good: About half of mottoes IN GOD WE TRUST (on Liberty's pedestal) and E PLURIBUS UNUM (on obverse ribbon) visible. Rim on both sides well defined.

F-12 Fine: Mottoes and LIBERTY legible but worn.

EF-40 Extremely Fine: Mottoes and LIBERTY sharp. Only slight wear on rims.

AU-50 About Uncirculated: Slight trace of wear on Liberty's left breast and left knee and on hair above ear, as well as on eagle's head, knee, and wing tips.

MS-60 Uncirculated: No trace of wear. Light blemishes.

MS-63 Choice Uncirculated: Some distracting contact marks or blemishes in prime focal areas. Impaired luster possible.

PF-63 Choice Proof: Reflective surfaces with only a few blemishes in secondary focal places. No major flaws.

1875-S, S Over CC

	Mintage	VG-8	F-12	EF-40	AU-50	MS-60	MS-63	PF-63
1873 . . . . (600). 396,900		$100	$105	$175	$250	$700	$2,000	$2,200
1873CC 124,500		200	250	650	1,250	6,500	15,000	
1873S 703,000		100	105	175	250	950	2,500	
1874 . . . . (700). 987,100		100	105	175	250	675	1,800	2,200
1874CC 1,373,200		200	250	550	700	2,200	5,000	
1874S 2,549,000		100	105	175	250	675	1,600	
1875 . . . . (700). 218,200		95	200	325	500	1,600	3,500	2,200
1875CC 1,573,700		200	225	375	500	1,800	2,600	
1875S 4,487,000		95	100	175	250	675	1,400	
1875S, S Over CC . . . . *		200	275	600	900	2,800	8,500	
1876 . . . . . . (1,152). 455,000		95	100	175	250	675	1,250	2,200
1876CC 509,000		250	350	500	950	5,500	13,500	

* Included in number above.

	Mintage	VG-8	F-12	EF-40	AU-50	MS-60	MS-63	PF-63
1876S 5,227,000		$95	$100	$175	$250	$675	$1,350	
1877 . . . . (510) 3,039,200		95	100	175	250	700	1,500	$2,200
1877CC 534,000		200	250	500	650	1,850	7,500	
1877S 9,519,000		95	100	175	250	675	1,500	
1878 . . . . (900)				800				2,200
1878CC **(a)** 97,000		450	750	2,500	4,000	12,000	15,000	
1878S 4,162,000		95	100	175	250	650	1,300	
1879 . . . . . . (1,541)				800				2,200
1880 . . . . . . (1,987)				850				2,200
1881 . . . . (960)				850				2,200
1882 . . . . . . (1,097)				850				2,200
1883 . . . . (979)				850				2,200
1884 **(b)** . . . . . . (10)								300,000
1885 **(b)** . . . . (5)								1,000,000

a. 44,148 trade dollars were melted on July 19, 1878. Many of these may have been 1878-CC. **b.** The trade dollars of 1884 and 1885 were unknown to collectors until 1908. None are listed in the Mint director's report, and numismatists believe that they are not a part of the regular Mint issue.

MORGAN (1878–1921)

George T. Morgan, formerly a pupil of William Wyon at the Royal Mint in London, designed the new dollar. His initial M is found at the truncation of the neck, at the last tress. It also appears on the reverse on the left-hand loop of the ribbon.

Sharply struck prooflike coins have a highly reflective surface and usually command substantial premiums.

VF-20 Very Fine: Two thirds of hair lines from top of forehead to ear visible. Ear well defined. Feathers on eagle's breast worn.

EF-40 Extremely Fine: All hair lines strong and ear bold. Eagle's feathers all plain but with slight wear on breast and wing tips.

AU-50 About Uncirculated: Slight trace of wear on the bust shoulder and hair left of forehead, and on eagle's breast and top edges of wings.

MS-60 Uncirculated: No trace of wear. Full mint luster present, but may be noticeably marred by scuff marks or bag abrasions.

MS-63 Choice Uncirculated: No trace of wear; full mint luster; few noticeable surface marks.

MS-64 Uncirculated: A few scattered contact marks. Good eye appeal and attractive luster.

MS-65 Gem Uncirculated: Only light, scattered contact marks that are not distracting. Strong luster, good eye appeal.

8 Tail Feathers, 1878, Philadelphia Only
Mintmark location on reverse, below wreath.

Most Proof Morgan dollars, where indicated in mintage records (quantity shown in parentheses), are valued by coin dealers approximately as follows:
Proof-60 – $600; Proof-63 – $1,400; Proof-65 – $3,000.

Most Uncirculated silver dollars have scratches or nicks because of handling of mint bags in shipping and storage. Coin dealers usually pay more than the listed prices for choice sharply struck pieces with full brilliance and without blemishes.

	Mintage	VF-20	EF-40	AU-50	MS-60	MS-63	MS-65
1878, 8 Feathers........(500).....749,500		$55	$60	$75	$125	$160	$1,000
1878, 7 Feathers........(250)...9,759,300		30	31	40	60	100	1,050
1878, 7/8 Clear Doubled Feathers..........*		30	31	37	125	175	1,750
1878CC....................2,212,000		80	95	120	300	340	1,250
1878S......................9,774,000		30	31	35	45	55	225
1879..............(1,100)..14,806,000		20	22	30	40	55	575
1879CC, CC Over CC..............756,000		175	425	1,200	3,000	4,750	20,000
1879O....................2,887,000		20	26	29	65	175	3,000
1879S......................9,110,000		20	22	29	40	45	110
1880..............(1,355)..12,600,000		22	24	29	35	55	475
1880CC......................495,000		140	170	220	400	450	850
1880O....................5,305,000		22	25	29	65	250	16,500
1880S......................8,900,000		20	22	28	35	40	110
1881..............(984)...9,163,000		20	22	28	35	45	500
1881CC......................296,000		250	265	285	380	425	650
1881O....................5,708,000		22	24	27	35	42	950
1881S....................12,760,000		20	22	27	35	40	110
1882..............(1,100)..11,100,000		20	22	27	35	45	350
1882CC....................1,133,000		65	80	100	150	185	380
1882O....................6,090,000		22	24	28	35	45	875
1882S....................9,250,000		20	22	27	38	40	110
1883..............(1,039)..12,290,000		20	22	27	38	45	130
1883CC....................1,204,000		65	80	100	150	185	380
1883O....................8,725,000		20	22	27	35	40	110
1883S....................6,250,000		20	30	75	650	2,000	30,000
1884..............(875)..14,070,000		20	22	27	35	45	225
1884CC....................1,136,000		90	110	115	150	185	380
1884O....................9,730,000		20	22	27	35	40	110
1884S....................3,200,000		22	32	175	6,500	26,000	175,000
1885..............(930)..17,787,000		20	22	27	35	42	110
1885CC......................228,000		450	460	465	575	625	850
1885O....................9,185,000		20	22	27	35	40	110
1885S....................1,497,000		30	37	60	175	225	1,400
1886..............(886)..19,963,000		20	22	27	35	40	110
1886O....................10,710,000		25	30	50	750	2,500	125,000
1886S......................750,000		50	75	100	250	375	1,750
1887..............(710)..20,290,000		20	22	27	35	40	110
1887O....................11,550,000		20	22	28	50	100	1,900
1887S....................1,771,000		20	22	27	90	180	1,800
1888..............(833)..19,183,000		20	22	27	35	42	135
1888O....................12,150,000		20	22	29	40	45	375
1888S......................657,000		95	110	120	240	300	2,250
1889..............(811)..21,726,000		20	22	28	35	40	200
1889CC......................350,000		800	2,000	5,000	18,000	38,500	240,000
1889O....................11,875,000		20	22	27	130	250	4,750

* Included in number above.

SILVER AND RELATED DOLLARS

	Mintage	VF-20	EF-40	AU-50	MS-60	MS-63	MS-65
1889S	700,000	$40	$45	$70	$180	$300	$1,500
1890 (590)	16,802,000	20	22	27	35	45	1,050
1890CC	2,309,041	65	90	140	360	700	3,750
1890O	10,701,000	20	22	29	50	65	1,500
1890S	8,230,373	20	22	26	40	65	850
1891 (650)	8,693,556	20	22	28	38	125	4,750
1891CC	1,618,000	65	90	130	380	550	3,500
1891O	7,954,529	20	22	27	120	250	5,250
1891S	5,296,000	20	24	28	55	100	1,200
1892 (1,245)	1,036,000	28	32	55	225	375	2,900
1892CC	1,352,000	160	275	450	950	1,650	6,000
1892O	2,744,000	20	25	45	200	300	5,000
1892S	1,200,000	75	225	1,250	27,500	52,000	115,000
1893 (792)	378,000	140	165	250	600	850	5,000
1893CC	677,000	425	875	1,800	3,300	6,250	55,000
1893O	300,000	225	350	525	2,250	5,000	120,000
1893S	100,000	4,000	6,500	15,000	90,000	165,000	500,000
1894 (972)	110,000	825	900	1,000	2,750	3,850	25,000
1894O	1,723,000	30	55	135	900	3,650	40,000
1894S	1,260,000	60	95	300	600	900	4,750
1895 (880)		20,000 (a)	22,500 (a)	30,000 (a)	37,500 (a)	50,000 (a)
1895O	450,000	230	360	675	11,500	36,000	135,000
1895S	400,000	550	750	1,200	2,800	4,500	18,500
1896 (762)	9,976,000	20	22	27	35	42	140
1896O	4,900,000	26	28	100	1,050	5,500	115,000
1896S	5,000,000	32	125	500	1,600	2,750	12,000
1897 (731)	2,822,000	20	22	27	35	45	200
1897O	4,004,000	20	30	60	600	3,500	45,000
1897S	5,825,000	20	22	29	55	85	400
1898 (735)	5,884,000	20	22	27	35	45	150
1898O	4,440,000	20	22	27	35	42	110
1898S	4,102,000	28	30	55	175	325	1,500
1899 (846)	330,000	100	130	145	180	200	600
1899O	12,290,000	20	22	28	35	42	110
1899S	2,562,000	26	35	90	280	375	1,400
1900 (912)	8,830,000	20	22	27	35	40	110
1900O	12,590,000	20	22	27	37	42	110
1900S	3,540,000	28	30	50	205	275	1,350
1901 (813)	6,962,000	32	60	160	2,250	12,500	325,000
1901O	13,320,000	24	26	29	37	42	120
1901S	2,284,000	28	35	125	350	600	2,500
1902 (777)	7,994,000	24	28	30	55	85	325
1902O	8,636,000	22	24	29	35	40	135
1902S	1,530,000	90	140	165	285	450	1,850
1903 (755)	4,652,000	32	33	35	45	55	200
1903O	4,450,000	240	245	250	300	325	450
1903S	1,241,000	110	220	1,200	3,500	5,000	7,500
1904 (650)	2,788,000	25	28	30	85	165	1,900

a. Values are for Proofs.

Chart continued on next page.

	Mintage	VF-20	EF-40	AU-50	MS-60	MS-63	MS-65
19040	3,720,000	$28	$30	$33	$40	$45	$110
1904S	2,304,000	50	130	335	1,700	3,200	7,000
1921	44,690,000	18	20	22	28	40	100
1921D	20,345,000	18	20	22	28	45	225
1921S	21,695,000	18	20	22	28	45	1,000

PEACE (1921–1935)

Anthony de Francisci, a medalist, designed this dollar. His monogram is located in the field of the coin under the neck of Liberty.

VF-20 Very Fine: Hair over eye well worn. Some strands over ear well defined. Some eagle feathers on top and outside edge of right wing visible.

EF-40 Extremely Fine: Hair lines over brow and ear are strong, though slightly worn. Outside wing feathers at right and those at top visible but faint.

AU-50 About Uncirculated: Slight trace of wear. Most luster present, although marred by contact marks.

MS-60 Uncirculated: No trace of wear. Full mint luster, but possibly noticeably marred by stains, surface marks, or bag abrasions.

MS-63 Choice Uncirculated: Some distracting contact marks or blemishes in prime focal areas. Impaired luster possible.

MS-64 Uncirculated: A few scattered contact marks. Good eye appeal and attractive luster.

MS-65 Gem Uncirculated: Only light, scattered, non-distracting contact marks. Strong luster, good eye appeal.

PF-65 Choice Proof: Satin surfaces, no noticeable blemishes or flaws.

Mintmark location on reverse, below ONE.

Most Uncirculated silver dollars have scratches or nicks because of handling of mint bags in shipping and storage. Coin dealers usually pay more than the listed prices for choice sharply struck pieces with full brilliance and without blemishes.

	Mintage	VF-20	EF-40	AU-50	MS-60	MS-63	MS-65	PF-65
1921	1,006,473	$70	$75	$80	$200	$300	$1,400	$75,000
1922	51,737,000	17	18	19	25	28	80	90,000
1922D	15,063,000	17	18	19	28	45	375	
1922S	17,475,000	17	18	19	28	55	1,500	
1923	30,800,000	17	18	19	25	28	80	
1923D	6,811,000	17	18	22	32	85	700	
1923S	19,020,000	17	18	19	29	45	3,750	
1924	11,811,000	17	18	19	25	28	85	
1924S	1,728,000	17	18	33	150	300	5,500	
1925	10,198,000	17	18	19	25	28	85	
1925S	1,610,000	17	18	22	43	160	15,000	
1926	1,939,000	17	18	20	30	50	325	

SILVER AND RELATED DOLLARS

	Mintage	VF-20	EF-40	AU-50	MS-60	MS-63	MS-65
1926D	2,348,700	$17	$19	$25	$50	$130	$600
1926S	6,980,000	17	19	25	35	55	600
1927	848,000	21	24	25	45	120	1,500
1927D	1,268,900	21	24	45	100	250	3,000
1927S	866,000	22	25	45	125	350	6,000
1928	360,649	180	210	250	325	500	2,500
1928S	1,632,000	22	25	35	100	325	12,500
1934	954,057	22	25	30	75	125	475
1934D	1,569,500	22	25	30	90	200	1,000
1934S	1,011,000	22	100	275	1,600	3,250	7,000
1935	1,576,000	22	25	30	50	75	450
1935S	1,964,000	22	30	50	175	300	850

EISENHOWER (1971–1978)
Eagle Reverse (1971–1974)

Honoring both President Dwight D. Eisenhower and the first landing of man on the moon, this design is the work of Chief Engraver Frank Gasparro, whose initials are on the truncation of the President's neck and below the eagle. The reverse is an adaptation of the official *Apollo 11* insignia.

Mintmark location is above date.

	Mintage	EF-40	MS-63	PF-63	PF-65
1971, Copper-Nickel Clad	47,799,000	$1.10	$1.75		
1971D, Copper-Nickel Clad	68,587,424	1.10	1.50		
1971S, Silver Clad . . . . (4,265,234)	6,868,530		7.50	$7.50	$12.00
1972, Copper-Nickel Clad	75,890,000	1.10	1.50		
1972D, Copper-Nickel Clad	92,548,511	1.10	1.50		
1972S, Silver Clad . . . . (1,811,631)	2,193,056		7.50	7.50	12.00
1973, Copper-Nickel Clad (a)	2,000,056	1.10	3.00		
1973D, Copper-Nickel Clad (a)	2,000,000	1.10	3.00		
1973S, Copper-Nickel Clad . . . . (2,760,339)				2.50	7.00
1973S, Silver Clad . . . . (1,013,646)	1,883,140		7.50	22.00	27.00
1974, Copper-Nickel Clad	27,366,000	1.10	1.25		
1974D, Copper-Nickel Clad	45,517,000	1.10	1.25		
1974S, Copper-Nickel Clad . . . . (2,612,568)				2.50	3.75
1974S, Silver Clad . . . . (1,306,579)	1,900,156		7.50	10.00	13.00

a. 1,769,258 of each sold only in sets and not released for circulation. Unissued coins destroyed at mint.

Bicentennial (1776–1976)

| Obverse | Reverse Variety 2 | Reverse Variety 1 |

Variety 1: Design in low relief, bold lettering on reverse.
Variety 2: Sharp design, delicate lettering on reverse.

	Mintage	EF-40	MS-63	PF-63	PF-65
1776–1976, Copper-Nickel Clad, Variety 1	4,019,000	$1.10	$3.00		
1776–1976, Copper-Nickel Clad, Variety 2	113,318,000	1.10	1.50		
1776–1976D, Copper-Nickel Clad, Variety 1	21,048,710	1.10	1.50		
1776–1976D, Copper-Nickel Clad, Variety 2	82,179,564	1.10	1.50		
1776–1976S, Copper-Nickel Clad, Variety 1 . .	(2,845,450)			$3.00	$5.50
1776–1976S, Copper-Nickel Clad, Variety 2 . .	(4,149,730)			2.50	3.75
1776–1976S, Silver Clad, Variety 1	11,000,000		7.50		
1776–1976S, Silver Clad, Variety 1	(4,000,000)			9.00	11.00

Eagle Reverse Resumed (1977–1978)

	Mintage	EF-40	MS-63	PF-63	PF-65
1977, Copper-Nickel Clad	12,596,000	$1.10	$1.50		
1977D, Copper-Nickel Clad	32,983,006	1.10	1.50		
1977S, Copper-Nickel Clad	(3,251,152)			$2.50	$4.25
1978, Copper-Nickel Clad	25,702,000	1.10	1.50		
1978D, Copper-Nickel Clad	33,012,890	1.10	1.50		
1978S, Copper-Nickel Clad	(3,127,781)			2.50	4.75

SUSAN B. ANTHONY (1979–1999)

| Filled S | Clear S |

	Mintage	MS-63
1979P, Narrow Rim	360,222,000	$1.10
1979P, Wide Rim	*	27.00
1979D	288,015,744	1.10

* Included in number above.

	Mintage	MS-65	PF-63	PF-65
1979S	109,576,000	$1.10		
1979S, Proof, Type 1	(3,677,175)		$2.50	$4
1979S, Proof, Type 2	*		20.00	40
1980P	27,610,000	1.10		
1980D	41,628,708	1.10		
1980S	20,422,000	1.10		
1980S, Proof	(3,554,806)		2.50	3
1981P	3,000,000	2.00		

	Mintage	MS-65	PF-63	PF-65
1981D	3,250,000	$2.00		
1981S	3,492,000	2.00		
1981S, Proof, Type 1	(4,063,083)		$2.50	$4
1981S, Proof, Type 2	*		35.00	75
1999P	29,592,000	2.50		
1999P, Proof	(750,000)		13.00	16
1999D	11,776,000	2.50		

* Included in number above.

SACAGAWEA (2000–2008)

The design of this coin was selected in national competition from among 120 submissions that were considered by a panel appointed by Treasury Secretary Robert Rubin. The adopted motif depicts Sacagawea, a young Native American Shoshone, as rendered by artist Glenna Goodacre. On her back she carries Jean Baptiste, her infant son. The reverse shows an eagle in flight, designed by Mint engraver Thomas D. Rogers Sr.

The composition exemplifies the spirit of Liberty, Peace, and Freedom shown by Sacagawea in her conduct as interpreter and guide to explorers Meriwether Lewis and William Clark during their famed journey westward from St. Louis to the Pacific.

These coins have a distinctive golden color and a plain edge to distinguish them from other denominations or coins of a similar size. The change in composition and appearance was mandated under the United States Dollar Coin Act of 1997.

Several distinctive finishes can be identified on the Sacagawea dollars as a result of the Mint attempting to adjust the dies, blanks, strikes, or finishing to produce coins with minimal spotting and a better surface color. One group of 5,000 pieces dated 2000 with a special finish were presented to sculptor Glenna Goodacre in payment for the obverse design. Unexplained error coins made from mismatched dies (a State quarter obverse combined with a Sacagawea dollar reverse) are extremely rare.

	Mintage	MS-65	PF-63	PF-65
2000P	767,140,000	$1.10		
2000D	518,916,000	1.10		
2000S	(4,097,904)		$3	$5
2001P	62,468,000	1.10		
2001D	70,939,500	1.10		
2001S	(3,183,740)		7	9
2002P (a)	3,865,610	1.25		
2002D (a)	3,732,000	1.25		
2002S	(3,211,995)		3	5
2003P (a)	3,080,000	1.50		

	Mintage	MS-65	PF-63	PF-65
2003D (a)	3,080,000	$1.50		
2003S	(3,298,439)		$3	$5
2004P (a)	2,660,000	1.50		
2004D (a)	2,660,000	1.50		
2004S	(2,965,422)		3	5
2005P (a)	2,520,000	1.50		
2005D (a)	2,520,000	1.50		
2005S	(3,344,679)		3	5
2006P (a)	4,900,000	1.50		
2006D (a)	2,800,000	1.50		

a. Not issued for circulation.

Chart continued on next page.

	Mintage	MS-65	PF-63	PF-65
2006S	(3,054,436)		$3	$5
2007P (a)	3,640,000	$1.50		
2007D (a)	3,920,000	1.50		
2007S	(2,577,166)		3	5

	Mintage	MS-65	PF-63	PF-65
2008P (a)	1,820,000	$2.00		
2008D (a)	1,820,000	2.00		
2008S	(2,169,561)		$6	$8

a. Not issued for circulation.

NATIVE AMERICAN (2009 TO DATE)

Obverse

Three Sisters (2009)

Great Law of Peace (2010)

Wampanoag Treaty (2011)

Trade Routes in the 17th Century (2012)

Treaty With the Delawares (2013)

Native Hospitality (2014)

Mohawk Ironworkers (2015)

Code Talkers (2016)

	Mintage	MS-65	PF-65
2009P, Three Sisters	39,200,000	$1.25	
2009D, Three Sisters	35,700,000	1.25	
2009S, Three Sisters	(2,179,867)		$3
2010P, Great Law	32,060,000	1.75	
2010D, Great Law	48,720,000	1.75	
2010S, Great Law	(1,689,216)		3
2011P, Wampanoag	29,400,000	2.00	
2011D, Wampanoag	48,160,000	2.00	
2011S, Wampanoag	(1,673,010)		3
2012P, Trade Routes	2,800,000	1.75	
2012D, Trade Routes	3,080,000	1.75	
2012S, Trade Routes	(1,189,445)		3
2013P, Treaty, Delawares	1,820,000	1.50	

	Mintage	MS-65	PF-65
2013D, Treaty, Delawares	1,820,000	$1.50	
2013S, Treaty, Delawares	(1,222,180)		$3
2014P, Native Hospitality	3,080,000	1.50	
2014D, Native Hospitality	2,800,000	1.50	
2014S, Native Hospitality	(1,144,154)		3
2015P, Mohawk Ironworkers	2,800,000	1.50	
2015D, Mohawk Ironworkers	2,240,000	1.50	
2015S, Mohawk Ironworkers	(974,883)		3
2015W, Mohawk Ironworkers	(84,059)		
2016P, Code Talkers		1.50	
2016D, Code Talkers		1.50	
2016S, Code Talkers			3

PRESIDENTIAL (2007–2016)

Four different coins, each bearing the image of a former U.S. president, are issued each year in the order that the presidents served. The size and composition of these coins is the same as that of the Sacagawea / Native American dollars that are also made each year. A companion series of ten-dollar gold bullion coins (listed in the Bullion section) honors the spouse of each president.

Presidential Dollars Reverse

Date, Mintmark, and Motto Incused on Edge (Motto Moved to Obverse in 2009)

	Mintage	MS-65	PF-65
2007P, Washington	176,680,000	$1.10	
2007D, Washington	163,680,000	1.10	
2007S, Washington	(3,965,989)		$2
2007P, J. Adams......	112,420,000	1.10	
2007D, J. Adams......	112,140,000	1.10	
2007S, J. Adams.......	(3,965,989)		2

	Mintage	MS-65	PF-65
2007P, Jefferson......	100,800,000	$1.10	
2007D, Jefferson......	102,810,000	1.10	
2007S, Jefferson.......	(3,965,989)		$2
2007P, Madison	84,560,000	1.10	
2007D, Madison	87,780,000	1.10	
2007S, Madison	(3,965,989)		2

	Mintage	MS-65	PF-65
2008P, Monroe	64,260,000	$1.10	
2008D, Monroe	60,230,000	1.10	
2008S, Monroe	(3,083,940)		$2
2008P, J.Q. Adams	57,540,000	1.10	
2008D, J.Q. Adams	57,720,000	1.10	
2008S, J.Q. Adams	(3,083,940)		2

	Mintage	MS-65	PF-65
2008P, Jackson........	61,180,000	$1.10	
2008D, Jackson	61,070,000	1.10	
2008S, Jackson........	(3,083,940)		$2
2008P, Van Buren	51,520,000	1.10	
2008D, Van Buren	50,960,000	1.10	
2008S, Van Buren	(3,083,940)		2

Note: Errors have been reported in the Presidential dollar series, including coins minted without edge lettering. Depending on their rarity, dealers may pay a premium for such errors.

	Mintage	MS-65	PF-65
2009P, Harrison	43,260,000	$1.10	
2009D, Harrison	55,160,000	1.10	
2009S, Harrison	(2,809,452)		$2
2009P, Tyler	43,540,000	1.10	
2009D, Tyler	43,540,000	1.10	
2009S, Tyler	(2,809,452)		2

	Mintage	MS-65	PF-65
2009P, Polk	46,620,000	$1.10	
2009D, Polk	41,720,000	1.10	
2009S, Polk	(2,809,452)		$2
2009P, Taylor	41,580,000	1.10	
2009D, Taylor	36,680,000	1.10	
2009S, Taylor	(2,809,452)		2

	Mintage	MS-65	PF-65
2010P, Fillmore	37,520,000	$1.10	
2010D, Fillmore	36,960,000	1.10	
2010S, Fillmore	(2,224,613)		$2
2010P, Pierce	38,220,000	1.10	
2010D, Pierce	38,360,000	1.10	
2010S, Pierce	(2,224,613)		2

	Mintage	MS-65	PF-65
2010P, Buchanan	36,820,000	$1.10	
2010D, Buchanan	36,540,000	1.10	
2010S, Buchanan	(2,224,613)		$2
2010P, Lincoln	49,000,000	1.10	
2010D, Lincoln	48,020,000	1.10	
2010S, Lincoln	(2,224,613)		3

	Mintage	MS-65	PF-65
2011P, A. Johnson	35,560,000	$1.10	
2011D, A. Johnson	37,100,000	1.10	
2011S, A. Johnson	(1,972,863)		$2
2011P, Grant	38,080,000	1.10	
2011D, Grant	37,940,000	1.10	
2011S, Grant	(1,972,863)		2

	Mintage	MS-65	PF-65
2011P, Hayes	37,660,000	$1.10	
2011D, Hayes	36,820,000	1.10	
2011S, Hayes	(1,972,863)		$2
2011P, Garfield	37,100,000	1.10	
2011D, Garfield	37,100,000	1.10	
2011S, Garfield	(1,972,863)		2

	Mintage	MS-65	PF-65
2012P, Arthur (a)	6,020,000	$1.10	
2012D, Arthur (a)	4,060,000	1.10	
2012S, Arthur	(1,438,743)		$3
2012P, Cleveland, Variety 1 (a)	5,460,000	1.10	
2012D, Cleveland, Variety 1 (a)	4,060,000	1.10	
2012S, Cleveland, Variety 1	(1,438,743)		3

a. Not issued for circulation.

	Mintage	MS-65	PF-65
2012P, Harrison (a)	5,640,000	$1.10	
2012D, Harrison (a)	4,200,000	1.10	
2012S, Harrison	(1,438,743)		$3
2012P, Cleveland, Variety 2 (a)	10,680,000	1.10	
2012D, Cleveland, Variety 2 (a)	3,920,000	1.10	
2012S, Cleveland, Variety 2	(1,438,743)		3

	Mintage	MS-65	PF-65
2013P, McKinley (a)	4,760,000	$1.10	
2013D, McKinley (a)	3,365,100	1.10	
2013S, McKinley	(1,488,798)		$2
2013P, T. Roosevelt (a)	5,310,700	1.10	
2013D, T. Roosevelt (a)	3,920,000	1.10	
2013S, T. Roosevelt	(1,503,943)		2

a. Not issued for circulation.

	Mintage	MS-65	PF-65
2013P, Taft (a)	4,760,000	$1.10	
2013D, Taft (a)	3,360,000	1.10	
2013S, Taft	(1,488,798)		$2
2013P, Wilson (a)	4,620,000	1.10	
2013D, Wilson (a)	3,360,000	1.10	
2013S, Wilson	(1,488,798)		2

	Mintage	MS-65	PF-65
2014P, Harding (a)	6,160,000	$1.10	
2014D, Harding (a)	3,780,000	1.10	
2014S, Harding	(1,373,569)		$3
2014P, Coolidge (a)	4,480,000	1.10	
2014D, Coolidge (a)	3,780,000	1.10	
2014S, Coolidge	(1,373,569)		3

a. Not issued for circulation.

	Mintage	MS-65	PF-65
2014P, Hoover (a)	4,480,000	$1.10	
2014D, Hoover (a)	3,780,000	1.10	
2014S, Hoover	(1,373,569)		$3
2014P, F.D. Roosevelt (a)	4,760,000	1.10	
2014D, F.D. Roosevelt (a)	3,920,000	1.10	
2014S, F.D. Roosevelt	(1,392,619)		3

	Mintage	MS-65	PF-65
2015P, Truman (a)	4,900,000	$1.10	
2015D, Truman (a)	3,500,000	1.10	
2015S, Truman	(1,191,876)		$3
2015S, Truman, Rev Pf	(16,812)		135
2015P, Eisenhower (a)	4,900,000	1.10	
2015D, Eisenhower (a)	3,645,998	1.10	
2015S, Eisenhower	(1,191,876)		3
2015S, Eisenhower, Ref Pf	(16,744)		65

	Mintage	MS-65	PF-65
2015P, Kennedy (a)	6,160,000	$1.10	
2015D, Kennedy (a)	5,180,000	1.10	
2015S, Kennedy	(1,191,876)		$3
2015S, Kennedy, Rev Pf.	(49,051)		25
2015P, L. Johnson (a)	7,840,000	1.10	
2015D, L. Johnson (a)	4,200,000	1.10	
2015S, L. Johnson	(1,191,876)		3
2015S, L. Johnson, Rev Pf	(23,905)		25

a. Not issued for circulation.

The design for the 2016 Ronald Reagan Presidential dollar was not finalized at the time of publication.

	Mintage	MS-65	PF-65
2016P, Nixon (a)		$1.10	
2016D, Nixon (a)		1.10	
2016S, Nixon			$3
2016P, Ford (a)		1.10	
2016P, Ford (a)		1.10	

	Mintage	MS-65	PF-65
2016S, Ford			$3
2016P, Reagan (a)		$1.10	
2016D, Reagan (a)		1.10	
2016S, Reagan			3
2016S, Reagan, Rev Pf			

a. Not issued for circulation.

GOLD DOLLARS

The Coinage Act of 1792 established the independent monetary system of the United States, with the dollar as its basic monetary unit. Silver dollar coins were made starting in 1794. Coinage of a gold dollar coin, however, was not authorized until the Act of March 3, 1849. Its weight was set at 25.8 grains, fineness .900.

The first type, struck until 1854, is known as the Liberty Head. In 1854 the gold dollar was made larger in diameter and thinner, while keeping the same weight. Along with that modification, the design was changed to a female wearing a feather headdress, generally referred to as the Indian Princess Head type. In 1856 this was changed slightly by enlarging the size of the head.

LIBERTY HEAD (1849–1854)

VF-20 Very Fine: LIBERTY on headband complete and legible. Knobs on coronet defined.
EF-40 Extremely Fine: Slight wear on Liberty's hair. Knobs on coronet sharp.
AU-50 About Uncirculated: Trace of wear on headband. Nearly full luster.
AU-55 Choice About Uncirculated: Evidence of friction on design high points.
MS-60 Uncirculated: No trace of wear. Light marks and blemishes.
MS-63 Choice Uncirculated: Some distracting contact marks or blemishes in prime focal areas. Impaired luster possible.

	Mintage	VF-20	EF-40	AU-50	AU-55	MS-60	MS-63
1849, Open Wreath, No L on Truncation 688,567		$145	$160	$200	$250	$450	$1,000
1849, Close Wreath . . . . *		145	160	165	175	325	950
1849C, Open Wreath 11,634		150,000	200,000	250,000	300,000		
1849C, Close Wreath . . . . *		700	1,350	1,750	2,500	6,500	11,500
1849D 21,588		1,050	1,350	1,750	2,300	3,500	8,000
1849O 215,000		150	180	250	385	650	2,300
1850 81,953		145	160	170	175	275	650
1850C 6,966		850	1,350	2,250	2,750	5,500	20,000
1850D 8,382		1,050	1,350	2,250	3,500	7,000	17,500
1850O 14,000		195	275	600	1,150	2,000	4,000
1851 3,317,671		145	160	170	175	250	400
1851C 41,267		900	975	1,450	1,600	2,250	4,250
1851D 9,882		1,000	1,350	1,750	2,250	3,500	10,000
1851O 290,000		150	170	180	240	500	1,400
1852 2,045,351		145	160	170	175	250	400
1852C 9,434		950	1,200	1,500	1,800	3,000	7,500
1852D 6,360		1,000	1,400	1,850	3,250	5,500	22,500
1852O 140,000		150	200	250	475	850	2,500
1853 4,076,051		145	160	170	175	250	400
1853C 11,515		850	1,100	1,750	2,250	3,500	8,000
1853D 6,583		950	1,250	2,000	3,000	5,500	17,500
1853O 290,000		145	175	200	240	450	1,400
1854 855,502		145	160	170	175	250	400
1854D 2,935		1,200	1,500	4,000	5,200	7,000	22,500
1854S 14,632		225	320	460	850	1,750	4,000

* Included in number above.

INDIAN PRINCESS HEAD, SMALL HEAD (1854–1856)

VF-20 Very Fine: Feather-curl tips on headdress outlined but details worn.
EF-40 Extremely Fine: Slight wear on tips of feather curls on headdress.
AU-50 About Uncirculated: Trace of wear on feathers, nearly full luster.
AU-55 Choice About Uncirculated: Evidence of friction on design high points. Most of original mint luster present.
MS-60 Uncirculated: No trace of wear. Light marks and blemishes.
MS-63 Choice Uncirculated: Some distracting contact marks or blemishes in prime focal areas. Impaired luster possible.
PF-63 Choice Proof: Reflective surfaces with only a few blemishes in secondary focal areas. No major flaws.

	Mintage	VF-20	EF-40	AU-50	AU-55	MS-60	MS-63	PF-63
1854	783,943	$250	$325	$425	$525	$1,150	$4,500	$125,000
1855	758,269	250	325	425	525	1,150	4,500	110,000
1855C	9,803	1,000	2,500	6,000	8,500	18,000		
1855D	1,811	5,000	10,000	20,000	25,000	37,500	70,000	
1855O	55,000	350	475	1,100	1,750	5,000	20,000	
1856S	24,600	575	900	1,850	2,100	5,000	21,000	

INDIAN PRINCESS HEAD, LARGE HEAD (1856–1889)

VF-20 Very Fine: Slight detail in curled feathers in headdress. Details worn smooth at eyebrow, hair below headdress, and behind ear and bottom curl.
EF-40 Extremely Fine: Slight wear above and to right of eye and on top of curled feathers.
AU-50 About Uncirculated: Trace of wear on feathers, nearly full luster.
AU-55 Choice About Uncirculated: Evidence of friction on design high points. Most of original mint luster present.
MS-60 Uncirculated: No trace of wear. Light marks and blemishes.
MS-63 Choice Uncirculated: Some distracting contact marks or blemishes in prime focal areas. Impaired luster possible.
PF-63 Choice Proof: Reflective surfaces with only a few blemishes in secondary focal places. No major flaws.

	Mintage	VF-20	EF-40	AU-50	AU-55	MS-60	MS-63	PF-63
1856	1,762,936	$180	$190	$200	$225	$275	$500	$20,000
1856D	1,460	3,000	4,500	5,500	6,750	20,000	45,000	
1857	774,789	180	190	200	225	275	450	8,500
1857C	13,280	850	1,100	2,250	2,750	7,500		
1857D	3,533	900	1,350	3,000	4,000	8,000		
1857S	10,000	375	450	850	1,100	3,500	14,000	
1858	117,995	200	215	220	225	275	700	5,000
1858D	3,477	800	1,500	2,250	3,000	5,500	15,000	

1873, Close 3

1873, Open 3

	Mintage	VF-20	EF-40	AU-50	AU-55	MS-60	MS-63	PF-63
1858S	10,000	$275	$375	$1,000	$1,300	$4,250	$11,000	
1859	(80) 168,244	180	200	220	225	300	550	$7,500
1859C	5,235	800	1,150	2,250	2,750	7,000	19,000	
1859D	4,952	950	1,300	2,100	2,500	6,750	16,500	
1859S	15,000	225	275	875	1,150	4,250	10,000	
1860	(154) 36,514	180	200	220	225	300	750	6,500
1860D	1,566	1,850	2,750	5,500	6,750	12,500	40,000	
1860S	13,000	275	375	575	775	2,000	4,500	
1861	(349) ...527,150	180	200	220	225	300	500	4,500
1861D	1,250	15,000	22,500	27,500	35,000	55,000	85,000	
1862	(35) .. 1,361,355	180	200	220	225	300	550	5,000
1863	(50) 6,200	650	1,250	2,250	2,800	4,000	8,000	7,500
1864	(50) 5,900	275	375	625	825	1,000	2,500	7,500
1865	(25) 3,725	300	400	650	850	1,150	2,500	7,500
1866	(30) 7,100	300	375	550	750	800	1,750	7,500
1867	(50) 5,200	300	375	500	650	800	1,650	7,000
1868	(25) 10,500	225	325	375	550	750	1,650	7,000
1869	(25) 5,900	275	375	500	600	775	1,500	7,000
1870	(35) 6,300	225	325	375	475	650	1,250	7,000
1870S	3,000	375	550	1,000	1,200	1,850	5,000	
1871	(30) 3,900	200	325	375	475	600	1,100	6,500
1872	(30) 3,500	200	325	375	475	675	1,500	7,500
1873, Close 3 ...	(25) 1,800	300	600	675	775	1,150	2,500	10,000
1873, Open 3	123,300	180	200	220	225	300	450	
1874	(20) 198,800	180	200	220	225	300	450	7,500
1875	(20) 400	2,250	3,000	3,750	5,000	7,500	12,500	15,000
1876	(45) 3,200	190	275	375	425	500	950	5,500
1877	(20) 3,900	190	275	375	425	500	1,100	5,000
1878	(20) 3,000	190	275	375	425	500	950	4,500
1879	(30) 3,000	190	225	250	275	350	800	4,500
1880	(36) 1,600	190	200	220	235	350	750	4,000
1881	(87) 7,620	190	200	220	235	350	550	4,000
1882	(125) 5,000	190	225	250	275	350	550	4,500
1883	(207) 10,800	180	200	225	235	350	550	4,000
1884	(1,006) 5,230	180	200	225	235	350	550	4,000
1885	(1,105) 11,156	180	225	250	275	350	550	3,750
1886	(1,016) 5,000	180	200	220	225	350	550	3,750
1887	(1,043) 7,500	180	200	220	225	350	550	3,750
1888	(1,079) 15,501	180	200	220	225	325	550	3,750
1889	(1,779) 28,950	180	200	220	225	300	450	3,750

Although authorized by the Act of April 2, 1792, coinage of quarter eagles ($2.50 gold coins) was not begun until 1796.

CAPPED BUST TO RIGHT (1796–1807)

F-12 Fine: Hair worn smooth on high spots. E PLURIBUS UNUM on ribbon weak but legible.
VF-20 Very Fine: Some wear on high spots.
EF-40 Extremely Fine: Only slight wear on Liberty's hair and cheek.
AU-50 About Uncirculated: Trace of wear on cap, hair, cheek, and drapery.
AU-55 Choice About Uncirculated: Evidence of friction on design high points. Some original mint luster.
MS-60 Uncirculated: No trace of wear. Light blemishes.

No Stars on Obverse (1796)   Stars on Obverse (1796–1807)

	Mintage	F-12	VF-20	EF-40	AU-50	AU-55	MS-60
1796, No Stars on Obverse	963	$40,000	$55,000	$70,000	$85,000	$100,000	$185,000
1796, Stars on Obverse	432	40,000	55,000	70,000	85,000	100,000	150,000
1797	427	10,000	15,000	25,000	35,000	45,000	95,000
1798	1,094	3,000	5,000	10,000	18,500	21,000	50,000
1802	3,035	3,000	5,000	10,000	14,500	17,500	25,000
1804, 13-Star Reverse	*	35,000	45,000	75,000	100,000	150,000	
1804, 14-Star Reverse	3,327	3,000	5,000	10,000	13,000	16,000	25,000
1805	1,781	3,000	5,000	10,000	13,000	16,000	25,000
1806, 6/4, 8 Stars Left, 5 Right	1,136	3,500	5,500	10,000	13,000	16,000	23,000
1806, 6/5, 7 Stars Left, 6 Right	480	4,500	6,500	12,000	15,000	30,000	60,000
1807	6,812	3,000	5,000	10,000	13,000	16,000	25,000

* Included in number below.

DRAPED BUST TO LEFT, LARGE SIZE (1808)

F-12 Fine: E PLURIBUS UNUM on reverse, and LIBERTY on headband, legible but weak.
VF-20 Very Fine: Motto and LIBERTY clear.
EF-40 Extremely Fine: All details of hair plain.
AU-50 About Uncirculated: Trace of wear above eye, on top of cap, and on cheek and hair.
AU-55 Choice About Uncirculated: Evidence of friction on design high points. Some original mint luster present.
MS-60 Uncirculated: No trace of wear. Light blemishes.

	Mintage	F-12	VF-20	EF-40	AU-50	AU-55	MS-60
1808	2,710	$20,000	$30,000	$50,000	$75,000	$95,000	$135,000

CAPPED HEAD TO LEFT (1821–1834)

Those dated 1829 to 1834 are smaller in diameter than the 1821 to 1827 pieces.

Large Diameter   Reduced Diameter

	Mintage	F-12	VF-20	EF-40	AU-50	AU-55	MS-60
1821	6,448	$4,500	$5,500	$7,500	$10,000	$14,000	$25,000
1824, 4 Over 1	2,600	4,500	6,000	7,500	9,500	13,000	27,500
1825	4,434	5,000	6,500	7,500	9,500	13,000	22,500
1826, 6 Over 6	760	5,000	6,500	8,000	12,000	22,500	40,000
1827	2,800	4,500	6,500	8,500	10,000	15,000	22,000
1829	3,403	4,000	5,000	6,500	8,500	10,000	15,000
1830	4,540	4,000	5,000	6,500	8,500	10,000	15,000
1831	4,520	4,000	5,000	6,500	8,500	10,000	15,000
1832	4,400	4,000	5,000	6,500	8,500	10,000	15,000
1833	4,160	4,000	5,000	6,500	8,500	10,000	15,000
1834, With Motto	4,000	10,000	12,500	15,000	25,000	30,000	40,000

CLASSIC HEAD, NO MOTTO ON REVERSE (1834–1839)

In 1834, the quarter eagle was redesigned. A ribbon binding the hair, bearing the word LIBERTY, replaced the Liberty cap. The motto was omitted from the reverse.

F-12 Fine: LIBERTY on headband legible and complete. Curl under ear outlined but no detail.

VF-20 Very Fine: LIBERTY plain; detail in hair curl.

EF-40 Extremely Fine: Small amount of wear on top of hair and below L in LIBERTY. Wear evident on wing.

AU-50 About Uncirculated: Trace of wear on coronet and hair above ear.

AU-55 Choice About Uncirculated: Evidence of friction on design high points. Some of original mint luster present.

MS-60 Uncirculated: No trace of wear. Light blemishes.

MS-63 Choice Uncirculated: Some distracting contact marks or blemishes in prime focal areas. Impaired luster possible.

Mintmark location.

	Mintage	F-12	VF-20	EF-40	AU-50	AU-55	MS-60	MS-63
1834, No Motto	112,234	$225	$375	$600	$925	$1,100	$2,500	$7,000
1835	131,402	225	375	600	925	1,100	2,500	7,750
1836	547,986	225	375	600	925	1,100	2,500	7,000
1837	45,080	275	500	750	950	1,150	2,750	10,500
1838	47,030	250	450	650	950	1,100	2,750	7,500
1838C	7,880	1,000	1,750	2,750	6,500	8,000	20,000	35,000
1839	27,021	375	650	1,000	1,500	1,850	3,500	20,000
1839C	18,140	1,100	2,000	2,600	4,500	7,000	17,500	50,000
1839D	13,674	1,200	2,000	3,400	6,000	8,000	25,000	40,000
1839O	17,781	375	675	1,200	2,000	3,000	5,500	22,500

LIBERTY HEAD (1840–1907)

Mintmark location.

4 Plain 4

4 Crosslet 4

	Mintage	VF-20	EF-40	AU-50	AU-55	MS-60	MS-63
1840	18,859	$275	$500	$1,600	$2,000	$4,500	$8,000
1840C	12,822	1,200	1,650	2,500	2,750	7,500	21,500
1840D	3,532	2,000	4,500	6,500	8,500	24,000	
1840O	33,580	275	500	1,250	1,500	6,500	18,000

Chart continued on next page.

161

	Mintage	VF-20	EF-40	AU-50	AU-55	MS-60	MS-63
1841	(unknown)	$45,000	$75,000	$95,000	$125,000		
1841C	10,281	1,000	1,350	2,250	2,750	$12,000	$32,000
1841D	4,164	1,550	3,000	6,000	7,500	18,500	35,000
1842	2,823	850	2,000	4,000	5,500	12,500	32,500
1842C	6,729	1,550	2,250	4,500	6,250	16,000	32,500
1842D	4,643	1,500	3,000	6,500	8,250	25,000	55,000
1842O	19,800	275	650	1,500	2,200	7,000	22,500
1843	100,546	275	300	500	750	1,500	4,500
1843C, Large Date	23,076	1,000	1,350	1,900	2,700	5,500	14,000
1843C, Small Date	2,988	1,850	3,250	5,750	8,500	20,000	
1843D	36,209	1,100	1,450	1,800	2,500	4,500	20,000
1843O	364,002	275	300	315	400	1,000	4,250
1844	6,784	275	500	1,350	1,800	5,000	15,000
1844C	11,622	1,250	1,650	3,500	4,500	12,500	32,500
1844D	17,332	1,350	1,350	2,000	2,500	4,500	18,000
1845	91,051	275	300	315	400	900	3,500
1845D	19,460	1,150	1,350	2,000	3,000	6,500	25,000
1845O	4,000	1,250	1,500	5,500	7,750	14,000	36,000
1846	21,598	275	300	500	750	3,500	16,500
1846C	4,808	1,300	2,000	3,750	5,500	12,500	25,000
1846D	19,303	1,300	1,850	2,750	3,500	6,500	22,000
1846O	62,000	275	325	750	950	3,000	12,500
1847	29,814	275	300	500	650	2,200	5,500
1847C	23,226	1,150	1,550	2,100	3,000	4,500	11,000
1847D	15,784	1,100	1,600	2,250	3,200	5,500	17,500
1847O	124,000	275	300	750	1,250	3,000	13,500
1848	6,500	375	550	1,250	1,450	3,500	11,000

CAL. Gold Quarter Eagle (1848)

In 1848, about 230 ounces of gold were sent to Secretary of War William L. Marcy by Colonel R.B. Mason, military governor of California. The gold was turned over to the Mint and made into quarter eagles. The distinguishing mark CAL. was punched above the eagle on the reverse side while the coins were in the die.

CAL. Above Eagle on Reverse (1848)

	Mintage	VF-20	EF-40	AU-50	AU-55	MS-60	MS-63
1848, CAL. Above Eagle	1,389	$25,000	$30,000	$40,000	$45,000	$62,500	$85,000
1848C	16,788	1,050	1,450	2,250	3,000	8,500	26,000
1848D	13,771	1,150	1,500	2,350	2,750	6,500	23,500
1849	23,294	275	300	550	650	1,500	4,750
1849C	10,220	1,100	1,550	3,500	4,500	12,500	35,000
1849D	10,945	1,150	1,650	2,250	3,000	9,500	26,000
1850	252,923	275	300	325	375	675	2,500
1850C	9,148	1,150	1,500	2,250	2,750	7,000	25,000
1850D	12,148	1,150	1,650	2,350	3,000	10,000	32,000

QUARTER EAGLES ($2.50)

	Mintage	VF-20	EF-40	AU-50	AU-55	MS-60	MS-63	PF-63
18500	84,000	$225	$300	$700	$850	$2,750	$10,000	
1851	1,372,748	200	225	275	285	325	800	
1851C	14,923	1,100	1,550	2,250	2,750	6,000	21,000	
1851D	11,264	1,200	1,650	2,500	3,000	6,750	25,000	
18510	148,000	250	325	500	650	2,500	9,500	
1852	1,159,681	200	225	275	285	325	850	
1852C	9,772	1,050	1,650	2,750	3,250	9,500	23,500	
1852D	4,078	1,200	2,250	4,500	5,500	11,000	34,000	
18520	140,000	285	300	550	750	3,250	8,000	
1853	1,404,668	200	225	275	285	325	800	
1853D	3,178	1,500	2,500	3,750	4,500	10,000	37,500	
1854	596,258	200	225	275	285	325	850	
1854C	7,295	1,050	1,500	3,000	4,500	8,500	30,000	
1854D	1,760	2,500	4,750	7,500	9,500	18,500	50,000	
18540	153,000	300	325	350	400	1,000	6,000	
1854S	246	150,000	250,000	325,000				
1855	235,480	200	225	275	285	325	1,000	
1855C	3,677	1,250	2,100	3,000	3,500	14,500	30,000	
1855D	1,123	2,750	5,500	8,500	11,000	35,000	65,000	
1856	384,240	200	225	265	275	300	1,000	$45,000
1856C	7,913	950	1,850	2,500	3,000	8,500	23,000	
1856D	874	5,000	8,500	22,500	27,500	50,000	100,000	
18560	21,100	275	475	850	1,150	4,500	20,000	
1856S	72,120	300	325	650	750	2,750	7,500	
1857	214,130	200	225	275	285	325	1,000	37,000
1857D	2,364	1,350	2,000	2,500	3,000	8,500	22,000	
18570	34,000	275	325	650	850	3,000	9,500	
1857S	69,200	300	325	650	850	3,000	10,000	
1858	47,377	225	240	285	300	700	1,150	25,000
1858C	9,056	1,050	1,500	2,500	3,000	7,000	25,000	
1859 (80)	39,364	225	235	285	325	850	2,250	15,000
1859D	2,244	1,250	2,000	2,500	4,000	12,500	45,000	
1859S	15,200	300	675	1,550	1,850	3,000	12,500	
1860 (112)	22,563	225	240	285	325	750	2,000	15,000
1860C	7,469	1,200	1,650	2,500	5,000	14,000	25,000	
1860S	35,600	275	450	750	900	2,500	10,000	
1861 (90)	1,283,788	200	225	275	300	700	1,250	15,000
1861S	24,000	325	600	2,000	3,000	5,000	12,000	
1862, 2 Over 1	*	650	1,350	2,750	3,500	6,500	10,000	
1862 (35)	98,508	275	400	1,250	1,550	5,000	11,000	13,500
1862S	8,000	500	1,350	3,000	4,000	12,500	25,000	
1863, Proof only (30)	40,000							50,000
1863S	10,800	375	1,000	2,250	3,500	9,000	20,000	
1864 (50)	2,824	5,500	12,500	20,000	27,500	45,000		12,500
1865 (25)	1,520	3,500	6,500	15,000	15,000	27,500		12,500
1865S	23,376	250	450	950	1,350	3,000	7,000	
1866 (30)	3,080	750	2,500	4,000	5,500	8,000	18,000	10,000
1866S	38,960	250	425	925	1,550	4,500	14,000	
1867 (50)	3,200	300	500	750	1,250	3,500	6,000	10,000
1867S	28,000	250	400	1,000	1,350	3,000	8,000	
1868 (25)	3,600	250	300	450	675	1,250	5,000	10,000

* Included in number below.

Chart continued on next page.

	Mintage	VF-20	EF-40	AU-50	AU-55	MS-60	MS-63	PF-63
1868S	34,000	$225	$275	$750	$950	$2,500	$8,000	
1869	(25)	4,320	225	325	450	850	2,000	7,500	$7,500
1869S	29,500	225	350	550	1,000	2,750	6,000	
1870	(35)	4,520	225	325	500	900	2,750	6,500	7,500
1870S	16,000	225	300	550	1,150	3,000	10,000	
1871	(30)	5,320	225	300	425	600	1,500	3,000	7,500
1871S	22,000	225	300	425	600	1,500	3,000	
1872	(30)	3,000	300	550	750	1,650	3,200	10,000	7,000
1872S	18,000	225	300	600	1,200	3,000	8,000	
1873	(25)	178,000	225	240	315	325	400	900	7,000
1873S	27,000	225	300	500	750	1,800	5,500	
1874	(20)	3,920	225	275	450	700	1,500	4,500	10,000
1875	(20)	400	2,750	4,000	7,500	9,000	18,000	30,000	25,000
1875S	11,600	225	300	500	850	2,500	6,000	
1876	(45)	4,176	225	450	600	1,100	2,250	4,500	6,500
1876S	5,000	225	400	600	1,300	2,000	6,750	
1877	(20)	1,632	225	550	750	1,150	2,000	6,500	6,500
1877S	35,400	225	275	300	325	425	1,750	
1878	(20)	286,240	225	240	275	300	350	650	9,000
1878S	178,000	225	240	275	300	350	1,250	
1879	(30)	88,960	225	240	275	300	350	750	6,500
1879S	43,500	225	240	275	300	800	3,250	
1880	(36)	2,960	325	350	500	650	1,000	2,500	6,500
1881	(51)	640	1,250	2,000	4,500	5,000	7,500	15,000	6,500
1882	(67)	4,000	225	300	325	375	600	2,000	5,000
1883	(82)	1,920	225	350	600	900	1,800	5,000	5,000
1884	(73)	1,950	225	300	425	575	1,000	2,500	5,000
1885	(87)	800	675	1,250	1,850	2,000	3,000	5,000	5,000
1886	(88)	4,000	225	300	325	375	750	2,000	5,000
1887	(122)	6,160	225	300	315	325	575	2,000	4,750
1888	(97)	16,001	225	240	275	325	375	550	4,750
1889	(48)	17,600	225	240	275	325	375	600	4,750
1890	(93)	8,720	225	240	275	325	375	1,000	4,750
1891	(80)	10,960	225	240	275	325	375	900	4,750
1892	(105)	2,440	245	265	275	325	450	1,500	4,750
1893	(106)	30,000	225	240	275	325	375	550	4,750
1894	(122)	4,000	250	275	325	350	425	1,250	4,750
1895	(119)	6,000	225	240	285	325	375	700	4,750
1896	(132)	19,070	225	240	250	275	375	525	4,750
1897	(136)	29,768	225	240	275	305	350	425	4,750
1898	(165)	24,000	225	240	275	305	350	425	4,750
1899	(150)	27,200	225	240	275	305	350	425	4,750
1900	(205)	67,000	225	240	260	285	300	350	4,750
1901	(223)	91,100	225	240	260	285	300	350	4,750
1902	(193)	133,540	225	240	260	285	300	350	4,750
1903	(197)	201,060	225	240	260	285	300	350	4,750
1904	(170)	160,790	225	240	260	285	300	350	4,750
1905	(144)	217,800	225	240	260	285	300	350	4,750
1906	(160)	176,330	225	240	260	285	300	350	4,750
1907	(154)	336,294	225	240	260	285	300	350	4,750

INDIAN HEAD (1908–1929)

American sculptor Bela Lyon Pratt, a former student of Augustus Saint-Gaudens, designed this coin and the similar five-dollar gold piece. It features no raised rim, and the main devices and legends are in sunken relief below the surface of the coin. President Theodore Roosevelt, who sought to improve the overall aesthetic quality of American coinage, was enthusiastic about the innovative new design. Collectors and the public were not as pleased. Some feared that the recessed design would collect dirt and germs—an unfounded concern. Over time the design has been recognized as a classic, and part of the early 20th-century renaissance of American coinage.

VF-20 Very Fine: Hair-cord knot distinct. Feathers at top of head clear. Cheekbone worn.
EF-40 Extremely Fine: Cheekbone, war bonnet, and headband feathers slightly worn.
AU-50 About Uncirculated: Trace of wear on cheekbone and headdress.
MS-60 Uncirculated: No trace of wear. Light blemishes.
MS-63 Choice Uncirculated: Some distracting contact marks or blemishes in prime focal areas. Impaired luster possible.
MS-64 Uncirculated: A few scattered contact marks visible. Good eye appeal and attractive luster.
Matte PF-63 Choice Proof: Few blemishes in secondary focal areas. No major flaws. Matte surfaces.

Mintmark location is on reverse, to left of arrows.

	Mintage	VF-20	EF-40	AU-50	MS-60	MS-63	MS-64	MATTE PF-63
1908 . . . . (236) 564,821		$200	$225	$250	$300	$600	$900	$7,500
1909 . . . . (139) 441,760		200	225	250	300	950	1,450	7,500
1910 . . . . (682) 492,000		200	225	250	285	650	1,100	7,500
1911 . . . . (191) 704,000		200	225	250	300	500	850	7,500
1911D 55,680		2,250	2,500	3,500	6,000	10,000	20,000	
1912 . . . . (197) 616,000		200	225	250	450	950	2,000	7,500
1913 . . . . (165) 722,000		200	225	250	350	525	900	7,500
1914 . . . . (117) 240,000		210	245	265	500	1,750	4,000	7,500
1914D 448,000		200	225	250	300	1,000	2,000	
1915 . . . . (100) 606,000		200	225	250	300	500	900	8,500
1925D 578,000		200	225	250	275	425	625	
1926 446,000		200	225	250	275	425	625	
1927 388,000		200	225	250	275	425	625	
1928 416,000		200	225	250	275	425	625	
1929 532,000		200	225	250	275	425	625	

The three-dollar gold piece was authorized by the Act of February 21, 1853. Coinage was struck beginning in 1854. It was never popular and saw very little circulation.

VF-20 Very Fine: Eyebrow, hair about forehead and ear, and bottom curl all worn smooth. Faint details visible on curled feather-ends of headdress.

EF-40 Extremely Fine: Light wear above and to right of eye, and on top of curled feathers.

AU-50 About Uncirculated: Trace of wear on top of curled feathers and in hair above and to right of eye.

AU-55 Choice About Uncirculated: Evidence of friction on design high points. Much of original mint luster present.

MS-60 Uncirculated: No trace of wear. Light blemishes.

MS-63 Choice Uncirculated: Some distracting contact marks or blemishes in prime focal areas. Impaired luster possible.

Mintmark location is on reverse, below wreath.

PF-63 Choice Proof: Reflective surfaces with only a few blemishes in secondary focal places. No major flaws.

	Mintage	VF-20	EF-40	AU-50	AU-55	MS-60	MS-63	PF-63
1854	138,618	$700	$900	$1,150	$1,250	$1,750	$3,000	$55,000
1854D	1,120	10,000	15,000	25,000	35,000	60,000		
1854O	24,000	875	1,750	3,000	3,500	25,000	55,000	
1855	50,555	700	900	1,200	1,500	1,750	4,000	30,000
1855S	6,600	950	1,850	5,000	7,500	25,000	65,000	
1856	26,010	700	1,000	1,250	1,800	2,000	5,000	25,000
1856S	34,500	750	1,150	2,250	4,500	8,500	20,000	
1857	20,891	700	975	1,250	2,000	2,500	6,000	25,000
1857S	14,000	775	1,750	4,500	6,000	15,000		
1858	2,133	825	1,300	2,000	3,500	7,000	15,000	18,500
1859	(80)...15,558	700	900	1,250	1,500	2,250	6,000	15,000
1860	(119)....7,036	725	950	1,300	1,650	2,500	6,000	10,000
1860S	7,000	775	1,500	5,000	7,500	17,500	40,000	
1861	(113)....5,959	700	900	1,500	1,750	5,500	9,000	12,000
1862	(35)....5,750	700	900	1,500	1,750	5,500	9,000	12,000
1863	(39)....5,000	750	950	1,500	1,750	5,500	9,000	12,000
1864	(50)....2,630	750	950	1,500	1,750	5,500	9,000	12,000
1865	(25)....1,140	1,750	3,000	4,500	6,500	10,000	16,000	15,000
1866	(30)....4,000	750	950	1,350	1,750	3,000	7,500	12,000
1867	(50)....2,600	750	950	1,350	1,750	3,000	10,000	12,000
1868	(25)....4,850	700	900	1,350	1,750	2,750	7,500	12,000
1869	(25)....2,500	700	900	1,350	1,750	3,000	10,000	12,000
1870	(35)....3,500	700	900	1,350	1,750	3,000	10,000	12,000
1870S (unique)		—						
1871	(30)....1,300	725	1,000	1,350	1,750	3,200	8,500	14,000
1872	(30)....2,000	725	1,000	1,350	1,750	3,200	8,500	12,000
1873, Open 3 (Original)	(25)		10,000	17,000				26,000
1873, Close 3		2,750	4,500	7,500	12,500	24,000	40,000	30,000
1874	(20)...41,800	650	800	1,000	1,100	1,750	3,000	22,000
1875, Proof only	(20)			40,000	50,000			100,000
1876, Proof only	(45)			15,000	20,000			40,000
1877	(20)....1,468	2,500	5,000	6,500	10,000	15,000	35,000	15,000
1878	(20)...82,304	650	800	1,000	1,100	1,750	3,000	15,000
1879	(30)....3,000	750	925	1,250	1,850	2,100	5,250	12,000
1880	(36)....1,000	750	1,350	1,750	1,900	2,500	6,000	12,000
1881	(54).....500	1,500	3,000	5,000	6,000	10,000	14,000	12,000
1882	(76)....1,500	750	950	1,350	1,750	2,500	5,750	10,000
1883	(89).....900	750	1,250	1,750	2,250	2,750	6,500	10,000
1884	(106)....1,000	750	1,350	1,750	2,250	2,750	7,500	10,000
1885	(109).....801	775	1,375	1,850	2,500	3,500	10,000	12,000
1886	(142)....1,000	750	1,250	1,850	2,250	3,250	10,000	10,000
1887	(160)....6,000	725	950	1,350	1,750	2,500	5,000	10,000
1888	(291)....5,000	700	900	1,150	1,300	2,200	3,250	10,000
1889	(129)....2,300	700	900	1,150	1,300	2,200	3,750	10,000

STELLA (1879–1880)

These pattern coins were first suggested by the Hon. John A. Kasson, then U.S. envoy extraordinary and minister plenipotentiary to Austria-Hungary. It was through the efforts of Dr. W.W. Hubbell, who patented the alloy goloid (used in making another pattern piece, the goloid metric dollar) that we have these beautiful and interesting coins.

The four-dollar Stella—so called because of the five-pointed star on the reverse—was envisioned by Kasson as America's answer to various foreign gold coins popular in the international market. The British sovereign, Italy's 20 lire, and the 20 pesetas of Spain were three such coins: each smaller than a U.S. five-dollar gold piece, they were used widely in international trade.

The Stella was one of many proposals made to Congress for an international trade coin, and one of only several that made it to pattern coin form (others include the 1868 five dollar and 1874 Bickford ten dollar).

Odds were stacked against the Stella from the start. The denomination of four U.S. dollars didn't match any of the coin's European counterparts, and at any rate the U.S. double eagle (twenty-dollar coin)—already used in international commerce—was a more convenient medium of exchange. The Stella was never minted in quantities for circulation.

There are two distinct types in both years of issue. Charles E. Barber is thought to have designed the Flowing Hair type, and George T. Morgan the Coiled Hair. They were struck as patterns in gold, aluminum, copper, and white metal. Only those struck in gold are listed.

Flowing Hair   Coiled Hair

	Mintage	EF-40	AU-50	PF-60	PF-63	PF-65
1879, Flowing Hair	(425+)	$70,000	$80,000	$100,000	$130,000	$175,000
1879, Coiled Hair *(12 known)*		125,000	150,000	200,000	400,000	650,000
1880, Flowing Hair *(17 known)*		75,000	85,000	115,000	135,000	325,000
1880, Coiled Hair *(8 known)*		200,000	275,000	350,000	650,000	1,000,000

While the 1856 Flying Eagle cent, the 1879 and 1880 four-dollar Stellas, and a few other patterns are listed in this book, there are more than 1,800 other trial pieces that were minted from 1792 to the present. These are listed in Whitman's *United States Pattern Coins* book and are a fascinating numismatic specialty. Most patterns are rare, and most were made in Proof formats.

The half eagle (five-dollar gold coin) was the first gold coin struck for the United States. It was authorized to be coined by the Act of April 2, 1792. The first type weighed 135 grains, of .91667 fineness. The weight was changed by the Act of June 28, 1834, to 129 grains, of .899225 fineness. Fineness became .900 by the Act of January 18, 1837.

CAPPED BUST TO RIGHT (1795–1807)

F-12 Fine: Liberty's hair worn smooth but with distinct outline. For heraldic type, E PLURIBUS UNUM faint but legible.
VF-20 Very Fine: Slight to noticeable wear on high spots such as hair, turban, and eagle's head and wings.
EF-40 Extremely Fine: Slight wear on hair and highest part of cheek.
AU-50 About Uncirculated: Trace of wear on cap, hair, cheek, and drapery.
MS-60 Uncirculated: No trace of wear. Light blemishes.
MS-63 Choice Uncirculated: Some distracting marks or blemishes in focal areas. Impaired luster possible.

Small Eagle Reverse (1795–1798)

1795
Obverse

1795
Reverse

1796, 6 Over 5

1797, 15 Stars

1797, 16 Stars

	Mintage	F-12	VF-20	EF-40	AU-50	AU-55	MS-60	MS-63
1795, Small Eagle	8,707	$13,500	$18,000	$23,000	$32,000	$40,000	$55,000	$125,000
1796, 6 Over 5	6,196	15,000	19,000	30,000	50,000	65,000	95,000	175,000
1797, 15 Stars	3,609	16,500	21,000	37,500	75,000	100,000	150,000	
1797, 16 Stars	*	16,000	20,000	34,000	70,000	90,000	145,000	
1798, Small Eagle *(6 known)*	100,000	150,000	300,000	450,000	750,000	—		

* Included in number above.

Heraldic Eagle Reverse (1795–1807)

	Mintage	F-12	VF-20	EF-40	AU-50	AU-55	MS-60	MS-63
1795, Heraldic Eagle	*	$10,000	$15,000	$20,000	$35,000	$40,000	$75,000	$150,000
1797, 7 Over 5	*	8,000	12,000	22,000	45,000	50,000	100,000	
1798, Large 8, 13-Star Reverse	24,867	3,000	4,000	6,000	8,500	11,000	20,000	
1798, Large 8, 14-Star Reverse	**	3,000	4,250	8,000	15,000	20,000	55,000	
1799	7,451	2,500	3,750	5,500	9,000	12,000	18,000	45,000
1800	37,628	2,500	3,750	5,500	7,500	8,500	11,000	25,000

* Included in number below. ** Included in number above.

	Mintage	F-12	VF-20	EF-40	AU-50	AU-55	MS-60	MS-63
1802, 2 Over 1	53,176	$2,750	$3,750	$5,500	$7,500	$8,500	$11,000	$25,000
1803, 3 Over 2	33,506	2,750	3,750	5,500	7,500	8,500	11,000	25,000
1804, All kinds.	30,475	2,750	3,750	5,500	7,500	8,500	11,000	25,000
1805	33,183	2,750	3,750	5,500	7,500	8,500	11,000	25,000
1806	64,093	2,750	3,750	5,500	7,500	8,500	11,000	25,000
1807	32,488	2,750	3,750	5,500	7,500	8,500	11,000	25,000

DRAPED BUST TO LEFT (1807–1812)

F-12 Fine: LIBERTY on cap legible but partly weak.
VF-20 Very Fine: Headband edges slightly worn. LIBERTY bold.
EF-40 Extremely Fine: Slight wear on highest portions of hair; 80% of major curls plain.
AU-50 About Uncirculated: Trace of wear above eye and on top of cap, cheek, and hair.
AU-55 Choice About Uncirculated: Evidence of friction on design high points. Some mint luster present.
MS-60 Uncirculated: No trace of wear. Light blemishes.
MS-63 Choice Uncirculated: Some distracting contact marks or blemishes in prime focal areas. Impaired luster possible.

	Mintage	F-12	VF-20	EF-40	AU-50	AU-55	MS-60	MS-63
1807	51,605	$2,000	$3,000	$4,000	$6,000	$7,000	$9,500	$20,000
1808, All kinds.	55,578							
1808, 8 Over 7		2,250	3,500	4,500	7,000	9,000	12,000	25,000
1808		2,000	3,000	4,000	6,000	7,000	9,500	20,000
1809, 9 Over 8	33,875	2,000	3,000	4,000	6,000	7,000	9,500	20,000
1810	100,287	2,000	3,000	4,000	6,000	7,000	9,500	20,000
1811	99,581	2,000	3,000	4,000	6,000	7,000	9,500	20,000
1812	58,087	2,000	3,000	4,000	6,000	7,000	9,500	20,000

CAPPED HEAD TO LEFT (1813–1834)

Large Diameter   Reduced Diameter

Large Diameter (1813–1829)

	Mintage	F-12	VF-20	EF-40	AU-50	AU-55	MS-60	MS-63
1813	95,428	$2,500	$3,000	$4,500	$6,500	$7,500	$9,000	$15,000
1814, 4 Over 3	15,454	3,500	5,000	6,000	8,500	10,000	15,000	25,000
1815	635	25,000	50,000	110,000	175,000	200,000	225,000	300,000
1818	48,588	3,500	5,000	8,500	11,000	13,000	16,000	32,500
1819	51,723	6,500	12,000	25,000	35,000	40,000	50,000	65,000
1820	263,806	4,000	5,500	9,500	11,500	14,000	16,000	28,000
1821	34,641	10,000	15,000	30,000	50,000	65,000	100,000	250,000
1822 *(3 known)*	17,796			3,000,000				
1823	14,485	3,500	5,000	10,000	12,000	15,000	20,000	40,000

Chart continued on next page.

	Mintage	F-12	VF-20	EF-40	AU-50	AU-55	MS-60	MS-63
1824 17,340		$4,000	$6,000	$24,000	$30,000	$35,000	$45,000	$65,000
1825, 5 Over Partial 4 29,060		4,000	6,000	20,000	25,000	30,000	40,000	60,000
1825, 5 Over 4 *(2 known)* . . . . *				300,000				
1826 18,069		4,000	6,200	15,000	20,000	25,000	30,000	52,000
1827 24,913		7,500	12,500	22,000	30,000	35,000	45,000	70,000
1828, 8 Over 7 *(5 known)* . . . .**		15,000	25,000	50,000	65,000	80,000	150,000	250,000
1828 28,029		14,000	20,000	30,000	40,000	50,000	90,000	170,000
1829, Large Date 57,442		12,500	25,000	50,000	65,000	75,000	120,000	275,000

* Included in number above. ** Included in number below.

Reduced Diameter (1829–1834)

	Mintage	F-12	VF-20	EF-40	AU-50	AU-55	MS-60	MS-63
1829, Small Date . . . .*		$25,000	$45,000	$60,000	$85,000	$100,000	$150,000	$200,000
1830 126,351		12,500	24,000	30,000	35,000	40,000	52,500	75,000
1831 140,594		12,500	24,000	30,000	35,000	40,000	52,500	75,000
1832, Curved-Base 2, 12 Stars *(5 known)* 157,487		85,000	125,000	225,000	350,000			
1832, Square-Base 2, 13 Stars . . . . . **		12,500	24,000	30,000	35,000	40,000	52,500	75,000
1833 193,630		12,500	24,000	30,000	35,000	40,000	52,500	75,000
1834 50,141		12,500	24,000	30,000	35,000	40,000	52,500	75,000

* Included in mintage for 1829, Large Date (previous page). ** Included in number above.

CLASSIC HEAD, NO MOTTO (1834–1838)

	Mintage	F-12	VF-20	EF-40	AU-50	AU-55	MS-60	MS-63
1834 657,460		$400	$475	$600	$900	$1,100	$3,000	$7,500
1835 371,534		400	475	600	1,000	1,200	3,200	7,500
1836 553,147		400	475	600	1,000	1,200	3,200	9,500
1837 207,121		400	500	650	1,300	1,500	3,500	12,000
1838 286,588		400	475	600	1,250	1,500	3,500	9,000
1838C 17,179		1,150	3,000	5,500	8,500	12,000	27,500	65,000
1838D 20,583		1,100	2,750	5,000	7,500	10,000	22,500	40,000

LIBERTY HEAD (1839–1908)
Variety 1 – No Motto Above Eagle (1839–1866)

VF-20 Very Fine: LIBERTY on coronet bold. Major lines show in curls on neck.

EF-40 Extremely Fine: Details clear in curls on neck. Slight wear on top and lower part of coronet and on hair.

AU-50 About Uncirculated: Trace of wear on coronet and hair above eye.

AU-55 Choice About Uncirculated: Evidence of friction on design high points. Some original mint luster.

MS-60 Uncirculated: No trace of wear. Light blemishes.

MS-63 Choice Uncirculated: Some distracting contact marks or blemishes in prime focal areas. Impaired luster possible.

Mintmark: 1839, above date;
1840–1908, below eagle.

PF-63 Choice Proof: Attractive reflective surfaces with only a few blemishes in secondary focal places. No major flaws.

HALF EAGLES ($5)

1842, Large Date   **Small Letters**   **Large Letters**

	Mintage	VF-20	EF-40	AU-50	AU-55	MS-60	MS-63	PF-63
1839	118,143	$425	$450	$675	$875	$2,500	$16,000	
1839C	17,205	1,350	2,250	3,500	5,000	12,500	40,000	
1839D	18,939	1,850	3,500	5,000	6,750	17,000		
1840	137,382	400	415	750	950	2,200	6,750	
1840C	18,992	1,250	2,000	3,500	5,000	15,000	40,000	
1840D	22,896	1,350	2,000	4,000	5,500	10,000	30,000	
1840O	40,120	400	415	1,100	1,500	6,500	27,500	
1841	15,833	400	415	900	1,100	3,000	7,000	
1841C	21,467	1,350	1,700	2,200	2,600	9,500	30,000	
1841D	29,392	1,350	1,750	2,200	2,600	8,000	20,000	
1842, Small Letters	27,578	400	415	1,350	1,550	8,500	15,000	
1842, Large Letters	*	525	1,100	1,850	2,250	7,500	16,000	
1842C, Small Date	27,432	5,000	12,500	20,000	25,000	50,000		
1842C, Large Date	*	1,250	1,700	2,200	2,600	9,500	25,000	
1842D, Small Date	59,608	1,250	1,600	2,200	2,600	9,500	25,000	
1842D, Large Date	*	1,950	4,000	8,500	12,500	32,500		
1842O	16,400	750	1,500	5,000	8,000	13,000	30,000	
1843	611,205	400	415	425	475	1,350	7,500	
1843C	44,277	1,350	1,650	2,500	3,500	7,300	22,500	
1843D	98,452	1,350	1,700	2,000	2,500	7,000	15,000	
1843O, Small Letters	19,075	450	1,000	1,500	2,000	12,500	32,500	
1843O, Large Letters	82,000	425	875	1,250	1,850	7,500	18,000	
1844	340,330	400	415	425	450	1,500	6,000	
1844C	23,631	1,350	2,000	3,500	4,500	13,500	27,500	
1844D	88,982	1,250	1,750	2,000	2,500	7,000	19,000	
1844O	364,600	400	415	425	575	3,250	9,500	
1845	417,099	400	415	425	450	1,500	7,000	
1845D	90,629	1,350	1,700	2,250	2,750	6,750	18,500	
1845O	41,000	450	550	1,850	2,500	6,000	17,500	
1846, Large Date	395,942	400	415	425	500	1,650	8,500	
1846, Small Date	*	400	415	425	450	1,350	7,500	
1846C	12,995	1,250	2,000	3,500	4,750	13,500	40,000	
1846D	80,294	1,250	1,750	2,500	3,500	7,500	15,000	
1846O	58,000	450	650	2,000	2,500	7,000	18,500	
1847	915,981	385	400	425	450	1,350	4,250	
1847C	84,151	1,300	1,600	2,250	2,750	7,500	20,000	
1847D	64,405	1,300	1,600	2,250	2,750	6,000	12,500	
1847O	12,000	1,350	3,000	5,500	7,000	18,000	25,000	
1848	260,775	385	400	425	450	1,450	8,000	
1848C	64,472	1,250	1,650	2,100	2,750	12,500	32,500	
1848D	47,465	1,350	1,750	2,100	2,750	8,500	18,500	
1849	133,070	385	400	475	575	1,850	9,000	
1849C	64,823	1,350	1,600	2,200	2,650	7,500	15,000	
1849D	39,036	1,350	1,650	2,250	2,750	9,500	20,000	
1850	64,491	385	450	675	825	2,500	14,000	

* Included in number above.

Chart continued on next page.

	Mintage	VF-20	EF-40	AU-50	AU-55	MS-60	MS-63	PF-63
1850C	63,591	$1,300	$1,550	$2,250	$2,650	$7,500	$13,000	
1850D	43,984	1,350	1,750	2,750	3,250	16,500		
1851	377,505	385	400	425	450	1,750	7,000	
1851C	49,176	1,250	1,650	2,350	2,800	8,000	30,000	
1851D	62,710	1,250	1,600	2,250	2,750	9,000	16,000	
1851O	41,000	500	1,000	2,600	3,250	8,000	15,000	
1852	573,901	385	400	425	450	1,200	5,500	
1852C	72,574	1,250	1,500	2,000	2,500	4,500	16,500	
1852D	91,584	1,250	1,650	2,100	2,650	7,000	18,000	
1853	305,770	385	400	425	450	1,250	6,000	
1853C	65,571	1,250	1,650	2,200	2,500	5,000	18,000	
1853D	89,678	1,300	1,750	2,300	2,600	5,250	15,000	
1854	160,675	385	400	425	450	1,500	6,000	
1854C	39,283	1,250	1,650	2,650	3,250	9,000	25,000	
1854D	56,413	1,250	1,500	2,100	2,600	6,000	20,000	
1854O	46,000	425	475	1,050	1,500	5,000	16,500	
1854S *(2 known)*	268			2,500,000				
1855	117,098	385	400	425	450	1,500	5,500	
1855C	39,788	1,250	1,650	2,250	2,650	9,000	30,000	
1855D	22,432	1,350	1,850	2,250	2,650	9,500	27,500	
1855O	11,100	550	1,550	3,000	3,500	13,500		
1855S	61,000	425	675	1,550	2,000	9,000		
1856	197,990	385	400	425	450	1,650	6,500	—
1856C	28,457	1,250	1,600	2,250	2,650	13,000	30,000	
1856D	19,786	1,250	1,750	2,500	3,000	7,500	25,000	
1856O	10,000	550	875	3,000	3,500	9,500		
1856S	105,100	425	475	700	975	4,500	18,500	
1857	98,188	385	400	425	450	1,500	5,500	—
1857C	31,360	1,250	1,650	2,250	2,650	5,250	20,000	
1857D	17,046	1,300	1,700	2,400	2,750	8,000	25,000	
1857O	13,000	550	1,000	2,750	3,500	10,000	32,500	
1857S	87,000	425	450	675	900	6,000	12,500	
1858	15,136	385	400	475	575	2,400	6,000	—
1858C	38,856	1,200	1,650	2,250	2,650	6,000	22,500	
1858D	15,362	1,250	1,750	2,450	2,850	8,000	23,000	
1858S	18,600	700	2,000	3,500	4,500	20,000		
1859 (80)	16,734	385	475	575	650	4,500	12,500	$40,000
1859C	31,847	1,250	1,650	2,500	3,250	8,500	27,000	
1859D	10,366	1,250	1,750	2,250	3,000	7,000	30,000	
1859S	13,220	800	2,000	3,250	4,500	16,000		
1860 (62)	19,763	385	450	750	900	2,500	10,000	30,000
1860C	14,813	1,500	1,850	2,600	3,500	8,000	15,000	
1860D	14,635	1,500	2,000	2,750	3,500	8,500	32,000	
1860S	21,200	650	1,400	3,000	3,850	16,000		
1861 (66)	688,084	385	415	425	450	1,300	5,000	30,000
1861C	6,879	1,500	2,500	4,500	6,000	16,000	55,000	
1861D	1,597	10,000	17,500	22,500	27,500	60,000	115,000	
1861S	18,000	650	2,500	3,500	5,000	24,000		
1862 (35)	4,430	500	1,400	2,400	2,850	12,000	28,000	30,000
1862S	9,500	2,000	3,500	5,500	6,750	27,500		
1863 (30)	2,442	800	2,500	3,500	4,500	16,000		25,000
1863S	17,000	1,000	2,750	5,000	7,000	22,000		
1864 (50)	4,170	500	1,250	2,750	3,500	8,000		25,000
1864S	3,888	3,000	12,000	18,000	20,000	32,500		
1865 (25)	1,270	900	3,000	6,750	7,750	13,500		25,000
1865S	27,612	750	1,500	3,000	3,850	10,000	20,000	
1866S	9,000	1,200	2,500	7,500	9,000	25,000		

Variety 2 – Motto Above Eagle (1866–1908)

VF-20 Very Fine: Half of hair lines above coronet missing. Hair curls under ear evident, but worn. Motto and its ribbon sharp.

EF-40 Extremely Fine: Small amount of wear on top of hair and below L in LIBERTY. Wear evident on wing tips and neck of eagle.

AU-50 About Uncirculated: Trace of wear on tip of coronet and hair above eye.

AU-55 Choice About Uncirculated: Evidence of friction on design high points. Some original mint luster present.

MS-60 Uncirculated: No trace of wear. Light blemishes.

MS-63 Choice Uncirculated: Some distracting contact marks or blemishes in prime focal areas. Impaired luster possible.

PF-63 Choice Proof: Reflective surfaces with only a few blemishes in secondary focal places. No major flaws.

	Mintage	VF-20	EF-40	AU-50	AU-55	MS-60	MS-63	PF-63
1866 . . . . (30). 6,700		$550	$950	$2,100	$2,500	$10,000		$17,500
1866S 34,920		750	1,800	4,500	6,500	15,000		
1867 . . . . (50). 6,870		425	1,000	2,250	2,750	7,500		17,500
1867S 29,000		750	1,500	4,000	5,500	20,000		
1868 . . . . (25). 5,700		500	650	1,850	2,250	6,500		17,500
1868S 52,000		425	950	2,200	2,750	12,500		
1869 . . . . (25). 1,760		650	1,450	2,750	3,500	10,000		17,500
1869S 31,000		400	1,050	2,400	3,500	14,000		
1870 . . . . (35). 4,000		550	1,250	1,500	1,850	11,000		17,500
1870CC 7,675		12,000	17,500	30,000	37,500	80,000		
1870S 17,000		700	1,500	4,000	6,500	16,000		
1871 . . . . (30). 3,200		625	1,100	1,900	2,500	6,500		17,500
1871CC 20,770		1,750	3,500	10,000	15,000	45,000	$77,500	
1871S 25,000		400	600	2,000	2,400	8,000		
1872 . . . . (30). 1,660		550	1,200	1,900	2,500	7,500	12,500	17,500
1872CC 16,980		2,500	4,500	12,000	17,500	40,000		
1872S 36,400		400	500	1,900	2,750	8,000		
1873 . . . . (25). 112,505		285	300	315	325	700	2,750	17,500
1873CC 7,416		3,000	8,500	18,000	25,000	45,000		
1873S 31,000		400	900	2,000	2,400	13,000		
1874 . . . . (20). 3,488		425	1,100	1,500	1,750	7,500	13,500	20,000
1874CC 21,198		800	1,500	6,750	8,750	27,500		
1874S 16,000		450	1,400	2,250	2,750	13,500		
1875 . . . . (20). 200		40,000	50,000	80,000	100,000			75,000
1875CC 11,828		1,500	3,500	8,500	11,500	35,000		
1875S 9,000		475	1,350	3,000	3,500	10,000		
1876 . . . . (45). 1,432		600	1,000	2,500	3,000	9,000	14,000	13,500
1876CC 6,887		1,500	3,750	9,000	11,500	35,000		
1876S 4,000		1,250	2,000	5,500	6,500	18,000		
1877 . . . . (20). 1,132		650	1,800	2,750	3,250	8,000	15,000	13,500
1877CC 8,680		1,100	2,500	7,750	10,000	35,000		
1877S 26,700		285	425	900	1,100	5,500	13,000	
1878 . . . . (20). 131,720		285	300	315	325	375	1,500	20,000
1878CC 9,054		3,000	5,750	12,500	15,000	55,000		
1878S 144,700		285	300	315	325	375	2,750	
1879 . . . . (30). 301,920		285	300	315	325	375	1,350	13,000
1879CC 17,281		750	1,100	2,750	3,500	17,500		
1879S 426,200		285	300	315	350	750	1,500	
1880 . . . . (36). . . . 3,166,400		285	300	315	325	375	700	12,000
1880CC 51,017		700	875	1,000	2,750	8,500	30,000	
1880S 1,348,900		285	300	315	325	375	500	

Chart continued on next page.

	Mintage	VF-20	EF-40	AU-50	AU-55	MS-60	MS-63	PF-63
1881 . . . . (42). . . . 5,708,802		$285	$300	$315	$325	$375	$450	$12,000
1881CC 13,886		650	1,250	5,000	7,500	16,500	50,000	
1881S 969,000		285	300	315	325	375	675	
1882 . . . . (48). . . . 2,514,520		285	300	315	325	375	450	11,000
1882CC 82,817		500	600	750	1,000	7,500	30,000	
1882S 969,000		285	300	315	325	375	450	
1883 . . . . (61). 233,400		285	300	315	325	375	1,000	11,000
1883CC 12,598		600	1,000	2,750	3,750	14,000		
1883S 83,200		285	300	315	325	450	1,800	
1884 . . . . (48). 191,030		285	300	315	325	375	1,200	11,000
1884CC 16,402		700	1,000	2,500	3,750	16,500		
1884S 177,000		285	300	315	325	375	1,100	
1885 . . . . (66). 601,440		285	300	315	325	375	700	10,000
1885S 1,211,500		285	300	315	325	375	450	
1886 . . . . (72). 388,360		285	300	315	325	375	675	10,000
1886S 3,268,000		285	300	315	325	375	450	
1887, Proof only (87).								32,500
1887S 1,912,000		285	300	315	325	375	675	
1888 . . . . (95). . . .18,201		285	300	315	325	400	1,100	10,000
1888S 293,900		285	300	315	325	550	2,000	
1889 . . . . (45). 7,520		285	300	315	325	600	1,800	10,000
1890 . . . . (88). 4,240		285	300	315	375	1,250	3,500	10,000
1890CC 53,800		600	675	800	875	1,300	6,000	
1891 . . . . (53). . . .61,360		285	300	315	325	375	1,200	9,500
1891CC 208,000		550	650	750	850	1,200	2,500	
1892 . . . . (92). 753,480		285	300	315	325	375	700	9,500
1892CC 82,968		550	650	750	850	1,500	5,000	
1892O 10,000		550	650	875	1,150	2,250	9,000	
1892S 298,400		285	300	315	325	375	1,500	
1893 . . . . (77). . . . 1,528,120		285	300	315	325	375	450	9,500
1893CC 60,000		500	550	650	850	1,150	5,000	
1893O 110,000		285	425	450	475	700	4,000	
1893S 224,000		285	300	315	325	400	675	
1894 . . . . (75). 957,880		285	300	315	325	375	500	9,500
1894O 16,600		285	425	450	475	850	4,500	
1894S 55,900		285	300	315	350	1,500	6,000	
1895 . . . . (81). . . . 1,345,855		285	300	315	325	375	450	9,500
1895S 112,000		285	300	315	350	1,850	3,500	
1896 . . . . (103). 58,960		285	300	315	325	375	500	8,500
1896S 155,400		285	300	315	375	750	3,500	
1897 . . . . (83). 867,800		285	300	315	325	375	450	8,500
1897S 354,000		285	300	315	350	550	3,250	
1898 . . . . (75). 633,420		285	300	315	325	375	500	8,500
1898S 1,397,400		285	300	315	325	375	800	
1899 . . . . (99). . . . 1,710,630		285	300	315	325	375	450	8,500
1899S 1,545,000		285	300	315	325	375	800	
1900 . . . . (230). . . . 1,405,500		285	300	315	325	375	450	8,500
1900S 329,000		285	300	315	325	375	1,000	
1901 . . . . (140). 615,900		285	300	315	325	375	450	8,500
1901S, 1 Over 0 3,648,000		285	300	315	325	375	1,100	
1901S . . . . *		285	300	315	325	375	450	
1902 . . . . (162). 172,400		285	300	315	325	375	450	8,500
1902S 939,000		285	300	315	325	375	450	
1903 . . . . (154). 226,870		285	300	315	325	375	450	8,500
1903S 1,855,000		285	300	315	325	375	450	

* Included in number above.

	Mintage	VF-20	EF-40	AU-50	AU-55	MS-60	MS-63	PF-63
1904 . . . . (136)	392,000	$285	$300	$315	$325	$375	$500	$8,500
1904S	97,000	285	300	315	325	500	2,250	
1905 . . . . (108)	302,200	285	300	315	325	375	450	8,500
1905S	880,700	285	300	315	325	450	1,300	
1906 . . . . (85)	348,735	285	300	315	325	375	450	8,500
1906D	320,000	285	300	315	325	375	450	
1906S	598,000	285	300	315	325	435	850	
1907 . . . . (92)	626,100	285	300	315	325	375	450	8,500
1907D	888,000	285	300	315	325	375	450	
1908	421,874	285	300	315	325	375	450	

INDIAN HEAD (1908–1929)

This type conforms in design to the quarter eagle of the same date. The sunken-relief designs and lettering make the Indian Head a unique series, along with the quarter eagle, in United States coinage.

VF-20 Very Fine: Noticeable wear on large middle feathers and tip of eagle's wing.

EF-40 Extremely Fine: Cheekbone, war bonnet, and headband feathers slightly worn. Feathers on eagle's upper wing show considerable wear.

AU-50 About Uncirculated: Trace of wear on cheekbone and headdress.

AU-55 Choice About Uncirculated: Evidence of friction on design high points. Much of original mint luster present.

MS-60 Uncirculated: No trace of wear. Light blemishes.

MS-63 Choice Uncirculated: Some distracting contact marks or blemishes in prime focal areas. Impaired luster possible.

Mintmark Location

Matte PF-63 Choice Proof: Matte surfaces with few blemishes in secondary focal places. No major flaws.

Coin dealers usually pay higher prices than those listed for scarcer coins with well-struck mintmarks.

	Mintage	VF-20	EF-40	AU-50	AU-55	MS-60	MS-63	MATTE PF-63
1908 . . . . (167)	577,845	$300	$325	$350	$365	$475	$850	$10,000
1908D	148,000	300	325	350	365	475	1,000	
1908S	82,000	450	500	550	600	950	6,000	
1909 . . . . (78)	627,060	300	325	350	365	475	900	10,000
1909D 3,423,560		300	325	350	365	475	750	
1909O	34,200	2,500	3,750	6,000	8,500	20,000	70,000	
1909S	297,200	300	325	350	365	1,150	10,000	
1910 . . . . (250)	604,000	300	325	350	365	475	850	10,000
1910D	193,600	300	325	350	365	475	2,250	
1910S	770,200	300	325	375	425	650	6,500	
1911 . . . . (139)	915,000	300	325	350	365	475	900	10,000
1911D	72,500	425	650	1,000	1,250	5,000	32,500	
1911S 1,416,000		300	325	375	500	650	3,250	
1912 . . . . (144)	790,000	300	325	350	365	475	950	10,000
1912S	392,000	300	325	375	475	1,100	12,500	
1913 . . . . (99)	915,901	300	325	350	365	475	750	10,000
1913S	408,000	300	325	375	550	1,750	13,500	
1914 . . . . (125)	247,000	300	325	350	365	475	1,550	10,000
1914D	247,000	300	325	350	365	475	1,750	
1914S	263,000	300	325	375	450	1,250	7,000	
1915 . . . . (75)	588,000	300	325	350	365	475	800	10,000
1915S	164,000	300	325	375	400	1,750	12,500	
1916S	240,000	300	325	375	400	550	4,000	
1929	662,000	7,500	10,000	12,500	17,500	22,500	37,500	

Coinage authorization, specified weights, and fineness of the eagle coins conform to those of the half eagle. The Small Eagle reverse was used until 1797, when the large, Heraldic Eagle replaced it.

CAPPED BUST TO RIGHT (1795–1804)

F-12 Fine: Details on turban and head obliterated.
VF-20 Very Fine: Hair lines in curls on neck and details under turban and over forehead worn but distinguishable.
EF-40 Extremely Fine: Definite wear on hair to left of eye and strand of hair across and around turban, as well as on eagle's wing tips.
AU-50 About Uncirculated: Trace of wear on cap, hair, cheek, and drapery.
AU-55 Choice About Uncirculated: Evidence of friction on design high points. Most of original mint luster present.
MS-60 Uncirculated: No trace of wear. Light blemishes.
MS-63 Choice Uncirculated: Some distracting contact marks or blemishes in prime focal areas. Impaired luster possible.

Small Eagle Reverse (1795–1797)

	Mintage	F-12	VF-20	EF-40	AU-50	AU-55	MS-60	MS-63
1795 5,583		$22,500	$25,000	$35,000	$45,000	$55,000	$80,000	$170,000
1796 4,146		25,000	27,000	40,000	50,000	57,500	87,500	225,000
1797, Small Eagle 3,615		27,500	35,000	55,000	100,000	150,000		

Heraldic Eagle Reverse (1797–1804)

	Mintage	F-12	VF-20	EF-40	AU-50	AU-55	MS-60	MS-63
1797, Large Eagle 10,940		$7,500	$10,000	$15,000	$17,000	$20,000	$40,000	$95,000
1798, 8 Over 7, 9 Stars Left, 4 Right . . . 900		10,000	15,000	25,000	37,500	50,000	105,000	195,000
1798, 8 Over 7, 7 Stars Left, 6 Right . . . 842		12,500	17,500	27,500	40,000	75,000	120,000	225,000
1799 37,449		6,500	8,500	12,000	16,000	17,500	22,500	50,000
1800 5,999		6,500	8,500	12,000	16,000	17,500	22,500	60,000
1801 44,344		6,500	8,500	12,000	16,000	17,500	22,500	50,000
1803 15,017		6,500	8,500	12,000	16,000	17,500	22,500	50,000
1804 3,757		12,500	17,000	25,000	35,000	47,500	65,000	125,000

LIBERTY HEAD, NO MOTTO ABOVE EAGLE (1838–1866)

In 1838 the weight and diameter of the eagle were reduced and the obverse and reverse were redesigned. Liberty now faced left and the word LIBERTY was placed on the coronet.

VF-20 Very Fine: Hair lines above coronet partly worn. Curls under ear worn but defined.

EF-40 Extremely Fine: Small amount of wear on top of hair and below L in LIBERTY. Wear evident on wing tips and neck of eagle.

AU-50 About Uncirculated: Trace of wear on tip of coronet and hair above eye.

AU-55 Choice About Uncirculated: Evidence of friction on design high points. Some of original mint luster present.

Mintmark is on reverse, below eagle.

MS-60 Uncirculated: No trace of wear. Light blemishes.

MS-63 Choice Uncirculated: Some distracting contact marks or blemishes in prime focal areas. Impaired luster possible.

PF-63 Choice Proof: Attractive reflective surfaces with only a few blemishes in secondary focal places. No major flaws.

	Mintage	VF-20	EF-40	AU-50	AU-55	MS-60	MS-63	PF-63
1838	7,200	$2,000	$4,750	$10,000	$12,500	$30,000	$75,000	
1839, Large Letters	25,801	850	1,500	4,000	5,000	20,000	40,000	
1839, Small Letters	12,447	1,100	2,300	4,500	6,000	22,000	70,000	
1840	47,338	800	875	950	1,200	7,000		
1841	63,131	800	825	875	1,000	5,500	22,000	
1841O	2,500	2,750	6,000	14,000	20,000	35,000		
1842	81,507	800	825	900	1,075	10,000	22,500	
1842O	27,400	850	950	2,000	2,500	15,000		
1843	75,462	800	825	1,000	1,250	12,000		
1843O	175,162	800	825	950	1,100	8,500	32,000	
1844	6,361	900	2,000	3,500	4,000	10,000		
1844O	118,700	825	850	1,250	1,550	8,750		
1845	26,153	800	825	1,250	1,550	10,000		
1845O	47,500	850	900	1,800	2,250	10,000	30,000	
1846	20,095	800	900	3,500	4,000	14,000		
1846O	81,780	825	875	2,500	3,250	10,000	25,000	
1847	862,258	700	750	850	875	2,500	15,000	
1847O	571,500	800	850	900	975	4,000	13,000	
1848	145,484	700	750	850	875	3,500	15,000	
1848O	35,850	850	900	2,350	3,000	12,500	20,000	
1849	653,618	700	750	850	875	2,500	12,000	
1849O	23,900	950	1,750	4,000	6,000	20,000		
1850	291,451	725	750	850	875	2,750	13,000	
1850O	57,500	850	875	1,250	1,500	12,000		
1851	176,328	700	750	850	875	3,000	15,000	
1851O	263,000	825	875	900	1,000	4,500	17,000	
1852	263,106	700	750	850	875	3,500	16,000	
1852O	18,000	850	950	2,500	3,250	18,000		
1853, 3 Over 2	201,253	800	950	1,500	1,750	10,000		
1853	*	700	750	850	875	2,500	13,000	
1853O	51,000	825	850	900	1,000	8,500		
1854	54,250	700	750	850	875	3,500		
1854O	52,500	800	825	850	1,450	6,500	23,000	
1854S	123,826	800	850	950	1,150	6,500	25,000	
1855	121,701	700	750	850	875	3,000	12,000	
1855O	18,000	900	1,250	4,750	6,500	18,000		

* Included in number above.

Chart continued on next page.

	Mintage	VF-20	EF-40	AU-50	AU-55	MS-60	MS-63	PF-63
1855S	9,000	$1,500	$2,300	$4,250	$6,000	$19,000		
1856	60,490	700	750	800	875	2,500	$12,000	
1856O	14,500	825	1,100	2,750	3,500	12,000		
1856S	68,000	800	825	900	1,100	6,000		
1857	16,606	700	800	1,250	1,450	7,000		
1857O	5,500	900	1,250	3,000	3,750	20,000		
1857S	26,000	825	900	1,500	1,850	7,000	13,000	
1858	2,521	3,500	6,000	8,500	10,500	25,000		$75,000
1858O	20,000	825	900	1,250	1,500	6,000	23,000	
1858S	11,800	1,100	2,000	3,000	3,750	22,000		
1859	(80) 16,013	800	825	900	950	6,000	12,000	45,000
1859O	2,300	3,250	7,500	15,000	20,000	40,000		
1859S	7,000	1,550	3,000	8,500	11,000	30,000		
1860	(50) 15,055	750	800	900	1,000	5,000	12,000	31,000
1860O	11,100	900	1,150	2,250	2,750	8,000		
1860S	5,000	1,850	3,250	8,000	10,000	27,500		
1861	(69) 113,164	750	800	850	900	4,000	12,000	30,000
1861S	15,500	1,000	1,850	4,000	5,000	25,000		
1862	(35) 10,960	800	850	1,500	1,750	8,000	18,000	30,000
1862S	12,500	1,250	2,250	3,250	4,000	26,500		
1863	(30) 1,218	2,750	5,500	8,500	10,000	32,500	50,000	30,000
1863S	10,000	1,250	2,500	6,000	8,500	16,500		
1864	(50) 3,530	1,250	2,500	5,000	8,000	12,000		30,000
1864S	2,500	10,000	25,000	45,000	60,000	80,000		
1865	(25) 3,980	1,300	2,500	4,000	6,000	24,000	37,500	30,000
1865S	16,700	2,350	4,000	11,000	12,500	32,000	50,000	
1866S	8,500	1,600	2,450	10,000	16,500	30,000		

LIBERTY HEAD, MOTTO ABOVE EAGLE (1866–1907)

VF-20 Very Fine: Half of hair lines over coronet visible. Curls under ear worn but defined. IN GOD WE TRUST and its ribbon sharp.
EF-40 Extremely Fine: Small amount of wear on top of hair and below L in LIBERTY. Wear evident on wing tips and neck of eagle.
AU-50 About Uncirculated: Trace of wear on hair above eye and on coronet.
AU-55 Choice About Uncirculated: Evidence of friction on design high points. Some of original mint luster present.

Mintmark is on reverse, below eagle.

MS-60 Uncirculated: No trace of wear. Light blemishes.
MS-63 Choice Uncirculated: Some distracting marks or blemishes in focal areas. Impaired luster possible.
PF-63 Choice Proof: Reflective surfaces with only a few blemishes in secondary focal areas. No major flaws.

	Mintage	VF-20	EF-40	AU-50	AU-55	MS-60	MS-63	PF-63
1866	(30) 3,750	$850	$1,500	$3,250	$4,000	$16,500		$27,500
1866S	11,500	1,200	2,750	4,750	6,500	17,500		
1867	(50) 3,090	1,100	1,650	2,500	3,500	15,000		27,500
1867S	9,000	1,500	3,500	5,000	6,500	25,000		
1868	(25) 10,630	650	750	1,050	1,200	10,000		27,500
1868S	13,500	1,000	1,300	2,250	2,500	13,000		
1869	(25) 1,830	1,100	1,600	2,500	3,000	18,000		27,500
1869S	6,430	1,050	1,500	2,750	3,250	13,000		
1870	(35) 3,990	825	950	1,450	1,650	12,500		25,000
1870CC	5,908	20,000	35,000	60,000	85,000			
1870S	8,000	825	1,350	3,250	4,500	20,000		
1871	(30) 1,790	1,000	1,600	2,500	3,000	11,000		25,000
1871CC	8,085	2,500	5,000	12,500	17,500	45,000		

EAGLES ($10)

	Mintage	VF-20	EF-40	AU-50	AU-55	MS-60	MS-63	PF-63
1871S	16,500	$875	$1,350	$3,000	$4,500	$15,000		
1872	(30)....1,620	1,400	2,000	5,000	6,000	10,000	$23,000	$25,000
1872CC	4,600	3,500	6,000	15,000	22,500	45,000		
1872S	17,300	700	750	1,100	1,500	11,000		
1873	(25).......800	5,000	12,000	17,500	22,500	45,000		27,500
1873CC	4,543	3,500	8,500	25,000	35,000	60,000		
1873S	12,000	900	1,300	2,500	3,000	15,000		
1874	(20)......53,140	600	650	675	725	1,200	4,500	27,500
1874CC	16,767	1,100	2,000	6,000	7,500	32,500		
1874S	10,000	875	1,550	3,250	3,500	25,000		
1875	(20).........100	55,000	100,000	150,000	225,000			115,000
1875CC	7,715	3,500	6,500	15,000	27,500	67,500	90,000	
1876	(45).......687	1,800	3,500	10,000	11,500	30,000		22,000
1876CC	4,696	2,850	5,000	12,500	14,500	40,000		
1876S	5,000	875	1,300	2,750	3,500	22,000		
1877	(20).........797	2,150	3,500	7,250	8,500	22,500		22,000
1877CC	3,332	2,500	5,500	10,000	12,500	35,000		
1877S	17,000	700	800	1,100	1,250	18,000		
1878	(20)......73,780	575	600	700	725	850	5,000	22,000
1878CC	3,244	2,750	6,750	13,500	15,000	45,000		
1878S	26,100	675	750	800	950	6,500	20,000	
1879	(30)....384,740	535	550	575	575	600	2,500	18,500
1879CC	1,762	4,750	8,750	17,500	20,000	45,000		
18790	1,500	1,600	3,500	8,500	10,000	27,000		
1879S	224,000	575	600	625	635	800	4,500	
1880	(36)....1,644,840	535	550	560	575	600	2,500	18,500
1880CC	11,190	900	950	1,250	1,550	10,000		
18800	9,200	750	800	1,100	1,350	5,500		
1880S	506,250	535	550	560	575	600	2,500	
1881	(40)....3,877,220	535	550	560	575	600	850	18,500
1881CC	24,015	850	950	1,100	1,250	4,000	15,000	
18810	8,350	750	850	975	1,150	5,000		
1881S	970,000	535	550	560	575	600	2,500	
1882	(40)....2,324,440	535	550	560	575	600	850	15,000
1882CC	6,764	900	1,150	2,500	2,750	15,000	30,000	
18820	10,820	800	850	1,000	1,150	4,250	12,500	
1882S	132,000	535	550	560	575	600	3,500	
1883	(40)....208,700	535	550	560	575	600	2,500	15,000
1883CC	12,000	850	1,000	2,250	2,750	12,000		
18830	800	5,000	12,000	20,000	25,000	55,000		
1883S	38,000	535	550	560	575	600	6,000	
1884	(45)......76,860	535	550	560	575	600	3,000	15,000
1884CC	9,925	900	1,150	2,300	3,000	8,000		
1884S	124,250	535	550	560	575	600	3,500	
1885	(65).....253,462	535	550	560	575	600	2,250	12,500
1885S	228,000	535	550	560	575	600	1,850	
1886	(60)....236,100	535	550	560	575	600	3,000	12,500
1886S	826,000	535	550	560	575	600	1,250	
1887	(80)......53,600	535	550	560	575	600	4,000	12,000
1887S	817,000	535	550	560	575	600	2,000	
1888	(75)....132,921	535	550	560	575	600	4,500	12,000
18880	21,335	535	550	560	575	600	4,000	
1888S	648,700	535	550	560	575	600	1,350	
1889	(45)......4,440	575	625	650	700	1,500	4,500	12,000
1889S	425,400	535	550	560	575	600	1,250	
1890	(63)......57,980	535	550	560	575	600	3,500	10,000
1890CC	17,500	900	925	950	1,000	1,750	8,500	
1891	(48)......91,820	535	550	560	575	600	2,500	10,000

Chart continued on next page.

	Mintage	VF-20	EF-40	AU-50	AU-55	MS-60	MS-63	PF-63
1891CC	103,732	$850	$900	$950	$1,000	$1,500	$5,500	
1892 (72)	797,480	535	550	560	575	600	750	$10,000
1892CC	40,000	850	925	1,000	1,050	2,500	7,500	
18920	28,688	800	815	825	835	900	5,000	
1892S	115,500	535	550	560	575	600	2,500	
1893 (55)	1,840,840	535	550	560	575	600	750	10,000
1893CC	14,000	850	925	1,000	1,250	5,000	15,000	
18930	17,000	800	815	825	850	1,000	4,500	
1893S	141,350	535	550	560	575	600	2,500	
1894 (43)	2,470,735	535	550	560	575	600	750	10,000
18940	107,500	575	600	625	675	685	4,000	
1894S	25,000	800	815	825	835	2,000	8,250	
1895 (56)	567,770	535	550	560	575	600	1,250	10,000
18950	98,000	575	600	625	635	725	4,250	
1895S	49,000	800	815	825	835	1,500	5,000	
1896 (78)	76,270	535	550	560	575	600	1,800	10,000
1896S	123,750	800	815	825	835	1,500	7,000	
1897 (69)	1,000,090	535	550	560	575	600	750	10,000
18970	42,500	535	550	560	575	750	3,500	
1897S	234,750	535	550	560	575	700	3,500	
1898 (67)	812,130	535	550	560	575	675	1,250	10,000
1898S	473,600	535	550	560	575	675	3,000	
1899 (86)	1,262,219	535	550	560	575	675	750	10,000
18990	37,047	535	550	560	575	800	3,500	
1899S	841,000	535	550	560	575	800	2,250	
1900 (120)	293,840	535	550	560	575	600	1,250	10,000
1900S	81,000	535	550	560	575	800	4,000	
1901 (85)	1,718,740	535	550	560	575	600	750	10,000
19010	72,041	535	550	560	575	700	2,500	
1901S	2,812,750	535	550	560	575	600	1,000	
1902 (113)	82,400	535	550	560	575	600	2,000	10,000
1902S	469,500	535	550	560	575	600	750	
1903 (96)	125,830	535	550	560	575	600	1,250	10,000
19030	112,771	535	550	560	575	700	2,250	
1903S	538,000	535	550	560	575	600	1,250	
1904 (108)	161,930	535	550	560	575	600	1,500	10,000
19040	108,950	535	550	560	575	700	2,500	
1905 (86)	200,992	535	550	560	575	600	750	10,000
1905S	369,250	535	550	560	575	600	3,500	
1906 (77)	165,420	535	550	560	575	600	1,200	10,000
1906D	981,000	535	550	560	575	600	750	
19060	86,895	535	550	560	575	700	3,000	
1906S	457,000	535	550	560	575	750	2,750	
1907 (74)	1,203,899	535	550	560	575	600	750	10,000
1907D	1,030,000	535	550	560	575	600	1,325	
1907S	210,500	535	550	560	575	750	3,750	

INDIAN HEAD (1907–1933)

VF-20 Very Fine: Bonnet feathers worn near band. Wear visible on high points of hair.

EF-40 Extremely Fine: Slight wear on cheekbone and headdress feathers. Slight wear visible on eagle's eye and left wing.

AU-50 About Uncirculated: Trace of wear on hair above eye and on forehead.

AU-55 Choice About Uncirculated: Evidence of friction on design high points. Much of original mint luster present.

MS-60 Uncirculated: No trace of wear. Light blemishes.

MS-63 Choice Uncirculated: Some distracting contact marks or blemishes in prime focal areas. Impaired luster possible.

Matte PF-63 Choice Proof: Matte surfaces with few blemishes in secondary focal places. No major flaws.

No Motto
Mintmark is above left tip of branch on 1908-D No Motto.

With Motto IN GOD WE TRUST
Mintmark is at left of arrow points.

Gem Uncirculated (MS-65) coins are rare, and dealers usually pay substantial premiums for them.

	Mintage	VF-20	EF-40	AU-50	AU-55	MS-60	MS-63
1907, Wire Rim, Periods	500	$12,500	$15,000	$17,500	$19,000	$23,000	$35,000
1907, Rounded Rim, Periods Before and After •E•PLURIBUS•UNUM•	50	30,000	35,000	45,000	50,000	75,000	100,000
1907, No Periods	239,406	625	675	700	750	950	2,750
1908, No Motto	33,500	625	675	750	775	975	3,250
1908D, No Motto	210,000	625	800	825	875	1,000	5,000

Variety 2 – Motto on Reverse (1908–1933)

	Mintage	VF-20	EF-40	AU-50	AU-55	MS-60	MS-63	MATTE PF-63
1908 (116)	341,370	$600	$625	$650	$675	$750	$1,250	$15,000
1908D	836,500	600	625	650	675	875	4,500	
1908S	59,850	800	825	850	950	2,500	8,500	
1909 (74)	184,789	600	625	650	675	750	2,500	16,000
1909D	121,540	600	625	650	675	1,000	3,500	
1909S	292,350	600	625	650	675	1,500	4,500	
1910 (204)	318,500	600	625	650	675	700	850	15,000
1910D	2,356,640	600	625	650	675	700	850	
1910S	811,000	600	625	650	675	1,000	6,500	
1911 (95)	505,500	600	625	650	675	700	1,000	15,000
1911D	30,100	900	950	1,150	2,200	5,500	25,000	
1911S	51,000	600	625	650	700	950	8,000	
1912 (83)	405,000	600	625	650	675	700	900	15,000
1912S	300,000	600	625	650	700	950	5,000	
1913 (71)	442,000	600	625	650	675	700	850	15,000
1913S	66,000	750	775	850	1,000	3,000	20,000	
1914 (50)	151,000	600	625	650	675	700	1,700	15,000
1914D	343,500	600	625	650	675	700	1,500	
1914S	208,000	600	625	650	700	950	5,000	
1915 (75)	351,000	600	625	650	675	700	1,150	16,000
1915S	59,000	600	700	750	900	2,250	14,000	
1916S	138,500	600	625	650	700	950	4,500	
1920S	126,500	8,500	12,500	15,000	17,500	30,000	70,000	
1926	1,014,000	600	625	650	660	675	800	
1930S	96,000	5,000	6,500	8,500	10,000	17,500	35,000	
1932	4,463,000	600	625	650	660	675	800	
1933	312,500	75,000	85,000	100,000	115,000	165,000	185,000	

This largest denomination of all regular United States issues was authorized to be coined by the Act of March 3, 1849. The coin's weight was set at 516 grains, and its fineness at .900. A single twenty-dollar gold pattern of 1849 resides in the Smithsonian.

LIBERTY HEAD (1850–1907)

VF-20 Very Fine: LIBERTY on crown bold; prongs on crown defined; lower half worn flat. Hair worn about ear.

EF-40 Extremely Fine: Trace of wear on rounded prongs of crown and down hair curls. Minor bagmarks.

AU-50 About Uncirculated: Trace of wear on hair over eye and on coronet.

AU-55 Choice About Uncirculated: Evidence of friction on design high points. Some of original mint luster present.

MS-60 Uncirculated: No trace of wear. Light blemishes.

MS-63 Choice Uncirculated: Some distracting marks or blemishes in focal areas. Impaired luster possible.

PF-63 Choice Proof: Reflective surfaces with only a few blemishes in secondary focal areas. No major flaws.

Without Motto on Reverse (1850–1866)

Mintmark is below eagle.

	Mintage	VF-20	EF-40	AU-50	AU-55	MS-60	MS-63	PF-63
1850	1,170,261	$1,650	$1,800	$2,500	$3,250	$8,500	$32,500	
1850O	141,000	1,750	3,000	5,500	10,000	35,000		
1851	2,087,155	1,450	1,500	1,625	1,675	3,250	17,000	
1851O	315,000	1,700	2,450	3,750	5,000	14,000		
1852	2,053,026	1,450	1,500	1,625	1,675	3,000	12,500	
1852O	190,000	1,700	2,500	3,500	5,000	15,500	35,000	
1853	1,261,326	1,450	1,500	1,625	1,675	3,250	16,000	
1853O	71,000	1,550	1,800	3,250	5,500	22,500		
1854	757,899	1,450	1,500	1,625	1,700	6,500	17,500	
1854O	3,250	80,000	150,000	275,000	300,000	500,000		
1854S	141,468	1,625	1,750	2,600	3,250	5,000	15,000	
1855	364,666	1,450	1,500	1,750	2,500	7,000	45,000	
1855O	8,000	2,750	11,000	27,500	30,000	65,000		
1855S	879,675	1,450	1,650	1,700	2,000	5,500	12,000	
1856	329,878	1,450	1,500	1,700	2,000	6,000	20,000	
1856O	2,250	100,000	175,000	300,000	350,000	500,000		
1856S	1,189,750	1,600	1,625	1,635	1,800	4,500	12,500	
1857	439,375	1,450	1,500	1,600	1,700	3,500	17,500	
1857O	30,000	2,000	2,500	5,500	7,500	30,000	80,000	
1857S **(a)**	970,500	1,600	1,625	1,650	1,700	3,000	6,500	
1858	211,714	1,600	1,625	1,700	2,500	4,500	25,000	
1858O	35,250	2,000	3,000	5,000	7,500	30,000		
1858S	846,710	1,600	1,650	1,750	2,000	7,500		
1859 (80)	43,597	1,650	2,000	3,250	5,500	22,500		$100,000
1859O	9,100	4,000	15,000	25,000	30,000	80,000		
1859S	636,445	1,600	1,625	1,635	1,700	3,750	25,000	
1860 (59)	577,670	1,600	1,625	1,635	1,655	2,750	10,000	75,000
1860O	6,600	4,000	10,000	25,000	35,000	100,000		
1860S	544,950	1,600	1,635	1,675	1,700	5,500	10,000	

a. Different size mintmarks exists; the Large S variety is rarest.

	Mintage	VF-20	EF-40	AU-50	AU-55	MS-60	MS-63	PF-63
1861 . . . . (66)	2,976,453	$1,600	$1,625	$1,635	$1,650	$2,750	$7,500	$75,000
1861O	17,741	3,500	12,500	30,000	40,000	70,000		
1861S	768,000	1,600	1,650	2,000	2,500	7,500	25,000	
1862 . . . . (35)	92,133	1,600	1,950	3,750	5,000	11,000	27,500	50,000
1862S	854,173	1,600	1,625	1,650	1,900	6,500	22,000	
1863 . . . . (30)	142,790	1,450	1,500	1,850	3,500	15,000	25,000	50,000
1863S	966,570	1,450	1,500	1,650	1,800	5,000	22,500	
1864 . . . . (50)	204,235	1,450	1,500	1,650	1,900	7,500		47,500
1864S	793,660	1,450	1,500	1,650	1,700	5,500	22,500	
1865 . . . . (25)	351,175	1,450	1,500	1,650	1,700	4,500	15,000	47,500
1865S	1,042,500	1,550	1,625	1,650	1,700	4,000	8,500	
1866S	120,000	3,500	12,000	35,000	55,000	125,000		

Motto Above Eagle (1866–1907)
Value TWENTY D. (1866–1876)

	Mintage	VF-20	EF-40	AU-50	AU-55	MS-60	MS-63	PF-63
1866 . . . . (30)	698,745	$1,300	$1,325	$1,400	$1,425	$5,500	$16,500	$42,500
1866S	842,250	1,300	1,325	1,635	3,250	11,250		
1867 . . . . (50)	251,015	1,300	1,325	1,400	1,425	2,150	12,500	42,500
1867S	920,750	1,300	1,325	1,400	1,500	7,500		
1868 . . . . (25)	98,575	1,500	1,600	1,750	1,900	7,500	37,500	42,500
1868S	837,500	1,300	1,325	1,400	1,600	8,500	30,000	
1869 . . . . (25)	175,130	1,300	1,325	1,400	1,425	6,000	16,250	42,500
1869S	686,750	1,300	1,325	1,400	1,425	5,500	32,500	
1870 . . . . (35)	155,150	1,300	1,625	1,635	1,750	6,500	35,000	42,500
1870CC	3,789	150,000	225,000	325,000	425,000			
1870S	982,000	1,300	1,325	1,400	1,425	3,500	22,500	
1871 . . . . (30)	80,120	1,300	1,325	1,400	1,425	3,500	16,000	40,000
1871CC	17,387	8,500	20,000	40,000	50,000	80,000		
1871S	928,000	1,300	1,325	1,400	1,425	3,250	16,000	
1872 . . . . (30)	251,850	1,300	1,325	1,400	1,425	2,500	16,500	40,000
1872CC	26,900	2,750	5,000	10,000	15,000	50,000		
1872S	780,000	1,300	1,325	1,400	1,425	2,250	15,500	
1873 . . . . (25)	1,709,800	1,300	1,325	1,400	1,425	1,600	8,500	42,500
1873CC	22,410	2,750	5,200	10,000	16,500	32,500		
1873S	1,040,600	1,300	1,325	1,400	1,425	1,750	12,500	
1874 . . . . (20)	366,780	1,300	1,325	1,400	1,425	1,700	12,000	42,500
1874CC	115,085	2,000	2,500	4,000	5,500	20,000	45,000	
1874S	1,214,000	1,300	1,325	1,400	1,425	1,600	16,000	
1875 . . . . (20)	295,720	1,300	1,325	1,400	1,425	1,600	8,500	67,500
1875CC	111,151	2,000	2,500	3,000	4,000	7,500	15,000	
1875S	1,230,000	1,300	1,325	1,400	1,425	1,600	9,500	
1876 . . . . (45)	583,860	1,300	1,325	1,400	1,425	1,600	8,500	42,500
1876CC	138,441	2,000	2,500	3,000	4,000	8,500	25,000	
1876S	1,597,000	1,300	1,325	1,400	1,425	1,600	8,500	

Chart continued on next page.

Value TWENTY DOLLARS (1877–1907)

	Mintage	VF-20	EF-40	AU-50	AU-55	MS-60	MS-63	PF-63
1877 . . . . (20) . .397,650		$1,200	$1,225	$1,250	$1,265	$1,285	$10,000	$30,000
1877CC 42,565		2,250	3,000	4,000	5,500	20,000		
1877S 1,735,000		1,200	1,225	1,250	1,265	1,285	13,000	
1878 . . . . (20) . .543,625		1,200	1,225	1,250	1,265	1,285	10,000	30,000
1878CC 13,180		3,000	5,500	10,000	15,000	35,000		
1878S 1,739,000		1,200	1,225	1,250	1,265	1,285	14,000	
1879 . . . . (30) . .207,600		1,200	1,225	1,250	1,265	1,285	11,000	30,000
1879CC 10,708		4,500	7,500	13,500	16,500	33,600		
18790 2,325		15,000	24,000	28,000	45,000	100,000	150,000	
1879S 1,223,800		1,200	1,225	1,250	1,265	1,750	25,000	
1880 . . . . (36) . . .51,420		1,200	1,225	1,250	1,265	3,250	16,500	30,000
1880S 836,000		1,200	1,225	1,250	1,265	1,285	11,000	
1881 . . . . (61) 2,199		12,500	20,000	27,500	35,000	85,000		30,000
1881S 727,000		1,200	1,225	1,250	1,265	1,285	14,500	
1882 . . . . (59) 571		20,000	40,000	65,000	75,000	100,000	175,000	30,000
1882CC 39,140		2,000	2,500	3,500	4,000	12,000	55,000	
1882S 1,125,000		1,200	1,225	1,250	1,265	1,285	11,000	
1883, Proof only . . . (92)								50,000
1883CC 59,962		2,000	2,500	3,500	4,000	7,500	25,000	
1883S 1,189,000		1,200	1,225	1,250	1,265	1,285	5,500	
1884, Proof only . . . (71)								45,000
1884CC 81,139		2,000	2,500	3,500	4,000	7,500	25,000	
1884S 916,000		1,200	1,225	1,250	1,265	1,285	5,000	
1885 . . . . (77) 751		15,000	20,000	30,000	35,000	55,000	87,500	35,000
1885CC 9,450		3,000	5,500	10,000	15,000	25,000	50,000	
1885S 683,500		1,200	1,225	1,250	1,265	1,285	3,750	
1886 . . . . (106) . . .1,000		25,000	45,000	55,000	65,000	90,000	125,000	30,000
1887, Proof only . . (121)		1,200						45,000
1887S 283,000		1,200	1,225	1,250	1,265	1,285	12,000	
1888 . . . . (105) . .226,161		1,200	1,225	1,250	1,265	1,285	6,500	27,500
1888S 859,600		1,200	1,225	1,250	1,265	1,285	3,500	
1889 . . . . (41) . . .44,070		1,200	1,225	1,250	1,265	1,285	9,000	27,500
1889CC 30,945		1,850	2,000	2,500	3,000	6,500	16,500	
1889S 774,700		1,200	1,225	1,250	1,265	1,285	4,500	
1890 . . . . (55) . . .75,940		1,200	1,225	1,250	1,265	1,285	7,000	27,500
1890CC 91,209		1,750	1,900	2,100	2,350	4,500	25,000	
1890S 802,750		1,200	1,225	1,250	1,265	1,285	4,500	
1891 . . . . (52) 1,390		6,400	10,800	17,500	20,000	50,000	100,000	27,500
1891CC 5,000		5,500	10,000	11,500	15,000	20,000	40,000	
1891S 1,288,125		1,200	1,225	1,250	1,265	1,285	2,500	
1892 . . . . (93) 4,430		1,750	2,350	3,750	5,000	10,000	27,000	27,500

DOUBLE EAGLES ($20)

	Mintage	VF-20	EF-40	AU-50	AU-55	MS-60	MS-63	PF-63
1892CC	27,265	$2,000	$2,500	$3,000	$3,500	$10,000	$27,500	
1892S	930,150	1,200	1,225	1,250	1,265	1,285	2,650	
1893	(59) 344,280	1,200	1,225	1,250	1,265	1,285	2,000	$27,500
1893CC	18,402	1,850	2,000	2,500	3,000	6,000	25,000	
1893S	996,175	1,200	1,225	1,250	1,265	1,285	2,200	
1894	(50) 1,368,940	1,200	1,225	1,250	1,265	1,285	1,600	27,500
1894S	1,048,550	1,200	1,225	1,250	1,265	1,285	2,350	
1895	(51) 1,114,605	1,200	1,225	1,250	1,265	1,285	1,500	27,500
1895S	1,143,500	1,200	1,225	1,250	1,265	1,285	1,550	
1896	(128) 792,535	1,200	1,225	1,250	1,265	1,285	1,500	27,500
1896S	1,403,925	1,200	1,225	1,250	1,265	1,285	1,550	
1897	(86) 1,383,175	1,200	1,225	1,250	1,265	1,285	1,500	27,500
1897S	1,470,250	1,200	1,225	1,250	1,265	1,285	1,500	
1898	(75) 170,395	1,200	1,225	1,250	1,265	1,285	4,000	27,500
1898S	2,575,175	1,200	1,225	1,250	1,265	1,285	1,350	
1899	(84) 1,669,300	1,200	1,225	1,250	1,265	1,285	1,350	27,500
1899S	2,010,300	1,200	1,225	1,250	1,265	1,285	1,500	
1900	(124) 1,874,460	1,200	1,225	1,250	1,265	1,285	1,350	27,500
1900S	2,459,500	1,200	1,225	1,250	1,265	1,285	1,800	
1901	(96) 111,430	1,200	1,225	1,250	1,265	1,285	1,350	27,500
1901S	1,596,000	1,200	1,225	1,250	1,265	1,285	2,500	
1902	(114) 31,140	1,200	1,225	1,250	1,265	1,285	9,000	27,500
1902S	1,753,625	1,200	1,225	1,250	1,265	1,285	2,000	
1903	(158) 287,270	1,200	1,225	1,250	1,265	1,285	1,350	27,500
1903S	954,000	1,200	1,225	1,250	1,265	1,285	1,550	
1904	(98) 6,256,699	1,200	1,225	1,250	1,265	1,285	1,350	27,500
1904S	5,134,175	1,200	1,225	1,250	1,265	1,285	1,350	
1905	(92) 58,919	1,200	1,225	1,300	1,450	2,000	10,000	27,500
1905S	1,813,000	1,200	1,225	1,250	1,265	1,285	2,500	
1906	(94) 69,596	1,200	1,225	1,250	1,265	1,285	5,500	27,500
1906D	620,250	1,200	1,225	1,250	1,265	1,285	3,000	
1906S	2,065,750	1,200	1,225	1,250	1,265	1,285	2,000	
1907	(78) 1,451,786	1,200	1,225	1,250	1,265	1,285	1,350	27,500
1907D	842,250	1,200	1,225	1,250	1,265	1,285	2,500	
1907S	2,165,800	1,200	1,225	1,250	1,265	1,285	2,200	

SAINT-GAUDENS (1907–1933)

The twenty-dollar gold piece designed by Augustus Saint-Gaudens is considered by many to be the most beautiful United States coin. The first coins issued were slightly more than 12,000 high-relief pieces struck for general circulation. The relief is much higher than that of later issues and the date 1907 is in Roman numerals. A few of the Proof coins were made using the lettered-edge collar from the Ultra High Relief version. These can be distinguished by a pronounced bottom left serif on the N in UNUM, and other minor differences. Flat-relief double eagles were issued later in 1907 with Arabic numerals, and continued through 1933.

The field of the rare, Ultra High Relief experimental pieces is extremely concave and connects directly with the edge without any border, giving it a sharp knifelike appearance. Liberty's skirt shows two folds on the side of her right leg; the Capitol building in the background at left is very small; the sun, on the reverse side, has 14 rays, as opposed to the regular high-relief coins, which have only 13 rays extending from the sun. High-relief Proofs are trial or experimental pieces.

VF-20 Very Fine: Minor wear on Liberty's legs and toes. Eagle's left wing and breast feathers worn.

EF-40 Extremely Fine: Drapery lines on chest visible. Wear on left breast, knee, and below. Eagle's feathers on breast and right wing bold.

AU-50 About Uncirculated: Trace of wear on nose, breast, and knee. Wear visible on eagle's wings.

AU-55 Choice About Uncirculated: Evidence of friction on design high points. Most of mint luster remains.

MS-60 Uncirculated: No trace of wear. Light marks or blemishes.

MS-63 Select Uncirculated: Some distracting contact marks or blemishes in prime focal areas. Impaired luster possible.

Matte PF-63 Choice Proof: Matte surfaces with only a few blemishes in secondary focal places. No major flaws.

Ultra High Relief Pattern, MCMVII (1907)

	PF-67
1907, Ultra High Relief, Plain Edge *(unique)*.	—
1907, Ultra High Relief, Lettered Edge.	—

No Motto IN GOD WE TRUST (1907–1908) and With Motto IN GOD WE TRUST (1908–1933)

High Relief, MCMVII (1907)

	Mintage	VF-20	EF-40	AU-50	AU-55	MS-60	MS-63	PF
1907, High Relief, Roman Numerals (MCMVII), Wire Rim	2,367	$6,000	$8,000	$9,000	$9,500	$12,000	$18,000	—

Arabic Numerals (1907–1933)

No Motto (1907–1908)

With Motto IN GOD WE TRUST (1908–1933)

Mintmark is on obverse, above date.

1909, 9 Over 8

DOUBLE EAGLES ($20)

	Mintage	VF-20	EF-40	AU-50	AU-55	MS-60	MS-63	MATTE PF-63
1907	.361,667	$1,200	$1,225	$1,250	$1,265	$1,450	$1,500	
1908	4,271,551	1,200	1,225	1,250	1,265	1,275	1,300	
1908D	.663,750	1,200	1,225	1,250	1,265	1,275	1,300	
1908, With Motto.. (101)	.156,258	1,200	1,225	1,250	1,265	1,300	1,750	$22,500
1908D, With Motto	.349,500	1,200	1,225	1,250	1,265	1,300	1,750	
1908S, With Motto	.22,000	1,700	2,500	5,500	5,750	9,000	17,000	
1909, 9 Over 8	*	1,200	1,225	1,250	1,265	1,275	3,500	
1909 (67)	.161,282	1,200	1,225	1,250	1,265	1,275	2,200	22,500
1909D	.52,500	1,500	1,600	1,650	1,675	2,000	5,500	
1909S	2,774,925	1,200	1,225	1,250	1,265	1,275	1,300	
1910 (167)	.482,000	1,200	1,225	1,250	1,265	1,275	1,300	22,500
1910D	.429,000	1,200	1,225	1,250	1,265	1,275	1,300	
1910S	2,128,250	1,200	1,225	1,250	1,265	1,275	1,650	
1911 (100)	.197,250	1,200	1,225	1,250	1,265	1,275	2,000	22,500
1911D	.846,500	1,200	1,225	1,250	1,265	1,275	1,300	
1911S	.775,750	1,200	1,225	1,250	1,265	1,275	1,300	
1912 (74)	.149,750	1,200	1,225	1,250	1,265	1,275	2,000	22,500
1913 (58)	.168,780	1,200	1,225	1,250	1,265	1,275	2,500	22,500
1913D	.393,500	1,200	1,225	1,250	1,265	1,275	1,600	
1913S	.34,000	1,450	1,500	1,550	1,600	1,750	3,500	
1914 (70)	.95,250	1,200	1,225	1,250	1,265	1,275	2,750	22,500
1914D	.453,000	1,200	1,225	1,250	1,265	1,275	1,300	
1914S	1,498,000	1,200	1,225	1,250	1,265	1,275	1,300	
1915 (50)	.152,000	1,200	1,225	1,250	1,265	1,275	1,900	25,000
1915S	.567,500	1,200	1,225	1,250	1,265	1,275	1,300	
1916S	.796,000	1,200	1,225	1,250	1,265	1,275	1,500	
1920	.228,250	1,200	1,225	1,250	1,265	1,275	1,600	
1920S	.558,000	12,000	15,000	22,000	27,500	40,000	75,000	
1921	.528,500	25,000	35,000	45,000	55,000	85,000	200,000	
1922	1,375,500	1,200	1,225	1,250	1,265	1,275	1,300	
1922S	2,658,000	1,550	1,600	1,650	1,700	2,000	4,250	
1923	.566,000	1,200	1,225	1,250	1,265	1,275	1,400	
1923D	1,702,250	1,200	1,225	1,250	1,265	1,275	1,300	
1924	4,323,500	1,200	1,225	1,250	1,265	1,275	1,300	
1924D	3,049,500	1,900	2,000	2,100	2,450	3,250	6,000	
1924S	2,927,500	1,900	1,950	2,000	2,350	3,250	8,000	
1925	2,831,750	1,200	1,225	1,250	1,265	1,275	1,300	
1925D	2,938,500	1,650	1,900	2,250	2,800	3,750	9,000	
1925S	3,776,500	1,800	2,250	2,850	3,250	7,850	13,000	
1926	.816,750	1,200	1,225	1,250	1,265	1,275	1,300	
1926D	.481,000	6,000	8,750	9,500	11,000	14,000	23,000	
1926S	2,041,500	1,850	2,000	2,350	2,750	3,000	4,500	
1927	2,946,750	1,200	1,225	1,250	1,265	1,275	1,300	
1927D	.180,000		250,000	300,000	350,000	500,000	850,000	
1927S	3,107,000	4,000	7,000	9,000	12,500	20,000	40,000	
1928	8,816,000	1,200	1,225	1,250	1,265	1,275	1,300	
1929	1,779,750	7,500	10,000	12,000	13,000	17,500	30,000	
1930S	.74,000	20,000	30,000	35,000	40,000	50,000	75,000	
1931	2,938,250	7,500	10,000	15,000	20,000	27,000	50,000	
1931D	.106,500	7,500	10,000	14,000	19,000	27,500	60,000	
1932	1,101,750	7,500	10,000	14,000	19,000	27,500	60,000	
1933	.445,500			*None placed in circulation.*				

* Included in number below.

Collecting United States commemorative coins is like gathering snapshots for an album of important events, places, and people in the nation's history. Because they represent so many different aspects of America—from wars and Olympic games to presidents and historical landmarks, every collector can assemble a set with its own special significance.

All U.S. commemorative coins are issued as legal tender, though in all cases the precious metal of the coins surpasses their face values. The weight and fineness for commemoratives follow those of standard-issue gold, silver, and clad coins.

CLASSIC COMMEMORATIVE SILVER AND GOLD

(1892–1893) World's Columbian Exposition Half Dollar

	Distribution	AU-50	MS-60	MS-63	MS-65
1892, World's Columbian Exposition half dollar	950,000	$15	$20	$50	$260
1893, Same type.	1,550,405	15	20	50	260

(1893) World's Columbian Exposition, Isabella Quarter Dollar

	Distribution	AU-50	MS-60	MS-63	MS-65
1893, World's Columbian Exposition, Chicago, quarter dollar . .	24,214	$275	$280	$320	$1,800

(1900) Lafayette Dollar

	Distribution	AU-50	MS-60	MS-63	MS-65
1900, Lafayette silver dollar	36,026	$350	$600	$1,150	$5,300

(1903) Louisiana Purchase Exposition

	Distribution	AU-50	MS-60	MS-63	MS-65
1903, Louisiana Purchase / Thomas Jefferson gold dollar	17,500	$375	$430	$570	$1,025
1903, Louisiana Purchase / William McKinley gold dollar	17,500	375	435	460	950

(1904–1905) Lewis and Clark Exposition

	Distribution	AU-50	MS-60	MS-63	MS-65
1904, Lewis and Clark Exposition gold dollar	10,025	$620	$700	$1,150	$3,700
1905, Lewis and Clark Exposition gold dollar	10,041	620	960	1,300	6,400

(1915) Panama-Pacific Exposition

	Distribution	AU-50	MS-60	MS-63	MS-65
1915S, Panama-Pacific Exposition half dollar	27,134	$290	$340	$500	$900
1915S, Panama-Pacific Exposition gold dollar	15,000	350	400	480	1,000
1915S, Panama-Pacific Exposition gold $2.50	6,749	1,100	1,360	3,025	4,600
1915S, Panama-Pacific Exposition gold $50 Round	483	30,000	45,000	63,000	120,000

Entry continued on next page.

(1915) Panama-Pacific Exposition

	Distribution	AU-50	MS-60	MS-63	MS-65
1915S, Panama-Pacific Exposition gold $50 Octagonal	645	$30,000	$44,000	$60,000	$120,000

(1916–1917) McKinley Memorial

	Distribution	AU-50	MS-60	MS-63	MS-65
1916, McKinley Memorial gold dollar.	15,000	$340	$360	$390	$1,000
1917, McKinley Memorial gold dollar.	5,000	360	460	590	1,200

(1918) Illinois Centennial

	Distribution	AU-50	MS-60	MS-63	MS-65
1918, Illinois Centennial half dollar	100,058	$90	$95	$100	$240

(1920) Maine Centennial

	Distribution	AU-50	MS-60	MS-63	MS-65
1920, Maine Centennial half dollar	50,028	$85	$95	$100	$240

(1920–1921) Pilgrim Tercentenary

With 1921 in Field
on Obverse

	Distribution	AU-50	MS-60	MS-63	MS-65
1920, Pilgrim Tercentenary half dollar.................. 152,112		$55	$65	$70	$130
1921, Same, With Date Added in Field 20,053		110	125	130	185

(1921) Missouri Centennial

With 2★4 in Field

	Distribution	AU-50	MS-60	MS-63	MS-65
1921, Missouri Centennial half dollar, "2★4" in Field 9,400		$410	$460	$675	$1,450
1921, Missouri Centennial half dollar, Plain................ 11,400		260	340	500	1,750

(1921) Alabama Centennial

Without 2X2 in Field

	Distribution	AU-50	MS-60	MS-63	MS-65
1921, Alabama Centennial half dollar, With "2X2" in Field of Obverse.....6,006		$200	$215	$290	$975
1921, Alabama Centennial half dollar, Plain........................16,014		120	135	270	800

Star in Field

(1922) Grant Memorial

	Distribution	AU-50	MS-60	MS-63	MS-65
1922, Grant Memorial, With Star* half dollar	4,256	$610	$825	$1,125	$4,150
1922, Same type, No Star in Obv Field	67,405	70	80	100	370
1922, Grant Memorial, With Star* gold dollar	5,016	1,050	1,100	1,200	1,700
1922, Grant Memorial, No Star in Obv Field	5,016	960	1,000	1,000	1,700

* Fake stars usually have a flattened spot on the reverse.

(1923) Monroe Doctrine Centennial

	Distribution	AU-50	MS-60	MS-63	MS-65
1923S, Monroe Doctrine Centennial half dollar	274,077	$38	$52	$85	$750

(1924) Huguenot-Walloon Tercentenary

	Distribution	AU-50	MS-60	MS-63	MS-65
1924, Huguenot-Walloon Tercentenary half dollar	142,080	$85	$90	$95	$170

(1925) Lexington-Concord Sesquicentennial

	Distribution	AU-50	MS-60	MS-63	MS-65
1925, Lexington-Concord Sesquicentennial half dollar.	162,013	$58	$65	$67	$260

(1925) Stone Mountain Memorial

	Distribution	AU-50	MS-60	MS-63	MS-65
1925, Stone Mountain Memorial half dollar.	1,314,709	$40	$45	$55	$125

(1925) California Diamond Jubilee

	Distribution	AU-50	MS-60	MS-63	MS-65
1925S, California Diamond Jubilee half dollar	86,594	$125	$130	$140	$400

(1925) Fort Vancouver Centennial

	Distribution	AU-50	MS-60	MS-63	MS-65
1925, Fort Vancouver Centennial half dollar	14,994	$200	$210	$230	$375

**(1926) Sesquicentennial
of American Independence**

	Distribution	AU-50	MS-60	MS-63	MS-65
1926, Sesquicentennial of American Independence half dollar	141,120	$60	$70	$85	$1,450
1926, Sesquicentennial of American Independence gold $2.50	46,019	280	320	480	1,800

(1926–1939) Oregon Trail Memorial

	Distribution	AU-50	MS-60	MS-63	MS-65
1926, Oregon Trail Memorial half dollar	47,955	$95	$110	$125	$160
1926S, Same type, S Mint	83,055	95	110	125	160
1928, Oregon Trail Memorial half dollar (same as 1926)	6,028	105	110	125	200
1933D, Oregon Trail Memorial half dollar	5,008	240	250	265	275
1934D, Oregon Trail Memorial half dollar	7,006	120	130	135	200
1936, Oregon Trail Memorial half dollar	10,006	105	115	125	170
1936S, Same type, S Mint	5,006	110	120	125	170
1937D, Oregon Trail Memorial half dollar	12,008	110	125	135	160
1938, Oregon Trail Memorial half dollar (same as 1926)	6,006				
1938D, Same type, D Mint	6,005	*Set:*	375	400	600
1938S, Same type, S Mint	6,006				
1939, Oregon Trail Memorial half dollar (same as 1926)	3,004				
1939D, Same type, D Mint	3,004	*Set:*	950	1,025	1,200
1939S, Same type, S Mint	3,005				
Oregon Trail Memorial half dollar, single type coin		95	110	130	160

(1927) Vermont Sesquicentennial

	Distribution	AU-50	MS-60	MS-63	MS-65
1927, Vermont Sesquicentennial (Battle of Bennington) half dollar	28,142	$170	$175	$190	$325

COMMEMORATIVES

(1928) Hawaiian Sesquicentennial

	Distribution	AU-50	MS-60	MS-63	MS-65
1928, Hawaiian Sesquicentennial half dollar	10,008	$1,200	$1,475	$1,700	$2,900
1928, Hawaiian Sesquicentennial, Sandblast Proof Presentation Piece	(50)			8,000	15,000

(1934) Maryland Tercentenary

	Distribution	AU-50	MS-60	MS-63	MS-65
1934, Maryland Tercentenary half dollar	25,015	$90	$105	$110	$135

(1934–1938) Texas Independence Centennial

	Distribution	AU-50	MS-60	MS-63	MS-65
1934, Texas Independence Centennial half dollar	61,463	$88	$90	$100	$135
1935, Texas Independence Centennial half dollar (same as 1934)	9,996				
1935D, Same type, D Mint	10,007	*Set:*	265	275	425
1935S, Same type, S Mint	10,008				
1936, Texas Independence Centennial half dollar (same as 1934)	8,911				
1936D, Same type, D Mint	9,039	*Set:*	265	275	425
1936S, Same type, S Mint	9,055				
1937, Texas Independence Centennial half dollar (same as 1934)	6,571				
1937D, Same type, D Mint	6,605	*Set:*	265	275	425
1937S, Same type, S Mint	6,637				

Chart continued on next page.

	Distribution	AU-50	MS-60	MS-63	MS-65
1938, Texas Independence Centennial half dollar (same as 1934)..... 3,780					
1938D, Same type, D Mint 3,775	Set:	$460	$480	$850	
1938S, Same type, S Mint.................................. 3,814					
Texas Independence Centennial half dollar, single type coin		$88	90	100	140

(1934–1938) Daniel Boone Bicentennial | 1934 Added on Reverse

	Distribution	AU-50	MS-60	MS-63	MS-65
1934, Daniel Boone Bicentennial half dollar.................... 10,007		$88	$95	$100	$120
1935, Daniel Boone Bicentennial half dollar.................... 10,010					
1935D, Same type, D Mint 5,005	Set:	285	300	400	
1935S, Same type, S Mint.................................. 5,005					
1935, Same as 1934 but Small 1934 on reverse................ 10,008					
1935D, Same type, D Mint 2,003	Set:	450	500	800	
1935S, Same type, S Mint.................................. 2,004					
1936, Daniel Boone Bicentennial half dollar (same as preceding) 12,012					
1936D, Same type, D Mint 5,005	Set:	300	350	500	
1936S, Same type, S Mint.................................. 5,006					
1937, Daniel Boone Bicentennial half dollar (same as preceding) 9,810					
1937D, Same type, D Mint 2,506	Set:	425	500	650	
1937S, Same type, S Mint.................................. 2,506					
1938, Daniel Boone Bicentennial half dollar (same as preceding) 2,100					
1938D, Same type, D Mint 2,100	Set:	650	750	1,000	
1938S, Same type, S Mint.................................. 2,100					
Daniel Boone Bicentennial half dollar, single type coin		85	95	100	115

(1935) Connecticut Tercentenary

	Distribution	AU-50	MS-60	MS-63	MS-65
1935, Connecticut Tercentenary half dollar 25,018	$140	$145	$150	$250

**(1935–1939)
Arkansas Centennial**

	Distribution	AU-50	MS-60	MS-63	MS-65
1935, Arkansas Centennial half dollar 13,012					
1935D, Same type, D Mint 5,505		*Set:*	$200	$205	$330
1935S, Same type, S Mint................................. 5,506					
1936, Arkansas Centennial half dollar (same as 1935 but 1936 on rev) 9,660					
1936D, Same type, D Mint 9,660		*Set:*	200	205	320
1936S, Same type, S Mint................................. 9,662					
1937, Arkansas Centennial half dollar (same as 1935) 5,505					
1937D, Same type, D mint 5,505		*Set:*	215	225	450
1937S, Same type, S mint................................. 5,506					
1938, Arkansas Centennial half dollar (same as 1935) 3,156					
1938D, Same type, D Mint 3,155		*Set:*	275	310	750
1938S, Same type, S Mint................................. 3,156					
1939, Arkansas Centennial half dollar (same as 1935) 2,104					
1939D, Same type, D Mint 2,104		*Set:*	475	550	1,275
1939S, Same type, S Mint................................. 2,105					
Arkansas Centennial half dollar, single type coin.......................		$60	65	68	100

**(1936) Arkansas
Centennial – Robinson**

	Distribution	AU-50	MS-60	MS-63	MS-65
1936, Arkansas Centennial (Robinson) half dollar 25,265	$75	$80	$90	$150

**(1935) Hudson, New
York, Sesquicentennial**

	Distribution	AU-50	MS-60	MS-63	MS-65
1935, Hudson, New York, Sesquicentennial half dollar 10,008	$480	$500	$560	$750

(1935–1936) California-Pacific International Exposition

	Distribution	AU-50	MS-60	MS-63	MS-65
1935S, California-Pacific International Exposition half dollar ...	70,132	$64	$68	$72	$85
1936D, California-Pacific International Exposition half dollar ...	30,092	65	68	72	90

(1935) Old Spanish Trail

	Distribution	AU-50	MS-60	MS-63	MS-65
1935, Old Spanish Trail half dollar.....................	10,008	$720	$740	$760	$850

(1936) Providence, Rhode Island, Tercentenary

	Distribution	AU-50	MS-60	MS-63	MS-65
1936, Providence, Rhode Island, Tercentenary half dollar	20,013	*Set:*	$200	$225	$325
1936D, Same type, D Mint	15,010				
1936S, Same type, S Mint.................	15,011				
Providence, Rhode Island, Tercentenary half dollar, single type coin ...		$62	68	72	95

(1936) Cleveland Centennial / Great Lakes Exposition

	Distribution	AU-50	MS-60	MS-63	MS-65
1936, Cleveland Centennial / Great Lakes Exposition half dollar	50,030	$64	$72	$80	$100

(1936) Wisconsin Territorial Centennial

	Distribution	AU-50	MS-60	MS-63	MS-65
1936, Wisconsin Territorial Centennial half dollar	25,015	$115	$120	$130	$160

(1936) Cincinnati Music Center

	Distribution	AU-50	MS-60	MS-63	MS-65
1936, Cincinnati Music Center half dollar	5,005				
1936D, Same type, D Mint	5,005	Set:	$600	$725	$950
1936S, Same type, S Mint.	5,006				
Cincinnati Music Center half dollar, single type coin		$190	200	240	300

(1936) Long Island Tercentenary

	Distribution	AU-50	MS-60	MS-63	MS-65
1936, Long Island Tercentenary half dollar 81,826		$50	$60	$65	$130

(1936) York County, Maine, Tercentenary

	Distribution	AU-50	MS-60	MS-63	MS-65
1936, York County, Maine, Tercentenary half dollar. 25,015		$105	$110	$120	$140

(1936) Bridgeport, Connecticut, Centennial

	Distribution	AU-50	MS-60	MS-63	MS-65
1936, Bridgeport, Connecticut, Centennial half dollar 25,015		$80	$85	$90	$125

(1936) Lynchburg, Virginia, Sesquicentennial

	Distribution	AU-50	MS-60	MS-63	MS-65
1936, Lynchburg, Virginia, Sesquicentennial half dollar. 20,013		$150	$155	$160	$200

(1936) Elgin, Illinois, Centennial

	Distribution	AU-50	MS-60	MS-63	MS-65
1936, Elgin, Illinois, Centennial half dollar	20,015	$125	$130	$135	$155

(1936) Albany, New York, Charter

	Distribution	AU-50	MS-60	MS-63	MS-65
1936, Albany, New York, Charter half dollar	17,671	$145	$145	$160	$195

(1936) San Francisco – Oakland Bay Bridge Opening

	Distribution	AU-50	MS-60	MS-63	MS-65
1936S, San Francisco–Oakland Bay Bridge Opening half dollar . .	71,424	$130	$135	$145	$180

(1936) Delaware Tercentenary

	Distribution	AU-50	MS-60	MS-63	MS-65
1936, Delaware Tercentenary half dollar	20,993	$145	$150	$160	$185

(1936) Columbia, South Carolina, Sesquicentennial

	Distribution	AU-50	MS-60	MS-63	MS-65
1936, Columbia, South Carolina, Sesquicentennial half dollar 9,007					
1936D, Same type, D Mint 8,009	Set:	$425	$435	$500	
1936S, Same type, S Mint. 8,007					
Columbia, South Carolina, Sesquicentennial half dollar, single type coin	$120	140	145	165	

(1936) Battle of Gettysburg Anniversary

	Distribution	AU-50	MS-60	MS-63	MS-65
1936, Battle of Gettysburg Anniversary half dollar 26,928	$320	$330	$340	$550

(1936) Norfolk, Virginia, Bicentennial

	Distribution	AU-50	MS-60	MS-63	MS-65
1936, Norfolk, Virginia, Bicentennial half dollar 16,936	$210	$212	$216	$225

(1937) Roanoke Island, North Carolina, 350th Anniversary

	Distribution	AU-50	MS-60	MS-63	MS-65
1937, Roanoke Island, North Carolina, 350th Anniversary half dollar	29,030	$120	$125	$130	$160

(1937) Battle of Antietam Anniversary

	Distribution	AU-50	MS-60	MS-63	MS-65
1937, Battle of Antietam Anniversary half dollar	18,028	$385	$400	$415	$450

(1938) New Rochelle, New York, 250th Anniversary

	Distribution	AU-50	MS-60	MS-63	MS-65
1938, New Rochelle, New York, 250th Anniversary half dollar	15,266	$210	$220	$230	$260

(1946) Iowa Centennial

	Distribution	AU-50	MS-60	MS-63	MS-65
1946, Iowa Centennial half dollar	100,057	$55	$60	$65	$85

(1946–1951) Booker T. Washington Memorial

	Distribution	AU-50	MS-60	MS-63	MS-65
1946, Booker T. Washington Memorial half dollar **(a)**	700,546				
1946D, Same type, D Mint	50,000	Set:	$40	$48	$120
1946S, Same type, S Mint.	500,279				
1947, Booker T. Washington Memorial half dollar (same as 1946)	6,000				
1947D, Same type, D Mint	6,000	Set:	55	60	150
1947S, Same type, S Mint.	6,000				
1948, Booker T. Washington Memorial half dollar (same as 1946)	8,005				
1948D, Same type, D Mint	8,005	Set:	55	60	165
1948S, Same type, S Mint.	8,005				
1949, Booker T. Washington Memorial half dollar (same as 1946)	6,004				
1949D, Same type, D Mint	6,004	Set:	50	60	240
1949S, Same type, S Mint.	6,004				
1950, Booker T. Washington Memorial half dollar (same as 1946)	6,004				
1950D, Same type, D Mint	6,004	Set:	55	105	195
1950S, Same type, S Mint.	62,091				
1951, Booker T. Washington Memorial half dollar (same as 1946) . .	210,082				
1951D, Same type, D Mint	7,004	Set:	50	60	175
1951S, Same type, S Mint.	7,004				
Booker T. Washington Memorial, single type coin		$10	12	15	35

a. Minted; quantity melted unknown.

(1951–1954) Carver/Washington Commemorative

	Distribution	AU-50	MS-60	MS-63	MS-65
1951, Carver/Washington half dollar	20,018				
1951D, Same type, D Mint	10,004	Set:	$45	$70	$235
1951S, Same type, S Mint.	10,004				
1952, Carver/Washington half dollar (same as 1951)	1,106,292				
1952D, Same type, D Mint	8,006	Set:	55	70	145
1952S, Same type, S Mint.	8,006				

	Distribution	AU-50	MS-60	MS-63	MS-65
1953, Carver/Washington half dollar (same as 1951)	8,003				
1953D, Same type, D Mint	8,003	*Set:*	$50	$60	$145
1953S, Same type, S Mint	88,020				
1954, Carver/Washington half dollar (same as 1951)	12,006				
1954D, Same type, D Mint	12,006	*Set:*	50	60	140
1954S, Same type, S Mint	42,024				
Carver/Washington half dollar, single type coin		$10	12	15	40

MODERN COMMEMORATIVES

(1982) George Washington 250th Anniversary of Birth

	Distribution	MS-67	PF-67
1982D, George Washington 250th Anniversary silver half dollar	2,210,458	$7	
1982S, Same type, S mint, Proof	(4,894,044)		$7

(1983–1984) Los Angeles Olympiad

	Distribution	MS-67	PF-67
1983P, Discus Thrower silver dollar	294,543	$18	
1983D, Same type, D Mint	174,014	18	
1983S, Same type, S Mint (1,577,025)	174,014	18	$18

Entry continued on next page.

(1983–1984) Los Angeles Olympiad

	Distribution	MS-67	PF-67
1984P, Olympic Coliseum silver dollar..	217,954	$18	
1984D, Same type, D Mint	116,675	19	
1984S, Same type, S Mint............................	(1,801,210) 116,675	19	$18
1984P, Olympic Torch Bearers gold $10	(33,309)		570
1984D, Same type, D Mint	(34,533)		570
1984S, Same type, S Mint..............................	(48,551)		570
1984W, Same type, W Mint..............................	(381,085) 75,886	570	570

(1986) Statue of Liberty Centennial

	Distribution	MS-67	PF-67
1986D, Statue of Liberty Centennial clad half dollar	928,008	$3	
1986S, Same type, S Mint, Proof........................	(6,925,627)		$3
1986P, Statue of Liberty Centennial silver dollar	723,635	15	
1986S, Same type, S Mint, Proof........................	(6,414,638)		14
1986W, Statue of Liberty Centennial gold $5.................	(404,013) 95,248	285	285

(1987) U.S. Constitution Bicentennial

	Distribution	MS-67	PF-67
1987P, U.S. Constitution Bicentennial silver dollar.......................... 451,629		$15	
1987S, Same type, S Mint, Proof....................... (2,747,116)			$15
1987W, U.S. Constitution Bicentennial gold $5 ....(651,659) 214,225		285	285

(1988) Seoul Olympiad

	Distribution	MS-67	PF-67
1988D, Seoul Olympiad silver dollar 191,368		$17	
1988S, Same type, S Mint, Proof....................... (1,359,366)			$15
1988W, Seoul Olympiad gold $5 ....(281,465) 62,913		285	285

(1989) Congress Bicentennial

	Distribution	MS-67	PF-67
1989D, Congress Bicentennial clad half dollar	163,753	$4	
1989S, Same type, S Mint, Proof. . . . . (767,897)			$4
1989D, Congress Bicentennial silver dollar	135,203	17	
1989S, Same type, S Mint, Proof. . . . . (762,198)			19
1989W, Congress Bicentennial gold $5 . . . . (164,690)	46,899	285	285

(1990) Eisenhower Centennial

	Distribution	MS-67	PF-67
1990W, Eisenhower Centennial silver dollar	241,669	$20	
1990P, Same type, P Mint, Proof. . . . . (1,144,461)			$18

(1991) Mount Rushmore Golden Anniversary

	Distribution	MS-67	PF-67
1991D, Mount Rushmore Golden Anniversary clad half dollar 172,754		$9	
1991S, Same type, S Mint, Proof. . . . . (753,257)			$7
1991P, Mount Rushmore Golden Anniversary silver dollar. 133,139		26	
1991S, Same type, S Mint, Proof. . . . . (738,419)			21
1991W, Mount Rushmore Golden Anniversary gold $5 . . . . (111,991) 31,959		285	285

(1991) Korean War Memorial

	Distribution	MS-67	PF-67
1991D, Korean War Memorial silver dollar. 213,049		$20	
1991P, Same type, P Mint, Proof. . . . . (618,488)			$16

(1991) United Service Organizations

	Distribution	MS-67	PF-67
1991D, USO silver dollar	124,958	$20	
1991S, Same type, S Mint, Proof	(321,275)		$16

(1992) XXV Olympiad

	Distribution	MS-67	PF-67
1992P, XXV Olympiad clad half dollar	161,607	$4	
1992S, Same type, S Mint, Proof	(519,645)		$4
1992D, XXV Olympiad silver dollar	187,552	23	
1992S, Same type, S Mint, Proof	(504,505)		22
1992W, XXV Olympiad gold $5	(77,313) 27,732	285	285

210

COMMEMORATIVES

(1992) White House 200th Anniversary

	Distribution	MS-67	PF-67
1992D, White House 200th Anniversary silver dollar 123,803		$16	
1992W, Same type, W Mint, Proof.........................(375,851)			$18

(1992) Christopher Columbus Quincentenary

	Distribution	MS-67	PF-67
1992D, Christopher Columbus Quincentenary clad half dollar 135,702		$6	
1992S, Same type, S Mint, Proof.........................(390,154)			$5
1992D, Christopher Columbus Quincentenary silver dollar...................... 106,949		24	
1992P, Same type, P Mint, Proof.........................(385,241)			20
1992W, Christopher Columbus Quincentenary gold $5 ....(79,730) 24,329		285	285

(1993) Bill of Rights

	Distribution	MS-67	PF-67
1993W, Bill of Rights silver half dollar.. 193,346		$12	
1993S, Same type, S Mint, Proof.......................... (586,315)			$10
1993D, Bill of Rights silver dollar... 98,383		24	
1993S, Same type, S Mint, Proof.......................... (534,001)			22
1993W, Bill of Rights gold $5 .... (78,651) 23,266		285	285

(1991–1995) 50th Anniversary of World War II

	Distribution	MS-67	PF-67
(1993P) 1991–1995 World War II clad half dollar .... (317,396) 197,072		$9	$10

(1991–1995) 50th Anniversary of World War II

	Distribution	MS-67	PF-67
(1993D) 1991–1995 World War II silver dollar	107,240	$28	
(1993W) Same type, W Mint, Proof	(342,041)		$28
(1993W) 1991–1995 World War II gold $5	(67,026) 23,672	285	300

(1994) World Cup Tournament

	Distribution	MS-67	PF-67
1994D, World Cup Tournament clad half dollar	168,208	$6	
1994P, Same type, P Mint, Proof	(609,354)		$6
1994D, World Cup Tournament silver dollar	81,524	28	
1994S, Same type, S Mint, Proof	(577,090)		22
1994W, World Cup Tournament gold $5	(89,614) 22,447	300	300

(1993 [1994]) Thomas Jefferson

	Distribution	MS-67	PF-67
1993 (1994) Thomas Jefferson silver dollar, P Mint.	266,927	$17	
1993 (1994) Same type, S Mint, Proof.	(332,891)		$15

(1994) Vietnam Veterans Memorial

	Distribution	MS-67	PF-67
1994W, Vietnam Veterans Memorial silver dollar.	57,290	$48	
1994P, Same type, P Mint, Proof.	(227,671)		$40

(1994) U.S. Prisoner of War Museum

	Distribution	MS-67	PF-67
1994W, U.S. Prisoner of War Museum silver dollar.	54,893	$48	
1994P, Same type, P Mint, Proof.	(224,449)		$28

(1994) Women in Military Service Memorial

	Distribution	MS-67	PF-67
1994W, Women in Military Service Memorial silver dollar	69,860	$22	
1994P, Same type, P Mint, Proof	(241,278)		$27

(1994) U.S. Capitol Bicentennial

	Distribution	MS-67	PF-67
1994D, U.S. Capitol Bicentennial silver dollar	68,332	$26	
1994S, Same type, S Mint, Proof	(279,579)		$24

(1995) Civil War Battlefield Preservation

	Distribution	MS-67	PF-67
1995S, Civil War Battlefield Preservation clad half dollar	119,520	$22	
1995S, Same type, S Mint, Proof	(330,002)		$20

(1995) Civil War Battlefield Preservation

	Distribution	MS-67	PF-67
1995P, Civil War Battlefield Preservation silver dollar	45,866	$38	
1995S, Same type, S Mint, Proof	(437,114)		$31
1995W, Civil War Battlefield Preservation gold $5	12,735	320	
1995W, Same type, W Mint, Proof	(55,246)		300

(1995) XXVI Olympiad

	Distribution	MS-67	PF-67
1995S, XXVI Olympiad, Basketball clad half dollar	171,001	$10	
1995S, Same type, S Mint, Proof	(169,655)		$9
1995S, XXVI Olympiad, Baseball clad half dollar	164,605	11	
1995S, Same type, S Mint, Proof	(118,087)		11
1996S, XXVI Olympiad, Swimming clad half dollar	49,533	65	
1996S, Same type, S Mint, Proof	(114,315)		18

COMMEMORATIVES

	Distribution	MS-67	PF-67
1996S, XXVI Olympiad, Soccer clad half dollar 52,836		$60	
1996S, Same type, S Mint, Proof.........................(112,412)			$50
1995D, XXVI Olympiad, Gymnastics silver dollar 42,497		30	
1995P, Same type, P Mint, Proof.........................(182,676)			18
1995D, XXVI Olympiad, Paralympics silver dollar............................ 28,649		28	
1995P, Same type, P Mint, Proof.........................(138,337)			25
1995D, XXVI Olympiad, Track and Field silver dollar 24,976		48	
1995P, Same type, P mint, Proof.........................(136,935)			25
1995D, XXVI Olympiad, Cycling silver dollar................................. 19,662		85	
1995P, Same type, P Mint, Proof.........................(118,795)			28
1996D, XXVI Olympiad, Tennis silver dollar 15,983		130	
1996P, Same type, P Mint, Proof.........................(92,016)			45
1996D, XXVI Olympiad, Paralympics silver dollar............................ 14,497		145	
1996P, Same type, P Mint, Proof.........................(84,280)			42
1996D, XXVI Olympiad, Rowing silver dollar 16,258		145	
1996P, Same type, P Mint, Proof.........................(151,890)			42
1996D, XXVI Olympiad, High Jump silver dollar............................. 15,697		150	
1996P, Same type, P Mint, Proof.........................(124,502)			26
1995W, XXVI Olympiad, Torch Runner gold $5 14,675		400	
1995W, Same type, W Mint, Proof.........................(57,442)			285
1995W, XXVI Olympiad, Stadium gold $5................................... 10,579		600	
1995W, Same type, W Mint, Proof.........................(43,124)			285
1996W, XXVI Olympiad, Flag Bearer gold $5 9,174		360	
1996W, Same type, W Mint, Proof.........................(32,886)			285
1996W, XXVI Olympiad, Cauldron gold $5 9,210		660	
1996W, Same type, W Mint, Proof.........................(38,555)			285

(1995) Special Olympics World Games

	Distribution	MS-67	PF-67
1995W, Special Olympics World Games silver dollar......................... 89,301		$23	
1995P, Same type, P Mint, Proof.........................(351,764)			$22

(1996) National Community Service

	Distribution	MS-67	PF-67
1996S, National Community Service silver dollar	23,500	$72	
1996S, Same type, S Mint, Proof	(101,543)		$22

(1996) Smithsonian Institution 150th Anniversary

	Distribution	MS-67	PF-67
1996D, Smithsonian Institution 150th Anniversary silver dollar	31,320	$43	
1996P, Same type, P Mint, Proof	(129,152)		$26
1996W, Smithsonian Institution 150th Anniversary gold $5	9,068	285	
1996W, Same type, W Mint, Proof	(21,772)		285

(1997) U.S. Botanic Garden

	Distribution	MS-67	PF-67
1997P, U.S. Botanic Garden silver dollar	58,505	$18	
1997P, Same type, P Mint, Proof	(189,671)		$26

(1997) Jackie Robinson

	Distribution	MS-67	PF-67
1997S, Jackie Robinson silver dollar	30,180	$50	
1997S, Same type, S Mint, Proof	(110,002)		$38
1997W, Jackie Robinson gold $5	5,174	950	
1997W, Same type, W Mint, Proof	(24,072)		360

(1997) Franklin D. Roosevelt

	Distribution	MS-67	PF-67
1997W, Franklin D. Roosevelt gold $5	11,894	$320	
1997W, Same type, W Mint, Proof	(29,474)		$285

(1997) National Law Enforcement Officers Memorial

	Distribution	MS-67	PF-67
1997P, National Law Enforcement Officers Memorial silver dollar	28,575	$75	
1997P, Same type, P Mint, Proof	(110,428)		$40

(1998) Robert F. Kennedy

	Distribution	MS-67	PF-67
1998S, Robert F. Kennedy silver dollar	106,422	$25	
1998S, Same type, S Mint, Proof	(99,020)		$42

(1998) Black Revolutionary War Patriots

	Distribution	MS-67	PF-67
1998S, Black Revolutionary War Patriots silver dollar	37,210	$52	
1998S, Same type, S Mint, Proof	(75,070)		$34

(1999) Dolley Madison

	Distribution	MS-67	PF-67
1999P, Dolley Madison silver dollar	89,104	$22	
1999P, Same type, P Mint, Proof	(224,403)		$21

COMMEMORATIVES

(1999) George Washington Death Bicentennial

	Distribution	MS-67	PF-67
1999W, George Washington Death Bicentennial gold $5	22,511	$285	
1999W, Same type, W Mint, Proof. . . . . (41,693)			$285

(1999) Yellowstone National Park

	Distribution	MS-67	PF-67
1999P, Yellowstone National Park silver dollar	82,563	$30	
1999S, Same type, S Mint, Proof. . . . . (187,595)			$30

(2000) Library of Congress Bicentennial

	Distribution	MS-67	PF-67
2000P, Library of Congress Bicentennial silver dollar	53,264	$17	
2000P, Same type, P Mint, Proof. . . . . (198,503)			$18
2000W, Library of Congress Bicentennial bimetallic (gold/platinum) $10.	7,261	850	
2000W, Same type, W Mint, Proof. . . . . (27,445)			625

(2000) Leif Ericson Millennium

	Distribution	MS-67	PF-67
2000P, Leif Ericson Millennium silver dollar	28,150	$45	
2000P, Same type, P Mint, Proof	(144,748)		$34

(2001) American Buffalo Commemorative

	Distribution	MS-67	PF-67
2001D, American Buffalo silver dollar	227,131	$100	
2001P, Same type, P Mint, Proof	(272,869)		$110

(2001) Capitol Visitor Center

	Distribution	MS-67	PF-67
2001P, U.S. Capitol Visitor Center clad half dollar	99,157	$12	
2001P, Same type, P Mint, Proof	(77,962)		$10

COMMEMORATIVES

(2001) Capitol Visitor Center

	Distribution	MS-67	PF-67
2001P, U.S. Capitol Visitor Center silver dollar...............................	35,380	$26	
2001P, Same type, P Mint, Proof..........................(143,793)............			$26
2001W, U.S. Capitol Visitor Center gold $5	6,761	650	
2001W, Same type, W Mint, Proof.........................(27,652)............			285

(2002) Salt Lake Olympic Games

	Distribution	MS-67	PF-67
2002P, Salt Lake Olympic Games silver dollar..............................	40,257	$26	
2002P, Same type, P Mint, Proof.........................(166,864)............			$24
2002W, Salt Lake Olympic Games gold $5	10,585	285	
2002W, Same type, W Mint, Proof.........................(32,877)............			285

(2002) West Point Bicentennial

See next page for chart.

	Distribution	MS-67	PF-67
2002W, West Point Bicentennial silver dollar	103,201	$15	
2002W, Same type, W Mint, Proof	(288,293)		$26

(2003) First Flight Centennial

	Distribution	MS-67	PF-67
2003P, First Flight Centennial clad half dollar	57,122	$8	
2003P, Same type, P Mint, Proof	(109,710)		$10
2003P, First Flight Centennial silver dollar	53,533	28	
2003P, Same type, P Mint, Proof	(190,240)		27
2003W, First Flight Centennial gold $10	10,009	570	
2003W, Same type, W Mint, Proof	(21,676)		570

(2004) Thomas Alva Edison

	Distribution	MS-67	PF-67
2004P, Thomas Alva Edison silver dollar	92,510	$20	
2004P, Same type, P Mint, Proof	(211,055)		$21

(2004) Lewis and Clark Bicentennial

	Distribution	MS-67	PF-67
2004P, Lewis and Clark Bicentennial silver dollar	142,015	$21	
2004P, Same type, P Mint, Proof	(351,989)		$21

(2005) Chief Justice John Marshall

	Distribution	MS-67	PF-67
2005P, Chief Justice John Marshall silver dollar	67,096	$26	
2005P, Same type, P Mint, Proof	(196,753)		$22

(2005) Marine Corps 230th Anniversary

	Distribution	MS-67	PF-67
2005P, Marine Corps 230th Anniversary silver dollar	49,671	$30	
2005P, Same type, P Mint, Proof	(548,810)		$30

(2006) Benjamin Franklin "Scientist"

	Distribution	MS-67	PF-67
2006P, Benjamin Franklin "Scientist" silver dollar	58,000	$22	
2006P, Same type, P Mint, Proof	(142,000)		$26

(2006) Benjamin Franklin "Founding Father"

	Distribution	MS-67	PF-67
2006P, Benjamin Franklin "Founding Father" silver dollar	58,000	$21	
2006P, Same type, P Mint, Proof	(142,000)		$21

(2006) San Francisco Old Mint Centennial

	Distribution	MS-67	PF-67
2006S, San Francisco Old Mint Centennial silver dollar	67,100	$28	
2006S, Same type, S Mint, Proof	(160,870)		$23
2006S, San Francisco Old Mint Centennial gold $5	17,500	285	
2006S, Same type, S Mint, Proof	(44,174)		285

COMMEMORATIVES

	Distribution	MS-67	PF-67
2007P, Jamestown 400th Anniversary silver dollar	81,034	$23	
2007P, Same type, P Mint, Proof	(260,363)		$22
2007W, Jamestown 400th Anniversary gold $5	18,623	285	
2007W, Same type, W Mint, Proof	(47,123)		285
2007P, Little Rock Central High School Desegregation silver dollar	124,678	20	
2007P, Same type, P Mint, Proof	(66,093)		22
2008S, Bald Eagle Recovery and National Emblem clad half dollar	120,180	8	
2008S, Same type, S Mint, Proof	(220,577)		10
2008P, Bald Eagle Recovery and National Emblem silver dollar	119,204	18	
2008P, Same type, P Mint, Proof	(294,601)		22
2008W, Bald Eagle Recovery and National Emblem gold $5	19,009	285	
2008W, Same type, W Mint, Proof	(59,269)		285
2009P, Louis Braille Bicentennial silver dollar	82,639	17	
2009P, Same type, P Mint, Proof	(135,235)		17
2009P, Abraham Lincoln Bicentennial silver dollar	125,000	20	
2009P, Same type, P Mint, Proof	(325,000)		21
2010W, American Veterans Disabled for Life silver dollar	78,301	22	
2010W, Same type, W mint, Proof	(202,770)		19
2010P, Boy Scouts of America Centennial silver dollar	105,020	19	
2010P, Same type, S Mint, Proof	(244,963)		23
2011S, Medal of Honor silver dollar	44,752	30	
2011P, Same type, P Mint, Proof	(112,883)		28
2011P, Medal of Honor gold $5	8,233	365	
2011W, Same type, W Mint, Proof	(17,999)		300
2011D, U.S. Army clad half dollar	39,442	40	
2011S, Same type, S Mint, Proof	(68,332)		22
2011S, U.S. Army silver dollar	43,512	30	
2011P, Same type, P Mint, Proof	(119,829)		27
2011P, U.S. Army gold $5	8,052	285	
2011W, Same type, W Mint, Proof	(17,148)		300
2012W, Infantry Soldier silver dollar	44,348	26	
2012W, Same type, W Mint, Proof	(161,151)		31
2012P, Star-Spangled Banner silver dollar	41,686	30	
2012P, Same type, P Mint, Proof	(169,065)		30
2012W, Star-Spangled Banner gold $5	7,027	320	
2012W, Same type, W Mint, Proof	(18,313)		295
2013W, Girl Scouts of the U.S.A. Centennial silver dollar	37,461	26	
2013W, Same type, W Mint, Proof	(86,353)		32
2013D, 5-Star Generals clad half dollar	38,097	14	
2013S, Same type, S Mint, Proof	(47,337)		18
2013W, 5-Star Generals silver dollar	34,639	36	
2013P, Same type, P Mint, Proof	(69,290)		40
2013P, 5-Star Generals gold $5	5,658	385	
2013W, Same type, W Mint, Proof	(15,843)		345

Chart continued on next page.

	Distribution	MS-67	PF-67
2014D, National Baseball Hall of Fame clad half dollar	176,446	$18	
2014S, Same type, S Mint, Proof	(257,173)		$18
2014P, National Baseball Hall of Fame silver dollar	131,924	32	
2014P, Same type, P Mint, Proof	(268,076)		44
2014W, National Baseball Hall of Fame gold $5	17,677	480	
2014W, Same type, W Mint, Proof	(32,427)		520
2014P, Civil Rights Act of 1964 silver dollar	24,720	36	
2014P, Same type, P Mint, Proof	(61,992)		40
2015D, U.S. Marshals Service 225th Anniversary clad half dollar	30,231	13	
2015S, Same type, S Mint, Proof	(76,549)		14
2015P, U.S. Marshals Service 225th Anniversary silver dollar	38,149	32	
2015P, Same type, P Mint, Proof	(124,329)		36
2015W, U.S. Marshals Service 225th Anniversary gold $5	6,743	320	
2015W, Same type, W Mint, Proof	(24,959)		325
2015P, March of Dimes 75th Anniversary silver dollar	24,742	32	
2015W, Same type, W Mint, Proof	(132,030)		28
2016P, Mark Twain silver dollar	18,759	40	
2016P, Same type, Proof	(48,362)		40
2016W, Mark Twain $5 gold coin	4,706	340	
2016W, Same type, Proof	(10,412)		340
2016D, National Park Service 100th Anniversary half dollar			
2016S, Same type, Proof			
2016P, National Park Service 100th Anniversary silver dollar			
2016P, Same type, Proof			
2016W, National Park Service 100th Anniversary $5 gold coin			
2016W, Same type, Proof			

GOVERNMENT COMMEMORATIVE SETS

Values are for commemorative coins and sets in all of their original packaging.

	Value
(1983–1984) Los Angeles Olympiad	
1983 and 1984 Proof dollars	$39
1983 and 1984 6-coin set. One each of 1983 and 1984 dollars, both Proof and Uncirculated gold $10 **(a)**	1,225
1983 3-piece collector set. 1983 P, D, and S Uncirculated dollars	52
1984 3-piece collector set. 1984 P, D, and S Uncirculated dollars	56
1983 and 1984 gold and silver Uncirculated set. One each of 1983 and 1984 Uncirculated dollar and one 1984 Uncirculated gold $10	615
1983 and 1984 gold and silver Proof set. One each of 1983 and 1984 Proof dollars and one 1984 Proof gold $10	615
(1986) Statue of Liberty	
2-coin set. Proof silver dollar and clad half dollar	17
3-coin set. Proof silver dollar, clad half dollar, and gold $5	300
2-coin set. Uncirculated silver dollar and clad half dollar	17
2-coin set. Uncirculated and Proof gold $5	570
3-coin set. Uncirculated silver dollar, clad half dollar, and gold $5	300
6-coin set. One each of Proof and Uncirculated half dollar, silver dollar, and gold $5 **(a)**	600

a. Packaged in cherrywood box.

	Value

(1987) Constitution

2-coin set. Uncirculated silver dollar and gold $5	$300
2-coin set. Proof silver dollar and gold $5.	300
4-coin set. One each of Proof and Uncirculated silver dollar and gold $5 **(a)**.	600

(1988) Seoul Olympiad

2-coin set. Uncirculated silver dollar and gold $5	300
2-coin set. Proof silver dollar and gold $5.	300
4-coin set. One each of Proof and Uncirculated silver dollar and gold $5 **(a)**.	600

(1989) Congress

2-coin set. Proof clad half dollar and silver dollar	23
3-coin set. Proof clad half dollar, silver dollar, and gold $5.	310
2-coin set. Uncirculated clad half dollar and silver dollar.	21
3-coin set. Uncirculated clad half dollar, silver dollar, and gold $5	305
6-coin set. One each of Proof and Uncirculated clad half dollar, silver dollar, and gold $5 **(a)**.	615

(1991) Mount Rushmore

2-coin set. Uncirculated clad half dollar and silver dollar.	28
2-coin set. Proof clad half dollar and silver dollar	34
3-coin set. Uncirculated clad half dollar, silver dollar, and gold $5	315
3-coin set. Proof half dollar, silver dollar, and gold $5.	320
6-coin set. One each of Proof and Uncirculated clad half dollar, silver dollar, and gold $5 **(a)**.	635

(1992) XXV Olympiad

2-coin set. Uncirculated clad half dollar and silver dollar.	28
2-coin set. Proof clad half dollar and silver dollar	28
3-coin set. Uncirculated clad half dollar, silver dollar, and gold $5	315
3-coin set. Proof half dollar, silver dollar, and gold $5.	315
6-coin set. One each of Proof and Uncirculated clad half dollar, silver dollar, and gold $5 **(a)**.	630

(1992) Christopher Columbus

2-coin set. Uncirculated clad half dollar and silver dollar.	30
2-coin set. Proof clad half dollar and silver dollar	25
3-coin set. Uncirculated clad half dollar, silver dollar, and gold $5	315
3-coin set. Proof half dollar, silver dollar, and gold $5.	310
6-coin set. One each of Proof and Uncirculated clad half dollar, silver dollar, and gold $5 **(a)**.	625

(1993) Bill of Rights

2-coin set. Uncirculated silver half dollar and silver dollar.	36
2-coin set. Proof silver half dollar and silver dollar	31
3-coin set. Uncirculated silver half dollar, silver dollar, and gold $5	320
3-coin set. Proof half dollar, silver dollar, and gold $5.	315
6-coin set. One each of Proof and Uncirculated silver half dollar, silver dollar, and gold $5 **(a)**. . . . . ·	635
"Young Collector" set. Silver half dollar.	20
Educational set. Silver half dollar and James Madison medal	25
Proof silver half dollar and 25-cent stamp.	15

(1993) World War II

2-coin set. Uncirculated clad half dollar and silver dollar.	37
2-coin set. Proof clad half dollar and silver dollar	38
3-coin set. Uncirculated clad half dollar, silver dollar, and gold $5	320
3-coin set. Proof clad half dollar, silver dollar, and gold $5.	335
6-coin set. One each of Proof and Uncirculated clad half dollar, silver dollar, and gold $5 **(a)**.	655
"Young Collector" set. Clad half dollar.	25
Victory Medal set. Uncirculated clad half dollar and reproduction medal	30

a. Packaged in cherrywood box.

Chart continued on next page.   **229**

	Value

(1993) Thomas Jefferson
3-piece set (issued in 1994). Silver dollar, Jefferson nickel, and $2 note $40

(1994) World Cup Soccer
2-coin set. Uncirculated clad half dollar and silver dollar. 34
2-coin set. Proof clad half dollar and silver dollar 27
3-coin set. Uncirculated clad half dollar, silver dollar, and gold $5 335
3-coin set. Proof clad half dollar, silver dollar, and gold $5. 325
6-coin set. One each of Proof and Uncirculated clad half dollar, silver dollar, and gold $5 **(a)**. 660
"Young Collector" set. Uncirculated clad half dollar. 12
"Special Edition" set. Proof clad half dollar and silver dollar 35

(1994) U.S. Veterans
3-coin set. Uncirculated POW, Vietnam, and Women in Military Service silver dollars 120
3-coin set. Proof POW, Vietnam, and Women in Military Service silver dollars. 95

(1995) Special Olympics
2-coin set. Proof Special Olympics silver dollar, 1995S Kennedy half dollar 110

(1995) Civil War Battlefield Preservation
2-coin set. Uncirculated clad half dollar and silver dollar. 60
2-coin set. Proof clad half dollar and silver dollar 51
3-coin set. Uncirculated clad half dollar, silver dollar, and gold $5 380
3-coin set. Proof clad half dollar, silver dollar, and gold $5. 350
6-coin set. One each of Proof and Uncirculated clad half dollar, silver dollar, and gold $5 **(a)**. 730
"Young Collector" set. Uncirculated clad half dollar. 40
2-coin "Union" set. Clad half dollar and silver dollar 100
3-coin "Union" set. Clad half dollar, silver dollar, and gold $5. 400

(1995–1996) Centennial Olympic Games
4-coin set #1. Uncirculated half dollar (Basketball), dollars (Gymnastics, Paralympics),
gold $5 (Torch Bearer) 440
4-coin set #2. Proof half dollar (Basketball), dollars (Gymnastics, Paralympics),
gold $5 (Torch Bearer) 330
2-coin set #1: Proof silver dollars (Gymnastics, Paralympics) 42
"Young Collector" set. Uncirculated Basketball, Baseball, Swimming, or Soccer half dollar. . . . . —
1995–1996 16-coin Uncirculated set. One each of all Uncirculated coins **(a)** 5,300
1995–1996 16-coin Proof set. One each of all Proof coins **(a)** 1,325
1995–1996 8-coin Proof silver dollars set. 250
1995–1996 32-coin set. One each of all Uncirculated and Proof coins **(a)** 4,250

(1996) National Community Service
Proof silver dollar and Saint-Gaudens stamp. 80

(1996) Smithsonian Institution 150th Anniversary
2-coin set. Proof silver dollar and gold $5. 310
4-coin set. One each of Proof and Uncirculated silver dollar and gold $5 **(a)**. 640
"Young Collector" set. Proof silver dollar. 70

(1997) U.S. Botanic Garden
"Coinage and Currency" set. Uncirculated silver dollar, Jefferson nickel, and $1 note. 175

(1997) Jackie Robinson
2-coin set. Proof silver dollar and gold $5. 400
4-coin set. One each of Proof and Uncirculated silver dollar and gold $5 **(a)**. 1,400
3-piece "Legacy" set. Baseball card, pin, and gold $5 **(a)**. 475

(1997) Franklin D. Roosevelt
2-coin set. One each of Proof and Uncirculated gold $5 575

a. Packaged in cherrywood box.

COMMEMORATIVES

	Value
(1997) National Law Enforcement Officers Memorial	
Insignia set. Silver dollar, lapel pin, and patch.	$140
(1998) Robert F. Kennedy	
2-coin set. RFK silver dollar and JFK silver half dollar	160
2-coin set. Proof and Uncirculated RFK silver dollars.	68
(1998) Black Revolutionary War Patriots	
2-coin set. Proof and Uncirculated silver dollars	86
"Young Collector" set. Uncirculated silver dollar	100
Black Revolutionary War Patriots set. Silver dollar and four stamps.	100
(1999) Dolley Madison Commemorative	
2-coin set. Proof and Uncirculated silver dollars	42
(1999) George Washington Death	
2-coin set. One each of Proof and Uncirculated gold $5	570
(1999) Yellowstone National Park	
2-coin set. One each of Proof and Uncirculated silver dollars	60
(2000) Leif Ericson Millennium	
2-coin set. Proof silver dollar and Icelandic 1,000 kronur	65
(2000) Millennium Coin and Currency Set	
3-piece set. Uncirculated 2000 Sacagawea dollar; Uncirculated 2000 Silver Eagle;	
George Washington $1 note, series 1999	75
(2001) American Buffalo	
2-coin set. One each of Proof and Uncirculated silver dollar	210
"Coinage and Currency" set. Uncirculated American Buffalo silver dollar, face reprint of 1899	
$5 Indian Chief Silver Certificate, 1987 Chief Red Cloud 10¢ stamp, 2001 Bison 21¢ stamp	150
(2001) U.S. Capitol Visitor Center	
3-coin set. Proof clad half dollar, silver dollar, and gold $5	280
(2002) Salt Lake Olympic Games	
2-coin set. Proof silver dollar and gold $5	310
4-coin set. One each of Proof and Uncirculated silver dollar and gold $5	620
(2003) First Flight Centennial	
3-coin set. Proof clad half dollar, silver dollar, and gold $10	610
(2003) Legacies of Freedom™	
Uncirculated 2003 $1 American Eagle silver bullion coin and an Uncirculated 2002 £2 Silver Britannia coin	55
(2004) Thomas A. Edison	
Edison set. Uncirculated silver dollar and light bulb.	55
(2004) Lewis and Clark	
Coin and Pouch set. Proof silver dollar and beaded pouch.	130
"Coinage and Currency" set. Uncirculated silver dollar, Sacagawea golden dollar, two 2005 nickels,	
replica 1901 $10 Bison note, silver-plated Peace Medal replica, three stamps, two booklets	70
(2004) Westward Journey Nickel Series™	
Westward Journey Nickel Series™ Coin and Medal set. Proof Sacagawea golden dollar,	
two 2004 Proof nickels, silver-plated Peace Medal replica	40
(2005) Westward Journey Nickel Series™	
Westward Journey Nickel Series™ Coin and Medal set. Proof Sacagawea golden dollar,	
two 2005 Proof nickels, silver-plated Peace Medal replica	25

Chart continued on next page.

	Value

(2005) Chief Justice John Marshall
"Coin and Chronicles" set. Uncirculated silver dollar, booklet, BEP intaglio portrait $45

(2005) American Legacy
American Legacy Collection. Proof Marine Corps dollar, Proof John Marshall dollar, 11-piece Proof set . . . 70

(2005) Marine Corps 230th Anniversary
Marine Corps Uncirculated silver dollar and stamp set 65

(2006) Benjamin Franklin
"Coin and Chronicles" set. Uncirculated "Scientist" silver dollar, four stamps,
Poor Richard's Almanack replica, intaglio print 50

(2006) American Legacy
American Legacy Collection. Proof 2006P Benjamin Franklin, Founding Father silver dollar; Proof
2006S San Francisco Old Mint silver dollar; Proof cent, nickel, dime, quarter, half dollar, and dollar   60

(2007) American Legacy
American Legacy Collection. 16 Proof coins for 2007: five state quarters; four Presidential dollars;
Jamestown and Little Rock Central High School Desegregation silver dollars; Proof cent, nickel,
dime, half dollar, and dollar. 95

(2007) Little Rock Central High School Desegregation
Little Rock Coin and Medal set. Proof 2007P silver dollar, bronze medal 110

(2008) Bald Eagle
3-piece set. Proof clad half dollar, silver dollar, and gold $5 315
Bald Eagle Coin and Medal Set. Uncirculated silver dollar, bronze medal 50
"Young Collector" set. Uncirculated clad half dollar. 12

(2008) American Legacy
American Legacy Collection. 15 Proof coins for 2008: cent, nickel, dime, half dollar, and dollar;
five state quarters; four Presidential dollars; Bald Eagle dollar. 95

(2009) Louis Braille
Uncirculated silver dollar in tri-folded package 35

(2009) Abraham Lincoln Coin and Chronicles
Four Proof 2009S cents and Abraham Lincoln Proof silver dollar. 90

(2012) Star-Spangled Banner
2-coin set. Proof silver dollar and gold $5. 325

(2013) 5-Star Generals
3-coin set. Proof clad half dollar, silver dollar, and gold $5 405
Profile Collection. Uncirculated half dollar and silver dollar, replica of
1962 General MacArthur Congressional Gold Medal 55

(2013) Theodore Roosevelt Coin and Chronicles
Theodore Roosevelt Proof Presidential dollar; silver Presidential medal; National Wildlife
Refuge System Centennial bronze medal; and Roosevelt print. 45

(2013) Girl Scouts of the U.S.A.
"Young Collector" set. Uncirculated silver dollar 40

(2014) Franklin D. Roosevelt Coin and Chronicles
Franklin D. Roosevelt Proof dime and Presidential dollar; bronze Presidential
medal; silver Presidential medal; four stamps; companion booklet 45

(2014) National Baseball Hall of Fame
"Young Collector" set. Uncirculated half dollar 40

COMMEMORATIVES

	Value

(2015) Harry S. Truman Coin and Chronicles
Harry S. Truman Reverse Proof Presidential dollar, silver Presidential medal,
    one stamp, information booklet. $160

(2015) Dwight D. Eisenhower Coin and Chronicles
Dwight D. Eisenhower Reverse Proof Presidential dollar, silver Presidential medal,
    one stamp, information booklet. 100

(2015) John F. Kennedy Coin and Chronicles
John F. Kennedy Reverse Proof Presidential dollar, silver Presidential medal,
    one stamp, information booklet. 45

(2015) Lyndon B. Johnson Coin and Chronicles
Lyndon B. Johnson Reverse Proof Presidential dollar, silver Presidential medal,
    one stamp, information booklet. 45

(2015) March of Dimes Special Silver Set
Proof dime and March of Dimes silver dollar, Reverse Proof dime. 55

PROOF COINS AND SETS

Proof coins can usually be distinguished by their sharpness of detail, high wire edge, and extremely brilliant, mirrorlike surface. Proofs are sold by the Mint at a premium.

Proof coins were not struck during 1943–1949 or 1965–1967. Sets from 1936 through 1972 include the cent, nickel, dime, quarter, and half dollar; from 1973 through 1981 the dollar was also included. From 1999 on, Proof sets have included the year's multiple quarter dollars, and since 2000 they have included the Mint's golden dollar coins. *Values shown are for original unblemished sets.*

Figures in parentheses represent the total number of full sets minted.

	Mintage	Issue Price	Current Value		Mintage	Issue Price	Current Value
1936	(3,837)	$1.89	$4,700	1980S	(3,554,806)	$10.00	$3.00
1937	(5,542)	1.89	2,000	1981S, Type 1	(4,063,083)	11.00	3.00
1938	(8,045)	1.89	820	1981S, Type 2	*	11.00	180.00
1939	(8,795)	1.89	760	1982S	(3,857,479)	11.00	2.50
1940	(11,246)	1.89	630	1983S	(3,138,765)	11.00	2.50
1941	(15,287)	1.89	590	1983S, Prestige set			
1942, Both nickels	(21,120)	1.89	660	(Olympic dollar)	(140,361)	59.00	30.00
1942, One nickel	*	1.89	570	1984S	(2,748,430)	11.00	3.00
1950	(51,386)	2.10	365	1984S, Prestige set			
1951	(57,500)	2.10	360	(Olympic dollar)	(316,680)	59.00	17.00
1952	(81,980)	2.10	150	1985S	(3,362,821)	11.00	2.00
1953	(128,800)	2.10	125	1986S	(2,411,180)	11.00	4.00
1954	(233,300)	2.10	65	1986S, Prestige set (Statue			
1955, Box pack	(378,200)	2.10	65	of Liberty half, dollar)	(599,317)	48.50	15.00
1955, Flat pack	*	2.10	90	1987S	(3,792,233)	11.00	2.50
1956	(669,384)	2.10	41	1987S, Prestige set			
1957	(1,247,952)	2.10	15	(Constitution dollar)	(435,495)	45.00	14.50
1958	(875,652)	2.10	20	1988S	(3,031,287)	11.00	3.00
1959	(1,149,291)	2.10	18	1988S, Prestige set			
1960, With Lg Date cent	(1,691,602)	2.10	19	(Olympic dollar)	(231,661)	45.00	19.00
1960, With Sm Date cent	*	2.10	20	1989S	(3,009,107)	11.00	2.50
1961	(3,028,244)	2.10	18	1989S, Prestige set			
1962	(3,218,019)	2.10	18	(Congressional half,			
1963	(3,075,645)	2.10	18	dollar)	(211,807)	45.00	20.00
1964	(3,950,762)	2.10	18	1990S	(2,793,433)	11.00	3.50
1968S	(3,041,506)	5.00	4	1990S, With No S cent	(3,555)	11.00	2,960.00
1969S	(2,934,631)	5.00	4	1990S, With No S cent			
1970S	(2,632,810)	5.00	7	(Prestige set)	*	45.00	3,200.00
1970S, With Sm Date cent	*	5.00	56	1990S, Prestige set			
1971S	(3,220,733)	5.00	2	(Eisenhower dollar)	(506,126)	45.00	17.00
1972S	(3,260,996)	5.00	2	1991S	(2,610,833)	11.00	2.75
1973S	(2,760,339)	7.00	6	1991S, Prestige set (Mt.			
1974S	(2,612,568)	7.00	7	Rushmore half, dllr)	(256,954)	59.00	23.50
1975S, With 1976 quarter,				1992S	(2,675,618)	11.00	2.50
half, and dollar	(2,845,450)	7.00	6	1992S, Prestige set			
1976S	(4,149,730)	7.00	4	(Olympic half, dollar)	(183,293)	56.00	28.00
1976S, 3-piece set	(3,998,621)	15.00	16	1992S, Silver	(1,009,586)	21.00	11.00
1977S	(3,251,152)	9.00	4	1992S, Silver Premier set	(308,055)	37.00	14.50
1978S	(3,127,781)	9.00	4	1993S	(2,409,394)	12.50	3.50
1979S, Type 1	(3,677,175)	9.00	4	1993S, Prestige set (Bill			
1979S, Type 2	*	9.00	32	of Rights half, dollar)	(224,045)	57.00	25.00

* Included in number above.

Year	Mintage	Issue Price	Current Value
1993S, Silver	(570,213)	$21.00	$18.50
1993S, Silver Premier set	(191,140)	37.50	22.50
1994S	(2,308,701)	12.50	3.00
1994S, Prestige set (World Cup half, dollar)	(175,893)	57.00	22.50
1994S, Silver	(636,009)	21.00	17.00
1994S, Silver Premier set	(149,320)	37.50	23.00
1995S	(2,010,384)	12.50	7.00
1995S, Prestige set (Civil War half, dollar)	(107,112)	57.00	54.00
1995S, Silver	(549,878)	21.00	35.00
1995S, Silver Premier set	(130,107)	37.50	36.00
1996S	(1,695,244)	12.50	4.75
1996S, Prestige set (Olympic half, dollar)	(55,000)	57.00	225.00
1996S, Silver	(623,655)	21.00	18.50
1996S, Silver Premier set	(151,366)	37.50	20.00
1997S	(1,975,000)	12.50	5.00
1997S, Prestige set (Botanic dollar)	(80,000)	48.00	38.00
1997S, Silver	(605,473)	21.00	22.50
1997S, Silver Premier set	(136,205)	37.50	22.50
1998S	(2,086,507)	12.50	6.50
1998S, Silver	(638,134)	21.00	15.00
1998S, Silver Premier set	(240,658)	37.50	17.50
1999S, 9-piece set	(2,543,401)	19.95	5.25
1999S, 5-piece quarter set	(1,169,958)	13.95	2.25
1999S, Silver 9-piece set	(804,565)	31.95	62.00
2000S, 10-piece set	(3,082,572)	19.95	3.50
2000S, 5-piece quarter set	(937,600)	13.95	1.50
2000S, Silver 10-piece set	(965,421)	31.95	21.50
2001S, 10-piece set	(2,294,909)	19.95	6.50
2001S, 5-piece quarter set	(799,231)	13.95	2.50
2001S, Silver 10-piece set	(889,697)	31.95	29.00
2002S, 10-piece set	(2,319,766)	19.95	4.50
2002S, 5-piece quarter set	(764,479)	13.95	2.00
2002S, Silver 10-piece set	(892,229)	31.95	21.50
2003S, 10-piece set	(2,172,684)	19.95	3.75
2003S, 5-piece quarter set	(1,235,832)	13.95	1.50
2003S, Silver 10-piece set	(1,125,755)	31.95	20.00
2004S, 11-piece set	(1,789,488)	22.95	6.50
2004S, 5-piece quarter set	(951,196)	15.95	2.50
2004S, Silver 11-piece set	(1,175,934)	37.95	21.00
2004S, Silver 5-piece quarter set	(593,852)	23.95	13.25
2005S, 11-piece set	(2,275,000)	22.95	2.75
2005S, 5-piece quarter set	(987,960)	15.95	1.50
2005S, Silver 11-piece set	(1,069,679)	37.95	21.00
2005S, Silver 5-piece quarter set	(608,970)	23.95	13.25
2006S, 10-piece set	(2,000,428)	22.95	4.75
2006S, 5-piece quarter set	(882,000)	15.95	1.50
2006S, Silver 10-piece set	(1,054,008)	37.95	21.00
2006S, Silver 5-piece quarter set	(531,000)	23.95	13.25
2007S, 14-piece set	(1,702,116)	26.95	9.50
2007S, 5-piece quarter set	(672,662)	13.95	3.50
2007S, 4-piece Presidential set	(1,285,972)	14.95	3.50

Year	Mintage	Issue Price	Current Value
2007S, Silver 14-piece set	(875,050)	$44.95	$24.00
2007S, Silver 5-piece quarter set	(672,662)	25.95	13.25
2008S, 14-piece set	(1,382,017)	26.95	21.00
2008S, 5-piece quarter set	(672,438)	13.95	18.50
2008S, 4-piece Presidential set	(836,730)	14.95	8.00
2008S, Silver 14-piece set	(763,887)	44.95	29.00
2008S, Silver 5-piece quarter set	(429,021)	25.95	13.25
2009S, 18-piece set	(1,482,502)	29.95	14.50
2009S, 6-piece quarter set	(630,976)	14.95	2.75
2009S, 4-piece Presidential set	(629,585)	14.95	5.25
2009S, Silver 18-piece set	(697,365)	52.95	31.00
2009S, Silver 6-piece quarter set	(299,183)	29.95	15.00
2009S, 4-piece Lincoln Bicentennial set		7.95	5.75
2010S, 14-piece set	(1,103,815)	31.95	22.50
2010S, 5-piece quarter set	(272,296)	14.95	8.00
2010S, 4-piece Presidential set	(535,397)	15.95	11.25
2010S, Silver 14-piece set	(585,401)	56.95	34.00
2010S, Silver 5-piece quarter set	(274,034)	32.95	13.50
2011S, 14-piece set	(1,098,835)	31.95	23.00
2011S, 5-piece quarter set	(152,302)	14.95	8.50
2011S, 4-piece Presidential set	(299,853)	19.95	19.00
2011S, Silver 14-piece set	(574,175)	67.95	44.00
2011S, Silver 5-piece quarter set	(147,901)	39.95	17.50
2012S, 14-piece set	(794,002)	31.95	88.00
2012S, 5-piece quarter set	(148,498)	14.95	9.50
2012S, 4-piece Presidential set	(249,265)	19.95	49.00
2012S, Silver 14-piece set	(395,443)	67.95	145.00
2012S, Silver 8-piece Limited Edition set	(44,952)	149.95	160.00
2012S, Silver 5-piece quarter set	(162,448)	39.95	17.50
2013S, 14-piece set	(802,460)	31.95	22.50
2013S, 5-piece quarter set	(128,377)	14.95	9.00
2013S, 4-piece Presidential set	(266,618)	19.95	14.50
2013S, Silver 14-piece set	(419,720)	67.95	46.00
2013S, Silver 8-piece Limited Edition set	(47,971)	149.95	120.00
2013S, Silver 5-piece quarter set	(138,451)	39.95	17.50
2014S, 14-piece set	(714,661)	31.95	22.50
2014S, 5-piece quarter set	(115,179)	14.95	10.50
2014S, 4-piece Presidential set	(229,415)	18.95	14.50
2014S, Silver 14-piece set	(429,493)	53.95	38.00
2014S, Silver 8-piece Limited Edition set	(42,614)	139.95	120.00
2014S, Silver 5-piece quarter set	(119,251)	41.95	24.00
2015S, 14-piece set	(632,037)	32.95	26.00
2015S, 5-piece quarter set	(95,545)	14.95	12.00
2015S, 4-piece Presidential set	(221,273)	18.95	15.00
2015S, Silver 14-piece set	(361,511)	53.95	43.00
2015S, Silver 5-piece quarter set	(97,119)	41.95	26.00
2016S, 14-piece set		32.95	26.00
2016S, 5-piece quarter set		14.95	12.00
2016S, 4-piece Presidential set		18.95	15.00
2016S, Silver 14-piece set		53.95	43.00
2016S, Silver 8-piece Limited Edition set		139.95	120.00
2016S, Silver 5-piece quarter set		41.95	26.00

UNCIRCULATED MINT SETS

Official Mint Sets are specially packaged by the government for sale to collectors. They contain Uncirculated specimens of each year's coins for every denomination issued from each mint. Sets from 1947 through 1958 contain two examples of each regular-issue coin. No official sets were produced in 1950, 1982, or 1983. Privately assembled sets are valued according to individual coin prices. Only official sets are included in the following list. Unlike the Proof sets, these are normal coins intended for circulation and are not minted with any special consideration for quality. From 1942 to 1946, groups of two coins from each mint were sold in a cloth shipping bag with only minimal protection. Very few of those mailing packages were saved by collectors.

	Mintage	Issue Price	Current Value		Mintage	Issue Price	Current Value
1947 P-D-S	5,000	$4.87	$1,600.00	1984 P-D	1,832,857	$7.00	$1.75
1948 P-D-S	6,000	4.92	950.00	1985 P-D	1,710,571	7.00	2.25
1949 P-D-S	5,000	5.45	1,250.00	1986 P-D	1,153,536	7.00	5.00
1951 P-D-S	8,654	6.75	1,000.00	1987 P-D	2,890,758	7.00	2.25
1952 P-D-S	11,499	6.14	900.00	1988 P-D	1,646,204	7.00	2.50
1953 P-D-S	15,538	6.14	700.00	1989 P-D	1,987,915	7.00	2.00
1954 P-D-S	25,599	6.19	400.00	1990 P-D	1,809,184	7.00	2.00
1955 P-D-S	49,656	3.57	260.00	1991 P-D	1,352,101	7.00	2.50
1956 P-D	45,475	3.34	300.00	1992 P-D	1,500,143	7.00	2.25
1957 P-D	34,324	4.40	455.00	1993 P-D	1,297,431	8.00	2.50
1958 P-D	50,314	4.43	285.00	1994 P-D	1,234,813	8.00	1.75
1959 P-D	187,000	2.40	31.00	1995 P-D	1,038,787	8.00	2.00
1960 P-D	260,485	2.40	27.00	1996 P-D, Plus			
1961 P-D	223,704	2.40	29.00	1996W dime	1,457,949	8.00	9.50
1962 P-D	385,285	2.40	28.00	1997 P-D	950,473	8.00	2.50
1963 P-D	606,612	2.40	23.00	1998 P-D	1,187,325	8.00	2.00
1964 P-D	1,008,108	2.40	20.00	1999 P-D (18 pieces)	1,243,867	14.95	4.75
1965*	2,360,000	4.00	5.75	2000 P-D (20 pieces)	1,490,160	14.95	4.75
1966*	2,261,583	4.00	5.25	2001 P-D (20 pieces)	1,116,915	14.95	4.75
1967*	1,863,344	4.00	5.75	2002 P-D (20 pieces)	1,139,388	14.95	5.00
1968 P-D-S	2,105,128	2.50	4.00	2003 P-D (20 pieces)	1,001,532	14.95	5.50
1969 P-D-S	1,817,392	2.50	4.00	2004 P-D (22 pieces)	842,507	16.95	5.50
1970 P-D-S	2,038,134	2.50	11.50	2005 P-D (22 pieces)	1,160,000	16.95	5.00
1971 P-D-S	2,193,396	3.50	2.25	2006 P-D (20 pieces)	847,361	16.95	5.00
1972 P-D-S	2,750,000	3.50	1.50	2007 P-D (28 pieces)	895,628	22.95	11.25
1973 P-D-S	1,767,691	6.00	7.50	2008 P-D (28 pieces)	745,464	22.95	22.50
1974 P-D-S	1,975,981	6.00	4.00	2009 P-D (36 pieces)	784,614	27.95	15.50
1975 P-D	1,921,488	6.00	5.00	2010 P-D (28 pieces)	583,897	31.95	14.50
1776–1976, 3-piece set	4,908,319	9.00	11.00	2011 P-D (28 pieces)	533,529	31.95	15.25
1976 P-D	1,892,513	6.00	5.00	2012 P-D (28 pieces)	392,224	27.95	46.00
1977 P-D	2,006,869	7.00	3.75	2013 P-D (28 pieces)	376,844	27.95	14.50
1978 P-D	2,162,609	7.00	4.00	2014 P-D (28 pieces)	345,813	27.95	14.50
1979 P-D	2,526,000	8.00	3.50	2015 P-D (28 pieces)	299,122	28.95	24.00
1980 P-D-S	2,815,066	9.00	4.00	2016 P-D (28 pieces)		28.95	24.00
1981 P-D-S	2,908,145	11.00	7.00				

Note: Sets issued from 2005 to 2010 have a special Satin Finish that is somewhat different from the finish on Uncirculated coins made for general circulation. * Special Mint Set.

AMERICA THE BEAUTIFUL™ SILVER BULLION COINS

Weight and purity incused on edge.
Actual size 3 inches.

	Mintage	MS	SP
25¢ 2010(P), Hot Springs National Park (Arkansas)	26,788	$85	
25¢ 2010P, Hot Springs National Park (Arkansas)	(33,000)		$90
25¢ 2010(P), Yellowstone National Park (Wyoming)	26,711	85	
25¢ 2010P, Yellowstone National Park (Wyoming)	(33,000)		90
25¢ 2010(P), Yosemite National Park (California)	26,716	85	
25¢ 2010P, Yosemite National Park (California)	(33,000)		90
25¢ 2010(P), Grand Canyon National Park (Arizona)	25,967	85	
25¢ 2010P, Grand Canyon National Park (Arizona)	(33,000)		90
25¢ 2010(P), Mount Hood National Park (Oregon)	26,637	85	
25¢ 2010P, Mount Hood National Park (Oregon)	(33,000)		90
25¢ 2011(P), Gettysburg National Military Park (Pennsylvania)	24,625	80	
25¢ 2011P, Gettysburg National Military Park (Pennsylvania)	(126,700)		125
25¢ 2011(P), Glacier National Park (Montana)	20,805	80	
25¢ 2011P, Glacier National Park (Montana)	(126,700)		125
25¢ 2011P, Olympic National Park (Washington)	18,345	80	
25¢ 2011P, Olympic National Park (Washington)	(104,900)		125
25¢ 2011(P), Vicksburg National Military Park (Mississippi)	18,528	80	
25¢ 2011P, Vicksburg National Military Park (Mississippi)	(58,100)		125
25¢ 2011(P), Chickasaw National Recreation Area (Oklahoma)	16,746	80	
25¢ 2011P, Chickasaw National Recreation Area (Oklahoma)	(48,700)		125
25¢ 2012(P), El Yunque National Forest (Puerto Rico)	17,314	120	
25¢ 2012P, El Yunque National Forest (Puerto Rico)	(24,000)		280
25¢ 2012P, Chaco Culture National Historical Park (New Mexico)	17,146	120	
25¢ 2012P, Chaco Culture National Historical Park (New Mexico)	(24,400)		280
25¢ 2012P, Acadia National Park (Maine)	14,978	120	
25¢ 2012P, Acadia National Park (Maine)	(25,400)		310
25¢ 2012(P), Hawai'i Volcanoes National Park (Hawaii)	14,863	120	
25¢ 2012P, Hawai'i Volcanoes National Park (Hawaii)	(20,000)		360
25¢ 2012(P), Denali National Park and Preserve (Alaska)	15,225	120	
25¢ 2012P, Denali National Park and Preserve (Alaska)	(20,000)		280

Note: The U.S. Mint produces the America the Beautiful™ 5-oz. silver coins in bullion and numismatic versions. The bullion version, which lacks the P mintmark, has a brilliant Uncirculated finish and is sold only through dealers. The numismatic version, with the P mintmark, has a matte or burnished finish (although it is not marketed by the Mint as "Burnished"). These coins, designated Specimens (SP) by grading services, are sold directly to the public.

SILVER BULLION

	Mintage	MS	SP
25¢ 2013(P), White Mountain National Forest (New Hampshire) 20,530		$80	
25¢ 2013P, White Mountain National Forest (New Hampshire) . . . .(35,000)			$95
25¢ 2013(P), Perry's Victory and International Peace Memorial (Ohio). 17,707		80	
25¢ 2013(P), Perry's Victory and International Peace Memorial (Ohio). . . . . .(30,000)			95
25¢ 2013(P), Great Basin National Park (Nevada) 17,792		80	
25¢ 2013P, Great Basin National Park (Nevada) . . . .(30,000)			95
25¢ 2013(P), Ft McHenry Nat'l Monument and Historic Shrine (Maryland). 19,802		80	
25¢ 2013P, Ft McHenry Nat'l Monument and Historic Shrine (Maryland) . .(30,000)			95
25¢ 2013(P), Mount Rushmore National Memorial (South Dakota). 23,547		80	
25¢ 2013P, Mount Rushmore National Memorial (South Dakota). . . . .(35,000)			95
25¢ 2014(P), Great Smoky Mountains National Park (Tennessee) 24,710		80	
25¢ 2014P, Great Smoky Mountains National Park (Tennessee) . . . .(33,000)			95
25¢ 2014(P), Shenandoah National Park (Virginia). 28,451		80	
25¢ 2014P, Shenandoah National Park (Virginia). . . . .(25,000)			95
25¢ 2014P, Arches National Park (Utah) 28,434		80	
25¢ 2014(P), Arches National Park (Utah) . . . .(22,000)			95
25¢ 2014(P), Great Sand Dunes National Park (Colorado) 24,103		80	
25¢ 2014P, Great Sand Dunes National Park (Colorado) . . . .(22,000)			95
25¢ 2014(P), Everglades National Park (Florida) 22,732		80	
25¢ 2014P, Everglades National Park (Florida) . . . .(34,000)			95
25¢, 2015(P), Homestead Nat'l Monument of America (Nebraska). 20,602		80	
25¢, 2015P, Homestead Nat'l Monument of America (Nebraska) . . . .(35,000)			95
25¢, 2015(P), Kisatchie National Forest (Louisiana) 19,168		80	
25¢, 2015P, Kisatchie National Forest (Louisiana) . . . .(42,000)			95
25¢, 2015(P), Blue Ridge Parkway (North Carolina) 17,461		80	
25¢, 2015P, Blue Ridge Parkway (North Carolina) . . . .(45,000)			95
25¢, 2015(P), Bombay Hook National Wildlife Refuge (Delaware). 17,339		80	
25¢, 2015P, Bombay Hook National Wildlife Refuge (Delaware) . . . .(45,000)			95
25¢, 2015(P), Saratoga National Historical Park (New York). 17,457		80	
25¢, 2015P, Saratoga National Historical Park (New York) . . . .(45,000)			95
25¢ 2016(P), Shawnee National Forest (Illinois).		80	
25¢ 2016P, Shawnee National Forest (Illinois).			95
25¢ 2016(P), Cumberland Gap National Historical Park (Kentucky)		80	
25¢ 2016P, Cumberland Gap National Historical Park (Kentucky)			95
25¢ 2016(P), Harpers Ferry National Historical Park (West Virginia).		80	
25¢ 2016P, Harpers Ferry National Historical Park (West Virginia).			95
25¢ 2016(P), Theodore Roosevelt National Park (North Dakota).		80	
25¢ 2016P, Theodore Roosevelt National Park (North Dakota).			95
25¢ 2016(P), Fort Moultrie at Fort Sumter National Monument (South Carolina)		80	
25¢ 2016P, Fort Moultrie at Fort Sumter National Monument (South Carolina)			95

Note: The U.S. Mint produces the America the Beautiful™ 5-oz. silver coins in bullion and numismatic versions. The bullion version, which lacks the P mintmark, has a brilliant Uncirculated finish and is sold only through dealers. The numismatic version, with the mintmark, has a matte or burnished finish (although it is not marketed by the Mint as "Burnished"). These coins, designated Specimens (SP) by grading services, are sold directly to the public.

$1 SILVER EAGLES

Values below are based on spot silver value of $15.50 per ounce.

	Mintage	Unc.	PF
$1 1986	5,393,005	$28	
$1 1986S	(1,446,778)		$36
$1 1987	11,442,335	17	
$1 1987S	(904,732)		36
$1 1988	5,004,646	18	
$1 1988S	(557,370)		36
$1 1989	5,203,327	17	
$1 1989S	(617,694)		36
$1 1990	5,840,210	17	
$1 1990S	(695,510)		36
$1 1991	7,191,066	17	
$1 1991S	(511,925)		36
$1 1992	5,540,068	18	
$1 1992S	(498,654)		36
$1 1993	6,763,762	18	
$1 1993P	(405,913)		50
$1 1994	4,227,319	27	
$1 1994P	(372,168)		112
$1 1995	4,672,051	22	
$1 1995P	(438,511)		41
$1 1995W	(30,125)		2,950
$1 1996	3,603,386	44	
$1 1996P	(500,000)		36
$1 1997	4,295,004	19	
$1 1997P	(435,368)		41
$1 1998	4,847,549	19	
$1 1998P	(450,000)		36
$1 1999	7,408,640	19	
$1 1999P	(549,769)		36
$1 2000(W)	9,239,132	18	
$1 2000P	(600,000)		36
$1 2001(W)	9,001,711	17	
$1 2001W	(746,398)		36
$1 2002(W)	10,539,026	17	

	Mintage	Unc.	PF
$1 2002W	(647,32)		$36
$1 2003(W)	8,495,008	$17	
$1 2003W	(747,831)		36
$1 2004(W)	8,882,754	17	
$1 2004W	(801,602)		36
$1 2005(W)	8,891,025	17	
$1 2005W	(816,663)		36
$1 2006(W)	10,676,522	17	
$1 2006W, Burnished (a)	468,020	41	
$1 2006W	(1,092,477)		36
$1 2006P, Reverse Proof	(248,875)		140
$1 2007(W)	9,028,036	17	
$1 2007 W, Burnished	621,333	18	
$1 2007W	(821,759)		38
$1 2008(W)	20,583,000	17	
$1 2008W, Burnished	533,757	28	
$1 2008W, Burnished, Reverse of 2007	47,000	370	
$1 2008W	(700,979)		38
$1 2009(W) (b)	30,459,000	17	
$1 2010(W)	34,764,500	17	
$1 2010W	(849,861)		38
$1 2011(W)(S)	40,020,000	17	
$1 2011W, Burnished	409,776	23	
$1 2011S, Burnished	99,882	190	
$1 2011W	(947,355)		38
$1 2011P, Reverse Proof	(99,882)		205
$1 2012(W)(S)	33,742,500	17	
$1 2012W, Burnished	226,120	41	
$1 2012W	(869,386)		38
$1 2012S, Reverse Proof	(224,981)		72
$1 2012S	(285,184)		40
$1 2013(W)(S)	42,675,000	17	
$1 2013W, Burnished	222,091	26	

a. "Burnished" refers to special American Eagle Uncirculated coins in silver, gold, and platinum sold directly by the U.S. Mint. Similar in appearance to ordinary Uncirculated American Eagle bullion coins, these coins can be distinguished by the presence of a mintmark and the use of burnished coin blanks. (Proof coins also have a mintmark but have highly reflective, mirrorlike surfaces.) **b.** No Proof dollars were made in 2009. Beware of alterations made privately outside the Mint.

SILVER BULLION

	Mintage	Unc.	PF
$1 2013W, Enhanced	281,310	$62	
$1 2013W	(934,812)		$38
$1 2013W, Reverse Proof	(281,310)		56
$1 2014(W)(S)	44,006,000	17	
$1 2014W, Burnished	253,169	26	

	Mintage	Unc.	PF
$1 2014W	(944,757)		$38
$1 2015(W)(S)		$17	
$1 2015W, Burnished		26	
$1 2015W			38

Anniversary Sets

	Unc.
1997 Impressions of Liberty Set **(a)**	
2006 20th Anniversary Silver Coin Set. Uncirculated, Proof, Reverse Proof	$195
2006W 20th Anniversary 1-oz. Gold- and Silver-Dollar Set. Uncirculated	1,220
2011 25th Anniversary Five-Coin Set. 2011W Uncirculated, Proof; 2011P Reverse Proof; 2011S Uncirculated; 2011 Bullion	460
2012 75th Anniversary of San Francisco Mint Two-Piece Set. S-Mint Proof and Reverse Proof silver dollars	105
2013 75th Anniversary of West Point Depository Two-Coin Set. W-Mint Enhanced Uncirculated and Reverse Proof silver dollars	95

a. See under "Gold Bullion Sets."

AMERICAN EAGLE GOLD COINS

Bullion values are based on spot gold at $1,150 per ounce.

$5 Tenth-Ounce Gold

	Mintage	Unc.	PF
$5 MCMLXXXVI (1986)....	912,609	$130	
$5 MCMLXXXVII (1987) ...	580,266	120	
$5 MCMLXXXVIII (1988)...	159,500	130	
$5 MCMLXXXVIII (1988)P.	(143,881)		$125
$5 MCMLXXXIX (1989)....	264,790	120	
$5 MCMLXXXIX (1989)P...	(84,647)		125
$5 MCMXC (1990).......	210,210	130	
$5 MCMXC (1990)P......	(99,349)		125
$5 MCMXCI (1991)	165,200	130	
$5 MCMXCI (1991)P	(70,334)		125
$5 1992	209,300	120	
$5 1992P	(64,874)		125
$5 1993	210,709	120	
$5 1993P	(58,649)		125
$5 1994	206,380	120	
$5 1994W	(62,849)		125
$5 1995	223,025	120	
$5 1995W	(62,667)		125
$5 1996	401,964	120	
$5 1996W	(57,047)		125
$5 1997	528,266	120	
$5 1997W	(34,977)		125
$5 1998	1,344,520	120	
$5 1998W	(39,395)		125
$5 1999	2,750,338	120	
$5 1999W	(48,428)		125
$5 1999W, Unc. Made from			
unpolished Proof dies..	14,500	.560	
$5 2000	569,153	120	
$5 2000W	(49,971)		125
$5 2001	269,147	120	

	Mintage	Unc.	PF
$5 2001W	(37,530)		$125
$5 2002	230,027	$120	
$5 2002W	(40,864)		125
$5 2003	245,029	120	
$5 2003W	(40,027)		125
$5 2004	250,016	120	
$5 2004W	(35,131)		125
$5 2005	300,043	120	
$5 2005W	(49,265)		125
$5 2006	285,006	120	
$5 2006W, Burnished	20,643	160	
$5 2006W	(47,277)		125
$5 2007	190,010	120	
$5 2007W, Burnished	22,501	235	
$5 2007W	(58,553)		125
$5 2008	305,000	120	
$5 2008W, Burnished	12,657	235	
$5 2008W	(28,116)		125
$5 2009	270,000	120	
$5 2010	435,000	120	
$5 2010W	(54,285)		125
$5 2011	350,000	120	
$5 2011W	(42,697)		125
$5 2012	315,000	120	
$5 2012W	(20,637)		125
$5 2013	535,000	120	
$5 2013W	(21,738)		125
$5 2014	565,500	120	
$5 2014W	(22,725)		125
$5 2015	980,000	120	
$5 2015W	(26,761)		125

$10 Quarter-Ounce Gold

	Mintage	Unc.	PF
$10 MCMLXXXVI (1986)...	726,031	$300	
$10 MCMLXXXVII (1987) ..	269,255	325	
$10 MCMLXXXVIII (1988)...	49,000	465	
$10 MCMLXXXVIII (1988)P..	(98,028)		$310

	Mintage	Unc.	PF
$10 MCMLXXXIX (1989)....	81,789	$465	
$10 MCMLXXXIX (1989)P..	(54,170)		$310
$10 MCMXC (1990).......	41,000	545	
$10 MCMXC (1990)P.....	(62,674)		310

	Mintage	Unc.	PF
$10 MCMXCI (1991)	36,100	$545	
$10 MCMXCI (1991)P	(50,839)		$310
$10 1992	59,546	405	
$10 1992P	(46,269)		310
$10 1993	71,864	405	
$10 1993P	(46,464)		310
$10 1994	72,650	405	
$10 1994W	(48,172)		310
$10 1995	83,752	405	
$10 1995W	(47,526)		310
$10 1996	60,318	405	
$10 1996W	(38,219)		310
$10 1997	108,805	300	
$10 1997W	(29,805)		310
$10 1998	309,829	300	
$10 1998W	(29,503)		310
$10 1999	564,232	300	
$10 1999W	(34,417)		310
$10 1999W, Unc. Made from unpolished Proof dies	10,000	1,150	
$10 2000	128,964	300	
$10 2000W	(36,036)		310
$10 2001	71,280	405	
$10 2001W	(25,613)		310
$10 2002	62,027	405	
$10 2002W	(29,242)		310
$10 2003	74,029	300	
$10 2003W	(30,292)		310
$10 2004	72,014	$300	
$10 2004W	(28,839)		310
$10 2005	72,015	300	
$10 2005W	(37,207)		310
$10 2006	60,004	300	
$10 2006W, Burnished	15,188	440	
$10 2006W	(36,127)		310
$10 2007	34,004	405	
$10 2007W, Burnished	12,766	450	
$10 2007W	(46,189)		310
$10 2008	70,000	300	
$10 2008W, Burnished	8,883	1,150	
$10 2008W	(18,877)		310
$10 2009	110,000	300	
$10 2010	86,000	300	
$10 2010W	(44,057)		310
$10 2011	80,000	300	
$10 2011W	(28,782)		310
$10 2012	76,000	300	
$10 2012W	(13,926)		310
$10 2013	122,000	300	
$10 2013W	(12,782)		310
$10 2014	118,000	300	
$10 2014W	(14,790)		310
$10 2015	158,000	300	
$10 2015W	(15,775)		310

$25 Half-Ounce Gold

	Mintage	Unc.	PF
$25 MCMLXXXVI (1986)	599,566	$600	
$25 MCMLXXXVII (1987)	131,255	800	
$25 MCMLXXXVII (1987)P	(143,398)		$615
$25 MCMLXXXVIII (1988)	45,000	1,225	
$25 MCMLXXXVIII (1988)P	(76,528)		615
$25 MCMLXXXIX (1989)	44,829	1,250	
$25 MCMLXXXIX (1989)P	(44,798)		615
$25 MCMXC (1990)	31,000	1,435	
$25 MCMXC (1990)P	(51,636)		615
$25 MCMXCI (1991)	24,100	2,300	
$25 MCMXCI (1991)P	(53,125)		615
$25 1992	54,404	700	
$25 1992P	(40,976)		615
$25 1993	73,324	600	
$25 1993P	(43,819)		615
$25 1994	62,400	600	
$25 1994W	(44,584)		615
$25 1995	53,474	860	
$25 1995W	(45,388)		615
$25 1996	39,287	880	
$25 1996W	(35,058)		615
$25 1997	79,605	600	
$25 1997W	(26,344)		615
$25 1998	169,029	$600	
$25 1998W	(25,374)		$615
$25 1999	263,013	600	
$25 1999W	(30,427)		615
$25 2000	79,287	600	
$25 2000W	(32,028)		615
$25 2001	48,047	780	
$25 2001W	(23,240)		615
$25 2002	70,027	600	
$25 2002W	(26,646)		615
$25 2003	79,029	600	
$25 2003W	(28,270)		615
$25 2004	98,040	600	
$25 2004W	(27,330)		615
$25 2005	80,023	600	
$25 2005W	(34,311)		615
$25 2006	66,005	600	
$25 2006W, Burnished	15,164	740	
$25 2006W	(34,322)		615
$25 2007	47,002	600	
$25 2007W, Burnished	11,455	780	
$25 2007W	(44,025)		615
$25 2008	61,000	600	

	Mintage	Unc.	PF
$25 2008W, Burnished	15,682	$740	
$25 2008W	(22,602)		$615
$25 2009	110,000	600	
$25 2010	81,000	600	
$25 2010W	(44,527)		615
$25 2011	70,000	600	
$25 2011W	(26,781)		615
$25 2012	71,000	600	

	Mintage	Unc.	PF
$25 2012W	(12,919)		$615
$25 2013	58,000	$600	
$25 2013W	(12,716)		615
$25 2014	46,000	600	
$25 2014W	(14,693)		615
$25 2015	75,000	600	
$25 2015W	(15,287)		615

$50 One-Ounce Gold

	Mintage	Unc.	PF
$50 MCMLXXXVI (1986)	1,362,650	$1,200	
$50 MCMLXXXVI (1986)W	(446,290)		$1,230
$50 MCMLXXXVII (1987)	1,045,500	1,200	
$50 MCMLXXXVII (1987)W	(147,498)		1,230
$50 MCMLXXXVIII (1988)	465,000	1,200	
$50 MCMLXXXVIII (1988)W	(87,133)		1,230
$50 MCMLXXXIX (1989)	415,790	1,200	
$50 MCMLXXXIX (1989)W	(54,570)		1,230
$50 MCMXC (1990)	373,210	1,200	
$50 MCMXC (1990)W	(62,401)		1,230
$50 MCMXCI (1991)	243,100	1,200	
$50 MCMXCI (1991)W	(50,411)		1,230
$50 1992	275,000	1,200	
$50 1992W	(44,826)		1,230
$50 1993	480,192	1,200	
$50 1993W	(34,369)		1,230
$50 1994	221,633	1,200	
$50 1994W	(46,674)		1,230
$50 1995	200,636	1,200	
$50 1995W	(46,368)		1,230
$50 1996	189,148	1,200	
$50 1996W	(36,153)		1,230
$50 1997	664,508	1,200	
$50 1997W	(32,999)		1,230
$50 1998	1,468,530	1,200	
$50 1998W	(25,886)		1,230
$50 1999	1,505,026	1,200	
$50 1999W	(31,427)		1,230
$50 2000	433,319	1,200	
$50 2000W	(33,007)		1,230
$50 2001	143,605	1,200	
$50 2001W	(24,555)		1,230
$50 2002	222,029	1,200	
$50 2002W	(27,499)		1,230

	Mintage	Unc.	PF
$50 2003	416,032	$1,200	
$50 2003W	(28,344)		$1,230
$50 2004	417,019	1,200	
$50 2004W	(28,215)		1,230
$50 2005	356,555	1,200	
$50 2005W	(35,246)		1,230
$50 2006	237,510	1,200	
$50 2006W, Burnished	45,053	1,245	
$50 2006W	(47,092)		1,230
$50 2006W, Reverse Proof	(9,996)		2,050
$50 2007	140,016	1,200	
$50 2007W, Burnished	18,066	1,280	
$50 2007W	(51,810)		1,230
$50 2008	710,000	1,200	
$50 2008W, Burnished	11,908	1,725	
$50 2008W	(30,237)		1,525
$50 2009	1,493,000	1,200	
$50 2010	1,125,000	1,200	
$50 2010W	(59,480)		1,230
$50 2011	857,000	1,200	
$50 2011W, Burnished	8,729	1,560	
$50 2011W	(48,306)		1,230
$50 2012	667,000	1,200	
$50 2012W, Burnished	6,118	1,600	
$50 2012W	(23,805)		1,230
$50 2013	743,500	1,200	
$50 2013W, Burnished	7,293	1,300	
$50 2013W	(24,709)		1,230
$50 2014	415,500	1,200	
$50 2014W, Burnished	7,902	1,300	
$50 2014W	(28,703)		1,230
$50 2015	626,500	1,200	
$50 2015W, Burnished	7,794	1,300	
$50 2015W	(28,673)		1,230

Gold Bullion Sets

	PF
1987 Gold Set. $50, $25	$1,875
1988 Gold Set. $50, $25, $10, $5	2,280
1989 Gold Set. $50, $25, $10, $5	2,450
1990 Gold Set. $50, $25, $10, $5	2,350
1991 Gold Set. $50, $25, $10, $5	2,300

	PF
1992 Gold Set. $50, $25, $10, $5	$2,280
1993 Gold Set. $50, $25, $10, $5	2,450
1993 Bicentennial Gold Set. $25, $10, $5, $1 silver eagle, and medal	1,100
1994 Gold Set. $50, $25, $10, $5	2,280

	PF
1995 Gold Set. $50, $25, $10, $5	$2,280
1995 Anniversary Gold Set. $50, $25, $10,	
$5, and $1 silver eagle	4,875
1996 Gold Set. $50, $25, $10, $5	2,280
1997 Gold Set. $50, $25, $10, $5	2,280
1997 Impressions of Liberty Set.	
$100 platinum, $50 gold, $1 silver	2,125
1998 Gold Set. $50, $25, $10, $5	2,280
1999 Gold Set. $50, $25, $10, $5	2,280
2000 Gold Set. $50, $25, $10, $5	2,280
2001 Gold Set. $50, $25, $10, $5	2,280
2002 Gold Set. $50, $25, $10, $5	2,280

	PF
2003 Gold Set. $50, $25, $10, $5	$2,280
2004 Gold Set. $50, $25, $10, $5	2,280
2005 Gold Set. $50, $25, $10, $5	2,280
2006 Gold Set. $50, $25, $10, $5	2,280
2007 Gold Set. $50, $25, $10, $5	2,280
2008 Gold Set. $50, $25, $10, $5	2,280
2010 Gold Set. $50, $25, $10, $5 (a)	2,280
2011 Gold Set. $50, $25, $10, $5	2,280
2012 Gold Set. $50, $25, $10, $5	2,280
2013 Gold Set. $50, $25, $10, $5	2,280
2014 Gold Set. $50, $25, $10, $5	2,280
2015 Gold Set. $50, $25, $10, $5	2,280

a. The U.S. Mint did not issue a 2009 gold set.

2006 20th Anniversary Sets

2006W $50 Gold Set. Uncirculated, Proof, Reverse Proof	$4,000
2006W 1-oz. Gold- and Silver-Dollar Set. Uncirculated	1,225

Gold Bullion Burnished Sets 2006–2008

	Unc.
2006W Burnished Gold Set. $50, $25, $10, $5	$2,280
2007W Burnished Gold Set. $50, $25, $10, $5	2,760
2008W Burnished Gold Set. $50, $25, $10, $5	3,880

AMERICAN BUFFALO .9999 FINE GOLD BULLION COINS

	Mintage	Unc.	PF
$5 2008W, Burnished	17,429	$325	
$5 2008W	(18,884)		$320
$10 2008W, Burnished	9,949	825	
$10 2008W	(13,125)		720
$25 2008W, Burnished	16,908	850	
$25 2008W	(12,169)		960
$50 2006	337,012	1,210	
$50 2006W	(246,267)		1,220
$50 2007	136,503	1,210	
$50 2007W	(58,998)		1,220
$50 2008	214,058	1,210	
$50 2008W	(18,863)		1,840
$50 2008W, Burnished	9,074	1,950	
$50 2009	200,000	1,210	

	Mintage	Unc.	PF
$50 2009W	(49,388)		$1,220
$50 2010	209,000	$1,210	
$50 2010W	(38,895)		1,220
$50 2011	174,500	1,210	
$50 2011W	(28,693)		1,260
$50 2012	132,000	1,210	
$50 2012W	(19,765)		1,280
$50 2013	239,000	1,210	
$50 2013W	(18,594)		1,280
$50 2013W, Reverse Proof	(47,836)		1,380
$50 2014	177,500	1,210	
$50 2014W	(20,557)		1,280
$50 2015	220,500	1,210	
$50 2015W	(16,593)		1,280

American Buffalo Gold Bullion Sets

	Unc.	PF
2008W Four-coin set ($5, $10, $25, $50)		$3,840
2008W Four-coin set ($5, $10, $25, $50), Burnished	$3,950	
2008W Double Prosperity set. Uncirculated $25 Buffalo gold and $25 American Eagle coins . .	1,850	

FIRST SPOUSE $10 GOLD BULLION COINS
Half-Ounce 24-Karat Gold

Martha Washington   Abigail Adams   Jefferson's Liberty   Dolley Madison

	Mintage	Unc.	PF
$10 2007W, Martha Washington . . . . (19,167) 17,661		$610	$615
$10 2007W, Abigail Adams . . . . (17,149) 17,142		610	615
$10 2007W, Thomas Jefferson's Liberty . . . . (19,815) 19,823		610	615
$10 2007W, Dolley Madison . . . . (17,943) 12,340		610	615
$10 2008W, Elizabeth Monroe. . . . . (7,800) 4,462		610	615
$10 2008W, Louisa Adams . . . . (6,581) 3,885		610	615
$10 2008W, Andrew Jackson's Liberty . . . . (7,684) 4,609		610	615
$10 2008W, Martin Van Buren's Liberty . . . . (6,807) 3,826		610	615
$10 2009W, Anna Harrison . . . . (6,251) 3,645		615	630
$10 2009W, Letitia Tyler . . . . (5,296) 3,240		615	670
$10 2009W, Julia Tyler . . . . (4,844) 3,143		615	670
$10 2009W, Sarah Polk. . . . . (5,151) 3,489		615	615
$10 2009W, Margaret Taylor . . . . (4,936) 3,627		615	615
$10 2010W, Abigail Fillmore . . . . (6,130) 3,482		615	650
$10 2010W, Jane Pierce . . . . (4,775) 3,338		615	615
$10 2010W, James Buchanan's Liberty . . . . (7,110) 5,162		615	615
$10 2010W, Mary Lincoln . . . . (6,861) 3,695		615	615
$10 2011W, Eliza Johnson. . . . . (3,887) 2,905		615	615
$10 2011W, Julia Grant. . . . . (3,943) 2,892		615	615
$10 2011W, Lucy Hayes . . . . (3,868) 2,196		615	670
$10 2011W, Lucretia Garfield . . . . (3,653) 2,168		615	615
$10 2012W, Alice Paul. . . . . (3,505) 2,798		615	615
$10 2012W, Frances Cleveland, Type 1 . . . . (3,158) 2,454		615	615
$10 2012W, Caroline Harrison . . . . (3,046) 2,436		615	615
$10 2012W, Frances Cleveland, Type 2 . . . . (3,104) 2,425		615	615
$10 2013W, Ida Mckinley . . . . (2,724) 2,008		615	615
$10 2013W, Edith Roosevelt . . . . (2,840) 2,027		615	615
$10 2013W, Helen Taft. . . . . (2,598) 1,993		615	615
$10 2013W, Ellen Wilson. . . . . (2,511) 1,980		615	615

GOLD BULLION

	Mintage	Unc.	PF
$10 2013W, Edith Wilson .... (2,464) 1,974		$615	$615
$10 2014W, Florence Harding........................... (2,372) 1,801		615	615
$10 2014W, Grace Coolidge .... (2,315) 1,797		615	615
$10 2014W, Lou Hoover .... (2,229) 1,779		615	615
$10 2014W, Eleanor Roosevelt .... (2,377) 7,886		615	615
$10 2015W, Elizabeth Truman .... (2,367) 1,654		620	615
$10 2015W, Mamie Eisenhower .... (2,595) 1,725		620	615
$10 2015W, Jacqueline Kennedy .... (11,123) 5,491		620	615
$10 2015W, Claudia Taylor "Lady Bird" Johnson .... (2,285) 1,475		620	615
$10 2016W, Pat Nixon...................................		620	615
$10 2016W, Betty Ford		620	615
$10 2016W, Nancy Reagan		620	615

MMIX ULTRA HIGH RELIEF GOLD COIN

A modern version of the famous United States 1907 Ultra High Relief double eagle gold pattern was produced in 2009 at the Philadelphia Mint. It was made as a tour de force to demonstrate how technical advances in minting techniques can now accommodate manufacturing such a coin. The original design was never made for commercial use because it was at that time impossible to make it in sufficient quantities.

The design used on these coins was the artistry of Augustus Saint-Gaudens. A version of it in much lower relief was used on double eagle coins minted from 1907 to 1933. In recreating the artist's attempt to mint a stunning coin in ultra high relief, the 2009 version was made in a slightly smaller diameter, and composed of 24-karat gold, thus making it easier to strike and maintain the fidelity of the design. Through 21st-century technology the original Saint-Gaudens plasters were digitally mapped by the Mint and used in the die-making process. The date was changed to 2009, and four additional stars were added to represent the current 50 states. The inscription "In God We Trust" was not used on the 1907 version.

The MMIX Ultra High Relief gold coins are 4 mm thick and contain one ounce of .999 fine gold. All are Uncirculated (business strikes). All are made at the West Point Mint, and packaged by the Mint in a special mahogany box.

MMIX Ultra High Relief Gold Coin
Photographed at an angle to show the edge,
lettered E PLURIBUS UNUM, and the depth of relief.

	Mintage	Unc.
MMIX Ultra High Relief $20 Gold Coin 114,427		$1,525

AMERICAN EAGLE PLATINUM COINS

The one-ounce American Eagle platinum coin is designated $100 and contains one ounce of pure platinum. Fractional denominations containing 1/2 ounce, 1/4 ounce, or 1/10 ounce are called $50, $25, and $10, respectively.

Bullion values are based on spot platinum at $1,050 per ounce.

Obverse for Bullion and Proof, All Years

Reverse for Bullion, All Years; for Proof in 1997

1998: Eagle Over New England. "Vistas of Liberty" series.

1999: Eagle Above Southeastern Wetlands. "Vistas of Liberty" series.

2000: Eagle Above America's Heartland. "Vistas of Liberty" series.

2001: Eagle Above America's Southwest. "Vistas of Liberty" series.

2002: Eagle Fishing in America's Northwest. "Vistas of Liberty" series.

2003.

2004.

2005.

2006: Legislative Branch. "Foundations of Democracy" series.

2007: Executive Branch. "Foundations of Democracy" series.

2008: Judicial Branch. "Foundations of Democracy" series.

2009: To Form a More Perfect Union. "Preamble to the Constitution" series.

2010: To Establish Justice. "Preamble to the Constitution" series.

2011: To Insure Domestic Tranquility. "Preamble to the Constitution" series.

2012: To Provide for the Common Defence. "Preamble to the Constitution" series.

2013: To Promote the General Welfare. "Preamble to the Constitution" series.

2014: To Secure the Blessings of Liberty to Ourselves and Our Posterity. "Preamble to the Constitution" series.

2015: Liberty Nurtures Freedom.

$10 Tenth-Ounce Platinum

	Mintage	Unc.	PF		Mintage	Unc.	PF
$10 1997	70,250	$95		$10 2001W	(12,174)		$90
$10 1997W	(36,993)		$90	$10 2002	23,005	$95	
$10 1998	39,525	95		$10 2002W	(12,365)		90
$10 1998W	(19,847)		90	$10 2003	22,007	95	
$10 1999	55,955	95		$10 2003W	(9,534)		90
$10 1999W	(19,133)		90	$10 2004	15,010	95	
$10 2000	34,027	95		$10 2004W	(7,161)		90
$10 2000W	(15,651)		90	$10 2005	14,013	95	
$10 2001	52,017	95		$10 2005W	(8,104)		90

	Mintage	Unc.	PF
$10 2006	11,001	$95	
$10 2006W, Burnished	3,544	275	
$10 2006W	(10,205)		$90
$10 2007	13,003	95	
$10 2007W, Burnished	5,556	145	

	Mintage	Unc.	PF
$10 2007W	(8,176)		$90
$10 2008	17,000	$95	
$10 2008W, Burnished	3,706	215	
$10 2008W	(5,138)		180

$25 Quarter-Ounce Platinum

	Mintage	Unc.	PF
$25 1997	27,100	$235	
$25 1997W	(18,628)		$250
$25 1998	38,887	235	
$25 1998W	(14,873)		250
$25 1999	39,734	235	
$25 1999W	(13,507)		250
$25 2000	20,054	235	
$25 2000W	(11,995)		250
$25 2001	21,815	235	
$25 2001W	(8,847)		250
$25 2002	27,405	235	
$25 2002W	(9,282)		250
$25 2003	25,207	235	
$25 2003W	(7,044)		250

	Mintage	Unc.	PF
$25 2004	18,010	$235	
$25 2004W	(5,193)		$250
$25 2005	12,013	235	
$25 2005W	(6,592)		250
$25 2006	12,001	235	
$25 2006W, Burnished	2,676	400	
$25 2006W	(7,813)		250
$25 2007	8,402	235	
$25 2007W, Burnished	3,690	400	
$25 2007W	(6,017)		250
$25 2007W, Frosted FREEDOM	(21)		—
$25 2008	22,800	235	
$25 2008W, Burnished	2,481	400	
$25 2008W	(4,153)		420

$50 Half-Ounce Platinum

	Mintage	Unc.	PF
$50 1997	20,500	$460	
$50 1997W	(15,431)		$500
$50 1998	32,415	460	
$50 1998W	(13,836)		500
$50 1999	32,309	460	
$50 1999W	(11,103)		500
$50 2000	18,892	460	
$50 2000W	(11,049)		500
$50 2001	12,815	460	
$50 2001W	(8,254)		500
$50 2002	24,005	460	
$50 2002W	(8,772)		500
$50 2003	17,409	460	
$50 2003W	(7,131)		500
$50 2004	13,236	460	

	Mintage	Unc.	PF
$50 2004W	(5,063)		$980
$50 2005	9,013	$460	
$50 2005W	(5,942)		500
$50 2006	9,602	460	
$50 2006W, Burnished	2,577	640	
$50 2006W	(7,649)		500
$50 2007	7,001	460	
$50 2007W, Burnished	3,635	575	
$50 2007W	(25,519)		500
$50 2007W, Reverse Proof			1,080
$50 2007W, Frosted FREEDOM	(21)		—
$50 2008	14,000	460	
$50 2008W, Burnished	2,253	800	
$50 2008W	(4,020)		840

$100 One-Ounce Platinum

	Mintage	Unc.	PF
$100 1997	56,000	$980	
$100 1997W	(20,851)		$1,025
$100 1998	133,002	980	
$100 1998W	(14,912)		1,025
$100 1999	56,707	980	
$100 1999W	(12,363)		1,025
$100 2000	10,003	980	
$100 2000W	(12,453)		1,025
$100 2001	14,070	980	

	Mintage	Unc.	PF
$100 2001W	(8,969)		$1,025
$100 2002	11,502	$980	
$100 2002W	(9,834)		1,025
$100 2003	8,007	980	
$100 2003W	(8,246)		1,025
$100 2004	7,009	980	
$100 2004W	(6,007)		1,025
$100 2005	6,310	980	
$100 2005W	(6,602)		1,025

	Mintage	Unc.	PF
$100 2006	6,000	$980	
$100 2006W, Burnished	3,068	1,540	
$100 2006W	(9,152)		$1,025
$100 2007	7,202	980	
$100 2007W, Burnished	4,177	1,360	
$100 2007W	(8,363)		1,025
$100 2007W, Frosted FREEDOM	(12)		—
$100 2008	21,800	980	
$100 2008W, Burnished	2,876	1,560	

	Mintage	Unc.	PF
$100 2008W	(4,769)		$1,600
$100 2009W	(7,945)		1,025
$100 2010W	(9,871)		1,025
$100 2011W	*(14,790)*		1,025
$100 2012W	(10,084)		1,025
$100 2013W	(5,745)		1,025
$100 2014	16,900	$1,080	
$100 2014W	(4,596)		1,075
$100 2015W	(3,881)		1,075

Platinum Bullion Sets

	Unc.
1997 Platinum Set. $100, $50, $25, $10.	$1,950
1998 Platinum Set. $100, $50, $25, $10.	1,950
1999 Platinum Set. $100, $50, $25, $10.	1,950
2000 Platinum Set. $100, $50, $25, $10.	1,950
2001 Platinum Set. $100, $50, $25, $10.	1,950
2002 Platinum Set. $100, $50, $25, $10.	1,950
2003 Platinum Set. $100, $50, $25, $10.	1,950
2004W Platinum Set. $100, $50, $25, $10	1,950
2005W Platinum Set. $100, $50, $25, $10	1,950
2006W Platinum Set. $100, $50, $25, $10	1,950
2006W Platinum Burnished Set. $100, $50, $25, $10	2,400
2007W Platinum Set. $100, $50, $25, $10	1,950
2007W Platinum Burnished Set. $100, $50, $25, $10	2,280
2008W Platinum Set. $100, $50, $25, $10	3,080
2008W Platinum Burnished Set. $100, $50, $25, $10	2,400

Prices are for original Uncirculated or Proof pieces with box and papers.

American Eagle 10th Anniversary Platinum Set

	Unc.
Two-coin set containing one Proof platinum half-ounce and one Enhanced Reverse Proof half-ounce dated 2007W. Housed in hardwood box with mahogany finish	$1,140

Learn More About Bullion Coins

In *American Silver Eagles: A Guide to the U.S. Bullion Coin Program*, U.S. Mint chief engraver John M. Mercanti reveals the historical, technical, artistic, and current market-driven secrets of these beautiful pieces. • In *American Gold and Platinum Eagles: A Guide to the U.S. Bullion Coin Programs*, Edmund C. Moy—the 38th director of the U.S. Mint—shares surprising, valuable facts gleaned from his extensive experience with precious metals • *American Gold and Silver: U.S. Mint Collector and Investor Coins and Medals, Bicentennial to Date*, by Dennis Tucker, gives illustrated histories, coin-by-coin studies, certified populations, values in multiple grades, and current market advice for all the remaining issues of the American bullion program. $29.95 each.

Call 1-800-546-2995 to order two for $50 postpaid, or all three
for $60 postpaid OR order individually online at Whitman.com
and mention code B7 for free shipping. Offers expire May 1, 2017.

Private coins were circulated in most instances because of a shortage of regular coinage. Some numismatists use the general term *private gold* to refer to coins struck outside of the United States Mint. In the sense that no state or territory had authority to coin money, *private gold* simply refers to those interesting necessity pieces of various shapes, denominations, and degrees of intrinsic worth which were circulated in isolated areas of our country by individuals, assayers, bankers, etc. Some numismatists use the words *territorial* and *state* to cover certain issues because they were coined and circulated in a territory or state. While the state of California properly sanctioned the ingots stamped by F.D. Kohler as state assayer, in no instance were any of the gold pieces struck by authority of any of the territorial governments.

The stamped ingots put out by Augustus Humbert, the United States assayer of gold, were not recognized at the United States Mint as an official issue of coins, but simply as ingots, though Humbert placed the value and fineness on the pieces as an official agent of the federal government.

TEMPLETON REID
Georgia Gold 1830

The first private gold coinage in the 19th century was struck by Templeton Reid, a jeweler and gunsmith, in Milledgeville, Georgia, in July 1830. To be closer to the mines, he moved to Gainesville, where most of his coins were made. Although weights were accurate, Reid's assays were not, and his coins were slightly short of claimed value. Accordingly, he was severely attacked in the newspapers and soon lost the public's confidence. His mint closed before the end of that October.

	VG	VF
1830, $2.50	$30,000	$70,000
1830, $5	75,000	150,000
1830, TEN DOLLARS	145,000	300,000
(No Date) TEN DOLLARS	150,000	350,000

California Gold 1849

1849 TEN DOLLAR CALIFORNIA GOLD *(unique, in Smithsonian collection)*. . . . .

THE BECHTLERS
RUTHERFORD COUNTY, NC, 1831–1852

Two skilled German metallurgists, Christopher Bechtler and his son August, and later Christopher Bechtler, Junior, a nephew of Christopher the elder, operated a private mint at Rutherfordton, North Carolina. Rutherford County, in which Rutherfordton is located, was a principal source of the nation's gold supply from 1790 to 1848.

Christopher Bechtler

	VF	EF	AU	Unc.
ONE DOLLAR CAROLINA, 28.G, N Reversed.	$1,000	$1,500	$2,500	$5,500
ONE GOLD DOLLAR N. CAROLINA, 28.G, No Star.	2,200	3,250	4,500	10,000
ONE GOLD DOLLAR N. CAROLINA, 30.G.	1,350	2,100	3,000	8,000
2.50 CAROLINA, 67.G., 21 CARATS.	3,000	5,000	6,500	11,000
2.50 CAROLINA, 70.G, 20 CARATS.	3,200	5,500	7,000	13,000
2.50 GEORGIA, 64.G, 22 CARATS.	3,500	6,000	8,000	15,000
2.50 NORTH CAROLINA, 75.G., 20 C., RUTHERFORD				
in a Circle. Border of Large Beads.	10,000	15,000	22,500	42,000
2.50 NORTH CAROLINA, 20 C. Without 75.G.	10,000	15,500	25,000	45,000

Without 150.G.

	VF	EF	AU	Unc.
5 DOLLARS NORTH CAROLINA GOLD, 150.G., 20.CARATS	$10,000	$17,000	$27,500	$50,000
Similar, Without 150.G.	—	—		
5 DOLLARS CAROLINA, RUTHERFORD, 140.G., 20 CARATS				
Plain Edge	3,250	5,000	6,500	11,000
Reeded Edge	8,500	15,000	20,000	32,000
5 DOLLARS CAROLINA GOLD, RUTHERF., 140.G., 20 CARATS,				
AUGUST 1, 1834	5,000	8,000	15,000	30,000
Similar, but "20" Distant From CARATS	3,250	5,500	6,500	13,000
5 DOLLARS CAROLINA GOLD, 134.G., 21 CARATS, With Star	3,000	4,000	5,000	8,500
5 DOLLARS GEORGIA GOLD, RUTHERFORD, 128.G., 22 CARATS	3,250	4,500	7,000	13,000
5 DOLLARS GEORGIA GOLD, RUTHERF, 128.G., 22 CARATS	3,250	4,500	7,000	13,000

August Bechtler

	VF	EF	AU	Unc.
1 DOL:, CAROLINA GOLD, 27.G., 21.C.	$800	$1,200	$1,600	$2,500
5 DOLLARS, CAROLINA GOLD, 134.G:, 21 CARATS	2,700	4,500	6,500	18,000

	VF	EF	AU	Unc.
5 DOLLARS, CAROLINA GOLD, 128.G., 22 CARATS	$6,250	$8,500	$15,000	$25,000
5 DOLLARS, CAROLINA GOLD, 141.G., 20 CARATS	5,500	8,000	13,000	22,000

NORRIS, GREGG & NORRIS
SAN FRANCISCO 1849

Numismatists consider these pieces the first of the California private gold coins. A newspaper account dated May 31, 1849, described a five-dollar gold coin struck at Benicia City, though with the imprint San Francisco, and the private stamp of Norris, Gregg & Norris.

	F	VF	EF	AU	Unc.
1849 Half Eagle, Plain Edge........................	$2,700	$3,600	$6,500	$9,000	$18,000
1849 Half Eagle, Reeded Edge......................	2,700	3,600	6,500	9,000	18,000
1850 Half Eagle, With STOCKTON Beneath Date *(unique, in Smithsonian collection)*					

MOFFAT & CO.
SAN FRANCISCO 1849–1853

The firm of Moffat & Co. was perhaps the most important of the California private coiners. The assay office they conducted was semi-official in character, and successors to this firm later sold its facilities to the Treasury Department, which used them to create the San Francisco Mint.

In June or July, 1849, Moffat & Co. began to issue small rectangular pieces of gold in values from $9.43 to $264. The $9.43, $14.25, and $16.00 varieties are the only known types. A similar ingot was made by the firm of Meyers & Company at this same time.

	EF
$9.43 Moffat Ingot *(unique, in Smithsonian collection)*..................................	—
$14.25 Moffat Ingot *(unique, in Smithsonian collection)*................................	—
$16.00 Moffat Ingot..	$75,000
$18.00 Meyers Ingot *(unique)*..	—

The dies for the five-dollar and ten-dollar pieces were cut by Albrecht Küner. The words MOFFAT & CO. appear on Liberty's coronet instead of the word LIBERTY as in regular United States issues.

	F	VF	EF	AU	Unc.
1849 FIVE DOL. *(all varieties)*	$900	$1,400	$1,900	$3,000	$7,000
1850 FIVE DOL. *(all varieties)*	900	1,500	2,000	3,200	8,000
1849 TEN DOL.	1,700	2,500	5,000	9,000	18,000
1849 TEN D.	1,800	2,900	6,000	11,000	22,000

UNITED STATES ASSAY OFFICE
Augustus Humbert
United States Assayer of Gold, 1851

When Augustus Humbert was appointed United States assayer, he placed his name and the government imprint on the ingots of gold issued by Moffat & Co. The assay office, a provisional government mint, was a temporary expedient to accommodate the Californians until the establishment of a permanent branch mint. The fifty-dollar gold piece was accepted as legal tender on a par with standard U.S. gold coins.

Lettered Edge Varieties

	F	VF	EF	AU	Unc.
1851 50 D C 880 THOUS., No 50 on Reverse. Sunk in Edge: AUGUSTUS HUMBERT UNITED STATES ASSAYER OF GOLD CALIFORNIA 1851	$12,000	$18,000	$35,000	$55,000	$110,000

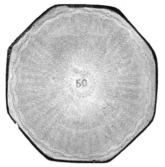

50 on Reverse

	F	VF	EF	AU	Unc.
1851 50 D C 880 THOUS, Similar to Last Variety, but 50 on Reverse	$13,000	$23,000	$37,500	$65,000	$125,000
1851 50 D C, 887 THOUS., With 50 on Reverse	12,000	20,000	35,000	55,000	110,000

Reeded Edge Varieties

 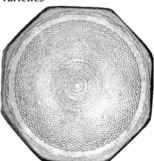

	F	VF	EF	AU	Unc.
1851 FIFTY DOLLS, 880 THOUS., "Target" Reverse	$8,000	$12,000	$18,000	$24,000	$55,000
1851 FIFTY DOLLS, 887 THOUS., "Target" Reverse	8,000	12,000	18,000	24,000	55,000
1852 FIFTY DOLLS, 887 THOUS., "Target" Reverse	8,500	13,000	19,000	27,000	57,500

Moffat & Co. proceeded in January 1852 to issue a new ten-dollar piece bearing the stamp MOFFAT & CO.

	F	VF	EF	AU	Unc.
1852 TEN D. MOFFAT & CO.	$2,000	$3,600	$7,000	$19,000	$39,000

	F	VF	EF	AU	Unc.
1852 TEN DOLS. 1852, 2 Over 1	$1,500	$2,750	$4,200	$8,000	$15,000
1852 TEN DOLS.	1,350	2,000	3,000	6,000	13,500

	F	VF	EF	AU	Unc.
1852 TWENTY DOLS., 1852, 2 Over 1	$3,750	$5,500	$9,500	$21,000	$55,000

United States Assay Office of Gold – 1852

The firm of Moffat & Co. was reorganized by Curtis, Perry, and Ward, who assumed the government contract to conduct the United States Assay Office of Gold.

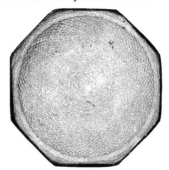

	F	VF	EF	AU	Unc.
1852 FIFTY DOLLS., 887 THOUS.	$7,500	$12,000	$18,000	$22,000	$46,000
1852 FIFTY DOLLS., 900 THOUS.	8,000	13,000	20,000	25,000	50,000

	F	VF	EF	AU	Unc.
1852 TEN DOLS., 884 THOUS.	$1,000	$1,650	$2,500	$4,000	$9,000
1853 TEN D., 884 THOUS.	3,500	7,000	13,500	18,000	35,000
1853 TEN D., 900 THOUS.	2,000	3,000	4,000	7,000	10,000
1853 TWENTY D., 884 THOUS.	3,500	5,000	9,000	14,000	25,000
1853 TWENTY D., 900 THOUS.	1,100	1,500	2,000	3,000	6,500

Moffat & Company Gold

The last Moffat issue was an 1853 twenty-dollar piece that is very similar to the U.S. double eagle of that period. It was struck after the retirement of John L. Moffat from Moffat & Company.

	F	VF	EF	AU	Unc.
1853, TWENTY D.	$2,200	$3,500	$5,500	$9,000	$20,000

CINCINNATI MINING & TRADING CO. (1849)

The origin and location of this company are unknown. It might have been organized in Ohio, and conducted business in California.

	EF	Unc.
1849 FIVE DOLLARS	—	—
1849 TEN DOLLARS.	$400,000	—

MASSACHUSETTS AND CALIFORNIA COMPANY

This company was believed to have been organized in Northampton, Massachusetts, in May 1849. Pieces with 5D are not genuine.

	F	VF	EF
1849 FIVE D.	$65,000	$95,000	$150,000

MINERS' BANK
SAN FRANCISCO 1849

The institution of Wright & Co., exchange brokers located in Portsmouth Square, San Francisco, was known as the Miners' Bank.

A ten-dollar piece was issued in the autumn of 1849, but the coins were not readily accepted because they were worth less than face value.

	VF	EF	AU	Unc.
(1849) TEN D.	$9,000	$16,500	$24,000	$45,000

J.S. ORMSBY
SACRAMENTO 1849

The initials J.S.O., which appear on certain issues of California privately coined gold pieces, represent the firm of J.S. Ormsby & Co. The firm struck both five- and ten-dollar denominations, all undated.

	VF
(1849) 5 DOLLS *(unique)*	—
(1849) 10 DOLLS *(4 known)*	$200,000

PACIFIC COMPANY, SAN FRANCISCO 1849

The origin of the Pacific Company is uncertain. All data regarding the firm are based on conjecture.

Edgar H. Adams wrote that he believed that the coins bearing the stamp of the Pacific Company were produced by the coining firm of Broderick and Kohler. The coins were probably hand struck with the aid of a sledgehammer.

	EF
1849, 1 DOLLAR *(2 known)*	—
1849, 5 DOLLARS *(4 known)*	$200,000
1849, 10 DOLLARS *(4 known)*	300,000

F.D. KOHLER
CALIFORNIA STATE ASSAYER 1850

The State Assay Office was authorized on April 12, 1850. That year, Governor Peter Burnett appointed F.D. Kohler, who thereupon sold his assaying business to Baldwin & Co. Kohler served at both the San Francisco and Sacramento offices. The State Assay Offices were discontinued when the U.S. Assay Office was established, on February 1, 1851. Ingots ranged from $36.55 to $150.00.

	EF
$36.55 Sacramento	—
$37.31 San Francisco	—
$40.07 San Francisco	—
$45.34 San Francisco	—
$50.00 San Francisco	—
$54.09 San Francisco	—

DUBOSQ & COMPANY
SAN FRANCISCO 1850

Theodore Dubosq, a Philadelphia jeweler, took melting and coining machinery to San Francisco in 1849.

	VF
1850, FIVE D.	$150,000
1850, TEN D.	150,000

BALDWIN & CO.
SAN FRANCISCO 1850

George C. Baldwin and Thomas S. Holman were in the jewelry business in San Francisco and were known as Baldwin & Co. They were the successors to F.D. Kohler & Co., taking over its machinery and other equipment in May 1850.

	F	VF	EF	AU	Unc.
1850, FIVE DOL.	$3,750	$6,200	$12,000	$18,000	$30,000
1850, TEN DOLLARS, Horseman Type	20,000	35,000	55,000	75,000	135,000

	F	VF	EF	AU	Unc.
1851, TEN D.	$6,500	$16,000	$22,000	$35,000	$85,000

	VF	EF	AU	Unc.
1851 TWENTY D.	$125,000	$300,000	—	—

SHULTZ & COMPANY
SAN FRANCISCO 1851

The firm, located in back of Baldwin's establishment, operated a brass foundry beginning in 1851. Judge G.W. Shultz and William T. Garratt were partners in the enterprise.

	F	VF
1851, FIVE D.	$17,000	$30,000

DUNBAR & COMPANY
SAN FRANCISCO 1851

Edward E. Dunbar operated the California Bank in San Francisco. Dunbar later returned to New York City and organized the famous Continental Bank Note Co.

	VF	EF
1851, FIVE D.	$115,000	$225,000

WASS, MOLITOR & CO.
SAN FRANCISCO 1852–1855

The gold-smelting and assaying plant of Wass, Molitor & Co. was operated by two Hungarian patriots, Count S.C. Wass and A.P. Molitor. They maintained an excellent laboratory and complete apparatus for analysis and coinage of gold.

	F	VF	EF	AU	Unc.
1852, FIVE DOLLARS	$2,100	$4,200	$9,000	$18,000	$32,000

Large Head   **Small Head**

	F	VF	EF	AU	Unc.
1852, TEN D., Large Head	$1,400	$2,000	$3,000	$6,000	$15,000
1852, TEN D., Small Head	3,200	4,250	10,000	16,000	38,500
1855, TEN D.	5,800	7,000	10,000	13,000	27,500

Large Head   **Small Head**

	F	VF	EF	AU	Unc.
1855, TWENTY DOL., Large Head	—	—	$250,000	—	—
1855, TWENTY DOL., Small Head	$6,500	$15,000	19,000	$27,500	$65,000

	F	VF	EF	AU	Unc.
1855, 50 DOLLARS	$12,000	$17,000	$25,000	$47,500	$95,000

KELLOGG & CO.
SAN FRANCISCO 1854–1855

When the U.S. Assay Office ceased operations, a period ensued during which no private firm was striking gold. The new San Francisco branch mint did not produce coins for some months after Curtis & Perry took the government contract. The lack of coin was again keenly felt by businessmen, who petitioned Kellogg & Richter to "supply the vacuum" by issuing private coin. Their plea was soon answered, for on February 9, 1854, Kellogg & Co. placed their first twenty-dollar piece in circulation.

	F	VF	EF	AU	Unc.	PF
1854, TWENTY D.	$1,600	$2,200	$3,000	$5,000	$12,500	
1855, TWENTY D.	1,650	2,500	3,300	5,000	13,500	
1855, FIFTY DOLLS						$375,000

OREGON EXCHANGE COMPANY
OREGON CITY 1849
The Beaver Coins of Oregon

On February 16, 1849, the territorial legislature passed an act providing for a mint and specified five- and ten-dollar gold coins without alloy. Oregon City, the largest city in the territory with a population of about 1,000, was designated as the location for the mint. However, Oregon was then brought into the United States as a territory. When the new governor arrived on March 2, he declared the coinage act unconstitutional. Still, a local company coined these private pieces.

	F	VF	EF	AU	Unc.
1849 5 D.	$15,000	$23,000	$35,000	$70,000	—
1849 TEN.D.	37,000	70,000	135,000	190,000	—

MORMON GOLD PIECES
SALT LAKE CITY, UTAH, 1849–1860

Brigham Young was the instigator of the coinage system and personally supervised the mint, which was housed in a little adobe building in Salt Lake City. The mint was inaugurated late in 1848 as a public convenience.

	F	VF	EF	AU	Unc.
1849, TWO.AND.HALF.DO.	$6,500	$11,000	$18,000	$30,000	$50,000
1849, FIVE.DOLLARS.	4,500	9,500	15,000	20,000	40,000

	F	VF	EF
1849, TEN.DOLLARS.	$125,000	$200,000	$300,000
1849, TWENTY.DOLLARS.	50,000	90,000	130,000

	F	VF	EF	AU	Unc.
1850, FIVE DOLLARS..............................	$5,000	$10,000	$15,000	$25,000	$48,000
1860, 5.D.....................................	10,000	16,500	22,000	35,000	50,000

COLORADO GOLD PIECES
Clark, Gruber & Co.
Denver 1860–1861

Clark, Gruber & Co. was a well-known private minting firm in Denver, Colorado, in the early 1860s.

	F	VF	EF	AU	Unc.
1860, 2 1/2 D	$850	$1,200	$1,800	$2,750	$6,500
1860, FIVE D	950	1,500	2,100	3,750	7,000

	F	VF	EF	AU	Unc.
1860, TEN D	$4,500	$6,500	$10,000	$17,500	$30,000
1860, TWENTY D.	30,000	70,000	125,000	200,000	350,000

	F	VF	EF	AU	Unc.
1861, 2 1/2 D...................................	$900	$1,400	$2,100	$3,500	$7,000
1861, FIVE D.	1,200	1,800	2,600	4,700	17,000
1861, TEN D....................................	1,250	1,850	2,750	4,800	14,000

267

	F	VF	EF	AU
1861, TWENTY D.	$10,000	$20,000	$30,000	$50,000

John Parsons & Company
Tarryall Mines – Colorado, 1861

Very little is known regarding the mint of John Parsons and Co., although it is reasonably certain that it operated in the South Park section of Park County, Colorado, near the original town of Tarryall, in the summer of 1861.

	VF
(1861) Undated 2 1/2 D.	$120,000
(1861) Undated FIVE D.	150,000

J.J. Conway & Co.
Georgia Gulch, Colorado, 1861

Records show that the Conway mint operated for a short while in 1861. As in all gold mining areas, the value of gold dust caused disagreement among the merchants and the miners. The firm of J.J. Conway & Co. solved this difficulty by bringing out its gold pieces in August 1861.

	VF
(1861) Undated 2 1/2 DOLL'S	$85,000
(1861) Undated FIVE DOLLARS	125,000
(1861) Undated TEN DOLLARS.	—

CALIFORNIA SMALL-DENOMINATION GOLD

There was a scarcity of small coins during the California Gold Rush and, starting in 1852, quarter, half, and dollar pieces were privately minted from native gold to alleviate the shortage. The need and acceptability of these pieces declined after 1856 and they then became popular as souvenirs. Authentic pieces all have CENTS, DOLLAR, or an abbreviation thereof on the reverse. The tokens are much less valuable. Modern restrikes and replicas (often having a bear in the design) have no numismatic value.

The values in the following charts are only for coins made before 1883 with the denomination on the reverse expressed as CENTS, DOL., DOLL., or DOLLAR.

Quarter Dollar – Octagonal

	EF-40	AU-50	MS-60
Liberty Head	$75	$100	$170
Indian Head	90	125	175
Washington Head	350	550	850

Quarter Dollar – Round

	EF-40	AU-50	MS-60
Liberty Head	$75	$100	$170
Indian Head	80	110	200
Washington Head	350	550	750

Half Dollar – Octagonal

	EF-40	AU-50	MS-60
Liberty Head	$75	$100	$175
Liberty Head / Eagle	400	600	1,000
Indian Head	85	125	270

Half Dollar – Round

	EF-40	AU-50	MS-60
Liberty Head	$85	$125	$225
Indian Head	75	110	185

Dollar – Octagonal

	EF-40	AU-50	MS-60
Liberty Head	$200	$300	$650
Liberty Head / Eagle	800	1,500	2,000
Indian Head	250	400	700

Dollar – Round

	EF-40	AU-50	MS-60
Liberty Head	$900	$1,350	$2,000
Indian Head	900	1,350	2,250

HARD TIMES TOKENS (1832–1844)

During the financial crises of 1832 to 1844 many government coins were hoarded, and privately made tokens were used out of necessity. The so-called Hard Times tokens of this period were slightly smaller and lighter than normal large cents. They were made of copper or brass and are of two general groups: political tokens whose theme centered on President Andrew Jackson's fight against the Bank of the United States, and tradesmen's cards, issued by merchants. Many different designs and varieties exist.

	VF	EF
Hard Times Tokens, 1832–1844, most common pieces	$10	$22

CIVIL WAR TOKENS (1860s)

Civil War tokens are generally divided into two groups: tradesmen's tokens, and anonymously issued pieces with political or patriotic themes. They came into existence only because of the scarcity of government coins and disappeared as soon as the bronze coins of 1864 met the public demand for small copper change.

These tokens vary greatly in composition and design. A number were more or less faithful imitations of the copper-nickel cent. A few of this type have the word NOT in very small letters above the words ONE CENT.

	F	VF	EF	Unc.
Copper or Brass Tokens	$5	$10	$15	$27
Nickel or German Silver Tokens	20	30	60	100
White-Metal Tokens	25	35	65	100
Copper-Nickel Tokens	30	50	80	125
Silver Tokens	80	150	225	400

Values shown are for the most common tokens in each composition.

In April 1899 control of the Philippine Islands was officially transferred from Spain to the United States, as a condition of the treaty ending the Spanish-American War. In July 1901 a civilian government (led by American judge William Howard Taft) replaced the islands' military administration; one of its first tasks was to sponsor a new territorial coinage that was compatible with the old Spanish issues, but also legally exchangeable for American money at the rate of two Philippine pesos to the U.S. dollar. The resulting coins—which bear the legend UNITED STATES OF AMERICA but are otherwise quite different in design from regular U.S. coins—today can be found in many collections, having been brought to the States as souvenirs by service members after World War II or otherwise saved.

The coins, introduced in 1903, also bear the Spanish names for the islands: FILIPINAS. Following Spanish custom, the dollar-sized peso was equivalent to 100 centavos. Silver fractions were minted in denominations of fifty, twenty, and ten centavos, and minor coins (in copper-nickel and bronze) included the five-cent piece, the centavo, and the half centavo.

Dies for the coins were made at the Philadelphia Mint. From 1903 to 1908 the coins were struck at the Philadelphia Mint (with no mintmark) and the San Francisco Mint (with an S mintmark). From 1909 through 1919, they were struck only at San Francisco. In the first part of 1920, one-centavo coins were struck in San Francisco; later in the year, a new mint facility was opened in Manila, and from that point into the early 1940s Philippine coins of one, five, ten, twenty, and fifty centavos were struck there. The coins produced at the Manila Mint in 1920, 1921, and 1922 bore no mintmark. No Philippine coins were struck in 1923 or 1924. The Manila Mint reopened in 1925; from then through 1941 its coinage featured an M mintmark.

Rising silver prices forced a reduction in the fineness and weight for each silver denomination beginning in 1907, and subsequent issues are smaller in diameter. The smaller size of the new silver issues led to confusion between the silver twenty-centavo piece and the copper-nickel five-centavo piece, resulting in a mismatching of dies for these two denominations in 1918 and again in 1928. A solution was found by reducing the diameter of the five-centavo piece beginning in 1930.

Japanese military forces advanced on the Philippines in 1942, prompting the civil government to remove much of the Philippine treasury's bullion to the United States. Nearly 16 million pesos' worth of silver remained, mostly in the form of one-peso pieces of 1907 through 1912. These coins were hastily crated and dumped into Manila's Caballo Bay to prevent their capture by Japan, then at war with the United States. The Japanese occupied the Philippines and did manage to recover some of the sunken coins (probably fewer than a half million). After the war, over the course of several years, more than 10 million of the submerged silver pesos were retrieved under the direction of the U.S. Treasury and, later, the Central Bank of the Philippines. Most of them show evidence of prolonged salt-water immersion, with dark corrosion that resists cleaning. This damage to so many coins has added to the scarcity of high-grade pre-war silver pesos.

Later during World War II, in 1944 and 1945, the U.S. Mint struck coins for the Philippines at its Philadelphia, Denver, and San Francisco mints.

The Philippines became an independent republic after the war, on July 4, 1946. Today the coins of 1903 to 1945, including a set of commemoratives issued in 1936, remain as interesting mementoes of a colorful chapter in U.S. history and numismatics.

The following are general descriptions of Philippine issues by type. For detailed date-by-date charts with mintages and retail values, see the *Guide Book of United States Coins, Deluxe Edition.*

BRONZE COINAGE UNDER U.S. SOVEREIGNTY (1903–1936)

Half Centavo   One Centavo

The bronze half centavo was struck from 1903 through 1908 (except for 1907), with some dates struck in Proof format only. Dealer buy prices for the most common pieces are $0.50 in EF to $12 in MS-63; for the most common Proofs, $20 to $60, depending on quality. The rarest Proof is the 1905, generally worth $50 to $150.

The bronze centavo was struck from 1903 through 1936. Dealers buy the most common pieces for $0.25 in VF to $10 in MS-63. The 1918-S, Large S, variety is the rarity of the series, valued from $50 (VF) to $650 (MS-63). Proofs were struck several years in the early 1900s; the most common Proofs bring buy prices of $30 to $40.

COPPER-NICKEL COINAGE UNDER U.S. SOVEREIGNTY
(1903–1935)

Large-Size Five Centavos   Reduced-Size Five Centavos
(1903–1928)   (1930–1935)

Copper-nickel five-centavo coins were struck by the millions in various years from 1903 through 1935. The most common dates are bought by dealers for $0.25 to $0.50 in VF, and for $10 to $20 in MS-63. The rare dates are the 1916-S ($20 to $425) and the 1918-S mule with the small-date reverse of the 20-centavo die ($150 to $3,500). Proofs were struck in some years of the early 1900s; the most common Proofs are bought by dealers for $17 to $35, depending on their state of preservation.

SILVER COINAGE UNDER U.S. SOVEREIGNTY (1903–1935)

Basic Design for Ten-, Twenty-, and
Fifty-Centavo and 1 Peso Pieces
(Large-size fifty centavos shown.)

Silver ten-centavo coins were struck by the millions in various years from 1903 through 1935. The most common dates are bought by dealers for their silver bullion value in VF, and for $12 to $15 in MS-63. The rarest dates are the 1909-S ($10 to $450) and the 1915-S ($6 to $200). Proofs were struck in some years of the early 1900s; the most common Proofs are bought by dealers for $20 to $30, depending on their state of preservation.

Silver twenty-centavo coins were struck in quantity in various years from 1903 through 1929. The most common dates are bought by dealers for their silver bullion value in VF, and for $25 to $30 in MS-63. There are several rarer dates in the series; the 1903-S, 1915-S, and the 1928-M mule (with a reverse of the 1903–1928 five-centavo die) are bought for $5 (VF) to $600 (MS-63). Proofs were struck in some years of the early 1900s; the most common Proofs are bought by dealers for $25 to $50, depending on their state of preservation.

Silver fifty-centavo coins were struck in quantity in various years from 1903 through 1921. The most common dates are bought by dealers for their silver bullion value in VF, and for $25 to $30 in MS-63. The rarest collectible date in the series, the 1905-S, is bought for $8 in VF but up to $800 in MS-63. Proofs were struck in some years of the early 1900s; the most common Proofs are bought by dealers for $40 to $50, depending on their state of preservation.

Silver pesos were struck in quantity in various years from 1903 through 1912. The most common dates are bought by dealers for their silver bullion value in VF, and for $50 to $60 in MS-63. There are several rarities in the series; the rarest, the 1906-S, is bought for $700 in VF and $10,000 or more in MS-63. Proofs were struck in some years of the early 1900s; the most common Proofs are bought by dealers for $75 to $100, depending on their state of preservation.

COINAGE UNDER THE COMMONWEALTH (1937–1945)

Basic Reverse Design for Commonwealth Coinage
(1936 peso shown.)

By 1935 the momentum for Philippine independence justified the creation of a Philippine Commonwealth, with full independence planned by 1946. Circulating coins struck for the commonwealth (1937–1945) featured the same basic obverse designs as those struck under U.S. sovereignty (1903–1936), and shared a common reverse design of an eagle-surmounted shield (the coat of arms of the commonwealth). All are fairly common, with mintages ranging from the millions to tens of millions, and dealer buy prices ranging from $0.05 to $2 in VF.

A set of three 1936-dated commemorative silver coins was issued to mark the beginning of the commonwealth. The fifty-centavo coin and one of the pesos feature busts of Philippine president Manuel L. Quezon and of outgoing U.S. governor-general Frank Murphy. The other peso has busts of Quezon and U.S. president Franklin D. Roosevelt. The fifty-centavo coin has a buy price of about $50 in MS-63, and the pesos of about $75 each.

These charts show the bullion values of common-date circulation-strike silver and gold coins. These are intrinsic values and do not reflect any numismatic premium a coin might have. The weight listed under each denomination is its actual silver weight (ASW) or actual gold weight (AGW). Dealers generally purchase common silver coins at around 15% below bullion value, and sell them at around 15% above bullion value. Nearly all U.S. gold coins have an additional numismatic premium beyond their bullion content. Gold bullion values here are based on AGW only; consult a coin dealer to ascertain current buy and sell prices.

Bullion Values of Silver Coins

Silver Price Per Ounce	Wartime Nickel .05626 oz.	Dime .07234 oz.	Quarter .18084 oz.	Half Dollar .36169 oz.	Silver Clad Half Dollar .14792 oz.	Silver Dollar .77344 oz.
$9.00	$0.51	$0.65	$1.63	$3.26	$1.33	$6.96
11.50	0.65	0.83	2.08	4.16	1.70	8.89
14.00	0.79	1.01	2.53	5.06	2.07	10.83
16.50	0.93	1.19	2.98	5.97	2.44	12.76
19.00	1.07	1.37	3.44	6.87	2.81	14.70
21.50	1.21	1.56	3.89	7.78	3.18	16.63
24.00	1.35	1.74	4.34	8.68	3.55	18.56
26.50	1.49	1.92	4.79	9.58	3.92	20.50
29.00	1.63	2.10	5.24	10.49	4.29	22.43
31.50	1.77	2.28	5.70	11.39	4.66	24.36
34.00	1.91	2.46	6.15	12.30	5.03	26.30
36.50	2.05	2.64	6.60	13.20	5.40	28.23
39.00	2.19	2.82	7.05	14.11	5.77	30.16

Bullion Values of Gold Coins

Gold Price Per Ounce	$5.00 Liberty Head 1839–1908 Indian Head 1908–1929 .24187 oz.	$10.00 Liberty Head 1838–1907 Indian Head 1907–1933 .48375 oz.	$20.00 1849–1933 .96750 oz.
$800	$193.50	$387.00	$774.00
850	205.59	411.19	822.38
900	217.68	435.38	870.75
950	229.78	459.56	919.13
1,000	241.87	483.75	967.50
1,050	253.96	507.94	1,015.88
1,100	266.06	532.13	1,064.25
1,150	278.15	556.31	1,112.63
1,200	290.24	580.50	1,161.00
1,250	302.34	604.69	1,209.38
1,300	314.43	628.88	1,257.75
1,350	326.52	653.06	1,306.13
1,400	338.62	677.25	1,354.50
1,450	350.71	701.44	1,402.88
1,500	362.81	725.63	1,451.25
1,550	374.90	749.81	1,499.63
1,600	386.99	774.00	1,548.00
1,650	399.09	798.19	1,596.38
1,700	411.18	822.38	1,644.75
1,750	423.27	846.56	1,693.13
1,800	435.37	870.75	1,741.50

Note: The U.S. bullion coins first issued in 1986 are unlike the older regular issues. They contain the following amounts of pure metal: silver $1, 1 oz.; gold $50, 1 oz.; gold $25, 1/2 oz.; gold $10, 1/4 oz.; gold $5, 1/10 oz.

The precursor to the best-selling *Guide Book of United States Coins* (the "Red Book") was *The Handbook of United States Coins With Premium List,* popularly known as the "Blue Book" because of its cover color. The mastermind behind the Blue Book was R.S. Yeoman, who had been hired by Western Publishing Company as a commercial artist in 1932. He distributed Western's Whitman line of "penny boards" to coin collectors, promoting them through department stores, along with children's books and games. He eventually arranged for Whitman to expand the line of penny boards into other denominations, giving them the reputation of a more serious numismatic endeavor rather than a "game" of filling holes with missing coins. He also developed these flat boards into a line of popular folders.

Soon Yeoman realized that coin collectors needed other resources and supplies for their hobby, and he began to compile coin mintage data and market values. This research grew into the Blue Book: now collectors had a coin-by-coin, grade-by-grade guide to the prices dealers would pay, on average, for U.S. coins. The first and second editions were both published in 1942, indicating the strong demand for this kind of hobby-related information.

In the first edition of the Red Book, published four years later, Whitman Publishing would describe the Blue Book as "a low-priced standard reference book of United States coins and kindred issues" for which there had been "a long-felt need among American collectors."

The Blue Book has been published annually (except in 1944 and 1950) since its debut. Past editions offer valuable information about the hobby of yesteryear as well as developments in numismatic research and the marketplace. Old Blue Books are collectible, but they are not yet as avidly sought as the Red Book, and most editions after the 12th can be found for a few dollars in VF or better condition. Major variants were produced for the third, fourth, and ninth editions, including perhaps the only "overdate" books in American numismatic publishing. Either to conserve the previous years' covers or to correct an error in binding, the cloth on some third-edition covers was overstamped "Fourth Edition," and a number of eighth-edition covers were overstamped "Ninth Edition." The third edition was produced in several shades of blue ranging from light to dark. Some copies of the fourth edition were also produced in black cloth—the only time the Blue Book was bound in other than blue.

Valuation Guide for Select Past Editions of the Blue Book

Edition	Date*		VF	New	Edition	Date*		VF	New
	Title-Page	Copyright				Title-Page	Copyright		
1st	1942	1942	$50	$100	7th	1949	1948	$10	$15
2nd.	1943	1942	25	55	8th	1950	1949	7	12
3rd	1944	1943	20	40	9th	1952	1951	4	7
4th	None	1945	20	40	10th	1953	1952	3	6
5th	None	1946	12	18	11th	1954	1953	2	4
6th	1948	1947	10	15	12th	1955	1954	2	4

* During its early years of production, the Blue Book's date presentation was not standardized. Full information is given here to aid in precise identification of early editions.

Combined with dealer's buying prices, auction data can help advanced collectors understand the modern market for high-end rarities.

It is important to understand that the following prices include a buyer's premium (a surcharge which the buyer pays the auction house over the final "hammer price," or winning bid; contemporary auction houses charge around 17.5%) and the seller's commission (a small percentage of the hammer price which the individual selling the coin pays to the auction house; this fee can sometimes be negotiated to less than 5%).

Rank	$Price	Coin	Grade	Firm	Date
1	$10,016,875	$1(s), 1794, Silver Plug, B-1 BB-1	PCGS SP-66	Stack's Bowers	January 2013
2	7,590,020	$20, 1933	Gem BU	Sotheby's/Stack's	July 2002
3	4,993,750	$1(s), 1794 PCGS	MS-66+	Sotheby's/Stack's Bwrs	September 2015
4	4,582,500	Prefed, 1787, Brasher dbln, EB on Wing	NGC MS-63	Heritage	January 2014
5	4,140,000	$1(s), 1804, Class I	PCGS PF-68	B&M	August 1999
6	3,877,500	$1(s), 1804, Class I	PCGS PF-62	Heritage	August 2013
7	3,737,500	5¢, 1913, Liberty Head (A)	NGC PF-64	Heritage	January 2010
8	3,737,500	$1(s), 1804, Class I	NGC PF-62	Heritage	April 2008
9	3,290,000	5¢, 1913, Liberty Head (A)	NGC PF-64	Heritage	January 2014
10	3,172,500	5¢, 1913, Liberty Head	PCGS PF-63	Heritage	April 2013
11	2,990,000	Prefed, 1787, Brasher, EB on Breast	NGC EF-45	Heritage	January 2005
12	2,990,000	$20, MCMVII, Ultra HR, LE (B)	PCGS PF-69	Heritage	November 2005
13	2,760,000	$20, MCMVII, Ultra HR, LE (B)	PCGS PF-69	Stack's Bowers	June 2012
14	2,585,000	$10, 1795, 13 Leaves, BD-4	PCGS MS-66+	Sotheby's/Stack's Bwrs	September 2015
15	2,585,000	Pattern 1¢, 1792, Birch Cent, LE, J-4	NGC MS-65RB	Heritage	January 2015
16	2,574,000	$4, 1880, Coiled Hair	NGC PF-67Cam	Bonhams	September 2013
17	2,415,000	Prefed, 1787, Brasher, EB on Wing	NGC AU-55	Heritage	January 2005
18	2,350,000	$2.50, 1808	PCGS MS-65	Sotheby's/Stack's Bwrs	May 2015
19	2,350,000	1¢, 1793, Chain AMERICA, S-4	PCGS MS-66BN	Heritage	January 2015
20	2,300,000	$1(s), 1804, Class III	PCGS PF-58	Heritage	April 2009
21	2,232,500	Pattern 25¢, 1792, copper, J-12	NGC MS-63BN	Heritage	January 2015
22	2,185,000	$10, 1907, Rounded Rim	NGC Satin PF-67	Heritage	January 2011
23	2,115,000	$20, MCMVII, Ultra HR, LE	PCGS PF-68	Heritage	January 2015
24	1,997,500	10¢, 1894-S	PCGS PF-66	Heritage	January 2016
25	1,997,500	Pattern 1¢, 1792 Silver Center, J-1	PCGS MS-64BN	Heritage	August 2014

KEY

Price: The sale price of the coin, including the appropriate buyer's fee.

Coin: The denomination/classification, date, and description of the coin, along with pertinent catalog or reference numbers. Abbreviations include: dbln = doubloon; HR = High Relief; J = Judd; LE = Lettered Edge; Pattern = a pattern, experimental, or trial piece; Prefed = pre-federal issue; S = Sheldon. Letters in parentheses, **(A)** and **(B)**, denote instances in which multiple sales of the same coin rank within the Top 25.

Grade: The grade of the coin, plus the name of the grading firm (if independently graded). NGC = Numismatic Guaranty Corporation of America; PCGS = Professional Coin Grading Service.

Firm: The auction firm (or firms) that sold the coin. B&M = Bowers & Merena; Soth = Sotheby's; Stack's Bowers or Stack's Bwrs = Stack's Bowers Galleries (the name under which Stack's and B&M merged in 2010; also encompasses the merger of Stack's and American Numismatic Rarities in 2006).

Date: The month and year of the auction.

Auction records compiled and edited by P. Scott Rubin.

A coin's "grade" is a classification of its physical condition—how much wear it has received. Such wear can come from being transported in bags from the coinage press to a storage vault, and from being circulated from hand to hand in everyday business transactions.

When you examine your coins for circulation wear, look for slight changes in color, surface texture, and sharpness of fine details. Signs of handling and abrasion are first seen on the highest parts of a coin's design. They become rounded or flattened, with fine details merging together in small spots. More and more circulation wears away the coin's mint luster (its brilliant shiny surface), starting on the highest areas, then the flat fields, and finally the recessed areas. The high details of the design continue to merge together, the coin's rim smoothes away, and finally the entire surface flattens.

A coin's grade is perhaps the single most important factor that affects its value. Supply (rarity) and demand are important, too, of course. But those factors being equal, an attractive, higher-grade coin of a particular type and variety will be worth more than a lower-grade example. Look at the 1901 Morgan silver dollar as an example. In Very Fine condition, a dealer might pay $30 for the coin. In About Uncirculated, its wholesale value jumps to $225. And in MS-63, you can expect to receive $9,000 or more.

THE LANGUAGE OF COIN GRADING

Coin grades are standardized to a 70-point scale, as endorsed by the American Numismatic Association. (For more on how this scale was developed, see *Grading Coins by Photographs* or *The Official ANA Grading Standards for United States Coins.*)

To grade any given coin:

1. determine its denomination (e.g., cent, dime, dollar)
2. determine what *type* it is (e.g., Indian Head cent, Barber quarter dollar)
3. find that coin type's grading standards in this book or in a grading-standards book
4. compare your coin with the text descriptions and photographs, and find the best match

Grades are assigned using an alphanumeric code—a combination of letters and numbers (for example, VG-8 or EF-40). The letters are abbreviations for these descriptions:

Abbrev.	Grade Description	Grade Number(s)	Notes
MS	Mint State	60–70	Mint State coins are collected in the full range from MS-70 (the highest quality within the grade), MS-69, MS-68, down to MS-60 (the lowest Mint State). Mint State is also known as *Uncirculated.*
AU	About Uncirculated	50–59	About Uncirculated grades usually are assigned as AU-58, AU-55, AU-53, and AU-50 (from highest quality within the grade to lowest).
EF	Extremely Fine	40–49	Typical Extremely Fine grades are EF-45 and EF-40.
VF	Very Fine	20–39	Typical Very Fine grades are VF-30 and VF-20.
F	Fine	12–19	Typical Fine grades are F-15 and F-12.
VG	Very Good	8–11	Typical Very Good grades are VG-10 and VG-8.
G	Good	4–7	Typical Good grades are G-6 and G-4.
AG	About Good	3	Below AG-3, the lowest coin grades are Fair-2 and Poor-1.

GRADING EXAMPLES FOR POPULAR
COIN TYPES (CIRCULATION STRIKES)

These descriptions and enlarged photographs show you three examples of grades for six popular coin types. Each is illustrated in Good, Very Fine, and Mint State. Understanding the level of wear in your coins will help you evaluate the offers you get from coin dealers when the time comes to sell.

Grading Wheat Cents

MS-65 (Gem Uncirculated)— No trace of wear. Barely noticeable blemishes. Nearly full red color.

MS-63 (Choice Uncirculated)— No trace of wear. Slight blemishes. Red-brown in color.

MS-60 (Uncirculated)—No trace of wear. Light blemishes. Brown or red-brown in color.

MS-65 (Mint State)

AU-50 (About Uncirculated)— There is slight wear on the cheek and jaw, and on the wheat stalks.

EF-40 (Extremely Fine)— Slight wear; all details are sharp.

VF-20 (Very Fine)—Lincoln's cheekbone and jawbone are worn but separated. The wheat heads have no worn spots.

VF-20 (Very Fine)

F-12 (Fine)—The wheat lines are worn but visible.

VG-8 (Very Good)—Only half of the lines are visible in the upper wheat heads.

G-4 (Good)—The date is worn but apparent. Lines in the wheat heads are missing. Rims are full.

G-4 (Good)

Grading Buffalo or Indian Head Nickels

MS-63 (Choice Uncirculated)—No trace of wear. Light blemishes.

MS-60 (Uncirculated)—No trace of wear. May have several blemishes.

AU-50 (About Uncirculated)—Traces of light wear are visible only on the high points of the design. Half of the original mint luster is present.

EF-40 (Extremely Fine)—The horn is lightly worn. Slight wear is seen on the Indian's hair ribbon.

VF-20 (Very Fine)—Much of the horn is visible. The Indian's cheekbone is worn.

F-12 (Fine)—The horn and tail are smooth but partially visible. The obverse rim is intact.

VG-8 (Very Good)—The horn is worn nearly flat.

G-4 (Good)—The legends and date are readable. The bison's horn does not show.

MS-65 (Mint State)

VF-20 (Very Fine)

G-4 (Good)

Grading Mercury Dimes

MS-63 (Choice Uncirculated)—No wear. Attractive mint luster.

MS-60 (Uncirculated)—No trace of wear. Light blemishes.

AU-50 (About Uncirculated)—There are slight traces of wear. Most mint luster is present.

EF-40 (Extremely Fine)—Only slight wear is seen on the diagonal bands. The braids and hair before the ear are clearly visible.

VF-20 (Very Fine)—The diagonal bands are definitely visible.

F-12 (Fine)—All the sticks in the fasces are defined. The diagonal bands are worn nearly flat.

VG-8 (Very Good)—Half of the sticks in the fasces are discernible.

G-4 (Good)—The letters and date are clear. The lines and bands in the fasces are obliterated.

MS-65 (Mint State)

VF-20 (Very Fine)

G-4 (Good)

Grading Liberty Walking Half Dollars

MS-63 (Choice Uncirculated)—No wear. Some distracting contact marks or blemishes in prime focal areas. Impaired luster possible.

MS-60 (Uncirculated)—No trace of wear. Light blemishes.

AU-50 (About Uncirculated)—There is slight trace of wear on Liberty's head, knee, and breasts, and on the eagle's claws and head.

EF-40 (Extremely Fine)—All skirt lines are bold.

VF-20 (Very Fine)—Skirt lines are sharp, including in the leg area. There is only a little wear on the breast and right arm.

F-12 (Fine)—All skirt lines are evident, but worn in spots. The details of the sandal below the motto remain clear.

VG-8 (Very Good)—The motto is distinct. About half of Liberty's skirt lines at the left are clear.

G-4 (Good)—The rims are defined. The motto IN GOD WE TRUST is legible.

MS-65 (Mint State)

VF-20 (Very Fine)

G-4 (Good)

Grading Morgan Dollars

MS-65 (Gem Uncirculated)—Only light, scattered contact marks that are not distracting. Strong luster, good eye appeal.

MS-64 (Uncirculated)—A few scattered contact marks. Good eye appeal and attractive luster.

MS-63 (Choice Uncirculated)—No trace of wear; full mint luster; few noticeable surface marks.

MS-60 (Uncirculated)—No trace of wear. Full mint luster is present, but may be noticeably marred by scuff marks or bag abrasions.

AU-50 (About Uncirculated)—Slight trace of wear on the bust shoulder and the hair to the left of the forehead, as well as on the eagle's breast and top edges of the wings.

EF-40 (Extremely Fine)—All hair lines are strong, and the ear is bold. The eagle's feathers are all plain, but with slight wear on the breast and wing tips.

VF-20 (Very Fine)—Two thirds of the hair lines from the top of Liberty's forehead to the ear are visible. The ear is well defined. The feathers on the eagle's breast are worn.

MS-65 (Mint State)

VF-20 (Very Fine)

G-4 (Good)

Over the years coin collectors and dealers have developed a special jargon to describe coins. Here are some terms frequently used within the hobby.

altered date—A false date on a coin; a date fraudulently changed to make a coin appear to be one of a rarer or more valuable issue.

bag mark—A surface mark, usually a small nick, acquired by a coin through contact with others in a mint bag.

blank—The formed piece of metal on which a coin design will be stamped.

bullion—Uncoined silver, gold, or platinum in the form of bars, ingots, or plate.

certified coin—A coin that has been graded, authenticated, and encapsulated in plastic by an independent third-party (neither buyer nor seller) grading service.

circulation strike—A coin intended for eventual use in commerce, as opposed to a Proof coin.

clad coinage—U.S. dimes, quarters, half dollars, and some dollars made since 1965. Each coin has a center core of pure copper and a layer of copper-nickel or silver on both sides.

die—A piece of metal engraved with a negative-image design and used for stamping coins.

die variety—Any minor alteration in the basic design of a coin type.

dipped coin—A coin that has been chemically cleaned to remove oxidation or foreign matter from its surfaces.

doubled die—A die that has been given two misaligned impressions from a hub (positive-image punch); also, a coin made from such a die.

encapsulated coin—A coin that has been authenticated, graded, and sealed in plastic by a professional third-party grading service.

error coin—A mismade coin not intended for circulation.

field—The background portion of a coin's surface not used for a design or legends.

fineness—The purity of gold, silver, or other precious metal, expressed in terms of one thousand parts. A coin of 90% pure silver is described as being .900 fine.

gem—A coin of exceptionally high quality, typically considered MS-65 or PF-65 or better.

intrinsic value—The bullion or "melt" value of the actual silver or gold in a precious-metal coin.

junk silver—Common-date silver coins in circulated grades, worth only their bullion value.

key coin—One of the scarcer or more valuable coins in a series.

legend—A principal inscription on a coin (e.g., E PLURIBUS UNUM).

luster—The brilliant or "frosty" surface quality of an Uncirculated coin.

mintmark—A small letter or other mark on a coin, indicating the mint at which it was made.

Mint set—A set of Uncirculated coins, packaged and sold by the U.S. Mint, containing one of each of the coins made for circulation at each of the mints in a particular year.

Mint State—The grade of a circulation-strike coin that has never been used in commerce, and has retained its original surface and luster; also called Uncirculated.

obverse—The front or face ("heads") side of a coin.

planchet—The blank piece of metal on which a coin design is stamped.

Proof—A coin struck for collectors by the Mint using specially polished dies and planchets.

Proof set—A set of each of the Proof coins made during a given year, packaged by the Mint and sold to collectors.

raw coin—A coin that has not been encapsulated by an independent third-party grading service.

reeded edge—The edge of a coin with grooved lines that run vertically around its perimeter, as seen on modern U.S. silver and clad coins.

reverse—The back or "tails" side of a coin.

rim—The raised outer portion of a coin that protects the design from wear.

slab—A hard plastic case containing a coin that has been graded and encapsulated by a professional grading service.

spot price—The daily quoted market value of a precious metal in bullion form.

third-party grading service—A professional firm that authenticates and grades a coin, encapsulating it in a protective hard plastic case; called *third-party* because it is neither the buyer nor the seller of the coin.

token—A privately issued piece, similar to a coin but not official legal tender, typically with an exchange value for goods or services.

type—A series of coins defined by a shared distinguishing design, composition, denomination, and other elements. For example, Barber dimes or Morgan dollars.

type set—A collection consisting of one representative coin of each type, of a particular series or period.

Uncirculated coin—A circulation-strike coin that has never been used in commerce, and has retained its original surface and luster; also called Mint State.

variety—A coin with a die characteristic that sets it apart from the normal issues of its type.

BIBLIOGRAPHY

Colonial Issues

Bowers, Q. David. *Whitman Encyclopedia of Colonial and Early American Coins*. Atlanta, GA, 2009.

Cents

Bowers, Q. David. *A Guide Book of Half Cents and Large Cents*. Atlanta, GA, 2015.

Bowers, Q. David. *A Guide Book of Lincoln Cents*. Atlanta, GA, 2008.

Snow, Richard. *A Guide Book of Flying Eagle and Indian Head Cents* (2nd ed.). Atlanta, GA, 2009.

Nickels and Dimes

Bowers, Q. David. *A Guide Book of Barber Silver Coins*. Atlanta, GA, 2015.

Bowers, Q. David. *A Guide Book of Buffalo and Jefferson Nickels*. Atlanta, GA, 2007.

Bowers, Q. David. *A Guide Book of Mercury Dimes, Standing Liberty Quarters, and Liberty Walking Half Dollars*. Atlanta, GA, 2015.

Bowers, Q. David. *A Guide Book of Shield and Liberty Head Nickels*. Atlanta, GA, 2006.

Flynn, Kevin. *The Authoritative Reference on Roosevelt Dimes*. Brooklyn, NY, 2001.

Quarter Dollars and Half Dollars

Bowers, Q. David. *A Guide Book of Barber Silver Coins*. Atlanta, GA, 2015.

Bowers, Q. David. *A Guide Book of Mercury Dimes, Standing Liberty Quarters, and Liberty Walking Half Dollars*. Atlanta, GA, 2015.

Bowers, Q. David. *A Guide Book of Washington and State Quarters*. Atlanta, GA, 2006.

Tomaska, Rick. *A Guide Book of Franklin and Kennedy Half Dollars* (2nd ed.). Atlanta, GA, 2012.

Silver Dollars

Bowers, Q. David. *A Guide Book of Morgan Silver Dollars* (4th ed.). Atlanta, GA, 2012.

Burdette, Roger W. *A Guide Book of Peace Dollars* (2nd ed.). Atlanta, GA, 2012.

Newman, Eric P., and Kenneth E. Bressett. *The Fantastic 1804 Dollar, Tribute Edition*. Atlanta, GA, 2009.

Standish, Michael "Miles," and John B. Love. *Morgan Dollar: America's Love Affair With a Legendary Coin*. Atlanta, GA, 2014.

Gold Coins

Bowers, Q. David. *A Guide Book of Double Eagle Gold Coins*. Atlanta, GA, 2004.

Bowers, Q. David. *A Guide Book of Gold Dollars* (2nd ed.). Atlanta, GA, 2011.

Fivaz, Bill. *United States Gold Counterfeit Detection Guide*. Atlanta, GA, 2005.

Garrett, Jeff, and Ron Guth. *Encyclopedia of U.S. Gold Coins, 1795–1933* (2nd ed.). Atlanta, GA, 2008.

Commemoratives

Bowers, Q. David. *A Guide Book of United States Commemorative Coins*. Atlanta, GA, 2008.

Proof and Mint Sets

Lange, David W. *A Guide Book of Modern United States Proof Coin Sets* (2nd ed.). Atlanta, GA, 2010.

Bullion Coins

Mercanti, John M., with Michael Standish. *American Silver Eagles: A Guide to the U.S. Bullion Coin Program* (2nd ed.). Atlanta, GA, 2013.

Moy, Edmund C. *American Gold and Platinum Eagles: A Guide to the U.S. Bullion Coin Programs*. Atlanta, GA, 2013.

Tucker, Dennis. *American Gold and Silver: U.S. Mint Collector and Investor Coins and Medals, Bicentennial to Date*. Atlanta, GA, 2015.

Tokens and Medals

Bowers, Q. David. *A Guide Book of Civil War Tokens* (2nd ed.). Atlanta, GA, 2015.

Bowers, Q. David. *A Guide Book of Hard Times Tokens*. Atlanta, GA, 2015.

Jaeger, Katherine, and Q. David Bowers. *100 Greatest American Medals and Tokens*. Atlanta, GA, 2007.

Jaeger, Katherine. *A Guide Book of United States Tokens and Medals*. Atlanta, GA, 2008.

U.S./Philippine Coins

Allen, Lyman L. *U.S. Philippine Coins*. Oakland Park, FL, 1998.

Shafer, Neil. *United States Territorial Coinage for the Philippine Islands*. Racine, WI, 1961.

Type Coins

Bowers, Q. David. *A Guide Book of United States Type Coins* (2nd ed.). Atlanta, GA, 2008.

Guth, Ron, and Jeff Garrett. *United States Coinage: A Study by Type*. Atlanta, GA, 2005.

Die Varieties

Fivaz, Bill, and J.T. Stanton. *The Cherrypickers' Guide to Rare Die Varieties (various editions and volumes)*. Atlanta, GA.